An Introduction to Holocaust Studies

Michael Bernard-Donals
University of Wisconsin

PEARSON

Prentice
Hall

Upper Saddle River, NJ 07458

Library of Congress Cataloging-in-Publication Data

Bernard-Donals, Michael F.
An introduction to Holocaust studies / Michael Bernard-Donals.
 p. cm.
 Includes bibliographical references and index.
 ISBN 0-13-183917-9
 1. Holocaust, Jewish (1939–1945)—Historiography.   2. Holocaust,
Jewish (1939–1945), in literature.   3. Memory.   I. Title.
 D804.348.B48 2005
 940.53'18'072—dc22

                                                        2005014361

VP/Editorial Director: Charlyce Jones Owens
Executive Editor: Charles Cavaliere
Editorial Assistant: Maria Guarascio
Director of Marketing: Heather Shelstad
Marketing Assistant: Jennifer Lang
Sr. Managing Editor: Joanne Riker
Production Liaison: Jan H. Schwartz
Manufacturing and Prepress Buyer: Ben Smith
Cover Design: Bruce Kenselaar
Cover Illustration/Photo: © Dorling Kindersley,
 Courtesy of the Collection Jewish Historical
 Museum, Amsterdam

Director, Image Resource Center: Melinda Reo
Manager, Rights and Permissions: Zina Arabia
Manager, Visual Research: Beth Brenzel
Manager, Cover Visual Research and Permis-
sions: Karen Sanatar
Photo Researcher: Julie Tesser
Image Permission Coordinator: Cynthia Vincenti
Composition/Full-Service Project Management:
 PineTree Composition, Inc./Linda Duarte
Printer/Binder: R.R. Donnelly, Harrisonburg
Cover Printer: Phoenix Color Corp.

Credits and acknowledgments borrowed from other sources and reproduced, with permission, in this textbook appear on appropriate page within text.

Pearson Prentice Hall is a trademark of Pearson Education, Inc.
Pearson® is a registered trademark of Pearson plc.
Prentice Hall® is a registered trademark of Pearson Education, Inc.

Pearson Education LTD., London
Pearson Education Singapore, Pte. Ltd
Pearson Education, Canada, Ltd
Pearson Education—Japan
Pearson Education Australia PTY, Limited

Pearson Education North Asia Ltd
Pearson Educación de Mexico, S.A. de C.V.
Pearson Education Malaysia, Pte. Ltd
Pearson Education, Upper Saddle River, New Jersey

10 9 8 7 6 5 4 3 2 1
0-13-183917-9

To my students

Contents

Preface VII

Part I: The Holocaust 1
Chapter 1: The Holocaust 3
Chapter 2: Holocaust Studies 20
Discussion Questions for Part I 39

Part II: History 41
Chapter 3: The Holocaust in History 43
Chapter 4: Narratives and Events 70
Chapter 5: Case Studies: History, Narrative, and the Problems
   of Evidence 95
Discussion Questions for Part II 119

Part III: Memory 121
Chapter 6: Memory, Witness, and Testimony 123
Chapter 7: The Language of the Witness: Diaries, Testimonies,
   and First-Person Narratives 141
Chapter 8: Case Studies: Testimony and the Problem
   of Authenticity 170
Discussion Questions for Part III 185

Part IV: Representation 187
Chapter 9: The Problem of Representation 189
Chapter 10: Picturing Atrocity 214
Chapter 11: Making Memory: Case Studies in Holocaust Art
and Architecture 239
Discussion Questions for Part IV 260

Part V: Teaching 261
Chapter 12: Conclusion: Some Thoughts about Teaching
after Auschwitz 263
Discussion Questions for Part V 275

Bibliography 277
Index 293

Preface

The Holocaust is a watershed event. It changed how we think of war, about humanity and inhumanity, about justice, and about history. For some writers and historians, the Holocaust defines the twentieth century. Because of the Nazi policy of Final Solution—whose aim was to eliminate the Jewish population of Europe and, eventually, the world—historians and social scientists, theologians and ethicists, writers and artists, have all had to reconsider not only a crucial aspect of their subject matter but also their methods of study and of representation. The Holocaust was an event, like any other event, that has had effects upon the generations that came after. But because of its magnitude, and because it pushed the limits of what we consider normal, it has also pushed the limits of the disciplines and methods through which we study events.

It is for this reason that "Holocaust studies" has evolved as a field of study. In part because it pushes the limits of so many conventions, and in part because it seems to affect just about every traditional subject area and genre of representation, scholars and writers have begun to think of the Holocaust as deserving attention not just from one or another disciplinary lens—historical, or anthropological, or ethical, or artistic—but from a multidisciplinary perspective. That multidisciplinary perspective takes as a given that it's simply impossible to pin the event down once and for all. It also takes as a given that a scholar or artist loses sight of the effects of the event if she limits herself to questions of "what happened." This is because the question of what happened is horrifying enough; but answering that question doesn't tell us anything about the effects of what happened. Those effects aren't just how the event made an impression on the people whose lives were directly affected by the Holocaust. Those effects are also visible on those who weren't there and who were born generations later. We can't read a story about a disaster, or see film footage of a war or an atrocity, we can't look at a photograph of a burned synagogue in Argentina or the war in Palestine without seeing a shadow of the Holocaust. And we can't study the history of the war in Iraq, or think about the ethics of the Human Genome Project, without also realizing that the questions we might ask about the Iraq war or about genetic classification are shaped by studies of the limits of warfare and of eugenics; they are shaped by the Holocaust as well.

This book isn't an introduction to the Holocaust; it's an introduction to Holocaust studies. It's not a book about what happened; there are many, many very good books that tell the story of the Holocaust. Instead, this is an introduction to the way the Holocaust has been studied, particularly in the last fifteen to twenty years. Or, to put it more specifically still, this book provides one way to see how the Holocaust has been studied over the last fifteen to twenty years. It includes a consideration of how questions about the history of the Holocaust have changed; it includes an examination of the words of survivors and perpetrators and how their recollections of what happened have been considered differently by different writers and thinkers; and it includes questions about whether some depictions of the Holocaust—artistic and academic—are better, more ethically acceptable, and more accurate, than others. It also takes seriously the question of why we ought to study the Holocaust (from any disciplinary perspective) at all: what does the Holocaust teach us, what does it teach us *about,* and what are the implications of teaching and learning about something as horrifying as the near-total destruction of a people?

Because the Holocaust has become the focus of so much writing, scholarship, and art over the last twenty years, no book on the subject could be exhaustive, this one included. No book on the Holocaust, let alone Holocaust studies, could take account of the full range of work done on the subject since the conclusion of World War II. Instead, this book—as the title implies—provides an overview of the trends that Holocaust scholars, writers, and artists have followed, and suggests some avenues for questioning some of the assumptions from which they work. It doesn't take into account all the writers and scholars who have taken the Holocaust as their subject; it doesn't introduce all the diarists and memoirists, novelists and poets who've turned their attention to the events; and it doesn't turn to all the filmmakers, architects, and visual artists who have thought long and hard about how the Holocaust has changed the nature of film, or architecture, or painting. The book does, however, provide representative examples from all of these fields (among others). And the book takes those examples as points of departure: readers can ask not just the questions the artists and writers have asked in their work—about ethics, genocide, history, humanity—but can also ask questions *of* those thinkers, writers, and artists. As the title of the book also suggests, this is not the introduction but *an* introduction; it's not only an overview of the field. It asks and prompts questions about the field, about its object of study, and about the appropriateness of some of the assumptions it makes—about art, about the academic disciplines, about ethics, and about genocide.

□ □ □

This book falls into three main sections. After two brief chapters outlining the events of the Holocaust and of the years immediately following in which Holocaust studies emerged, the first section involves the question of history: what history is, how it defines its object, what challenges the Holocaust offers to history and historiography, and what we can and can't learn from investigating the Holocaust through a primarily historical lens. One way to think about history is as a tool for making clear what happened and when it happened; another is to think about it as a way of weaving together events into coherent and understandable stories. History is both what happened and the story of what happened. In the case of the Holocaust, because what happened seems so counterintuitive and horrifying, what do historians do when confronted with the need to say what happened in a language that is both intuitive and understandable? The problem historians face is the same problem any thinker or scholar faces: how do you handle an object of knowledge that seems to defy any of the categories you'd place it in so we can make sense of it?

This historical problem is mirrored in those who were in the midst of the disaster: its eyewitnesses. The second section of the book involves how Holocaust studies treats eyewitnesses and the testimonies produced by them. One can think of eyewitness testimonies as a piece of evidence, among many other kinds of evidence, through which to understand the Holocaust. But testimony, like other kinds of evidence, is by its nature incomplete and doesn't, by itself, explain the nature of what the witness saw. Eyewitness testimony is complicated by the witness's memory—which is usually only partial and is always shaped by other events—and by the language into which the witness must cram what she saw. What happens when the witness forgets? What happens when the witness is traumatized and—either by choice or because of shock—has nothing to say? And what happens when a witness can't find the words to say what happened and so finds other words, and other events, through which to explain herself and her circumstances?

If history and testimonies can't provide a sense of what happened, maybe other genres, and other methods, do. The third section of this book takes seriously the possibility that if the academic disciplines and the words of the witnesses themselves are fallible instruments with which to understand the events of the Holocaust, maybe literature and the other arts do a better job. What is it, exactly, that these other media do, and are they appropriate—if we take art, in its old-fashioned recipe, as that which both instructs and delights—in the case of the Holocaust? Decades ago the philosopher Theodor Adorno said that to write poetry after Auschwitz is barbaric, seeming to imply that any representation of atrocity that provides pleasure to the spectator should be ruled out of bounds. But another way to think of Adorno's pronouncement is to say that any representation of or "after" Auschwitz should be barbaric, that it should offer a sense of the effects of atrocity rather than to copy what it tries to represent. But this is a troubling place to be left, with the idea that we learn best about what happened during the Holocaust not through traditional modes of representation—the academic disciplines or testimony—but by being shocked or repulsed. This doesn't accord with traditional notions of learning, notions that suggest that by understanding the past we have the opportunity for a brighter future. Learning about the Holocaust, we like to think, will prevent future atrocities, future Holocausts. But with anti-Semitism on the rise, instances of torture and barbarity in the news, and a long string of genocides following in the wake of the Holocaust, this formulation doesn't seem to have been borne out. I've tried to draw some lessons from this conclusion in the final chapter.

This book is meant to introduce students to the different ways we've come to understand the Holocaust, and is also meant to give students an opportunity to ask questions about them. While its chapters and sections can stand on their own—each one provides a bibliography and questions for discussion, and each one could be supplemented with enough primary material to fill an entire course or semester—its arc is one I've followed myself in courses on Holocaust studies and Holocaust representation. Making our way through what we generally think of as the best and most accurate means of understanding of the Holocaust (the academic disciplines and the words of survivors), my students and I are often left with more questions than answers. And while narrative, poetic, and artistic representations don't answer those questions any more adequately than the more academic genres, they seem to do a better job giving a sense of the effect of the Holocaust. This may not be the same thing as *learning about* the Holocaust; but it may supplement the more academic language we sometimes use with a more complicated, and sometimes far more troubling, sense of what happened, and it may implicate us far more.

Acknowledgments

I've relied on many people over a number of years as I've worked through some of the material in this book. They have given me patience, they've provided direction, and, more than anything else, they've helped me see the importance of the work; not just of writing about, but especially of teaching about the Holocaust. My response to those who ask how I can spend my time on such a difficult subject is that I have the support of an outstanding group of teachers, scholars, and writers, all of whom understand that limit events, and this particular limit event—the Shoah—make clear just how high the stakes of learning really are.

Among those who've been remarkable in their support have been my good friends and colleagues Richard Glejzer and Janet Alsup. It was with Professor Alsup that I first co-taught some of the material that has found its way into this book; it was with Professor Glejzer that I first seriously examined the problems inherent in Holocaust representation. The three of us, in different combinations and at different times, have presented some of the issues and questions that arise in the book at colloquia, conferences, and lectures. Rich and Janet also continue to be good friends and marvelous colleagues.

I'm also grateful to others with whom I've had conversations about this material, sometimes in person but most often through my writing. They include Dominick La Capra, with whom I've had a productive and running argument on questions of the "Holocaust sublime;" Berel Lang, whose discussions of the ethical stakes of historical and fictional representations of the Holocaust have haunted me since I read his book, *Act and Idea in the Nazi Genocide,* for the first time; Geoffrey Hartman, whose erudition can only be matched by his generosity;

Cliff Spargo, whose work on mourning and whose good company continue to teach me a great deal about endurance; and other, anonymous readers of parts of this book while it was in proposal and draft form for their smart questions, their intellectual prescience, and their insistence that the questions I ask in this book *matter.*

But more than anyone, it's been the students I've taught over the last ten years or so who've been my best teachers. The arc of the book you're about to read—beginning with history, continuing through questions of witness and testimony, and concluding with representation—mirrors the arc of a class I first co-taught in 1994 at the University of Missouri, and have myself taught twice at the University of Wisconsin in 2001 and again in 2003. In graduate seminars at both institutions, I was able to further probe the historical, political, and philosophical dimensions of those questions. The undergraduate classes, entitled "Writing (and) the Holocaust," included some of the very best students I've ever had the good fortune to teach. Those students, as well as those enrolled in my graduate seminars, were nothing short of excellent teachers. Through their sometimes very tough and probing questions, I came to understand more clearly than before why it's so important to ensure that this generation—a generation for whom genocide is less a horror than a recurring theme on CNN—catch a glimpse of what Maurice Blanchot has called "the disaster," the destructiveness of what humans can bring upon themselves for apparently no good reason at all. It's these students' questions that resonate most clearly in my ears, and that keep me honest and engaged in the work.

Some of the material you'll see in this book will look familiar to readers of *Between Witness and Testimony* and some of my essays on the Holocaust. I'm grateful for the opportunity to present that material in a pedagogical context. Charles Cavaliere at Prentice Hall deserves a special note of thanks for his confidence in the project and his willingness to see it through. I also wish to thank Jan Schwartz who has patiently guided me through the production process, and to Linda Duarte at Pine Tree Composition for her meticulous work on bringing the typescript to life as a book. I can't thank Stephanie Kerschbaum enough for her work on the book's index. I'm also grateful to the University of Wisconsin and its Institute for Research in the Humanities for giving me a semester to work on some of the material that would find its way into this book.

Last, but certainly not least, I wish to thank my family—Ruth and Syd Bernard, and to Hannah and my children, Avi, Miryam, and Shoshana—for their support, love, and patience.

About
the Author

Michael Bernard-Donals is the Nancy Hoefs Professor of English at the University of Wisconsin–Madison, where he is also an affiliate member of the Mosse-Weinstein Center for Jewish Studies. He is the coeditor, coauthor, or author of five other books, two of which are on the Holocaust and the ways it is represented in art, architecture, film, and literature. He teaches courses on literary theory, rhetoric, ethics, and the Holocaust. He lives in Madison with his wife, Hannah, and their three children.

I | THE HOLOCAUST

CHAPTER 1 | # The Holocaust

The Holocaust might best be defined as the systematic destruction of European Jews implemented by the National Socialist government in Germany and its allies during World War II. As a policy, it was known in Germany as the "Final Solution of the Jewish Question"; the "question"—of what to be done with Jews living in the midst of non-Jewish cultures—had been around in Germany, as it had been in Europe and the Americas, for as long as Jews had lived there. That the Final Solution took place in Germany, the most industrially advanced country in Europe, raises a number of other questions, among them the relation between industrial society and anti-Semitism, German cultural understanding of non-Germans, and particularly of Jews, other countries' and cultures' apparent inaction in the face of the concentration and later the liquidation of Jews in Germany and German-occupied and -allied countries. But because the "Jewish question" to which a final solution had to be found—and which Hitler and those in the National Socialist government of Germany implemented—was at least a thousand years old, the question of where to begin a history of the Holocaust is a difficult one to answer.

There are many very good histories of the Holocaust—among them Raul Hilberg's pathbreaking *The Destruction of the European Jews,* published initially in 1961; currently Saul Friedlander is writing a three-volume history, *Nazi Germany and the Jews,* the first volume of which (published in 1998) covers the years 1933–39—and chronologies of the events are widely available. This chapter considers of some of the key historical moments of the Holocaust and examines why they are worth studying. It is impossible to isolate the history of the Holocaust

3

from a broader study of it. So while there's a difference between a history of the Holocaust and "Holocaust studies"—which focuses upon *how* the events are described, studied, and understood, not on the events themselves—it's worth knowing the events' historical timeline.

PRELUDE

But how far back does that history go? One could argue you'd have to go back as far as Judaism's dispersion from its homeland to the far reaches of Europe and Asia after the destruction of the second Temple in Jerusalem to fully grasp its character in the early twentieth century in central Europe. With the Temple destroyed, Jews reconstituted their religious and cultural practice so that it could continue while essentially inside non-Jewish (primarily Christian and, later, Islamic) cultures. Before the end of the European middle ages, Jewish communities had already been established in England, in what is now France, Germany, Italy, the central European regions of Russia and Belarus, and in the southern Mediterranean including Greece, Turkey, north Africa, and west-central Asia (including Baghdad and Damascus). There, Jewish communities had to design agreements with what were essentially their national hosts, agreements that allowed Jewish practice and guaranteed their protection in the midst of a mainly Christian and sometimes-hostile environment. Hundreds of communities in Europe had by turns flourished and been persecuted in waves of an anti-Semitism that originated in the years after Jesus's death over the non-Christian Jews' apparent failure to accept what Christians adopted as a new covenant and—eventually—an entirely new religion (see Figure 1–1).

By the eighteenth and nineteenth centuries, the outlines of central European Jewish culture had already been established. Jews formed communities in urban centers and often, either by choice or by decree, lived separately from the broader secular or religious community. In most places laws were passed that prohibited Jews from participating in some aspects of communal life, including but not limited to banning them from owning land, joining the medical or legal professions, holding property over a certain value, or living outside designated areas of a community or city. (The term "ghetto" has its origins in sixteenth-century Venice, when the Jewish members of its community were told they could live only inside the walled area near the city's iron foundry, or *getto*.) Because of restrictions that often limited Jews' contact with non-Jews, Jews turned to one another for economic, religious, and cultural support; when Jews were allowed to work among and with non-Jews, they did so in the professions into which they were allowed—selling of merchandise and, in some cases, animal products (eggs, hides); textile manufacturing; and the handling, lending, and changing of money. They were

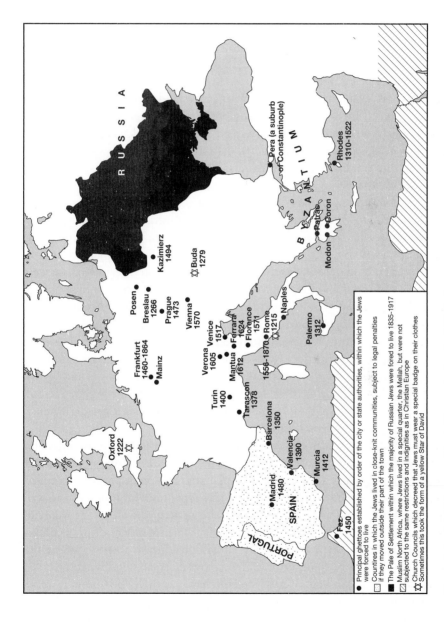

Figure 1–1 Jewish communities in Europe during the Middle Ages.

often educated in their own communities where they received not only religious training but also apprenticeships in the trades.

By the late nineteenth and early twentieth century, the concentrations of Jews in western Europe were mainly in the cities, and this sometimes changed the character of these communities. The growth of political reform movements in the late eighteenth century extended earlier enlightenment (or Haskalah) ideals, particularly the one highlighting the importance of interweaving Jewish tradition with a modern and politically secular sensibility. As a result, many urban Jewish communities made an effort to update their practices and worldviews so that they would be more in line with the contemporary national cultures in whose midst they lived. This, the advocates of this movement believed, would help Jews become more fully accepted as members of civil communities. Within two years of the Revolution in France, Jews were "emancipated," which meant that they were given—for the first time—the full range of rights and obligations due all citizens. Within twenty years, Jews were granted Emancipation in Holland and Prussia, and by 1870 full rights were granted to Jews in Italy, Austria-Hungary, and Switzerland. With this shift over the course of just under a century, Jews became integrated into the cultures and economies of western and central Europe: by that time, 30 to 40 percent of tradespeople involved in the textile industry were Jewish, as were 16 percent of doctors and 11 percent of lawyers. Jews were active in the financial and banking industry, as well as in other professions. Though there were continually arguments over just how full the "full citizenship" rights should be—there was an argument in British parliament in 1847 over whether Lionel de Rothschild should be seated, emancipation was withdrawn in the German states according to one of the articles of the Congress of Vienna in 1815, and a series of anti-Jewish riots erupted in Germany in 1819—and though anti-Semitism continued to boil just beneath the surface of these developments (and sometimes erupted), Jews had a place, and a face, in the western European landscape.

Things were different in the east. While a significant Jewish community also flourished there—in Russia, Poland, Belarus, and the Baltic region—it was mainly (though certainly not exclusively) a rural phenomenon, with Jews concentrated largely in smaller towns and villages (*shtetls*), in some cases forming majorities of the population. The Reform movements of the western part of Europe were not as influential in the east. In part because of the influence of Hasidism (a combination of folk belief, mysticism, and more traditional Jewish observance) and the dissolution of rabbinical authority in the regions of Poland and western Russia in the 1760s, Judaism had a very different character there. Because of a more marked difference in the eastern Jews' way of life, as well as their separation both geographically and religiously from non-Jews, anti-Jewish sentiment tended to be more virulent and violent in the east, as Jews were easier to identify *as* Jews. After Poland's partition in 1772 (between Austria-Hungary, Russia, and Prussia), Russia's Catherine the Great showed some friendliness toward those Jews inside Russia's new boundaries. By 1791 there was enough animosity toward Jews by merchants and others who saw them as a threat to competition that Catherine was asked to restrain settlement. In 1804 she did, restricting Jews to settle a swath of territory known as the "Pale of settlement," which stretched from Odessa in the south to Vilna in the north, and which included the cities of Lodz, Kiev, and Warsaw. Waves of pogroms against Jews overtook the region between the early nineteenth and early twentieth centuries, often during times of economic hardship. According to some scholars who have paid attention to this period—including Josef Yerushalmi and Eva Hoffman, to name only two—this led to the belief among some eastern European Jews that while borders and fortunes may change, the Jews would survive.

What all of this presaged for the mid-twentieth century was a clear distinction—of culture, of religion, and even of language—between an eastern Jewish culture that appeared (or was believed to be) different in character from rural and Christian culture, and a western Jewish culture large parts of which were becoming complementary to, if not assimilated with, the prevailing western culture and economy. It also led to the lessening, if not the elimination, of the more virulent kinds of anti-Semitism in the west, until the last quarter of the nineteenth century, without an equal lessening—and perhaps even a rise—in anti-Semitism in the east. Finally, it makes clear that there had been a culture of separation of Jewish culture from broader, national cultures, one that by the beginning of the twentieth century led to questions about Jews' affiliation with the nation or state in which they resided; their participation in, or their "ownership" of, the national economy, particularly in the west; and a set of precedents (ghettos, exclusionary laws, Jewish councils separate from but beholden to national governments, a culture of discrimination) that would come to play a major role in National Socialist Jewish policy.

THE JEWISH QUESTION

By the last thirty years of the nineteenth century, western European Jews had become full participants in their nations' lives. But with the defeat of France by Prussia in 1871 and the world economic collapse of 1873, matters took a turn for the worse. During these years, the anti-Semitism that was held at bay in the west, and that emerged periodically in the east with varying degrees of violence and hatred, became more pronounced, in part because Jews were an obvious target. They were "others," in the estimation of some not quite nationals but not quite foreigners whose religion and cultural practices (in spite of assimilation) made them an object of some suspicion when an object of blame or scorn was needed.

After the economic collapse of 1873, Germany fell into economic stagnation (as did much of the rest of the economically developed world), and because Jews had become prominent in the financial marketplace, some suspected that Jews might be responsible for the collapse and failure of recovery measures. In Germany in 1878, the Christian Social party, led by Adolf Stocker, realized that in order to get votes from the workers and small shopkeepers who were most severely affected by the crisis, the rhetoric of Jewish "arrogance," "control" of the press, and "finance capitalism," could lead to a rise in the representation from that party. By 1893, explicitly anti-Semitic parties in Germany elected sixteen members to the Reichstag. In the east during the economic turmoil, particularly in Poland and Russia, significant numbers of Jewish tradespeople and workers began to sympathize with the workers' reform movements, culminating eventually in socialist and communist parties by the early twentieth century. The formation of the Bund (the General Union of Jewish Workers) in Vilna in 1897—the same year of the first Zionist Congress—joined workers with radical intellectuals. Their common project was to revolutionize the economy for a more equitable and just society, and to help make coercive and imperial states—and Russia was seen as just such a state—to disappear. These developments helped to create an ideological (rather than a primarily religious) anti-Semitism, one based on an increased suspicion that Jews could not be counted on to join forces with members of their national community for the common good. Jewish socialists on the one hand and a "cabal" of Jewish plutocrats on the other were seen as specters of political and economic crisis on the European landscape of the late nineteenth century.

At about the same time there was a growth of racial anti-Semitism. Alfred Dreyfus was the only Jew on the General Staff of the French Army when he was accused of treason in 1894. Some of the suspicion against Dreyfus was a misplaced symptom of long-simmering French humiliation for the defeat at the hands of the Germans in the Franco-Prussian war, but much of that suspicion was also the result of French anti-Semitism. Though Dreyfus was eventually acquitted of the charges against him (the evidence had been forged), the question of his guilt or innocence polarized France for nearly a decade (and some suggest it informs French anti-Semitism today). In Russia, after the assassination of Tsar Alexander II by socialist revolutionaries, violent pogroms sponsored by the government—eventually culminating the "May Laws" of 1882—seriously curtailed Jewish settlement in the Pale and formally reversed a comparably liberal policy toward Jews. State-sponsored anti-Semitism came to a peak in Russia with the trial of Mendel Beilis in 1911 for ritual murder. When Beilis, like Dreyfus, was finally exonerated, it pushed anti-Semitic feeling into the background, but it did not disappear. A corrupt social-Darwinist racial pseudo-theory and the beginnings of the eugenics movement emerged clearly in the last decade of the nineteenth century: Houston Chamberlain's *Foundations of the Nineteenth Century*, published in 1899, theorized that the Jew was a social parasite that could only sustain itself by feeding off a national host, and this image was proof of the Jew's cultural inferiority. *The Protocols of the Elders of Zion,* a Russian forgery purported to be the minutes of a meeting for Jewish world domination, was published in the first decade of the twentieth century and widely circulated as genuine.

During World War I, Jews fought in the Armies of both sides: Germany, France, Britain, the United States, and Russia, among other countries. After the German defeat and the Versailles Treaty—which demilitarized Germany and exacted severe reparations payments that would hamstring the German economy and its eventual territorial designs by the third decade of the new century—many Germans again looked for scapegoats, and found many who had "stabbed Germany in the back" both during the war and after it. These included Jews, particularly "Jewish Bolsheviks" who sympathized with the Russian Revolution of 1917 and who were seen as a destabilizing force in the German political and economic systems. In 1917, the British Government—which had been given mandatory control over Palestine—declared its intention to establish a national home for Jews there. With the redrawing of the European map after the war, large numbers of Jews were concentrated in the east: in Poland (over three million), Romania (nearly a million), Hungary (nearly half a million), Lithuania and Latvia (nearly 200,000), Czechoslovakia and Austria (half a million), and the Soviet Union (nearly three million). For a time after the war, Jewish intellectual and artistic culture flourished, particularly in the German Weimar Republic, but this ended with the world economic collapse of 1929.

Even during the height of the Jewish-German renaissance of 1924–29, there were significant pockets of anti-Jewish animosity, not to mention anti-Semitism: Adolf Hitler, who had fought in World War I and had been demoralized by its aftermath, combined anti-Communism with anti-Semitism in forming the National Socialist party in the 1920s, and attempted a coup-d'etat in Munich in 1923. By the eve of the economic collapse, the Nazis had 800,000 votes in national elections; two years later they'd collected six million, and by 1932, 14 million (nearly 38 percent of the electorate). This support had been gained by promising a resurgence of German military, territorial, and cultural supremacy in Europe; by promising to heal the country's economic ills; and by instilling a kind of pride (or arrogance) in German peoplehood at the expense of non-German, inferior peoples (Slavs and, most important, Jews).

What had become apparent by 1932 throughout Europe was that in spite of strong anti-Semitic feelings, and even programmatic anti-Semitic political agendas, Jews had gained a secure foothold in national political dialogues. This didn't mean that Jews could rest assured: in the 1920s, Zionists in Europe and the United States understood that there was a greater need than ever to establish a safe national home for Jews outside the non-Jewish cultural centers that were productive but nonetheless perilous. The rise of the National Socialist party in Germany, as well as other fascist or fellow-traveling parties in Italy, Romania, and even the United States, was enough for some Jews to seek permits to emigrate to safer locations in the 1920s and early 1930s. But even with the sometimes virulent and racist animosity—sometimes murderous in the east—toward Jewish communities during the early years of the twentieth century, Jews thought of themselves as members of a national polity, particularly in the west. Even when their orthodoxy or religious observance maintained a distinction between their practice and their participation in a national home, most nonetheless believed that persecution was part and parcel of their condition, and that they would persevere.

The Holocaust

In early 1933, with a political stalemate in the German Reichstag, an ailing Chancellor Hindenburg, the hero of the Franco-Prussian war, appointed Hitler as a compromise leader. In the March elections that followed the appointment, the National Socialists gained 44 percent of the vote, the largest for a single party but smaller than the total of left-socialist and progressive parties. With Hitler as Chancellor and the Nazis in control of the legislature, the party quickly consolidated its power. Civil liberties were suspended and the government was given dictatorial powers right after the election; social institutions were merged into a more or less monolithic state bureaucracy, and by that summer all competing political parties had been eliminated. Trade unions were replaced by a government-controlled "labor front," and after book burnings in 1933, a number of scientists, intellectuals, and artists who were seen as posing a threat to the party were either arrested, deported, or "persuaded" to emigrate. (By this time, however, a number of countries had put a severe cap on immigration, particularly the immigration of European Jews.) A large number of those who fled early on were Jewish. In 1934 officials of the SA (*Sturmabteilung*), the party's paramilitary storm troopers, were purged (in what was called the "night of the long knives"), paving the way for an expansion of the role of the SS (*Schutzstaffeln*) or guard troops, what would become the Nazi elite under Heinrich Himmler. The army and police were merged in 1935, and the Army itself was brought under the direct command of the Fuhrer in 1938. Large public works projects were begun, and military factories were built and began production, in direct contravention of the Versailles Treaty. Germany occupied the Rhineland (which had been under League of Nations control) in 1936, supported Franco's fascists in the Spanish Civil War in 1937, annexed Austria in 1938, and in that same year—with the approval of British, French, and Italian ministers who thought the move would put an end to Hitler's expansionist aims—annexed the Sudenten portions of Czechoslovakia, which contained large numbers of ethnic Germans. (In 1939, Germany annexed what remained of the Czech portion of the country.)

In 1933, Hitler's position on Germany's Jews was well-known (it was spelled out in some detail in *Mein Kampf,* which was written while he was in prison for the Munich putsch attempt) and he began to implement "solutions" to the Jewish question in Germany almost as soon as the National Socialists took power. In fact, many scholars have actively questioned whether Hitler's aims for expansion and ultimately war were driven by his anti-Jewish policies, effectively making the war one of the elimination of Jews in Europe. There's a strong argument to be made for this case, based upon the National Socialist government's policies for Jews between 1933 and 1938 alone, the first stage of the Holocaust (generally referred to as "disenfranchisement"); the second stage, "concentration," took place between 1938 and 1941; with the final stage, "deportation and liquidation," beginning in late 1941 and concluding with the end of the war. A series of laws, collectively known as the Nuremburg Laws, was passed between 1935 and 1938. Among them were laws that stripped Jews of citizenship rights, that banned "race mixing" (relations between Jews and non-Jews of the opposite sex), that Aryanized Jewish businesses (stripping Jews of ownership and placing it instead in Aryan "managers"); Jews were identified racially and Jews' passports were marked with a "J" for easy identification. In 1938 all Jewish communal organizations were placed under direct Gestapo (state police) control, and Jews were ordered to register all foreign and domestic property. All of these measures and others like them—many if not most of which were modeled upon anti-Jewish measures historically taken from the middle ages into modernity, as have been documented by Hilberg and others—effectively reduced Jews to second-class status, and made them an obvious minority; they also made every aspect of Jewish life in Germany, and eventually those areas that came under German jurisdiction between 1933 and 1938, visible to the national bureaucracy and made them easier to control. Essentially, the first stage in solving the Jewish question was to gather them firmly under the control of the state government, and to remove their property and eventually their status as citizens and people. Whatever status Jews had achieved in the century leading up to the rise of the Nazis was systematically undermined in Germany within five years. By 1938, about half of Germany's Jews and two thirds of Austria's had left their countries. Once the Germans invaded Poland, precipitating declarations of war, any chance of Jews leaving German Europe was effectively halted: the German government stopped issuing emigration visas, and other nations (and their territories, including the British mandate in Palestine's) closed their borders to those trying to leave Germany and German-occupied countries. (This latter action was a reflection of the results of the Evian Conference on Emigration, held in 1938, which was ostensibly to discuss an equitable distribution of Jewish refugees among countries in the West but which had the effect of demonstrating, in sometimes horrifying language, their insensitivity to the plight of German Jews by severely limiting immigration. The Australian representative famously reported that his country "did not have a Jewish problem and did not want to import one.") In addition to these measures, political dissidents were rounded up and placed in concentration camps built specifically for the purpose of housing political prisoners for long periods. Many homosexuals (mostly men) and other "social undesirables" including the Sinti and Roma ("gypsies"), along with the disabled and the mentally ill, were either imprisoned, sent to sanatoriums, or systematically killed; others seen as threats to the government, including Jehovah's Witnesses, were banned and some were eventually sent to concentration camps.

The shift from disenfranchisement to a policy of physical isolation and concentration was marked by *Kristallnacht* ("the night of broken glass"), a "spontaneous"—though in actuality a government-sponsored and -coordinated—pogrom that took place throughout Germany on the night of November 9–10 in 1938. Jewish shops and synagogues were looted and burned, Jews were beaten and murdered on the streets, and businesses that weren't looted (and some that were) were soon afterward expropriated. By the end of 1940, when Germany had successfully invaded Poland, France, Holland, Belgium, and Luxembourg, German policies had been extended to those countries; Italy, Romania, and Hungary had allied themselves with Germany, and they too instituted anti-Jewish measures, though in some cases (like Hungary) they were put into practice sporadically. At this point in the war, it was not clear how the Jewish problem would be resolved: there were plans circulated in ministerial and government circles that involved the deportation of Jews to Madagascar, the large island off the southeastern coast of Africa, or to Palestine under a German or pro-German authority; accompanying the invasion of Poland were plans for its depopulation and German settlement in the area, with the aim of German colonization (Hitler claimed that Germans in central Europe needed *lebensraum,* living space, to further its cultural aims) and as a place to settle Germany's and other occupied countries' Jews, now disenfranchised and largely without property. But with the German occupation of Poland came the question of what to do with its three million Jewish residents. This question became even more acute with Germany's abrogation of the nonaggression pact it had signed with Soviet Russia and its massive invasion of the country in the summer of 1941.

A great deal of debate in Holocaust studies, and in Holocaust history in particular, has been devoted to whether the Final Solution was a decision implemented on the orders of Hitler and dictated throughout the ranks of the SS, the Gestapo, and the German armed forces in explicit terms, or whether its implementation was inferred by officers close to Hitler based upon his anti-Semitic ideology and his orders for resettlement, and thereby implicit. Maybe Hitler's insistence upon the Russian invasion was driven not by war aims alone (though it is clear that by 1941 the German army needed the petroleum that could only be acquired by invading the Russian southwest) but by his intent to rid the world of Jews, beginning with Europe and western Russia. Regardless, with the invasion of the Soviet Union the German bureaucracy had to deal not only with millions upon millions of Slavs who were deemed racially inferior to Aryan Germans, but also with nearly five million Jews in the Soviet Union and Poland alone. The formation of the *Einsatzgruppen,* mobile killing squads, was one such "solution": the squads followed the major movements into the Soviet Union by the German army, rounded up military and local government leaders, along with members of Jewish communities en masse, and killed them. Usually these killings were at gunpoint: those rounded up were taken in groups to a pit dug by soldiers, or in some cases dug by those detained, and were shot at the edge of the pit. Then another group was brought to the pit, and the process was repeated until the pit was filled. (In Babi Yar, near Kiev, an estimated 33,000 were killed this way, most of them Jews.)

But this method of killing was highly labor intensive and deemed inefficient; by late 1941, members of the SS had experimented with the use of toxic gas to kill larger numbers of individuals—in the T-4 campaign designed to exterminate the mentally ill and the handicapped, among others, and in experiments with Soviet prisoners of war—and by December 1941, the first campaign designed specifically to detain and murder Jews had been initiated at Chelmno, in occupied Poland, in which Jews who had been rounded up from neighboring cities and towns were loaded onto vans modified to vent exhaust fumes into their closed cargo bays. The vans were driven into the forest outside Chelmno where, once the Jews inside had been asphyxiated by the gas, the bodies were unloaded and burned. By this point, other concentration camps in and around Germany were being modified to accept Jewish inmates, and by 1942, six extermination camps were in operation, all in Poland, and all designed to eliminate Jews and other "undesirables."

The process of concentration, begun in the late 1930s, was made formal in a decree in 1941 code-named "Night and Fog," the results of which were that Jews would be concentrated in designated cities, primarily in the east (though there were Jewish ghettos and transport camps in western Europe as well, notably in France and Holland), from whence they would disappear as into the night and fog. In several of these cities, at least during the first months after the establishment of the ghettos, Jews tried valiantly to retain some measure of autonomy and social cohesion. The occupying powers formed Jewish Councils (or *Judenrate*), modeled on autonomous councils that originated in the middle ages, to establish authority in the ghettos and to exert a modicum of local control when Nazi policy had to be carried out. Some ghettos established aid societies, hospitals, musical and drama groups, and orphanages; most contained Bundist, Zionist, and other political and social organizations as there had been in the towns and villages from which the ghettos' populations had been drawn. The ghettos provided a local forced-labor pool for German industry and the war effort; many of those thus "employed" died of malnutrition and exhaustion. As the ghettos' existence continued on into early 1942, conditions worsened: in Warsaw during its most overcrowded period, each resident took in only 200 calories a day; 400,000 residents were concentrated in an area of less than 100 acres. People died not only of malnutrition but also of diseases that spread like wildfire because of the residents' weakness.

By the summer of 1942, the infrastructure of the Final Solution was finally in place: the Reichsbahn (the German national railroad) had built lines (where they did not already exist) that ran from various transport camps in France, Holland, Italy, and Germany (as well as, later, Romania, Hungary, and Greece) to the six liquidation camps: Chelmno (in operation from 1941 to 1943 in which nearly 400,000 were eventually killed); Belzec (in operation from 1941 to 1943 in which 600,000 were killed); Sobibor (in operation from 1942 until a prisoner uprising in 1943 forced it to close, in which nearly 200,000 were killed); Majdanek (in operation between 1942 and 1943 where 125,000 were killed); Treblinka, physically the largest of the extermination camps (in operation between 1942 and late 1943 where 800,000 were killed); and Auschwitz-Birkenau, a network of several camps (including the Buna and Monowitz work camps) that was originally intended, near the beginning of the war, to be a "model" camp (in operation from early 1942 to late 1944 where between 1 and 1.6 million were killed, see Figure 1-2).

Much has been written about the infrastructure required to maintain the operation of the death camps, particularly after late 1942 when the tide of the war in the east was turning and the German armed forces could well have used its resources to defend its western front. To pursue the Final Solution so single-mindedly is seen as evidence that Hitler was insane or inept as a general; that the Nazi policy was what drove the war; that it was the very bureaucratization of the Final Solution that made it not only thinkable but eminently "doable" for the German military and for those Germans who knew what was happening. A great deal else has been written about the large numbers of Jews who were killed without, or so it seemed, very much resistance: that the Jewish Councils were complicit with Hitler; that a Jewish culture of nonresistance or "martyrology" allowed the Germans to make short work of the killing; that there was resistance but that it was easily defeated by the overwhelming force of the German military machine (though the months-long Warsaw Ghetto uprising is an exception worth noting); that the long process of desubjectification and expropriation from 1933 to 1941 prevented many if not most Jews from thinking of themselves as humans worth saving. What is clear is that for many Jews, the long history of persecu-

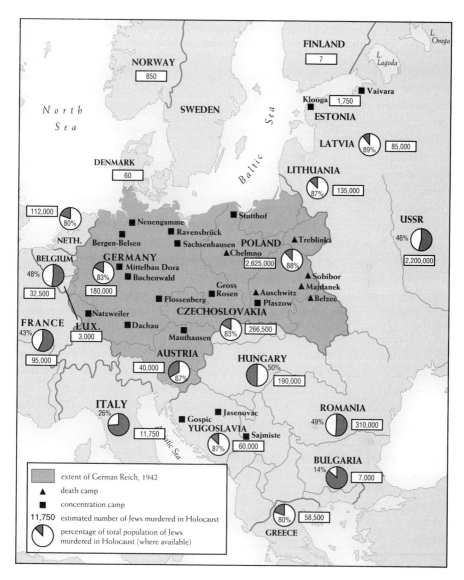

Figure 1–2 Major camps in 1942.

tion and survival, coupled with a more recent history of emancipation and the granting of full citizenship rights by their countries of residence, kept them from thinking that their persecution *as Jews* would be carried to the extremes to which it was carried, or that they would not ultimately be recognized as German (or French, or Hungarian) citizens worthy of protection by their home governments or by the international community. In fact there *was* resistance—Jewish organizations in the United States and in Europe worked with underground movements inside and outside the ghettos; Jewish paramilitary organizations in Europe and in Palestine actively fought both the Germans and their allies, and (in the case of the Irgun in Palestine) against British colonials. There were many non-Jews throughout Europe who risked their lives (and sometimes gave them) to hide Jews, to help them emigrate, or to otherwise secure their safety against tremendous odds. Some clergy and church members spoke out against the actions against Jews to their congregations and their ecclesiastical superiors; some were heeded, while others (like Pastor Niemoller in Germany) were eventually imprisoned for treason. A number of Jewish organizations took great pains to bring the concentration and extermination to the attention of both the British and the American governments during the war. The stunned disbelief with what they were hearing, coupled with the strong belief that winning the war would be the quickest way to end the atrocities, led British and American officials to turn aside request for assistance or military actions against the camps. But German military technology—along with years of anti-Semitism, a culture of suspicion of Jews, and a strong ideology of nativism and xenophobia—made such resistance ineffective.

In military terms, the tide of the war turned in early 1943, when the Nazi siege of Stalingrad was broken, Rommel's North Africa campaign was defeated by American and British forces, and the Allied offensive in Italy began (see Figure 1–3). Once it was clear to the Nazi generals that defeat (probably from the east) was possible, Himmler made arrangements for the extermination camps to be erased from history: bodies that were buried in mass graves in the early 1940s were exhumed and burned, and as the Red Army made its way westward, some of the camps ceased operation. But at the same time the war was being lost, and the invading Soviet armies were only tens of miles away from some of the concentration and death camps, the trains to Auschwitz still ran. In 1944, after the Nazis took direct control of Hungary, nearly 450,000 of its Jews were deported to Auschwitz between May 14 and July 8 of that year.

In Hungary, as in other parts of the Reich, the policy of extermination kicked into its highest gear not at the beginning of the war but at its end, which was when the resources used to carry it out (the trains, the manpower, the logistical support) might have been used by Hitler's generals to maintain its defensive positions on the war's two fronts and sue for peace from a position of strength. (Fully two-thirds of the exterminations were carried out *after* 1942.) It speaks to the depth of the ideological conviction of Hitler and of many—if not most—of his highest-ranking officials that the war against the European Jews must be won, even if the territorial aims of the war would be lost. In Raul Hilberg's terms, it speaks to both the failure of originality in the policy of the Final Solution and, ultimately, its evil genius: the Nazi policy against the Jews was, at its beginnings, modeled closely on historical measures taken against the Jews; and that at its end, in the

Figure 1–3 Europe, 1943.

turn to systematic murder, the Final Solution's "innovation," made the Holocaust unique among the countless pogroms against Jews.

In early 1945, Auschwitz was liberated by the Soviet army. By that time, most of the death camps had been evacuated and their inmates had been moved—on long "death marches" in which thousands died of exhaustion and starvation—farther west, sometimes to Germany proper, to concentration camps originally created for political and other prisoners. When the war in Europe finally drew to a close in the late spring, Allied forces were shocked by the conditions they found when they happened upon the camps. In most cases, the highest-ranking Nazis had already escaped, and they left behind thousands upon thousands of starving prisoners, and many thousands of corpses. Those who had survived the marches to the camps in greater Germany often suffered terribly from dysentery and typhus; others, when fed by sympathetic American and British soldiers, died because their bodies couldn't handle the food after starving for so long. By some estimates, more than half of those who survived in the camps to the end of the war (hundreds of thousands) died of disease in the weeks and months after the camps' liberations. Almost immediately after the surrender of the Nazis, the Allied authorities moved to transform many of the concentration camps into temporary refuges for those displaced by the war (Displaced Persons', or DP, camps). During the first year after the war's end, 250,000 Jewish refugees made their way to the DP camps. Originally, no provision had been made for separating Jewish DP camp residents from non-Jewish residents, but after a number of incidents of anti-Semitic violence, the authorities moved to segregate the camp populations. A number of those who survived the war decided to forgo the DP camps in favor of returning to their former homes, only to encounter the same (if not more virulent) anti-Semitic hostility and violence that they'd experienced during the early war years. In the Polish town of Kielce, more than forty Jews who had returned to their homes were murdered in a pogrom in the summer of 1946. While there were some relatively rare instances of individuals finding members of their families alive (in some cases decades later), most in the DP camps found themselves to be the only surviving members of their families.

In 1933, there was a thriving Jewish culture in Europe, one that was varied religiously, economically, geographically, and socially. After one hundred years of integration into western European political culture—with full voting rights, and representation in parliaments, government cabinets, and the military, along with the medical and legal professions, in the boardrooms of major corporations, along with more common social locations as shopkeepers, teachers, parents, and leaders of social organizations—Jews had come to feel themselves as members of a culture, if not completely secure members. In western and central Europe before the war, there were over nine million Jews. Of these nine million, somewhere over half a million emigrated (though some of them, like Anne Frank and her family, left for countries that would later be overrun by the Nazis), several hundred thousand died during the concentrations in the ghettos, around a million were killed by the *Einsatzgruppen* during the Nazis' push into the Soviet Union, and around three and a half million were killed in the death camps. When the war was over, two thirds—somewhere around six million—of the continent's Jews had been killed in under a decade. Ninety percent of Poland's three million Jews were killed, and of those who survived, most left after the war (see Figure 1–4). It is not an overstatement to say that Jewish culture was changed irrevocably with the Holocaust. It extinguished a Yiddish-speaking shtetl culture in eastern Europe altogether (though some of it remains, somewhat anachronistically, in the desert climate of Jerusalem). A thriving professional, intellectual and artistic class that existed in places like Berlin, Paris, Rome, and Budapest, not to mention Salonika and Amsterdam, disappeared, and has only in the last decade or so begun to reappear. The centers of Jewish culture are no longer in Europe but in the United States, Argentina, and Israel.

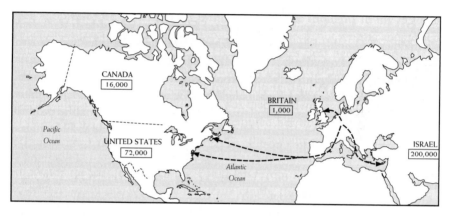

Figure 1–4   Jewish emigration, during and after World War II. *Adapted from Martin Gilbert 1982.*

CHAPTER 2

Holocaust Studies

In the years immediately following the end of the War, particularly once the camps had been liberated and the full effects of the destruction—both of non-Jewish Europe and of Jewish culture there—had begun to be felt, one of the reactions from people who saw what had happened was stunned silence. Among liberators and victims alike, a strong common sentiment was that what had happened was simply too horrible to be put into words, and even if it could be, no one would want to hear about it. Those who lived in the first and second generation after the Holocaust repeatedly say that the survivors' instinct was to keep the humiliation of the atrocity to themselves for fear that it would contaminate the lives that they were trying to build (or rebuild) after the destruction. Children often never heard directly what their parents went through, and only understood that something awful had happened from the odd scoldings having to do with wasting food, overreactions to apparent and small injustices, terrible nightmares, and the obvious fact that these children had no grandparents, no uncles, no cousins. Hundreds of thousands of survivors eventually left Europe to make new lives for themselves in the United States and in Israel, others stayed in Europe, and still others departed to be with relatives in Australia, South America, and wherever they could to rebuild their lives. The immediate aftermath of the Holocaust could be characterized as a kind of silent exile.

It's not true that "Holocaust studies" began immediately after the war. In fact, as a field Holocaust studies is a relatively recent phenomenon, probably only a decade or so old. There were those, however, who believed it was imperative to study the events of the Holocaust, to determine what had happened, and to find a way to explain the apparently unexplainable.

AFTERMATH

The Allied armed forces, which had together liberated the camps, were responsible for exacting justice from those who had carried out the war, both against Europe and against its Jews. To do so, they set up a tribunal in which to judge those who were responsible for the destruction. Precedents for war crimes trials had been established at the 1919 Paris peace conference at the end of World War I, at which moral culpability had been established for war crimes at the highest levels of government. As early as 1943, President Roosevelt in the United States, Prime Minister Churchill in Great Britain, and representatives of the other Allied Powers—having received reports of the atrocities that comprised the Final Solution—had begun discussions over how to try those responsible. Once the full measure of the war had been taken at its conclusion, and once the atrocities had been seen in some detail in the United States, Britain, and the Soviet Union—through newspaper and newsreel images, reports in major newsmagazines, and some eyewitness accounts made public—a process for the trials began in earnest. In October 1945, a set of formal indictments was signed against the major Nazi leaders, who would be brought before an International Military Tribunal. Negotiations took place between October 1945 and the summer of 1946 to ensure that those judging the guilt or innocence of the accused would have evidence to do so, and would use that evidence to understand the nature of the atrocities. No one wanted the Nuremberg tribunal to be a show trial.

In all, twenty-four Nazi officials, including the Polish Governor General Hans Frank (who was responsible for carrying out the policy of the Final Solution in Poland), along with Hitler confidants Goring, Hess, Bormann, and Speer, were put on trial. (Himmler and Hitler had committed suicide; other major figures, including Adolf Eichmann—the chief bureaucrat of the Final Solution—had escaped before they could be brought to trial.) The charges were for conspiracy, crimes against peace, war crimes, and crimes against humanity.

The trial made clear not just the facts of the Holocaust, but also the extent to which the Holocaust was a policy inextricably linked to the Nazis' war aims. Though much has been made of the officers' claim on the stand that in carrying out a policy of murder they were simply "following orders," it was also made clear—and this has been substantiated as more and more records from Soviet and American archives have become available over the last twenty years—that those orders were very often implied, not stated explicitly, and that it was up to local officials to determine the means by which those implied policies should best be carried out. To repeat a claim made by Hilberg, there was a certain dastardly originality with which Nazi officers contrived the mechanics of the Final Solution. As Hans Frank made clear in a meeting he had with his officers in 1942, what else could "eliminating" the Jews concentrated in Poland's ghettos mean? The trial made visible the damage done to the German language by the architects of the Holocaust: the words *murder, policy of extermination,* or even *Jew* were rarely if ever used; instead, "special treatment," "*endlosung*" (Final Solution), and "piece" (or "item") were used instead, providing just enough camouflage—at least in their own consciences—to allow those charged with "plausible deniability."

In 1946, Rafael Lemkin—a Polish Jewish lawyer who had emigrated to the United States five years earlier—went to Nuremberg to lobby for the inclusion of the term "genocide" in the articles of indictment against the Nazi war criminals. Lemkin had coined the term "genocide"—the killing of a people—years earlier, and defined it as the "destruction of the national pattern of the oppressed people" and the "imposition of the national pattern of the oppressor": the target group was stripped of its identity or physically exterminated in a purposeful eradication of a group, based upon that group's identity, separate from any other act of aggression. But while Lemkin managed to get the term inserted into the third count ("war crimes") of the Nuremberg indictments, he was unable to convince any of the prosecutors that the term could stand on its own as a description of what happened to the Jews during the war and—this was Lemkin's precedent—the Armenians during the Turkish campaign against them in 1915 and 1916. (It was that earlier genocide that Hitler referred to, infamously, when describing his campaign against the Jews—he asked rhetorically, "who, after all, remembers the Armenians?")

Part of the debate that circulates around the question of the Holocaust's "uniqueness"—whether it is a crime unlike all other crimes because of who it targeted and how it was carried out, or whether it is a species of crime that has been committed throughout history and will continue to be committed unless forbidden by statute or aggression—is put in terms of the word *genocide.* The Nuremberg trials convinced portions of the world that the Nazis' crimes against the Jews were brutal beyond comprehension and a violation of the normative values of humankind. But "crimes against humanity" was so vague a term that it could not be equated or squared with some of the descriptions of indignities provided by witnesses during the evidentiary hearings. Lemkin's pursuit of the term "genocide," and the eventual adoption by the United Nations of a Genocide Convention in 1948 (which the United States Senate did not finally ratify until a full forty years later) raised the stakes. It meant that the Holocaust could be understood not as an act that was subsidiary to the Nazis' war aims, but could instead be thought of as a separate and distinct species of aggression meant to destroy either a group or the character of a group simply because of who they were. The Holocaust historian Yehuda Bauer rightly believes this fact renders the Holocaust not unique but unprecedented: as a crime against humanity, the Holocaust was simply one set of events among many others whose intent was to destroy Jews; as a genocide, it was the most "successful" instance of such a destruction, and was perhaps unique only in the instruments through which its aims were accomplished, instruments that ran precisely *counter to* the logic of war.

NATIONAL EFFECTS

Germany

In addition to the Nuremberg trials, the Allied forces occupying Germany and the rubble of the European continent had to contend with the remnants of the Nazi party and its ideology, which was all-encompassing and infiltrated nearly every aspect of Germans' lives. Their "de-Nazification" of Germany was an attempt to root out party members who held office in the various German states, those who held judgeships, and particularly those who were members of the armed forces. Many were brought to trial and "reeducated" about the crimes that were committed by the party and the nation. But de-Nazification was complicated by the Cold War: the Soviet Union occupied much of eastern Europe, held the areas of Germany they had invaded (including its capital, Berlin), and seemed intent on designing or imposing national constitutions modeled on the one that existed in Russia. The Americans, British, and French occupied the western portion of Europe, including the large western portion of Germany. It became clear that it would be nearly impossible to reconcile the two opposing models of governance, and by 1947 it was also evident that Stalin wanted to keep the two portions of Germany divided (into what eventually became the German Federal Republic in the west and the German Democratic Republic in the east). It became important to keep qualified individuals on judiciaries and in local and state governments and as a result, de-Nazification became a lower-order priority after that year.

Konrad Adenauer—the leader of the Christian Democratic party in West Germany who became Chancellor in 1949—made sure that the new West German constitution included a balance of power that would prevent a recurrence of the stagnation that helped Hitler rise to power in 1933. He also tilted the country's economy and cultural organizations toward Europe and the United States. One of the results of a weakening of de-Nazification and a pro-western alliance was a very strong Holocaust education program in the West German schools, one that laid not just responsibility for the war but also the destruction of Europe's Jewish culture at the feet of the German government and its people. To this day,

Germany has a peculiar relation to the Holocaust and to Jews: on the one hand, even members of the current generation are especially sensitive to German culpability (which was formalized in 1952 with a reparations agreement in which the German government paid reparations to Israel and Jewish organizations); on the other hand, for a long time German scholars and intellectuals were hesitant to confront the details of that culpability because it could conceivably upset the paradigm in which they had learned about and interiorized their national self-identity. Moreover, the result of a downplayed de-Nazification program meant that many of those who were functionaries in the Final Solution maintained positions of authority in Germany, and some of those responsible for the war and for the Holocaust acquired asylum—often by illegal, though sometimes through state-sanctioned, means—throughout Europe, South America, and the United States.

Israel/Palestine

One of the regions of the world that was most greatly affected by the Holocaust was Palestine. Since the Balfour Declaration in 1918, when Britain committed to establishing a Jewish homeland in its Palestinian mandate, Zionism as a movement had a much more focused goal: paired with its ideological resolution (the forging of national identity) was now a territorial one (through the establishment of borders and a government). Palestine had been one of the primary destinations of those emigrating from Germany and other parts of Europe until emigration was halted at Evian in 1938 and the invasion of Poland in 1939. But for at least a thousand years it had been a predominantly Arab and Islamic region, and those who emigrated there joined a minority Jewish population. Jews and Arabs served together on municipal councils and on irrigation and forestation efforts there, but since the 1920s there had been many instances of violence, Jew against Arab and Arab against Jew. The pretexts for violence differed over the years—arguments over land and water rights, disputes over the justice of the British authorities, and charges of favoritism from one side or the other. During the years of the war different Jewish paramilitary organizations (the Irgun, a right-wing Zionist group led initially by Ze'ev Jabotinsky; the Lohamei Herut Israel, an anti-British group; and the Hagana, the main underground Palestinian force, controlled by the Jewish Agency for Palestine) fought armed Arab Palestinian groups and the British for autonomy. Throughout the war, immigration to Palestine continued, though on a far smaller scale than it had before the Polish invasion, and—because the British had closed the country to immigrants—almost entirely illegally. After the war, Jewish organizations and the United States pressed the British to resume their immigration policy to Palestine, requesting that 100,000 Jews be allowed to enter, but the British refused. This led to an upsurge in armed rebellion by the various paramilitary groups, and it also led to indignation by the Jewish Agency for Palestine (organized in the late 1920s), which pressed for immigration as well as for the creation of a Jewish state. With the help of the Jewish Agency, along with other Jewish organizations in Europe and the United States, boatloads of immigrants from the European DP camps tried to reach Palestine. Some arrived at their destination, while others were turned back by the British navy. In 1947 an American wartime transport ship renamed the *Exodus* was caught on its approach to Palestine by the British, but its commander and passengers would not be turned back. As a result, British soldiers boarded the ship and violently forced those aboard—some of them in terrible condition—to disembark and to board other ships destined (ironically) for Germany. The publicity generated by the incident was particularly bad for the British, who finally turned the "Jewish question" of Palestine over to the recently created United Nations. Refugees from Europe continued to come to Palestine, and after a UN-sponsored partition plan was rejected by the Arab residents in 1947, Israel declared independence. That declaration was followed by a nearly year-long war, after which the country's borders were established.

Though the creation of the state of Israel was a clear result of the events of the Holocaust, the state's early character was not shaped by the immigrants from the DP camps. During the first decades of independence there was marked (though sometimes understated) animosity between the "sabras"—native Israelis—and the immigrants from Europe. Those who declared the state's independence thought of themselves as long-time pioneers linked to the Zionist movement who had come (or whose parents had come) to Palestine during the mandatory period or even before. The founders of the state and its first-generation residents saw themselves as heroic, struggling first against the British and the country's Arab residents (who opposed partition and the declaration of statehood) and then against the massed Arab armies that attempted to prevent the Jewish separation of Palestine. The struggle after independence was not a military but an agrarian and industrial one, in which the nation attempted to establish a military and an economic infrastructure, begin an agricultural program (and to enhance that which already existed), and provide housing for those who continued to stream in, particularly in the country's first decade of existence. Among those who arrived were the remainder of a European Jewish community that—according to some sabras—allowed themselves to be slaughtered by the Nazis and who, when they mustered any resistance, failed to rise up against their tormentors. They pointed to the Jewish Councils, which they saw as co-conspirators with the Nazis, as an example of the moral decrepitude of European Jewish culture. By contrast, they saw in themselves a new model, "New Jews" who could throw off their colonial oppressors (the British), their Arab tormentors, and win a war for independence. Against the heroism and the socialist ideal of the sabras, their newly arrived European counterparts—often pale, undernourished, unable to speak Hebrew, and unable to fend for themselves without help from the foundling social welfare system—were seen as something of an embarrassment. But this should not have been the case: as Benny Morris, Tom Segev, and others have pointed out, the victory in the war for independence was helped out as much by Cold War politics, the Arab armies' ineptitude, and sheer luck as it was by valor and military ingenuity.

Still, the Holocaust exerted a unique kind of pressure on Israel's political, military, and domestic affairs. One of the most obvious signs of this pressure is the complex of buildings outside the city of Jerusalem on Mount Herzl (named after the founder of the Zionist movement), the Yad Vashem Heroes' and Martyrs' Memorial Authority. Originally established by an order of Israeli parliament in 1953, it was meant to provide a monument to those who died at the hands of the Nazis and to those who resisted. Later on the Authority set up a historical museum, in which visitors could walk through a chronological series of displays meant to follow the events of the Holocaust as they led to the creation of the state of Israel. Yad Vashem now also has a strong educational mission: young Israeli soldiers, during the training that they receive before serving the required two years in the Armed Forces, come to Yad Vashem as one of the requisite stations along the way to national education. (Another requisite site is Masada, where the last holdouts against the Romans in 70 CE committed suicide rather than be taken prisoners.) More than fifty-five years after the founding of the state, and more than sixty since the end of the Holocaust, it is impossible to visit or live in Israel without seeing its palpable signs.

France

In France, the signs of the Holocaust are less visible, but they are certainly palpable, and form another point of focus for Holocaust studies. France has a peculiar historical relation to the Final Solution: the northern and western parts of France were occupied by the Nazis immediately following their invasion of the country in 1940, while the southeastern region was unoccupied. With its seat of government in the town of Vichy, from which the unoccupied region took its name, Vichy France was allied with Nazi Germany under the leadership of Marshal Henri Phillipe Pétain, the leading general during France's victory in World War I. When France was quickly invaded, its government went into exile in London, and during the four years between the Nazi invasion and the Allied counterinvasion on D-Day (June 6) 1944, general Charles de Gaulle led the Free French essentially by radio broadcast across the English Channel. To be sure, there was French resistance, and to this day there are arguments in that country over just how successful the resistance was and just how responsible those forces were in turning the tide of the war in the west. But there is still a great deal of

bitterness in France over the complicity of the Vichy government and over the degree to which French citizens collaborated with their Nazi "captors."

Part of the argument has to do with France's treatment of its Jews. Between
1944 and 1955, the country went through a purge of national memory under the
leadership of (by then) President de Gaulle: collaborators were put on trial and
thrown out of their jobs, atrocities committed by French collaborators on other
(resistance and resistance-oriented) French citizens were made public, while other
atrocities committed by the resistance were covered up. What resulted was a ten-
year shift in memory in which France became the mythical land of resistance
against the Nazis and in which the country took part in its own liberation. But
as Serge Klarsfeld, a French Nazi hunter, put it, "De Gaulle had to give France
back its honor, he had to uplift and reunify the nation by burying the profound
differences between those who supported the Vichy government and those who
sided from the beginning with the Resistance. After all, most of the victims in
France were Jews. He didn't think it was worth torturing the nation's souls just
for them" by reminding them of this unpleasant fact. In fact, Vichy passed its own
race laws against the Jews, and set up its own concentration-camp system without being ordered to do so by the Germans. Jews in the Nazi-occupied part of
France were less likely to be deported to Auschwitz than those in the unoccupied
south; Jews in Vichy were more likely to be victims of anti-Jewish violence than
were those in Paris. There was a great deal of anti-Semitism in Vichy as well as
in France during and before the war; the popularity of Pétain not only in Vichy
but throughout France in 1940 was due in part to his victories in World War I
and in part to his nativist French sentiments. When Marcel Ophuls released his
long film, *The Sorrow and the Pity,* in 1972—a film that emphasized the anti-
Semitism and cowardice of the Vichy period—it was banned in France for almost
a decade. For at least 30 years after the war, silence was the most palpable reminder of the Holocaust in France. Another film, *Night and Fog,* created by Alain
Resnais in 1955—emphasizing the chronology and the systematicity of the Holocaust—cuts back and forth between black-and-white footage of the camps and
of the transports and color footage of the decrepit camps and rail lines today.
What it fails to mention is the fact that France had its own concentration and
trasport camps, and that those who were the Holocaust's victims were Jews. (The
word is not used once in the film; only "prisoners" or "victims.") In other words,
though clearly about the Holocaust, *Night and Fog* depicts the silence in France
that resulted from its ambivalent position toward Jews.

United States

Until the Eichmann trial, there was a great deal of silence after the Holocaust in
the United States as well. In fact, the term "Holocaust" was not widely adopted
to refer to the destruction of European Jewry during the war until the early 1960s.

For the same reasons the survivors in Israel were reluctant to say what had happened to them—embarrassment, a sense that they wouldn't be believed, a determination to move on—so were the survivors who came to the States. A greater number came than would otherwise have come had Britain agreed, in 1946, to a U.S.-sponsored plan to allow 100,000 Jews from Europe into Palestine. Instead, two thirds of those who emigrated from Europe came to the United States. But very much like the experience of survivors in Israel, those in the United States felt isolated: few Jewish organizations set up support networks for Holocaust victims, and even fewer non-Jewish organizations felt the need to do so. Only one other group in the United States shared some of their experiences—the soldiers who had liberated the camps—but their memories too were mainly kept to themselves. Part of this was because non-Jewish Americans failed to recognize the significance of the events for their Jewish fellow-citizens; part of this is, undoubtedly, also the result of a low- to mid-frequency anti-Semitism that lingered in the American consciousness, something that may have accounted for some Americans' sense that the "displaced persons," the more common term for Jewish victims of the Nazi years who had come to the United States, were victimized because they were weak and vulnerable in the first place.

In the 1950s, Raul Hilberg was completing a comprehensive book on the Final Solution. He'd gone through countless documents in U.S. and German archives, had traveled throughout Europe to do his research, and had collected a huge amount of evidence to support his thesis. But when he approached publishers, his book was rejected time and time again. He submitted it to the press at Yad Vashem, which was one of the few outlets for Holocaust-related material, but it was rejected even there. To this day, Hilberg refuses to say why, but Yehuda Bauer has speculated that it was because of a strand in his thesis that argued that the Jewish Councils played a role in the destruction of Jews throughout Europe. His book was eventually published in the United States in 1961, in the midst of the Eichmann trial. Partly for these reasons, the book got quite a bit of press in reviews, most of it negative.

This shouldn't have been the case. Hilberg's book is now recognized as a masterpiece. It documents, from the very beginnings of the Third Reich, the genesis of the Nazis' plans for the Jews, the possible routes the Final Solution could have taken but for circumstance and the directions—sometimes quite unexpected— that the war's progress took. It also establishes the historical precedents for the Final Solution, examining the early modern origins of the yellow star, the ghettos, the Jewish Councils, and the Nuremberg laws. Hilberg's book was most criticized for its apparent omission of the perspective of Jewish victims themselves. When it was accounted for, it was done through the perspective of the *Judenrate,* not from those of individuals in the ghettos or camps or in hiding. This was not surprising: in the 1950s there were very few written memoirs or diaries available, and so those individual perspectives were simply not in the archives or in public view. The documents detailing the Nazis' policy, however, were available because they had been collected by the Allied armies as they closed in on Berlin in 1944 and 1945. (The Nazis, moreover, were meticulous recordkeepers, to the point of recording the names and ages of individuals transported to the camps and killed there.) In any event, Hilberg's book was the first of many historical accounts of the Holocaust, and it provided a blueprint for the methodologies of those who would follow.

A PERIOD OF TRANSITION

Hilberg's book was published in the same year as the Eichmann trial, 1961, and that year forms something of a watershed in the perception and the study of the Holocaust. (Peter Novick's influential book, *The Holocaust in American Life*, calls that year a "transition" point in the event's history after the war.) Adolf Eichmann, the chief bureaucrat of the Final Solution, managed to escape Europe after the war, and lived for nearly a decade in Argentina before he was captured in Buenos Aires in 1960 by agents of the Israeli government. In the spring and summer of 1961 he was put on trial in Jerusalem for fifteen counts, including war crimes, crimes against humanity, and crimes against the Jewish people.

Eichmann's trial was very different from the Nuremberg tribunal fifteen years earlier. For one thing, the trial was not held under international jurisdiction but in an Israeli court. The particularity of the venue meant that, unlike the accused in Nuremberg, Eichmann was sitting among those who survived the crimes for which he was accused as well as a large group of those who founded the state of Israel to ensure that nothing like the Final Solution could be perpetrated again. The Eichmann trial was different also in that it was broadcast throughout the world—on television in its entirety in Israel, and in its entirety on radio in the United States and in portions on TV—to a vastly larger audience, many of which either did not know or did not want to know about the atrocities committed in the name of Nazism. David Ben Gurion, Israel's Prime Minister and one of the founders of the state, knew this. He saw the trial as an opportunity to make clear to the world once and for all what had happened to the Jews of Europe. As much as this was a trial to determine the guilt or innocence of the Final Solution's chief bureaucrat, it was also putting Germany, and the world, on trial for its complicity in anti-Semitism and mass murder.

Hannah Arendt, a political theorist and philosopher who escaped from Germany in 1933 and eventually came to the United States in 1941, covered the trial for the *New Yorker* magazine and published a longer account of the proceedings in 1963 under the title *Eichmann in Jerusalem: A Report on the Banality of Evil.* She was interested not only in reporting on the trial, but on the difficulty of bringing a man to justice who didn't see himself as particularly horrible, or his actions as exceptional. Her book also asked serious questions about the fairness of the trial itself, about the wisdom of the prosecution's strategy of bringing witnesses forward who had no direct knowledge of Eichmann's part in the Final Solution but who were witnesses instead to its horrors. And she also asked probing questions about the relation between the machinery of death Eichmann put into motion and the inability—or failure—of Jews to resist it. One of Arendt's conclusions—in part based on her groundbreaking earlier work, *The Origins of Totalitarianism* (1951)—was that "The trouble with Eichmann was precisely that so many were like him, and that the many were neither perverted nor sadistic, that they were, and still are, terribly and horrifyingly normal" (276). People were troubled by her thesis about the "banality of evil" (a thesis that is misunderstood even today). They were troubled even more by her conclusion that, by focusing on crimes against the Jewish people, "at no point . . . did the Jerusalem trial ever mention the possibility that extermination of whole ethnic groups—the Jews, the Poles, or the Gypsies—might be more than a crime against the Jewish or the Polish or the Gypsy people, that the international order, and mankind in its entirety, might have been grievously hurt and endangered" (275–6).

The great success of the trial, in the eyes of many, was that it pointed to the particularity of the Holocaust as a crime aimed at Jews; Arendt saw this as its signal failure. Because the trial was "staged" for the world, it could not, like the Nuremberg trials, create a link between the intent of the Final Solution—an intent focused on racial purity and aimed primarily against Jews—and the effect of the Holocaust on others whose complicity was manifested by inaction (which is, after all, "horrifyingly normal"). And because Hilberg's book seemed to make at least the same implicit point about the machinery of the Final Solution—that those who implemented it failed to see the horror behind its details, and that those who were caught up in it were unable to resist it in any significant way—both Arendt and Hilberg were seen as somehow wrong.

Two years after the Eichmann trial, Arendt's thesis on the "banality of evil" seemed to be confirmed in the work of Stanley Milgram, a young psychology professor at Yale University who was interested in questions of complicity and conformity. Milgram's work was influenced in part by his background as a first-generation Jewish American and his identification with the suffering of fellow Jews at the hands of the Nazis. His work could be seen as an attempt to fathom how the Holocaust could have happened. In his study, he found that an average, presumably normal group of New Haven, Connecticut, residents would readily inflict very painful and perhaps even harmful electric shocks on innocent victims. The subjects believed they were part of an experiment supposedly dealing with the relationship between punishment and learning. An experimenter—who used no coercive powers beyond a stern aura of efficiency—instructed participants to shock a learner by pressing a lever on a machine each time the learner made a mistake on a word-matching task. Each subsequent error led to an increase in the intensity of the shock in 15-volt increments, from 15 to 450 volts. In fact, the "shock box" was a prop and the learner an actor who did not actually get shocked. A majority of the subjects continued to obey to the end—believing they were delivering 450-volt shocks—simply because the experimenter told them to. Although subjects were told about the deception afterward, the experience was a very real and powerful one for them during the laboratory hour itself. Milgram's experiment, the results of which were published in 1963, showed that ordinary people could be induced to act destructively even in the absence of physical coercion, and humans don't have to be evil or aberrant to act in ways that are reprehensible and inhumane.

Eight years later, in 1971, Philip Zimbardo of Stanford University ran a similar experiment. Twenty young men were told that they would role-play as prisoners or guards in the basement of the psychology department at the university. Prisoners lived there day and night. Guards worked eight-hour shifts. Half of the subjects were randomly selected to be guards and half to be prisoners. Prisoners underwent mock arrests, and went through a formal arrest procedure exactly as they would arrest potential criminals, and were blindfolded so that they would not be aware of where they were going when they were taken from the police station down to the prison basement. They were stripped naked, allegedly to be deloused. When the blindfold was taken off, the guards stood laughing at and ridiculing each prisoner. The experiment had to be halted after seven days, because too many people became severely distressed, guards abused and dehumanized the inmates, and the previously normal, healthy prisoners had extreme stress reactions. Zimbardo had not anticipated that a benign group of students, knowing they were involved in what was essentially a game, would become so transformed. Zimbardo's aborted experiment seemed to confirm the extent to which circumstances themselves, like those involving dehumanization and concentration, and not ideology, could in fact turn evil and yet be "horrifyingly normal."

There were other early studies that were undertaken during the "silent" years. Viktor Frankl's book *Man's Search for Meaning,* published in 1963, was written from the perspective of his experience in the camps. In the book—somewhat the reverse of Milgram—he depicts the camps, particularly Auschwitz, as laboratories for the life one must live in the normal world. The death camp was a "testing ground" where "some of our comrades behaved like swine while others behaved like saints." The upshot of his observations is that "Man has both potentialities in himself"—to behave like a hero or a villain—though "which is actualized depends upon decisions but not on conditions" (Frankl 212). His focus upon the conditions of the camps and their effect upon human behavior has been complicated since the early 1960s (most notably by Tzvetan Todorov in *Facing the Extreme,* published in 1997), but his study was among the first to consider the relation between a life of suffering in the camps and the "normal" life outside them as important. Bruno Bettelheim, also a victim of a concentration camp for a short time, was the head of the University of Chicago's Orthogenic School for troubled children. He began directing the program in 1944, only six years after spending time in Buchenwald and Dachau; his experiences there affected his work in profound ways. Bettelheim believed that a child's disturbed behavior did not need to be cured, because it was a way of expressing her sense of the world and of herself. The Orthogenic School provided an insulated environment, away from the pressures of family, that provided therapy, education, understanding, and discipline, in which the child might abandon her abnormal expression of self and her world and forge a more realistic relationship with the world. This way of thinking about behavior was of a piece with his writing that it was a sort of abnormal, "ghetto thinking" on the part of Jews that led, at least in part, to making the Holocaust possible in the first place. His "Individual and Mass Behavior in Extreme Situations," published in 1943, was the earliest firsthand testimony of the atrocities taking place in Nazi Germany, and certainly the first scholarly—or, to Bettelheim's critics (and there are now many), pseudo-scholarly—account of those atrocities as a manifestation of human behavior.

In the decades after the Holocaust, a number of philosophical and theological writings—focusing mainly on the question of evil and the scheme in which such evil was possible—were published. Emil Fackenheim's famous "614th Commandment," a reference to the commandments given to the Jewish people on Sinai and to the additional commandment ("give Hitler no posthumous victories") required by the Holocaust, is a distillation of the post-Holocaust theology he works out more fully in his books *God's Presence in History* and *The Jewish Return into History: Reflections in the Age of Auschwitz and a New Jerusalem.* He essentially argues, as do many others who follow his work, that in order to understand the Holocaust, we have to divorce that understanding from an understanding of God. While it is true that the Holocaust is a watershed event that provides Jews with an urgent need to forge new ways to survive, it is not clear the extent to which it provides a new way to understand theodicy, the question of why evil exists in a divinely given world. Another religious focus of attention is the question of the role of the established churches—primarily the Catholic church, but also the Protestant denominations of central Europe—in the implementation of the Final Solution. Among these early works are Saul Friedlander's *Pius XII and the Third Reich* (1966), Gunter Lewy's *The Catholic Church and Nazi Germany* (1964), and Franklin Littell's *The German Church Struggle and the Holocaust* (1974).

The Emergence of Holocaust Studies

Holocaust studies, as a field, emerged in the late 1960s or early 1970s, and the events of those decades heightened interest in the events of the Holocaust enough to encourage the formation of a community of scholars—albeit still often un-recognized as a community—whose objects of study were the events of the Holocaust. This community saw its work not only as understanding the Holocaust—insofar as it could be understood—but to focus on the methodologies that would make the event visible, to expand the boundaries of those disciplines, and to encourage the borrowing of one anothers' methodologies when confronted with the extreme circumstances of those events.

But why did the field emerge only in the 1960s and 1970s? In part, it had to do with the early work done by those like Arendt, Hilberg, Milgram, and others who pioneered studies of the circumstances that led to a generation of silence. These individuals and others like them began finally to suggest that there were ways of making sense of the events of the war years, and that it was important to understand their effects on the victims. In part, however, the field's emergence in those years had to do with historical events that, while having little to do with the Holocaust as such, overlapped with some of the same concerns Holocaust historians and other scholars had. One of these events was the 1967 Six-Day War. Paired with the Yom Kippur War of 1973, and seen in the context of the Suez Crisis of 1956, the Six-Day War seemed to catapult Israel from an odd anomaly on the world stage—a pseudo-socialist experiment in democracy, one that sprang from Zionist roots but that pledged itself to a multiethnic but firmly Jewish state—to a world power capable of protecting its (Jewish) citizens from an on-slaught of national power bent on eliminating it. For its first thirty years of exis-tence, Israel struggled through the need to assimilate Jews from all over the world, and in particular Jews from the ruins of Europe, to a Middle Eastern and decid-edly socialist culture. The founders of the state, largely Bundists and other left-leaning and pro-labor men and women who'd settled there in the years before the war, were intent on creating a society that was communitarian, egalitarian, and whose economy was based on its indigenous resources (which, at the state's in-ception, were few). It attempted to do this in the face of Arab anger over the state's ejection of a majority of its Arab population and the destruction of its vil-lages, and a sense that Israel was trying to erase Palestine's Arab and Islamic (not to mention bicultural) identity. Israel had fought a war for independence that it could very easily have lost were it not for two ceasefires that allowed its armies to catch their collective breath. Moreover, it had always seemed a tenuous creation on a sliver of land between its vastly more populous and heavier-armed Arab neighbors and the Mediterranean.

The United States saw Israel as a bulwark against the increasingly left-oriented Arab States (Iraq, Syria, and Nasser's nonaligned Egypt) and thus an ally worth protecting after the Suez crisis. The crisis was sparked by Gamel Abdel Nasser's nationalization of the Suez Canal, which infuriated the British, who had built it in the late nineteenth century, because Nasser's action seemed to threaten the passage of trade through the canal. The French, who had been selling military hardware to Israel, joined with the British, and armies from the two nations seized the Egyptian port of Alexandria and convinced Israel to advance on the Suez peninsula in late October of that year. In the United States, President Eisenhower was unwilling to support what he saw as an ill-conceived scheme that might possibly bring the Soviet Union into the melee. Eventually the three armies withdrew and were replaced by a UN force, on the urging of the United States. The crisis, however bungled, proved three things. First, it proved that Israel, which had easily crushed the Soviet-armed Egyptian army, was a military force to be contended with; second, it proved to Eisenhower that the country might be used as a bulwark against a possible Soviet alliance with anti-Israel Arab states; and third, it suggested to Israel's neighbors that—because of its alliance with the west—it was a proto-colonialist state that posed to them a threat.

This led to an alliance between Egypt, Syria, and Iraq in the short-lived "United Arab Republic," and an increase in the militarization of these states for a war with Israel to destroy it. In May 1967, Nasser asked the UN to withdraw its troops from the Suez, where they'd been since 1956; he did so to clear the way for his own invasion of Israel from the south. Israel's generals saw this along with Syrian and Iraqi preparations, and on June 4 Israel launched a preemptive war. It was a swift and crushing defeat, in which Israel captured the Golan Heights from the Syrians, the entire Suez Peninsula from the Egyptians, and the West Bank of the Jordan River (and the biggest prize of all, the Old City of Jerusalem) from Jordan. In 1973, on the first day of Yom Kippur, the combined Arab armies attacked Israel again, and in the first several days of the war, had taken Israeli territory, inflicted heavy damage on the Israeli air force, and scared the generals and the prime minister into asking the United States for aid, which it received in the form of $2.2 billion in military hardware. After three weeks of war, a ceasefire was declared. By that time, Israel had recaptured all its territory and it had fought the Arab armies to a standstill. Though the United States, intervention may have finally turned the tide of the war, the 1967 and 1973 Israeli wars (each of which had amassed huge support throughout the Jewish community abroad) proved that Jews could fight and win wars, and could by themselves resist a threat of annihilation successfully. If there is a myth of invincibility in the Israeli Armed Forces that has survived its more recent wars of attrition, it was born in 1967 and matured in 1973. And if one needed to pinpoint the time at which the Palestinian crisis was born, it was with the Israeli capture, during the 1967 and 1973 wars, of the portion of Jordan that contained vast numbers of Palestinian refugee camps. From this point on, the Israeli wars of survival were seen by the Palestinians who lost their lands in 1948 as colonial wars to cleanse the land of non-Jews.

These wars also created an intense feeling of pride among Jews worldwide, but particularly in the United States and Israel. They convinced the Holocaust's silent generation that they need not remain embarrassed or guilty. According to Judith Miller, author of *One by One by One,* "because Jews no longer felt so absolutely vulnerable, they could finally confront the period of their most intense vulnerability. . . . [T]he growing awareness of the Holocaust in the wake of the 1967 war led children of Holocaust survivors and other young Jews to feel that they had a special obligation to try to right perceived wrongs," and "transformed the Holocaust into a quasi-religious event, a sign not only of suffering, but also of resurrection" (223). Almost as a corrective to Hilberg's *The Destruction of the European Jews,* Lucy Dawidowicz published *The War Against the Jews* in 1975. Its author was a researcher with the YIVO Institute for Jewish Learning in Vilna (and later New York) and a professor of Holocaust history at Yeshiva University. In her book Dawidowicz split her attention between the machinery of the Final Solution and the fate of the Jews during the war, seeing "the Holocaust" and "the Final Solution" as two interrelated but separate phenomena. In contrast to Hilberg, she gave over a good portion of her book to Jewish resistance during the Holocaust—the Warsaw Ghetto Uprising, attempts to destroy crematoria in the death camps, connections between Polish and Jewish undergrounds and residents of ghettos and camps—in response to the new Jewish paradigm of heroism and resistance borne of the Six-Day and Yom Kippur Wars.

In 1978 President Carter—responding to initiatives by congressmen, Jewish organizations, and Holocaust survivors who had become American businesspeople, philanthropists, and public figures—authorized the President's Commission on the Holocaust. The Commission, chaired by Holocaust survivor and author Elie Wiesel, was charged to make recommendations on how the United States should commemorate the Holocaust. That the United States should commemorate the event at all, an event that took place in Europe and that the United State did arguably nothing to prevent, was a major change in public perception of the event. It had, by the late 1970s, become "Americanized." Within ten months, the Commission recommended the construction of a museum and living monument in the capital, Washington, D.C., which would eventually become the United States Holocaust Memorial Museum, which opened on Holocaust Remembrance Day in 1993. Celebrating Holocaust Remembrance Day in the United States also signaled a major shift. It had been a day of memory written into the secular/religious calendar of Israel at around the same time the Yad Vashem Heroes' and Martyrs' Remembrance Authority was initiated. Now, in the United States, it had become an opportunity for Jews and non-Jews alike to reflect on what happened during the war years and on what had happened since—Cambodia, Bosnia, Rwanda. Edward Linenthal has aptly chronicled how the fifteen-year process of defining and building the national memorial to the Holocaust became a process of arguing over what the Holocaust was (and wasn't): a genocide modeled after the Armenian genocide of 1914–15; a genocide against all the non-Aryan peoples of Europe; a concerted effort to eliminate Jews from the world; one of several anti-Jewish pogroms, the latest of which—the wars against Israel in 1967 and 1973—had been prevented; and many other possibilities. The Museum eventually contained a huge archive of historical documents, and sponsored a significant number of research fellowships, teaching forums, and public events, all of which suggests that the Holocaust had by the 1990s become a real object of public and intellectual scrutiny. The Fortunoff Video Archive of Holocaust Testimonies was founded at Yale University in 1981 and opened in 1982, and the Survivors of the Shoah Foundation (sponsored by Steven Spielberg and led by the former Director of the USHMM, Michael Berenbaum) was begun in 1994 in recognition that the memories of those who survived would not be available very much longer, and that those memories in some cases provided the only direct link to the events of the Holocaust themselves. Perhaps also in view of the demise of private if not public memory—but also knowing full well that the Holocaust had become highly visible in the popular imagination—NBC produced a week-long miniseries, *Holocaust,* in 1978 that traced the lives of several European Jewish characters (and that of one Nazi officer) through a set of (imagined) events. Steven Spielberg created *Schindler's List,* perhaps the best-known film about the Holocaust, in 1993, which won the Academy Award for Best Picture in 1994 and was offered as a tool for Holocaust education by Spielberg himself. (Perhaps the best Holocaust film ever made, Claude Lanzmann's ten-hour-long *Shoah*—shown in 1983 on, and made for, French television—is not often shown in the United States.)

Over the last twenty years, the attention garnered by the events of the Holocaust has also produced a backlash. It's taken two forms, one cultural and one intellectual, though they're linked. In cultural terms, the freedom to talk about the Holocaust as a historical phenomenon in both the United States and in Europe, but particularly in France, led to a spike in the incidents of anti-Semitism in both countries. It was almost as if people had had enough of the Holocaust and whatever cultural guilt it might have created. In 1978 in France, Robert Faurisson, a professor of literature at the University of Lyon, denounced the "Holocaust lie." He claimed that the gas chambers never existed, and that the Final Solution was not policy (nor was there such a policy in France). He went on to say that the popularization of the Holocaust was the result of a campaign by a "Jewish lobby," in particular by Serge Klarsfeld, who finally had Klaus Barbie (the chief of the Gestapo in occupied Lyon who was convicted in absentia for war crimes) extradited to France. Faurisson was also reacting to books and essays that had been writ-ten in the 1960s and 1970s that had begun to expose the "myth" that France's Jews had been exterminated by the Nazis alone, and made clear that the anti-Semitism that lay dormant in France before the war exploded during the years of occupa-tion and of Vichy with deadly consequences for 75,000 of France's Jews. France's anti-Semitism was coupled with nativist anxiety about an influx of hundreds of thousands of immigrants from north Africa—one of the consequences of France's long war over its colony in Algeria—250,000 of whom were Jews who migrated from that region during the 1950s and 1960s. By the 1980s, there were arguments in the French legislature between rightists and Gaullists, who were insisting that France never had a Jewish "problem," and left-leaning parties including the So-cialists and the Communists, to denounce such claims as ignorance and their propagators as "fascists." During the 1980s, there was also an increase in popu-larity of the French National Front, led by Jean-Marie Le Pen, which coupled anti-Arab sentiment with anti-Semitic language. Members of the National Front, some of whose thugs dressed in Nazi garb, perpetrated acts of anti-Arab and anti-Jewish violence during those years. In short, because France was becoming more critical of its history and the cultural memory that had been forged to contain it, the movement to preserve its "mythical" national memory became violently op-posed to anything that might threaten it. To go to the root of the myth, and to argue that there was no anti-Semitism in France and that its Holocaust (or any Holocaust, for that matter) never occurred, seemed one sure way to secure the myth.

The politics involved in the backlash against the Holocaust (what Peter Novick calls "Holocaust consciousness") in the United States were similar to what hap-pened in France, but took a different tack. Whereas in France Holocaust denial and anti-Semitism could be traced to France's history, in the United States the backlash could just as easily be traced to Israel's. As in France, the victories by Is-rael in 1967 and 1973 seemed to provide survivors of the war and of the Holo-caust an occasion to speak about what had happened, but they also provided a pretext for denying it: the Israeli victories unleashed among survivors and skep-tics alike an awareness of the link between the Holocaust's destruction of the Jews and the more recent wars' guarantee of Jewish survival, at least in Israel. In the United States, the media seemed to become saturated with images and stories of the Holocaust: the British multipart "World at War" series, broadcast on Public Television in the 1970s, featured an hour devoted to the Holocaust (with its im-ages of the camps and of the heaps of bodies found by the liberators). The movie *Sophie's Choice,* an adaptation of William Styron's novel that involves a camp pris-oner forced to choose which of her children to send to death, captivated Amer-ican audiences in 1982. Elie Wiesel had already become something of a celebrity for his visibility in debates surrounding the humanitarian agenda of the Carter administration. More than anything else, the United States' perceived tilt toward Israel in world affairs, and the perception that this tilt was the result of lobbying by Jewish Americans in government, the media, and business, produced an awareness of the Holocaust that had a double edge, neither of which was wholly positive. On one edge was the fact that the Holocaust came to be associated with nearly any atrocity, or crisis, or conflagration in the media. As Peter Novick notes, the Televangelist Jim Bakker called the accusations of mismanagement of his media empire a "holocaust," and pro-life activists called abortion a holocaust of the unborn. It became so extreme that the actual event of the Holocaust began to lose its specificity and, some would argue, its moral force. On the other edge was the connection between Holocaust awareness and "Israel awareness," a connection that led to charges that U.S. foreign policy in particular, and American Jews in general, were unwilling to acknowledge the unjustness of Israel's Palestinian policy, and were unwilling to criticize Israel at all. This led, in some circles, to an anti-Israeli sentiment that bordered on anti-Semitism.

The intellectual facet to the backlash can be seen in two controversial books published around the same time: Peter Novick's *The Holocaust in American Life* (1999) and Norman Finkelstein's *The Holocaust Industry: Reflections on the Exploitation of Jewish Suffering* (2000). Using different methodologies and choosing different objects of focus, Novick and Finkelstein would concur that the Holocaust has perhaps too prominent a place in Jewish self-understanding and cultural identification. They also agree that it figures as iconic in most non-Jews' ideas about suffering, anti-Semitism, and politics. Finkelstein is critical of nearly every use of the term "Holocaust" that isn't tied directly to the testimonies of those who were there and to actual historical documents, whereas Novick seems to be more interested in the effects of the term's infiltration into various American (and other) discourses. Both scholars are suspicious of the "popularity" of the Holocaust as an object of study and of the American cultural imagination. The fact that the Holocaust seems to be a compulsory, if also perfunctory, unit in public school curricula and on university course websites—and the fact of this book—seem to be evidence that the term "Holocaust" may have lost its usefulness as a description of the events that took place in Europe over a half century ago.

□ □ □

Some of the chapters that follow will respond directly to the questions raised by Novick and Finkelstein. More to the point, all of the chapters will provide some productive ways to examine not just the events of the Holocaust but the ways in which those events are made visible in the historical, cultural, and popular imagination in the United States and elsewhere. While Novick and Finkelstein may be right to say that the Holocaust may in fact be too much of a presence in our everyday discourse, it's not right to say that we should therefore remove it—to some extent or perhaps completely—from our vocabulary. What's far more crucial, I think, is to discover how the Holocaust has been represented in the various disciplines in which it is studied and the vocabularies we use to describe it, and what the strengths and weaknesses of those representations and the moral and ethical demands those representations make (and don't make) on those who create and use them. We'll begin with the question of history—the main debates that historians engage in when discussing the Holocaust—but we'll press on the term "history" itself in productive and sometimes disturbing ways. From there we'll move to consider the promise and problems inherent in the privileging of eyewitnesses to the Holocaust: how do the genres their authors use—the ways they tell their stories—affect our understanding of them, and are there better and worse ways to say what happened during the Holocaust? And we'll confront the question of whether the event itself puts so much pressure on language that it stands in the way of what we can learn from such testimony. Finally, we'll turn our attention to what happens when we move away from "what happened" and focus instead on what individuals—artists, writers, photographers, and liars—imagine happened. In short, rather than spend time examining the Holocaust alone, the remainder of this book will pay attention to how those examinations change the nature of the event itself, both for good and for ill.

DISCUSSION QUESTIONS, Part I

1. In what ways is the Holocaust historically "unique"? In what ways is it like other historical events?

2. Why is it necessary to know about Jewish life in Europe in order to understand the Holocaust?

3. To what extent is the Holocaust defined by its destruction of Europe's Jews? To what extent does that definition become enriched (or broadened, or narrowed) when we consider other groups who were targeted for destruction?

4. To what extent does historical evidence "count" differently than evidence in theology, or the arts, or the sciences? Are such distinctions relevant in our understanding of the Holocaust? Why or why not?

5. Is America's Holocaust different from Israel's or Germany's? In what ways? How do these differences enrich or problematize what we know about the Holocaust?

6. What, if anything, does the Holocaust tell us about the human condition?

7. What's the diference between "Holocaust studies" and a history of the Holocaust?

8. How do the academic disciplines—philosophy, literature, history, religious studies, anthropology/sociology, the sciences—see the Holocaust differently from one another?

9. How problematic is the fact that different countries "use" the Holocaust as part of building a national identity? (Is using events like the Holocaust inevitable?)

10. How has the Holocaust changed history? How has it changed how we see the present? (Has it really changed history at all?)

II | HISTORY

CHAPTER 3

The Holocaust
in History

The Holocaust has undergone a profound change in the last sixty years. The issues that have been considered central to its history have also undergone profound shifts since the event's immediate aftermath. But acknowledging these shifts in focus is not, of course, to say that the Holocaust *as an event* has changed. The Holocaust happened, and the numbers—of the dead; of the vast array of camps; the records kept by the Wehrmach, the SS, and the German Reichsbahn; the accounts of survivors—seem often to speak for themselves.

But what it does mean is that what we know about the event, the *shape* of the event in historical terms, has shifted and those shifts have had a profound impact on the event's implications for us and for how we study, and write, history. To cite one example that I'll come back to, Yehuda Bauer has recently suggested that if we see the Holocaust as one among many instances of genocide in the 20th century and in the centuries before it, the historical stakes of the event become both lower and higher: lower because the Holocaust, on such a historical accounting, is deprived of its "unique" status among events of history; and higher, because the lessons one can learn from studying its history have farther reaching and more contemporary implications. So, though the numbers seem to speak for themselves, what each individual hears them say may be quite different.

This chapter provides an overview of some of the significant contemporary debates that surround the history of the Holocaust. These include, among others, the question of the event's "uniqueness" and its specifically Jewish character; the intentionalist/functionalist debate over precisely who or what bureaucracies dictated and shaped the outcome of the Final Solution; how the intentionalist/func-

43

tionalist debate became superseded, particularly in work coming out of Germany, by a sort of anthropological or sociological "thick description" of the conditions in which the Final Solution became policy; the argument between Christopher Browning and Daniel Goldhagen over the complicity of Germans in the destruction of Europe's Jews and that argument's "popularization;" the growing awareness of the victimization of non-Jews, particularly homosexual men and the T-4 campaign (ended officially in 1941) against the disabled, and the inception of the study of gender and the differences it implied in the treatment and the coping strategies of women; and how what Primo Levi called a moral "gray zone" complicates the tripartite division of focus on perpetrator, victim, and bystander. But my intention is not only to lay out these changes of focus for those interested in the study of the Holocaust. It is to note how each changes the historical questions one can ask about the event itself, including what counts as evidence, what options are available to historians in their choices of perspective, method, and language, and what (if any) risks are involved in certain historical lines of argument.

□ □ □

UNIQUENESS

Whether or not the events comprising the Final Solution were unique historical events began as early as 1943. Rafael Lemkin, a refugee from Poland who had become a lawyer in New York, that year began to receive information about the persecution of Jews and others, and on that basis formulated the term "genocide." It asserted as genocidal any act that aims at the total extermination of a people, and included as descriptors "extreme deprivation, destruction of educational institutions, interference in religious life, general denationalization," and moral poisoning of cultural life (cited in Berenbaum 20).

Lemkin's definition was to a certain degree the basis of the United Nations' Convention on Genocide, which was approved in 1948 after the conclusion of the Nuremburg War Crimes trial. That convention reads in part:

> [G]enocide means any of the following acts committed with the intent to destroy, in whole or in part, a national, ethnical or religious group, as such:
>   (a) killing members of the group; (b) causing serious bodily or mental harm to members of the group; (c) deliberately inflicting on the group conditions of life calculated to bring about its physical destruction in whole or in part; (d) imposing measures intended to prevent births within the group; (e) forcibly transferring children of the group to another group.

The difference between the two definitions—Lemkin's and the one adopted by the UN—is that intentions count, not just the outcome. Under Lemkin's definition the subordination of Africans and American-born blacks during the three hundred years of legal African slavery in this country would count as genocide. It would not under the UN's, because the intent of the African slave trade was not to destroy a people, only to enslave it and thereby change its character (if one can even use the term "only" here).

In other words, the UN's definition of genocide narrows the historical events that might qualify it for prosecution. And it also seemed to narrow those crimes or actions that might be seen to be in the same moral league with the Holocaust. Under Lemkin's definition, the Holocaust is not historically unique; under the UN's, it may well have been (up until, at any rate, more recent times). It's possible to ask whether the regime of Pol Pot in Cambodia, or the ethnic cleansing of large swaths of the former Yugoslavia by Slobodan Milosevic, or the brutal killing of a million Hutus by Tutsi nationalists in Rwanda, qualify as genocides, or even Holocausts, under these definitions.

The issue of the Holocaust's uniqueness has presented not only historical questions but also moral and theological ones. Emil Fackenheim, whose philosophical work on Jewish thought and culture in many ways directly responds to the Holocaust (during which he was imprisoned in the Sachenhausen concentration camp), suggests that we have categories in philosophy and theology—those having to do with radical evil—that explain the intention and the results of the events that comprised the Holocaust even if history doesn't. Fackenheim wonders whether it is productive to describe anything as unique, since doing so would run counter to the human impulse to explain in general terms any events at all. Theological or philosophical categories aside, however, Fackenheim goes on to suggest that it is the facts of the event—the numbers—that (in Michael Berenbaum's terms) present "a configuration without parallel in history" (*Holocaust* 2). Because of its intention (its goal was, for Fackenheim, the total destruction of the Jewish people), its comprehensiveness (all Jews, no matter what age and by what definition), and its scope and systematicity, it is possible to say that the extremity of the Holocaust may require not an elimination of previous categories (evil, the divine, genocide) but a reconsideration of them. It is because of the historical facts of the event that Judaism has had to in many cases rethink portions of its theology, and this led Fackenheim to insist that we should add a new commandment to those found in the Torah (the first five books of the bible): Jews must not hand Hitler a posthumous victory, which—for Fackenheim—means that Jews must not ignore their status as Jews, and that they must not forget that it was this status that led to their near destruction. For Fackenheim, then, and for others who understand the Holocaust as *historically* unique, it is the facts of the event that prove its uniqueness, and it is the burden of the historian to lay bare those facts and the facts of other atrocities in order to make that uniqueness clear.

And historians have done just that, both by comparing the Holocaust to other genocides, and by examining the Final Solution itself in the context of National Socialist racial and national policies, and of the regime's conduct of the war. On the latter front, Yehuda Bauer has surveyed a large number of documents that lay out Nazi territorial policy in the eastern territories (Poland, Ukraine, Russia) in order to explain how the Slavic peoples—who were seen as racially inferior to northern, Germanic people—were treated in comparison to Jews. As the German armies rushed into the east, Heinrich Himmler—in consultation with Erhard Wetzel—had to decide whether to "germanize" the 130 million ethnic Poles, Ukranians, and Russians who could be assimilated into the Reich without "corrupting" the race, or to eliminate them by transporting them to areas outside the German area of control or killing them. (For political and logistical reasons, Wetzel wrote of the plan to Himmler, it is "obvious that the Polish question cannot be solved in such a way that one would liquidate the Poles in the same manner as the Jews" [quoted in Bauer, "Place" 23].) So as Bauer puts it, the Slavic policy was a genocide, but not a holocaust. The case is similar with respect to the Roma (or, to use the language of the time, gypsies): there is a great deal of evidence to suggest that they were concentrated and eliminated nearly wholesale under the same "racial purity" laws that were used to destroy the Jews. (Sybil Milton has written a number of esays on the treatment of the Roma; Henry Friedlander's work on the same subject appears in *The Origins of the Nazi Genocide*.) Nonetheless, others have argued—on the basis of recently acquired documents and a book written by Michael Zimmerman—that Himmler was interested in preserving the "unique" racial qualities of the Roma, and while many "gypsies" were liquidated, it was only those who were not of "pure" Roma or Sinti descent. (The irony here, of course, is that it was the "pure" Roma who were to be preserved, while it was the "pure" Jews who were scheduled for destruction.) Again, though there was persecution and even possibly genocide, it was not a "holocaust."

As for comparisons with other genocides, it is the Armenian genocide of 1915–16 that is most often raised as a foil to claims that the Holocaust of 1939–45 is historically unique (see Henry Friedlander's work on the comparison in *The Origins of the Nazi Genocide*; Kevork Dadrian's long essay on the documentation of the Armenian massacre is an extremely useful source.) A largely Christian minority in Islamic Ottoman Anatolia (after the first world war and the dissolution of the Ottoman Empire, the central region of Turkey), the Armenians numbered nearly two million, and—like the Jews of Germany—were an important facet of the society, having attained a strong economic middle, and even stronger intellectual, class. In the midst of World War I (which was being lost in Turkey) and amid rising nationalist and racial tensions, they were seen as standing in the way of a "greater Turkey," and—again like the case of the Jews during the Holocaust—their intellectual and political leaders were "removed" or executed. This was followed, in 1915 and early 1916, by the expulsion of huge portions of the Armenian population to the southeastern part of the country (which is largely desert), the disarmament, enslavement, and eventual murder of Armenian soldiers in the Ottoman army, which resulted in anywhere from 800,000 to 1.1 million deaths. Unlike the Holocaust, in which the Jews were seen as the central problem facing Germany and the world in the late 1930s, the Armenians were, at worst, a potentially insurrectionist segment of the Turkic world. The Armenian massacre could be justified as an attempt—if a wholly brutal one—to quell an uprising. The Jews weren't a political, let alone a military, threat.

This has led Bauer to proclaim that the Holocaust is not unique, but unprecedented. "To say that the Holocaust is inexplicable," he argues, "is to justify it" (38), reasoning that by cordoning it off from other historical events—tragedies, genocides, destructions of people in war or outside of martial contexts—we fail to learn anything from it, and are unable to note differences between it and those other events. By noting its unprecedented nature, on the other hand, we are forced to ask, "Unprecedented compared with what?" While the Holocaust may be a genocide under Raphael Lemkin's definition because it aimed at the expulsion or destruction of a people, defined in national, ethnic or religious terms, or its leadership, the destruction of the European Jews between 1933 and 1945 under the National Socialist regime in Germany is unprecedented in both its scope and its motivating ideology. What distinguishes the Holocaust from other genocides, in other words, was the fact that the former aimed at the destruction of *all* members of an ethnic/national/religious group. The Holocaust was also unprecedented in its motivation: while other genocides were undertaken for what Bauer calls "pragmatic ends"—Armenians were killed to quell incipient revolution; American Indians were killed to open the west; the Muslims in Bosnia were "cleansed" for the purpose of Serbian territorial integrity—the destruction of the Jews of Europe was the product of "a pure, abstract antisemitic ideology in the context of biological racism." Jews were put to death for the crime of being born Jews, Bauer tells us. The Holocaust, then, is both particular—it was a crime against Jews—and universal. Because the monumental crime against the Jews was a crime perpetrated by humans against humans, it is also the most universal of crimes: if it could happen once in one of the most civilized countries in Europe, surely it could happen again. (As in an argument recently and cogently made by Giorgio Agamben, Bauer says that the Holocaust is horrifying not because of its inhumanity but precisely because of its *humanity*: the horrible was made possible; the possible was made manifest.) Moreover, the Holocaust is not the unfathomable horror—beyond reason—that some scholars have made it out to be. Far from it: the events had clearly identifiable causes, there is plenty of documentation to support what we know about them (and there's more to be had since the opening of the Soviet archives), and it's people like Saul Friedlander, Daniel Goldhagen, and Christopher Browning who have done the most to explain those events in a language that defies mystification. The problem isn't that we don't have enough information; it's that we haven't found a paradigm in which to make sense—to produce knowledge—of it, not yet anyway. The biggest obstacle to eventually producing knowledge of the events is mystification: we're ignoring what we can learn from the events while trying to use them as grist for political or academic mills.

□ □ □

ANTISEMITISM

If the Holocaust *is* distinguishable from other genocides, one of its characteristics may be its motivation. Ethnic and religious animosities are nothing new to the twentieth century. But what may set the Holocaust apart from other pogroms, ethnic cleansing campaigns, and expulsions is the anti-Semitism that fomented it in Germany, parts of Europe, North America, and the Middle East. The extent to which anti-Semitism is a direct or indirect cause of the Holocaust is a subject open to fierce debate.

The question, however, isn't whether anti-Semitism played a role in the Holocaust. It undoubtedly did. The question is how deep-seated that anti-Semitism was, and in what ways it affected the motivations of those in Germany, Europe, and other parts of the world who implemented—or stood by during—the Final Solution. The term "anti-Semitism" itself is only about 130 years old, coined by Wilhelm Marr in his nationalist volume *Der Sieg des Judentums das Germanthum* (The Victory of Jewry over Germanness). In it he blamed Germany's and the world's economic problems on a cabal of Jews. But anti-Semitism has been around, at least officially, since the establishment of Christianity and its indignation over Jews' refusal to see the historical Jesus's teachings as categorically distinct from Judaism. (A very good introduction is provided by Robert Wistrich's book, *Antisemitism: The Longest Hatred,* which begins with the Greco-Roman world and works its way up to the contemporary Middle East, Europe, and the United States.)

Matters become especially complicated in the nineteenth century, particularly in Germany and France. "Emancipation" in Napoleonic France granted Jews full rights as citizens in return for the guarantee, authorized by a rabbinical board, that the laws specific to Judaism would not conflict or interfere with the laws of France. By the time of the defeat of Napoleon in 1815, Jews had become well integrated into the national life of France, and eventually Prussia (Germany became unified in 1871), Holland, Austria-Hungary, and other countries in western Europe. In part because of this integration, middle- and upper-class Jewish citizens became well-ensconced in the financial, mercantile, and industrial economies; and in part because of Jewish reform movements and the growth of what would eventually become Zionism, Jews became more and more secular, aligning themselves in many cases with workers and workers' rights, and in some cases with the interests of the financial class. With the economic depression of 1873, and with a growing suspicion of those who aligned themselves with the increasing agitation for reform for workers in England, France, and Germany, Jews became persecuted for a number of contradictory reasons, because of their links to communism and because of their links to capitalism.

At the same time as antipathy against some Jews was growing because of their increased integration with German, French, and English society, a new strand of anti-Semitism made itself visible: racial anti-Semitism. Marr had portrayed Jews as those who have "corrupted all standards, have banned all idealism from society, dominate commerce, push themselves ever more into state services, rule the theatre, form a social and political phalanx" (quoted in Massing 9). Others like Houston Chamberlain (in a book entitled *The Foundations of the Nineteenth Century*, published in 1899) twisted Charles Darwin's notions of natural selection into a "social Darwinist" theory that transposed the notion of survival of the fittest to races and cultures from species. Borrowing from fields such as biology, psychology, and even stockbreeding, the racial and social Darwinist anti-Semitism of the late nineteenth century held that Jews were a "breed apart," unable—not unwilling—to become full citizens of the nations in which they resided. Chamberlain managed to read the milleniums-old antipathy toward Jews and their geographical and social mobility into evidence that their racial separateness was characterized by an inability to settle or remain loyal, that they were parasitic upon nation-states, and that there would be an inevitable struggle beween the inherently superior Aryan races and those who were inferior, particularly Jews.

And yet this racist anti-Semitism was far from widespread in the mid- to late-nineteenth century. Albert Lindemann studied three separate anti-Semitic episodes in Europe and the United States between 1890 and 1920—the Dreyfus affair in France, the Beilis trial in Russia, and the Frank lynching in the United States—and concluded that while anti-Semitism had disastrous effects in all three countries, it was not nearly as monolithic or widespread as we have presumed. His analysis reveals that while there were racists of all stripes in all three countries, there existed fine gradations of anti-Semitism: while there were many who were suspicious of individual Jews' rising through the ranks of the military and the business world, those same people were not Jew-haters. Lindemann concludes that the exoneration of Dreyfus and the lynching of Frank (though not the acquittal of

Beilis) had the effect of an anti-anti-Semitic backlash, whereby anti-Jewish intellectuals were shunned by the public once the charges in the cases were proved
false and the base motives of those bringing the charges were brought to light. Lindemann's work, alongside that of Zygmunt Bauman in *Modernity and the Holocaust,* suggests that the Holocaust may have been motivated by an anti-Semitism
that had lain dormant in Europe for fifty years, but it was only one of several
economic, political, and social causes that combined to bring about the circumstances of the Final Solution.

World War I and its aftermath complicate matters even further. With the defeat of Germany and with the terms of the treaty that ended the war, the economic
and political conditions in that country reached a crisis. There's been significant
disagreement over whether it was the war reparations agreed under the Versailles
Treaty that caused the economic difficulties in Germany between 1920 and 1924
and again between 1930 and 1933. The withdrawal of Russia from the war in
1917 after the Soviet revolution, and the eventual success of the Bolsheviks over
the czarists during the four-year-long Russian civil war, led to a fear of "Jewish
Bolshevism." There were many Jews of Russian descent that had left the country
between 1880 and 1917 and settled in Poland, Germany, and France, and this
combined with a lingering sense that Jewish financiers, liberals, and pacifists
played a part in the German defeat (it became known as the "Jewish stab in the
back" of Germany). These facts led to a rise in anti-Semitic feeling in Europe
and in the United States, where restrictive immigration laws passed in 1921 and
1924 slowed immigration into the country drastically. *The Protocols of the Elders
of Zion,* a forgery created in Russia in the 1890s and circulated in Russia in 1905,
purportedly recording a Jewish plot to manipulate the world's economy and its
presses, was widely circulated after World War I.

A disenchanted group of German Nationalists, among them a former corpo-
ral in the German army named Adolf Hitler, formed the National Socialist party.
It combined nationalism, anti-communism, and racial anti-Semitism, and it eventually became one of the largest parties in Germany by the early 1930s. The extent to which the anti-Semitism of the National Socialists drove its pursuit of
power is greatly disputed, as is the extent to which Hitler's anti-Semitism was
made policy once Hitler was appointed German chancellor in 1933. What is clear,
however, is that for Hitler, the Jews had already gained control over the inferior
Slavs of Russia and Poland, and for that reason a campaign against both Communism and the Jewish "race" became a single campaign against anti-German
ideology. Coupled with what Uta Gerhard has called Nazism's anti-state ideology—"the intent . . . [to replace the civil service] with an ideological party bureaucracy" (cited in Bauer, *Rethinking* 84)—National Socialism focused intently
on the creative spirit of the German people to bolster its economy, a rejection of
all things non-Germanic (particularly anything associated with foreign influences,

which they associated most clearly with Jews), and a cultivation of a belief in the *Volk,* the collectivity of the people seen as identical to the state and the party.

Raul Hilberg's *The Destruction of the European Jews,* which focuses almost exclusively on the bureaucratic measures taken in the Final Solution, begins with a brief history of anti-Semitic laws and opinions from early Christendom through the early twentieth century. He argues that while the Holocaust may have been unprecedented in its systematicity, it relied on well-established anti-Semitic edicts and laws. From forced conversions in the middle ages, to their ghettoization in Breslau, Germany, to decrees by the Muslim caliph Omar that Jews specially mark their clothing for easy identification, the Nazis were relying on a long history of anti-Semitism for its anti-Jewish legislation and the infamous Nuremburg Laws of the middle 1930s. The difference, according to Hilberg, is that the decrees this time around were based on race rather than religion.

Arguing exactly the reverse, Goetz Aly has argued that while Hitler and many of those in the Nazi regime were anti-Semites, the pursuit of the Final Solution was more likely the result of the planning and expertise of a relatively small group of well-respected academics and specialists. In "The Planning Intelligentsia and the 'Final Solution,'" Aly writes that "both expulsions and compulsory 'germanization' were carried out according to calculated economic, as opposed to racial-biological criteria" (141). The creation of a "release valve," in the form of the territories to the east, provided a way for the Germans to "dejudaize" their economy through mass deportations, which entailed disease, death by starvation, and exposure for those who were displaced—Russians, Ukrainians, and Poles—as well as for those deported. Omer Bartov has taken issue with this idea, since it doesn't account for the continuation of the Final Solution even through the later stages of the war, when it was clear that the Germans would lose and that their resources could be better directed to the defense of the homeland rather than the liquidation of the Jews.

□ □ □

EUTHANASIA

Nazi anti-Semitic policy and its euthanasia policy of the 1930s and early 1940s were both driven by notions of racial purity and the inherence of human inequality, and both were given a legitimacy by geneticists, cultural anthropologists, and psychiatrists in the 1920s and 1930s. Robert Proctor provides a sinister description of the corruption of scientific research driven by ideological policy after the Nazis' rise to power. (The same thing happened during the 1930s in Soviet Russia, with disastrous—though not explicitly murderous—consequences.) Henry

Friedlander has argued that because the Nazi regime was inherently racist, and not exclusively anti-Semitic, the euthanasia campaign provides evidence that the Holocaust was not unique and that it cannot be said to be an exclusively Jewish tragedy. Nonetheless, others—notably Michael Burleigh—have suggested that the euthanasia campaign was a "dress rehearsal" for the larger-scale killings of Jews in the east, and so it's worth analyzing.

The Nazi race laws began from the premise that northern germanic or Aryan peoples were superior to those of other geographical regions, and that any corruption of the "race"—either by ethnic intermingling or by genetic defect—should be avoided or, where it had already occurred, eliminated. It was this latter problem, genetic defect, that was the focus of the T-4 campaign (so named because the bureaucracy that acted as an umbrella, or front, for the euthanasia killings were housed at 4 Tiergartenstrasse in Berlin). Early on it was the job of physicians and scientists to define the conditions under which such "defects" might be detected. It was the job of the propaganda ministry to assure German citizens that any action was for the protection and security of their racial purity if not their general well-being. In the early 1930s, the definition was primarily reserved for those with physical or mental disabilities: the blind, the deaf, and the mute; epileptics and the mentally retarded; the senile and alcoholics; and those with physical abnormalities. At the beginning of the campaign for racial purity, those identified under the policy were institutionalized; under a law passed in 1933, several hundred thousand disabled people were sterilized over the next decade.

Michael Burleigh has suggested that the T-4 campaign was in part the result of radical changes in the profession of psychiatry as practiced in Germany between the wars. During and immediately after the war, there was a large influx of psychiatric patients into the hospitals due to "shell shock" (what we now call posttraumatic stress disorder) and other effects of combat. Tens of thousands of these patients died of malnutrition and neglect in institutions, political "enemies" were labeled psychopaths and sent not to prison but to mental hospitals, and the sheer number of those institutionalized suggested that the medical profession was simply not able to do its job. During the 1920s, a group of reformers suggested that, rather than keep patients in failing institutions, outpatient care and occupational therapy might provide a better and more cost-efficient way to integrate patients into the world (and the economy). While such new policies worked, the new National Socialist government was not pleased with the results: with its focus on productivity, many of those on work-release were seen as marginally- or noncontributing members of society and thus as expendable.

Given this cultural and racialist context, it was not surprising that the regime would pass a law allowing for the sterilization of the mentally ill. What was surprising is the extent to which the propaganda efforts of the regime were so successful. Even as early as 1925, a poll was conducted by Ewald Meltzer, the director of a mental institution in Germany, asking adults whether they would approve "the painless curtailment of the life of [their] child if experts had established that it is suffering from incurable idiocy" (cited in Burleigh 121). Nearly three-quarters of those polled responded that they would, and the SS security service in the 1930s used the results in its reports. In order to organize and run the killing operations themselves, the T-4 bureaucracy was set up in August 1939. That bureaucracy would identify, register, select, transfer, and kill a group of people targeted at 70,000.

By August 1941 more than that number were killed under the program, at which point it was "officially" ended. The reason most often given for the conclusion of the T-4 campaign is resistance by the churches in Germany, under the auspices of which some of the early euthanasia killings had been done. (The "Inner Mission," the Protestant social welfare agency under which the various churches engaged in ministries, institutions for the poor and handicapped, and other public works, convened a standing conference on eugenics in 1931.) As this suggests, there was no univocal voice raised within the churches in Germany—Catholic or Protestant—against the killings. A concordat between the church and the National Socialist government meant that any resistance from the Catholic clergy would be local. More to the point, officials in other churches tried to square the policy with church teachings. Rudolf Boeckh, a doctor at a Lutheran asylum, wrote that "the most severe forms of idiocy and the totally grotesque disintegration of the personality had nothing to do with the countenance of God," and "we should not maintain these travesties of human form . . . but rather we should return them to the Creator" (cited in Burleigh 134). What may have most rankled church leaders in charge of hospitals and institutions, rather than theological issues, was that Nazi lay officials were taking over the decision-making process about who would be killed and by what means. The vastness of numbers of those killed, and the thinness of the pretexts used, meant that by the late 1940s the euthanasia program seemed, to those in charge of the institutions themselves, to be spinning out of control. In December 1940, Pope Pius XII issued a condemnation of the killing of "life unworthy of life" (though the Catholic bishop who was closest to both the Vatican and to the National Socialist regime would be negotiating with Eichmann, well into 1943, for the exemption of non-Aryan Christians from deportation to the killing centers). This suggested that the Vatican, while against euthanasia, wasn't willing to condemn the Nazi program as such. Very little seemed to affect the campaign until the late summer of 1941 when Bishop Clemens August Graf von Galen gave a sermon in which he condemned the program in harsh terms:

> Woe to mankind, woe to our German nation if God's holy commandment "Thou shalt not kill!", which God proclaimed on Mount Sinai amid thunder

and lightning, which God our Creator inscribed in the conscience of mankind from the very beginning, is not only broken, but if this transgression is actually tolerated, and permitted to go unpunished. (Burleigh 140)

The wide dissemination of the sermon finally had some effect on Nazi leadership. But while the T-4 killing centers closed in August 1941, the program itself continued: the "children's euthanasia" program—which began the affair—continued, as did the gassing of adult concentration camp prisoners in facilities originally used to kill people in the euthanasia program (it went on to claim another 70,000 victims, by at least one estimation). Burleigh and Henry Friedlander note that the head of the euthanasia program, Viktor Brack, had met with Himmler in 1941, whose expertise was needed to begin the extermination program aimed at Jews in the late fall and early winter of that year.

The questions thus raised by the euthanasia "dress rehearsal for the Holocaust" are several: whether the T-4 program is evidence that the liquidation of Jews was simply one facet of a broad ideological program of racial "cleansing," one that included not only Jews but also Slavs, the Roma, the disabled, and those of marginal social standing; whether the campaign, like the Final Solution, was driven by evil intention or was the culmination of several factors including physicians', functionaries', and intellectuals' accommodation to an ideology whose (invisible) end was murder, along with economic necessity and bureaucratic mismanagement; and whether resistance by people of goodwill could have stopped the Holocaust as it appears, at least on the face of it, that resistance from the pulpit and public demonstrations halted the T-4 campaign.

□ □ □

INTENTIONALISM/FUNCTIONALISM

One of the results of the debate, particularly in Germany, over anti-Semitism's role in the Final Solution was that research took two main emphases during the late 1960s and early 1970s. One group, interested in the role played by Hitler and his ideological colleagues in the leadership of the National Socialist party, saw a direct line between their racialist and anti-Semitic intentions and the implementation of the Final Solution. Another group, wishing to understand the ground on which such intentions might be translated into a full-fledged policy, and interested not just in leadership or even the bureaucracies that carried out the policy but also the individuals and groups who were complicit with or unwilling to resist it, analyzed the function played by the various individuals, groups, and agencies. This bifurcation of scholarship politicized even more the question of Germany's guilt: could a group of ideological zealots lead the country down the path of war and genocide, or were there other factors, including the willingness of political groups and individuals to go along with the policy for whatever reasons? It also raised questions about the strength and coherence of the narrative framework built to contain history's fact.

The quarrel between the intentionalists and the functionalists had, in the beginning, mainly to do with the role of the Fuhrer in the execution of the Final Solution, but it has fundamentally to do with how historians name events and weave them into a workable narrative. In order to sort through the events of history, historians need a way to distinguish the documents that form the detritus of those events from the events themselves. It is one thing, for instance, to examine the documents from the SS and the ministries of transport and from the regional governments in order to determine the intent of those government officials, something that lies outside the documents themselves. It is another thing, though, to substitute those documents for intention itself, as if to say that it is possible to read, in those documents, the intentions of the leaders. The intentionalist/functionalist argument is also a debate over whether it is ultimately possible to see in documents the act or event that lies beyond the document.

In the early 1970s in Germany, Karl Dietrich Bracher and Eberhard Jäckel published a pair of books that set off the debate. Much of Bracher's *The German Dictatorship* traced the destruction of Jews in Europe during World War II back to an idea Hitler raised during the first war, and suggested that Hitler's ideas were far more central to German and Austrian national ideology in the twentieth century. For Bracher, the Final Solution was the principal aim of the war for Hitler. Jäckel, in two books on the Fuhrer, argued that Hitler had a plan for the elimination of Jews from Europe almost fifteen years before he became the leader of Germany, and suggested that it was on Hitler's insistence that the Holocaust was carried out.

In the United States, intentionalist writers like Lucy Dawidowicz tended like their German counterparts to see causal connections between historical events. Dawidowicz suggested, for example, that as early as his writings in *Mein Kampf* Hitler understood that any war would have to be a twofold one, for territorial gain and for the annihilation of Judaism. Dawidowicz's argument, like Jäckel's and Bracher's, hangs on the reconstruction of documentary evidence, recovered from archival records left by the SS, particularly individual reports from Heydrich, Himmler, and those in their employ. It also took account of speeches made by high officials of the Reich, including Hitler's speeches in the Reichstag invoking the massacre of Armenians during World War I and other virulently anti-Semitic statements made at public rallies. In part founded upon the logic through which a national bureaucracy would run, and in part founded upon the idea that one's statements provide a sense of one's intentions, the historian is forced to extrapolate intention through documents and testimony "originating outside the inner circle" of those involved in policymaking. "Like the man in Plato's cave, he sees only the reflection and shadows, but not reality" (Browning 99). Intentionalist history substitutes the shadows for the historical reality, in part because the question with which the historian begins—"from what point of origin did the final solution come?"—predetermines the answers and the evidence that may be adduced.

    The functionalists try to circumvent the problem by avoiding the question of intention altogether. Christopher Browning has pointed to Martin Broszat as an "ultrafunctionalist" on the question of the Final Solution. Broszat argues, in *The Hitler State,* that local pogroms and spontaneous actions against the Jews, particularly in eastern Europe, were not the result of an orderly plan that originated with officers of the German government. They were instead a collective response to an ideological set of circumstances that included anti-Semitism fomented by but that did not originate with Hitler, a panic and anger over the losses on the eastern front in the early 1940s, and a lingering question about the link between Bolshevism and Zionism. Hans Mommsen, in an essay in the German historical journal *Geschichte und Gesellschaft,* argued that Hitler's anti-Semitism was a kind of propagandistic act designed to whip the German hierarchy and citizenry into a nationalist furor. Hitler, argued Mommsen, was an unorganized and erratic leader, and really didn't have a plan for the destruction of the Jews of Europe. Like Dawidowicz, Broszat and other less radical functionalist historians like Mommsen resort to an incomplete documentary record and understand a relation that lies behind or beyond the language of the records themselves. But rather than attribute a single motive—a single shadow on the wall of Plato's cave—to the various utterances that can be found in the speeches and memos, the functionalists attribute a number of motives to those utterances. Furthermore, they examine the cultural and material context in which those utterances were made. But the same problem occurs in functionalism that does in intentionalism: at a certain point in the reconstruction of the context in which the policy of the Final Solution was formed, a substitution takes place. The material (in the form of reports and memos by Heydrich, Himmler, and others) is replaced by reality, a reality that in this case is not a reality of intention but of material circumstance. And, like the intentionalist substitution, the functionalist one limits the kinds of evidence that may be accounted for in the analysis, because the "network" of material (like the logical sequence of the same material in intentionalism) all responds to the same general question, "what is to be done with the Jews," a question (troublingly) posed by people like Heydrich, Himmler, SS functionaries, and local authorities.

    For a number of reasons that I'll explain below, the debate between intentionalism and functionalism more or less dissolved in the late 1980s, and scholarship on the history of the Holocaust began to turn its focus away from large, explanatory narratives that sought to explain the sweep of the Holocaust, and toward its component parts, their complex relation to one another, and to individuals who were party to the implementation of the Holocaust or who were caught in the malestrom.

□ □ □

CULTURE, GENDER, NATIONALITY

Since the intentionalism/functionalism debate, the Holocaust has come to be seen more clearly as a crime not only against Jews but against others the Nazis deemed unworthy of inclusion in the Aryan thousand-year Reich, particularly those whose gender, social status, and geographical point of origin affected their place in Germany society. Among non-Jewish groups affected by the National Socialist "national purity" laws, homosexual men suffered from the very beginnings of the new regime. Along with the poor, the homeless, and the habitually criminal, gay men were seen as socially deviant in the Reich Criminal Code established in 1933 and enacted fully by 1934. Because the Reich was particularly interested in upholding a "healthy popular morality" (Michael Burleigh's term) and emphasizing full participation in the economic well-being of the state, those seen as participating only marginally in the work-world, those whose sexual activities failed to provide for the hereditary "pureness" of its Aryan offspring, and those convicted of sex crimes were imprisoned, and by 1938 habitually sent to concentration camps.

As Burleigh suggests, homosexuality, like Jewishness, wasn't necessarily a descriptor of one's identity and public association. It was more a name used to marginalize those whose social status was deemed threatening and, as a result, had to be desubjectified so as to be rendered less threatening and susceptible to attack. The irony here is that there were highly placed (and in some instances well-known) gay men within the party—the SA (the Storm Troopers') leader Ernst Rohm was, for the time, openly gay—and, as Burleigh suggests, there were pronounced homoerotic "pathologies" in the movement itself. Nonetheless, a charge of homosexuality functioned in much the same way that a charge of hidden Jewishness did: it tainted the moral and racial purity of the person accused. As such, existing legislation was enforced much more strictly from the inception of the Criminal Code to the beginnings of the Final Solution: in 1934, just over 750 men were convicted and imprisoned for homosexual "offenses"; by 1936 over four thousand had been imprisoned, and by 1938 that figure had doubled. Most who finished their prison sentences were not returned to their homes but were

transferred instead to concentration camps, where they were given special in-
signias that identified them for their offense (as all prisoners were: prisoners of war
were distinguished from habitual criminals, political criminals, and, eventually,
Jews), in some camps with a pink triangle. Estimates of gay men who died in the
camps range from several hundred to several thousand. A good review of the recent research on the fate of gay men can be found in Günter Grau's "Final Solution of the Homosexual Question?" and Rüdiger Lautmann's "The Pink Triangle."

The treatment of women, and their role in resisting the fate of themselves and
their families in particular, has also come under scrutiny in the last several decades.
One of the reasons such scholarship has come only recently is that the leadership
in many of the Jewish political movements in Europe—the Bund, the various
Zionist parties and efforts, and even in the socialist and communist movements—
included few, if any, women, though their participation in less official roles was
pronounced. More to the point, religious life in the more traditional households
restricted women to supporting roles, as wives, mothers, and—in the cases of the
ultra-orthodox households—supporting yeshiva study for their husbands and
sons through certain sanctioned jobs. What prominence women had in Zionist
circles was in activities related to social welfare: the Women's Zionist Organization, Hadassah, the Youth Aliyah movement, and refugee organizations included
women in leadership roles, including Henrietta Szold, who headed Hadassah in
the United States and later worked for Youth Aliyah in Palestine.

But because women's roles were primarily restricted to the home, and because
the Nazi regime similarly restricted women to *Kinder, Küche, Kirche* (children,
the kitchen, and the church), Jewish women were largely invisible to the Nazis
except as members of the "weaker sex" and so were often liquidated, along with
their younger children, before their husbands, brothers, or older sons. In part because they were under the Nazi radar, women sometimes took positions of power
in the concentration camp hierarchy and in some of the resistance movements
that sprang up in the ghettos and the camps. Some of the complexities of these
women's positions have been taken up in a very good anthology of essays compiled by Dalia Ofer and Leonore Weitzman, entitled *Women in the Holocaust.*
Partly out of necessity—there were simply few people willing or able to take on
the dangerous work of active resistance—and partly because women were not
marked (by circumcision) as Jews and so could move more freely in Nazi-occupied
territory, women acted as go-betweens from ghetto to ghetto. The scholar
Rachel Brenner has widened a definition of resistance to include the act of living and writing. Bauer's definition of unarmed resistance—*amidah*, in Hebrew
meaning literally "standing" or "standing up for"—includes acts that sanctify
life rather than work actively against certain destruction either personal or political. Both he and Brenner suggest that women had an important, if sometimes
invisible, role in organizing education, sustaining morale, and otherwise finding

ways under the harshest conditions to provide a meaningful life for themselves and for their families.

Finally, studies of the Holocaust have been profoundly affected by national perspectives. This is true in the countries on whose territories the war was fought and from whose homes Jews were deported. It is also true in those countries that have served as points of immigration for Jews and others who survived the disaster and fled abroad, particularly Israel and the United States. Germany in particular has had a very difficult time dealing historically with its culpability in the Holocaust as a perpetrator nation. This was complicated by the division of the country into western (American- and European-influenced) and eastern (Soviet-influenced) sectors. For the first dozen years after partition (in 1949), most East German historians who dealt with the Holocaust at all tended to see it as one facet of a larger crime perpetrated by fascism upon democratic socialism. Many of the monuments in eastern Germany and in Poland (which was also part of the communist bloc until 1989) on the sites of concentration and death camps note only that German fascism perpetrated a crime upon the people of the nation (of Germany, Poland, and other countries in Europe), and up until recently few mentioned Jews at all. After the Eichmann trial in 1961 and again after the fortieth anniversary of Kristallnacht in 1978, the East German government offered limited reparations to Jewish victims who had lived in the territory occupied at the time by the GDR (though the offer was rejected).

As in the east, West German scholarship on the Holocaust didn't begin to emerge until the "denazification" program of the late 1940s and early 1950s had been substantially concluded. In 1960, Wolfgang Scheffler's *Judenverfolgung im Dritten Reich* ("The Persecution of the Jews in the Third Reich") unleashed a flood of new studies by scholars like Martin Broszat. Most traced the strand of anti-Semitic ideology through National Socialist doctrine, but several were written on the reaction of Jews in Germany and elsewhere to the National Socialist rise to power and their eventual capitulation to the Final Solution. Both kinds of work, however, had the effect of isolating the responsibility for the Holocaust upon the anti-Semitic Nazi elites, particularly in the person of Hitler, and focused on the Jews as a monolithic category that was treated almost as an organic whole (the irony being that this was precisely how Jews were seen in National Socialist doctrine).

Things changed in Germany during the 1970s as the struggle between the intentionalist scholars of the 1960s and the younger "functionalists" heated up and culminated in the *Historikerstreit*. The functionalists, arguing that there were several complicated factors in play in Germany that led to the Holocaust—factors that were hundreds, not dozens, of years in the making—were more willing to see ordinary Germans as having a hand in the persecution and eventual eliminationist policies of the Reich. This seemed too much for some conservative thinkers, and they adopted a functionalist approach to contextualize the Holocaust in other events of both the war and German history so as to relativize (some might argue trivialize) the enormity of the Holocaust. (Ironically, attention paid to the "ordinary German" tends to obscure the role of militant Nazis and elites.) As I suggested earlier, the struggle between the intentionalists and the functionalists in Germany was the symptom of a much greater struggle over the guilt of Germany and what it owed to the world in general and Jews in particular.

As in Germany, much of the scholarship that has emerged in France has been focused on the question of French complicity in the murder of a significant portion of its Jews, and in particular on how Vichy could have been more enthusiastic in carrying out the Nazi policy of Final Solution than the Nazi-occupied part. Over a hundred anti-Semitic laws were passed by the Vichy regime, not at the request of the German government but of its own accord, that were in some instances more draconian than those that were enforced in Nazi-occupied countries like Hungary and Slovakia. While seventy percent of France's Jews survived the war—a far higher proportion than in other European countries—many of them were deported from unoccupied soil, and even their deportations were not slowed by the French resistance. Very little was written about the Holocaust in France until the arrest and trial of four prominent perpetrators—Klaus Barbie, Paul Touvier, René Bousquet, and Maurice Papon—in the 1980s and 1990s. Since that time, a number of French public intellectuals (chief among them Alain Finkielkraut and Pierre Vidal-Naquet) have put forward some penetrating, and in some instances damning, arguments about an ongoing strain of French anti-Semitism that was as pronounced, if not more pronounced, than that which had existed in Germany and had been around at least since the Dreyfus affair a century earlier. The American scholar Richard Golsan, in *Memory, the Holocaust, and French Justice,* and the French historian Henry Rousso, in *The Vichy Syndrome,* have examined some of the reasons why French anti-Semitism has not been scrutinized thoroughly in that country and explored the consequences for France at a time when immigrants of other nationalities have become, in Finkielkraut's terms, its contemporary "jews."

As I suggested earlier, Holocaust scholarship has been most widely written and circulated in the United States and in Israel. The Holocaust has had an especially central place in the history of Israel. Before the founding of the state, Palestine was seen as a potential homeland for Jews who wished to leave the dangers of Europe, and there had been active military and political movements there—some of which acted in secret with the German authorities against the occupying British—both before and during the war. Immediately after the war, with Palestine closed by the British to immigration, thousands of Jews sailed, on makeshift passenger boats, from ports in Europe to the Palestinian coast, only to be turned back by the British authorities. Within three years of the founding of the state of

Israel in 1948, nearly a quarter million Jews, mostly from Europe and about half of them Holocaust survivors, had arrived.

In the Israeli founding national mythology, Israel became the refuge for Jews and Judaism after the catastrophe of the Holocaust; this redemptive history is well established through Yad Vashem and other organizations, and is inculcated in young men and women who serve in the armed forces by trips to Yad Vashem and to Masada, a two thousand-year-old mountaintop fortress in the Judean desert on which Jews committed suicide rather than be overrun by secularizing Roman forces in the first century C.E. Much of the historical work that came out of Israel in the three decades after the founding of the state has been of this redemptive sort: Yehuda Bauer's early work includes titles like *Out of the Ashes* and *Jews for Sale*. The first argues that the Holocaust's impact on its victims who emigrated to the United States and to those who had already found a home there by the beginning of the war was instrumental in the founding, and the valorization, of the Jewish State in Israel. The second depicts the efforts of organizations and individuals in the United States and abroad to negotiate with Nazi officials in order to save Jews. Israel Gutman, another don of Israeli Holocaust history, has written extensively on the heroism of Jewish resisters, particularly in the Warsaw ghetto. Yet while most survivors living in Israel during the early years of the state were silently overwhelmed by feelings of guilt and shame, "sabras," native Palestinian-born Jews, wanted little to do with them and wondered why they had not done more to mitigate their fate.

This tendency changed after the Eichmann trial in 1961 and the Kastner affair in the 1950s, during which Rudolf Kastner—who was accused of collaboration with the Nazis—brought suit against his accuser, Malkiel Gruenwald. Both trials made public the very complicated relation between European Jews, the Jews of Palestine, and the Nazis. It also forced scholars to recognize that the Holocaust—its memory and history—was largely shaped and in some instances "distorted" (Segev) by its entanglement with Israeli history and politics. Like Peter Novick in connection with American Jews (in *The Holocaust in American Life*), Tom Segev has concluded that the Holocaust has become separated from its historical occurrence in order to justify Israel's founding, and as a point of connection for otherwise nonreligious Jews. Segev worries that the Holocaust "often encourages insular chauvinism and a sense that the Nazi extermination of the Jews justifies any act that seems to contribute to Israeli security" (517). Some Israeli historians who have taken up the charge to untangle Israeli history from the history of the Holocaust include Yehuda Elkana, who suggests that the Holocaust is better forgotten than used as a political and ideological mill through which the grist of six million dead is run. Dalia Ofer castigates the historical work coming out of Yad Vashem for an ideological narrowness of focus. Perhaps the most sophisticated and complete history of the Holocaust published in Israel is

Leni Yahil's *The Holocaust,* which comprehensively reexamines some of the debates covered here by going over a huge body of documents, some of them new at the time of her research.

□ □ □

PERPETRATOR, VICTIM, BYSTANDER

In the sixty years since the end of World War II, but particularly since the publication of Hilberg's *The Destruction of the European Jews* in 1961, the emphasis on the study of the Holocaust has shifted among the categories of actors proposed in Hilberg's work. Study of the perpetrators focused particularly on members of the political and military elite of the Third Reich who created and then carried out the policy of the Final Solution. Study of the victims included not only Jews, the largest category killed and arguably the primary target of the killing, but also those considered by the Nazis either as culturally or racially "impure" or those whose territories had to be yielded due to German expansion. Most recently, scholars have begun studies of bystanders who, for whatever reasons, refused to take action to prevent the killing or did not know or wished not to know about what went on in their midst. Until the late 1960s the assumption had been that there was a distinction between the military and ideological elite and the rank-and-file members of the Wehrmacht. The officers and party members had been the ideological zealots who instigated the policy of extermination, whereas the army had been a professionally trained and well-disciplined corps removed ideologically, if not actually, from the crimes of their superiors. By the 1970s, scholarship began to focus upon the lives of those who were rounded up into the ghettos, sent to the camps, and killed, as well as those who survived in hiding or who actively resisted their tormentors. Recently the focus has been on "ordinary Germans" and others who were not actively involved in the killing but played a role in it nonetheless, participating in a climate of anti-Semitism or failing to participate in public life at all out of fear of the consequences that would return to them as a result of "meddling." Daniel Jonah Goldhagen's 1996 book *Hitler's Willing Executioners: Ordinary Germans and the Holocaust* was, again, only the most visible—and perhaps the most controversial—of a number of recent studies on those whose myopic obsession with "Jewish Question" may have allowed the Holocaust to continue past the point of no return in 1941.

The focus on the ideological elite—members of the SS and Hitler's inner circle of officers and apparatchiks—diverted attention away, however, from the inextricable links between the Nazi policy with regard to the Jews and the conduct and strategic execution of the war. Hans-Heinrich Wilhelm has written on the col-

laboration between the Wehrmach and the Einsatzgruppen; Klaus-Jürgen Müller
has looked at the relationship of the Wehrmach with the Nazi state; and a number of writers are working with documents from Potsdam's Institute for Military
History. Together this group of scholars has suggested that there was close collaboration between the policies of the German army and the policies of the Reich,
and that the army was in fact a tool, well known to its officers, of the clearing of
the east. (Most of the work cited above has not been translated into English; work
in English by Alexander Dallin and Robert O'Neill is valuable, but it doesn't
account for troves of documentation unearthed in the last decade or so.) This
collaboration was characterized by a willingness to provide the army's officers
and troops ideological training, its role in substantially changing the rules of engagement to favor the killing of civilians and the infliction of terror (in many
cases by using local anti-Semites as proxies), and its willing participation in and
planning of executions on a scale of the Einsatzgruppen push through western
Russia in the early 1940s. All of the above makes a great deal of sense if one understands that the clearing of the east, the removal of Europe's Jews, and the eventual reconfiguration of the political and the racial map of Europe were a central
aim of the War. It's not surprising, therefore, that the army's recruits would have
participated (if not entirely enthusiastically, once they knew what it entailed) in
the eliminationist facet of the war's aims.

At least at the beginning. Once some of the perpetrators saw what clearing
the east meant, they had second thoughts. Even Himmler himself was "visibly
moved" by the shooting of a hundred Jews in the Einsatzgruppe B, and wondered whether the officer in charge was right when he said that "these men [sol-
diers] are finished for the rest of their lives!" (Hilberg 218). The focus of much
of Christopher Browning's work, and particularly his *Ordinary Men: Reserve Police Battalion 101 and the Final Solution in Poland,* cites documents and reports
by the members of a detachment of order police and suggests that some of those
who carried out the policies of the Reich were at best ambivalent and at worst destroyed by what they did. Browning's work appeared in the early 1990s; work on
the rank-and-file perpetrators began in Germany in the middle 1980s, and culminated in an exhibit that has been presented in Austria and Germany in the
1990s entitled "The War of Annihilation: Crimes of the Wehrmacht 1941–44,"
which displayed photographs and documents chronicling the army's participation
in the Final Solution. Omer Bartov has also examined the Wehrmach's role in
atrocities (see *Eastern Front 1941–45: German Troops and the Barbarisation of
Warfare;* and *Hitler's Army: Soldiers, Nazis, and War in the Third Reich*). Between
Browning's work in the United States and the work of Hannes Heer and Klaus
Naumann (the scholars, of Hamburg's Institut fur Sozialforschung, who organized the exhibit) among others in Germany, the idea of the perpetrator in Germany has been vastly widened. Not only were those at the top of the National

Socialist state apparatus responsible for the destruction of the Holocaust, but also German officers, German soldiers, and—in many instances—bystanders who were not attached in any way to Germany's war effort.

The literature focusing on the victims of the Final Solution has been torrential in the last decade. Much of it has been published in the form of memoirs and novels, about which I'll have a great deal more to say in the second part of this book. Hilberg was taken to task for reserving only a small part of his book, and an even smaller section in his book's conclusion, to the lives of the victims of the Holocaust. What attention Hilberg focused on Jews was focused on the *Judenräte,* the Jewish councils into whose hands the SS placed the governance and, ultimately, the fate of those placed into ghettos before the last stage of the Final Solution (see also his essay, "The Ghetto as a Form of Government"). A good deal of research in the last decade or two has sought to reverse Hilberg's picture of the Jewish councils and police, including books of *responsa,* rulings by rabbis in the councils meant to determine how to act justly, and according to Jewish law, in the most horrible of circumstances (see, for instance, Ephraim Kaye's recent work). Other research has illuminated the role of ghetto "rulers," like the infamous Rumkowski, with letters and diaries found after the war that present a more complicated version of those, like Jan Karski and Immanuel Ringelblum, who saw firsthand the impossible situation into which such leaders were put.

Most people who know something about the Holocaust, if not its historical complexity, are familiar with the writing of those, like Primo Levi and Elie Wiesel (Jews who survived the privations of the camps and the gas chambers), and like Tadeusz Borowski and Jean Amery (whose political activities caused their arrest and deportation). Their testimonial accounts of victimization are compelling both in their detail and their "literariness." What they may not know, however, are the many other accounts written by survivors who simply wanted to record, as well as they could, their memories of those years for their children and grandchildren, and occasionally for a larger audience. The diary kept by Anne Frank, a young German Jew whose family fled to Holland and was eventually sent to Auschwitz and who died in Bergen Belsen toward the end of the war after spending a good deal of it in hiding, is the best known account of a life in hiding. Another diary that has gotten some attention in the last several years is that of Etty Hillesum, who volunteered to work, as a member of a Jewish council, at a Dutch transit camp in Westerbork and saw firsthand the lives of those who would be, as she too eventually was, sent to the east to be killed. Accounts of the camps are fairly well known as well, including the account of Filip Mueller, who was taken from the general camp population at Auschwitz to be a member of the Sonderkommando, a special detachment of Jewish prisoners whose task it was to deliver the gassed bodies of camp inmates to the crematoria. Editions of a number of diaries and chronicles have also been published in the last decade and a half, most of which have been translated into English. Two of the most extensive are *A Cup of Tears,* the diary of Abraham Lewin who survived for two years in the Warsaw ghetto before being transported to Treblinka and killed, and Avraham Tory, who lived in the Kovno ghetto before and during its liquidation and afterward escaped (*Surviving the Holocaust: The Kovno Ghetto Diary*).

Taken together, these writings present a complicated picture of the Jewish world that was lost during the Holocaust, the psychology of those who were interned and killed, and the enormity of the toll it took upon those who lived through to the camps' liberation and those who did not. One compelling study involves not only an examination of the writing that came out of the camps during the Final Solution but also the gulags during the Stalinist reign of terror in Soviet Russia before and after the war. In *Facing the Extreme,* Tzvetan Todorov concludes that though the aim of the SS in the camps, no less than the racial laws of the early and mid-1930s and the terror and deportations of the later 1930s and early 1940s, was to dehumanize Jews in accordance with Nazi race theory, there evolved a complicated set of very human relations among the sufferers of the privations. Those relations involved the will to survive and the basest of human action, along with the need for intimacy, contact, and kindness. Like the picture that emerges with closer study of the perpetrators of the Final Solution, what we have learned about the victims of the Holocaust suggests that some resisted their fate and others could not begin to understand what was happening to them enough to do so. Some acted generously and others acted hatefully, and the vast majority acted in both manners at different times and under different circumstances.

The lives of the victims before the Holocaust have also recently become the subject of study. Several writers have tried to reconstruct the vitality of Jewish culture not only in the cities in Germany, France, Italy, and Poland among other locations for which there is a record, but also the small villages, towns, and *shtetls* of central and eastern Europe, where records were harder to come by and were the easiest to destroy. Part of the focus of the first volume of Saul Friedlander's proposed three-volume study of the Holocaust is to make clear why the persecutions of the early years of the National Socialist regime were both unsurprising—both urban and rural Jews were well aware of the anti-Semitic tendencies of some of their neighbors—and a blow so severe as to hardly be believed (Friedlander, *Nazi Germany and the Jews*). A number of books focusing on *shtetl* life (one, simply entitled *Shtetl* by Eva Hoffman, is a very good introduction) also suggest both the peril in which rural Jews often found themselves, but also the rich and often modern daily life, a life that involved close relations—both personal and economic—with their non-Jewish neighbors, social and political organizations, and a feeling of situatedness in the civil life of the local government in which they played a vital part. These studies have given a great deal of nuance to the lives of survivors and the dead that, in the years immediately following the Holocaust and for decades after, portrayed them as victims both pitiable and, as a result, inherently virtuous.

The question of complicity on the part of the United States came up, most recently, in the discussions that eventually led to building the United States Holocaust Memorial Museum in Washington, D.C., in 1993. The legislation that authorized the U.S. Holocaust Memorial Council to conceive of the building and museum included language that would make clear the United States' role in the Holocaust, though it was at the time understood that the role it played was that of liberator and sanctuary. Yet as Edward Linenthal explains in his outstanding analysis of the process that led to the museum's creation (*Preserving Memory*), it became apparent that the United States had arguably been complicit in the process that led up to the Holocaust and even, perhaps, in prolonging it. The monument facing the Mall in Washington, which is—Americans like to say—the country's front yard, takes account of America's unwillingness to actively participate in the Evian conference of 1938, during which representatives of over a dozen countries met to discuss opening their immigration policies to allow Jews from Germany and other parts of Europe to leave. The Americans believed that to increase substantially the number of Jews who could enter the country might fan the flames of nativism and isolationism, which had the effect of arousing anti-Semitism in the country. (Austrialia's and Britain's representatives made much the same case.)

The museum also lays out the argument over whether it was possible for the United States to have bombed the train routes in and out of Auschwitz, thereby stopping the transports and slowing, if not stopping, the killing in the early part of 1944. In 1942, a World Jewish Congress representative in Geneva sent a cable to the WJC in New York and London making clear that Jews were in mortal danger, and Stephen Wise, the recognized leader of Zionist movements in the United States, was told, upon hearing news of the cable, to refrain from going public. The U.S. State Department was trying to balance anti-Semitism at home with an escalating war effort that was not going in the Allies' favor (Hitler was moving on Stalingrad and Cairo, and the Japanese were attacking at Midway). The complaint that American forces should have bombed the camps in Poland is made moot by the fact that it was only in late 1943 that they had air bases that would have allowed their long-range bombers to attack Auschwitz, and even then it would have diverted the effort from the buildups in England and North Africa for the attacks to come in the summer of 1944. But the fact is that even with the information about the gas chambers, that information was dismissed because it was simply beyond belief or, worse, seen as an effort at "stoking us up," in the words of the British Joint Intelligent Committee chairman (Breitman, *Official Secrets* 119). Either because they couldn't, or were unwilling to, believe that the Germans were trying to kill all the Jews of Europe, Americans will have to wrestle with their roles both as the liberators of the camps and as failing to prevent the destruction in the first place.

The question of complicity had been much in the forefront of the minds of those in Germany, France, and the rest of Europe who were alive during the war as it is for their children and grandchildren. For many Germans born after the war, and in particular those who came of age in the 1960s and 1970s, the focus on German culpability began to wear a bit thin, for—members of this generation asked— why should they be blamed for the crimes of their parents and grandparents? An interesting illustration of the mixed feelings individual Germans had about where to lay blame for the Holocaust appears in the chapter of Primo Levi's *The Drowned and the Saved* entitled "Letters from Germans." Upon publication of the German-language version of *Survival in Auschwitz,* Levi received hundreds of letters: some of them were guilt-ridden, others displayed crude forms of denial, while still others were furious with Levi for opening old wounds. In spite of a great deal of historical scholarship that came out of Germany in the 1960s and 1970s—two (Bracher, Sauer, and Schultz's *The National Socialist Ascendance to Power* and Broszat's *The National Socialist World View;* neither has yet been translated into English) took on the relationship among anti-Semitism, National Socialist ideology, and the everyday lives and circumstances of ordinary Germans—many in a reunified Germany have an exceptionally vexed relation to their own history.

Goldhagen's thesis, that ordinary Germans had been inculcated in an "eliminationist" anti-Semitic ideology that saw Jews as destructive and so could be easily moved to accept a more radical "exterminationist" view, came only ten years after the *Historikerstreit* (the "historians' debate"). The debate dealt with the memory of the Holocaust, and German complicity in it, in the context of the broader history of Germany's path to and conduct of World War II. Ernst Nolte, in his speech "The Past that will not Pass," argued that the Final Solution was linked to fears among members of the Nazi leadership that a Soviet occupation of Germany would lead to their extermination. Andreas Hilgruber's *Zweierlei Untergang (Two Kinds of Ruin)*, published in the same year as Nolte's speech, made a similar argument. Hilgruber suggested that the Holocaust was a secondary catastrophe to the destruction of civilians and eventually the Wehrmacht by the Soviets in the early 1940s. The philosopher Jürgen Habermas, along with the historians Eberhard Jäckel and Hans Mommsen, vehemently disagreed. In an essay entitled "A Kind of Settlement of Damages: The Apologetic Tendencies in German History Writing," Habermas lambasted Hilgruber and Nolte for willfully erasing the shame of Auschwitz from the collective memory of the German people, and for trying to destroy "the only reliable foundation for our ties to the West" (43–4). The debate died down after the early 1990s, but with the reunification of the country and plans to include, in a rebuilt downtown Berlin, a monument to the Holocaust,

Godlhagen's book simply poured gasoline on the already-burning question of Germany's guilt.

He writes, essentially, that the anti-Semitism that was common in Germany by the 1930s "moved many thousands of 'ordinary Germans'—and would have moved millions more, had they been appropriately positioned—to slaughter Jews" (72), and that it was this anti-Semitism, and nothing particular to National Socialist ideology, which allowed the German people to either actively participate or to stand by while the killing took place. The book was translated quickly into German, and had an immediate effect. Older Germans took issue with the claim that there was something inherent in the German psyche (or, at least, a German proclivity toward anti-Semitism) that drove its citizens to mass murder. Younger Germans, who had in many instances felt the burden of "too much" Holocaust in the schools and in the public presses, were quick to support the "Goldhagen thesis" out of a sense that the education they'd had about the events of the war were one-sided and that their parents had tried to sweep its detail under the historical rug. Goldhagen's book was criticized by many historians not so much because his argument is wrong but that it relied too much on secondhand accounts and ignored evidence that would make for a more nuanced treatment of the subject. But Yehuda Bauer, who had initially criticized the book, eventually came around to approving of it because it raised the question of ordinary people's complicity in the act of genocide (see *Rethinking* 102). Bauer himself has argued that it was the intellectual elite, and not ordinary Germans, who had to be persuaded by the exterminationist ideology of the National Socialist party, and that this consensus among the elite would provide a justification for "ordinary Germans" to participate.

Primo Levi's musings about the "gray zone" inhabited by members of the *sonderkommando* (among others), found in his book *The Drowned and the Saved,* teases out the roles of perpetrator, victim, and bystander in the camps, and suggests that they sometimes do not have well-defined boundaries: a person could in fact occupy all three positions at once. Giorgio Agamben takes up this moral ambiguity in his *Remnants of Auschwitz,* a book far more philosophical than historical. He sees in the figure of the *Muselmann* (in camp language, the inmate who had lost that "reserve of strength," and therefore would die or be killed) as a paradigm for a kind of border state, where one is neither victim nor perpetrator, where a person is both bereft of the ability to act and is nonetheless compelled to act. In spite of Dominick La Capra's disagreements with Agamben, the position of the *Muselmann* at Auschwitz "radically undermin[es] and deligitimat[es] all pre-existing ethics and all postwar discourses relying on traditional notions of ethics as well as any and every ethics related to dignity and conformity to a norm" (xx). In fact, the figure of the *Muselmann* as the one who can't bear witness for himself, but must be described by others (those who survived), is not the exception for Agamben. He is evidence of the "remnant of Auschwitz," those aspects of dehumanization and the limits of our ability to understand how anyone might have acted under the extreme duress of the Lager, something that "Auschwitz" (not as historical specificity but as a new reality in the post-1945 world) has introduced into the present: "the sight of *Muselmänner* is an absolute new phenomenon, unbearable to human eyes" (Agamben 51). While there are problems with this notion, it suggests that even the categories that seemed so useful to us in describing the primary actors during the Holocaust, at least in philosophcal terms (and perhaps in historical ones as well), may well break down under their own weight, requiring us to find better terms to describe the complexity and the extremity of the circumstances that individuals faced. Agamben is right: the historical fact of the Holocaust, and its effects upon the history of today, forces historians and those interested in history to deal with new and horrifying categories that we would rather not face, that are "unbearable to human eyes" while they remain, shockingly, human.

| CHAPTER 4 | N a r r a t i v e s |
| | a n d   E v e n t s |

On the afternoon of 3 August 1942, the liquidation of the ghetto in Warsaw had been underway for nearly two weeks. We know this because we have access to two sets of documents. There are those left by leaders and bureaucrats of the Polish General Government, Nazi officials, and those responsible for following out the policy of the Final Solution. And there are those written by Jews in the ghetto, including members of the Jewish councils, and the residents who had not died of starvation or violence and who frequently recorded the events in diaries. In a meeting in July of that year, Hans Frank, the governor of the Polish General Government, said

> I want to say to you quite openly that we shall have to finish with the Jews one way or another. . . . Certainly, a major migration is about to start. But what is to happen to the Jews? Do you think they will actually be resettled in the *Ostland* villages? We were told in Berlin: Why all this trouble? We can't use them in the *Ostland* either; liquidate them yourselves. (quoted in Hilberg, *Destruction* 308)

This record allows us today to see the logistics of the deportations: a train would run daily between Warsaw and the center at Treblinka carrying no fewer than five thousand Jews from the ghetto. The directives presented to the *judenrat* in early July, of which we also have records, made clear what was to follow: all residents of the Warsaw ghetto were to report voluntarily to the Umschlagplatz (literally, "transshipment point," but understood by residents as "gathering place"), with the exception of those registered for certain kinds of "valuable" work in industry, the ghetto bureaucracy, and those who were not fit for removal. Those in the ghetto were told that the deportations would total no more than about 60,000 people; in the end nearly eighty percent of the population of the ghetto—over 300,000 of the 380,000 Jews crammed into the corner of Warsaw—would be in Treblinka by the beginning of 1943.

Somewhere in the ghetto, Abraham Lewin, who was born in Warsaw fifty years earlier, was writing in a diary that he had kept probably since the establishment of the ghetto in 1940. That diary, along with several others written by members of the Oneg Shabbas organization (which was formed with the expressed purpose of recording "the martyrology of the Jews of Poland"), was eventually buried in a milk can in a basement in the ghetto. That diary, along with the remembrances of those who survived the deportations and the camps, provide another set of historical documents: a perspective far different from those who were in charge of the Final Solution, a far less formal, and certainly less bureaucratic, picture of life in the ghetto, before and during the deportations. Some of the details from those testimonies are horrifying. In one account, from Martin Gilbert's history of the Holocaust, a witness records the following:

> Several vans went by, loaded with Jews, sitting and standing, hugging sacks that contained whatever pitiful belongings they had managed to gather at the last moment. Some stared straight ahead vacantly, others mourned and wailed, wringing their hands and entreating the Jewish police who rode with them. Women tore their hair or clung to their children, who sat bewildered among the scattered bundles, gazing at the adults in silent fear. Running behind the last van, a lone woman, arms outstretched, screamed:
> "My child! Give me back my child!"
> In reply, a small voice called from the van.
> "Mama! Mama!" (qtd. in Gilbert 393)

The documents left by the perpetrators and the victims provide the historian with the outlines of the events—their chronology, a sense of cause and effect, a cast of primary characters, and a range of smaller and less visible characters who are for their invisibility no less effected by what happened. And yet none of these documents could possibly provide the historian, and certainly not the reader, anything other than a glimpse of the events they purport to describe. Those events, gleaned from the leavings of history, have to be set into a coherent order, so that we aren't simply left with the great swirling chaos that the events must have felt like to those who were there. But the historian also has to face the fact that whatever order she provides, there will be an inevitable gap between the documentary evidence, what the witnesses saw, and our perspective on the events. In the historian Siegfried Kracauer's words, the historian has to "establish the relevant evidence as impartially as possible" and she must "try to render intelligible the material thus secured" (47). But even as eminent a historian as Kracauer admits that these two tasks are impossible to separate, and that the events of history

are so variegated and chaotic that any successful combination of the two in a coherent historical account might also just be impossible.

One assumption that generally prevails among historians is that the event
somehow makes itself present or visible in historical writing, or that the events
have an effect upon writing. In the words of Louis Mink, after all historiographical options have been considered, "the conviction returns that the past is after all
there, with a determinateness beyond and over against our partial reconstruc-
tions" (93). Mink suggests that the paradox of history is both that it is *made* and
that it *happens.* What he means is that history is both the events that occur and
the historian's understanding (and writing) of them. The paradox can't be solved.
Instead, we "oscillate" between its two irreconcilable poles, history as what happened and history as writing. In this chapter I lay out this assumption about history, how historians understand the relation between the different kinds of
documentary evidence and the events, and suggest what effects this paradox has
on how scholars, and how we, understand the Holocaust. While it's true that
there is a "presentness" to the events of history, and particularly the events of the
Holocaust (which still exert a certain amount of pressure on us right now), the
most important question of all is *how* the presentness makes itself felt or recognized in historical writing. In other words, just how does an event like the Holocaust exert its presence over us, in spite of our recognition that any writing about
the event is after all a construction?

□ □ □

History *versus* Narrative (Berel Lang)

As we saw in the previous chapter, a number of the arguments over the history
of the Holocaust amount to disagreements over method: how do historians account for evidence, how much explanatory power do certain kinds of evidence
have over others, how much can we rely on eyewitness testimony, how are events
related causally, and so on. But a number of the disagreements over the history
of the event have as much to do with the idea of history as a mode of representation as they do with history as a method of research. Some of the disagreements
over the history of the Holocaust—or, rather, over its alternative histories, or the
histories of its component parts—have to do with the relation between history
as an event and history as the representation of events. For Berel Lang, a philosopher and historian of ideas as well as a prolific writer on the events of the Holocaust, the relation between the two is inseparable. More to the point, the question
of how best to make clear the events of the Holocaust is a deeply moral one, because the events of the Holocaust were unprecedented and because they have so

profoundly affected the world in which you and I and others work and write. For Lang, the problem isn't so much whether certain kinds of evidence matter more than others, or whether certain historical narratives are better able to represent the events than others; instead, what matters is the *effect* those historical accounts have on the current generation, and the extent to which those accounts are honest about their successes and failures.

The title of Lang's 1990 book, *Act and Idea in the Nazi Genocide,* tells part of the story: the Final Solution's destruction of the Jews of Europe was not merely an act, a historical event, nor was it merely an idea that the world has had to get used to since the end of World War II. It was, instead, an act that was motivated by an idea or—maybe more accurately—it was an enacted idea. As we saw in the debate between the intentionalist and the functionalists, the issue at stake was whether the events of the Final Solution were motivated or unmotivated—whether they were directed by an individual or group of individuals, or whether they came about through a series of disparate and unconnected policies, actions, and decisions that, taken cumulatively, resulted in the Holocaust. For Lang, this is the wrong question: all events are motivated by an idea, and it is the particularity of the interconnection of act and idea that interests him in this book. How were the historical events of the Holocaust, in their particularity, made present—represented—to historical consciousness, and how does the work and the writing of the historian (and the historically-conscious writer of fiction) responsibly account for that particularity? Of course, this isn't just a question about what happened. It's also a question of what happens in the here and now. Just as the Final Solution was the enactment of an idea—an idea motivated by the demonization of Jews as a group and by the apotheosis of the German nation as a race and a people—writing the history of the Final Solution is also the enactment of an idea. We have to account, in historical writing, both for the past and for the present. Lang puts it this way: memory, like history,

> insists on the present as a means to the past; without that basis, if memory did not originate in the active voice of the present—"I [now] remember"—it would not be memory that was disclosed, but an imaginary or hypothetical set of events, the beginning of fiction. The act of memory, moreover, cannot be carried on vicariously; each self must remember for itself, and thus the retelling is always, for each person, begun anew. (xiii)

Writing the history of the Final Solution depends on how the historian understands and interprets the evidence, testimonies, and causal relations among events and individuals' motivated actions. Those actions and testimonies, like the writing itself, are intentional.

They're intentional in that both depend on acts of definition. In the Nazi decision to concentrate its war effort (or part of it) on the extermination of the Jews

of Europe, this definitional act took two forms. First, it required the desubjectification of its victims; second, it required the corporatization of the perpetrators. "Genocide singles [victims] out by their identification with a group quite
apart from any choices they have made of identity or character and indeed aside
from all individual characteristics other than the biological feature(s) which (allegedly) mark them as group members" (15). As we saw in the previous chapters, Jews ceased to be individuals in the Third Reich. They became, by law and
by habit, members of an organism—a "bacillus," in the terms of high Nazi
officials—that had to be stamped out. They became, in other words, defined
not as individuals but as a corporate entity, which is far easier to identify and to
get rid of than nine million individuals that had, one by one, to be killed. The
same was true of the Nazi state. Speaking of Raphael Lemkin's definition of the
term "genocide" in the 1940s, Lang says that "the opprobrium attached to the
term 'genocide' seems also to have the connotation of a corporate action—as if
this act or sequence of acts would be a lesser fault, easier to understand if not to
excuse if one person rather than a group were responsible for it. A group (we sup-
pose) would be bound by a public moral code; decisions made would have been
reached collectively" (12). The only way the Final Solution could have happened, Lang argues, is if these definitions—of Jews as collectivity, of the German
people as a group of corporate actors—were accepted, and it is the responsibility of the historian to make sure that his writing of the events remains true to
these definitions. In the same way that the destruction of Jews was motivated,
in part or in total, by these definitions, so the writing of history must also be motivated by such definitions.

     This being the case, the problem of history is a problem of language, Lang in-
sists. This doesn't mean that history is reducible to language. Acts of history may
be motivated by an idea, and those ideas are in turn enacted through language and
through definitions ("Jews" as nonpeople, for example). But those acts exert a
pressure on the here and now, and on the historian writing in the here and now.
The historian has to ensure that the events he presents make visible both "enact-
ments" to the reader: the enactment of the Nazi destruction—the "then" part of
the equation—and the historian's enactment of the writing of history and his
own motivations—the "now" part. The single most important task of history is
"to establish a bare chronicle of the event—what *happened*"—but such a chronicle "would be as extensive as the events it was intended to explain and would be
no more coherent than they were individual" (81). So compression and artifice
are inevitable. One way to trace the relation between act and idea in the Final Solution, argues Lang, is to pay attention at least as much to the ways language was
as "deformed" by the event—*endlösung*, Final Solution, in place of extermination of the Jews; *sonderbehandlung*, special treatment, for killing; *stück*, piece, for
corpse—as people and objects were deformed or destroyed.

The need to pay attention to both form and content, act and idea, historical event and the medium in which it is represented, is overall a *moral* necessity because of the uniqueness—or the unprecedentedness—of the event of the Holocaust itself. No representation of the Nazi genocide escapes the risk or the likelihood of failure, no matter how compelling, because representation implies agency—the ability of the writer, or historical actors, to freely determine the outcomes of events. But the Final Solution was by definition a series of events in which the actors and events—Jews, those who implemented the exterminations, the exterminations themselves—had no agency because they were deprived of such agency. We know what happened during the Holocaust, the argument goes, so any attempt to write those events in a way that "detracts from" or "adds to" those events is morally inexcusable. Lang insists that the only way to write history is to show the events' deformation of history and of language as it affects the language of the historical narrative. "Writings about the Nazi genocide have two subjects, not one, and readers of those writings cannot avoid considering the one in order to judge what they know of the other." Those two subjects—the events of the Holocaust and writing about the events of the Holocaust—must interanimate and visibly affect one another.

But what constraints should there be on the writer? If her job is to say what happened and also to say something about her own sense of what happened, then what limits are there on how the writer makes clear her intention, or makes clear how she understands what happened? Why couldn't she depict the Holocaust in historically accurate terms through, say, a comedy? Why not depict perpetrators as less than evil (as some said Hannah Arendt had done in her controversial book *Eichmann in Jerusalem*)? If "the literary structure . . . becomes an assertion or an idea" of the event, then "the constraints and possibilities of literary representation, on the one hand, and the historical and then the moral character of what the representations are 'of,' on the other hand, converge" (120). The enormity of the events of the Holocaust, for Lang, suggest that there must be a "moral correlative" between the constraints placed upon the writing of history and the moral character of the subject itself. The historical constraints—getting it right—trump all other considerations, which explains for Lang why in all genres of writing (historical narrative, narrative fiction, memoir and diary, poetry) writers feel the need to assert that what they're writing about "really happened," and happened the way they say it happened (a point I'll come back to in the second and especially the third sections of this book).

"Documentary and historical writings about the genocide have been more adequate and more compelling—in sum, more *valuable*—than the imaginative writings about the subject" (140). That's because they don't add or subtract from the events they depict. Lang lists three reasons why this is the case. First, imaginative writing, unlike historical writing, "establishes a literary field or space between the

writer and his writing and between that writing and what is written 'about'"
(142). By using figures of speech—metaphors, similes, turns of phrase—the author seems to suggest that there are "alternate possibilities," that things were not
quite how history says they were. This kind of figurative turn "impinges on the
content of that subject [that is, the Holocaust], adding itself and the decisions it
presupposes" (143). Second, imaginative writing—unlike historical writing—
draws attention away from the object being represented and focuses it instead
on the literariness of the depiction. This "literary particularity" makes the reader
notice both the aesthetic nature of the representation in addition to the thing
being represented. Finally, by drawing attention away from the events of the
Holocaust and drawing it instead (or also) to the vehicle of representation, it dis-
tracts the reader's attention at the same time from the context of the events. "Figurative discourse 'estranges' the subject of representation—and with this separation,
a process of generalization begins" in which what is being represented—the killing
of individuals or groups; the deprivations associated with the camps and ghettos;
the machinery of the Final Solution—can be substituted for more general kinds
of actions. The person killed, or the person doing the killing or simply standing
by, can be substituted for "humankind" or "man in general" (or, in Lang's view,
worse, the reader himself) (144). Historical writing is the most valuable kind of
writing about the event because it doesn't add to the events depicted; "the effect
of the addition is . . . to misrepresent the subject and thus . . . to diminish it" (145).
Moreover, because literary representations tend to focus on individual actors—
main characters who seem to take on a life of their own—they misrepresent the
corporate nature of the Final Solution, whereby Jews were deprived of "a life of
their own," and whereby the responsibility of the killing was placed as much on
"the fatherland" as it was on its individual citizens.

Though Lang's argument about the supremacy of history to other forms of
writing is compelling, it also presents some problems. Take Lang's first point,
that historical representation is most apt to represent with some degree of accuracy the desubjectification of victims, while other sorts of representation may
give the impression that historical actors were more free to act than they actually
were. It's a strong point, but it implies that perpetrators' and bystanders' motivations were equally monolithic to those of the victims. Lang writes that "if the
Nazi genocide involves a knowing commitment to evil in principle beyond the
psychological motives of its individual agents, the difficulties of literary representation will also be encountered there. Few literary characters choose evil for
its own sake" (148). This is a pretty broad statement: do we know that perpetrators and bystanders were indeed committed knowingly to evil in principle? And
is it true that literary representations are any less apt than historical ones to present evil characters with mixed motives? In fact, this is precisely what got Hannah Arendt into trouble in her depiction of Eichmann: while the Israeli court

and the world watching the trial wanted to see Eichmann as the embodiment of evil, Arendt saw him as something more like a clerk, whose petty bureaucratic difficulties and his inability to tell the truth appeared as evidence not of "a knowing commitment to evil" but, quite the reverse, a blithe ignorance of it. And if it's true that literary representation provides a glimpse of individual actors free to choose their fate while Jews during the Holocaust rarely had such freedom, it's also true that they had personal lives—ones that were put under fierce pressure, to be sure, during the ordeal of the event, and which were constrained immeasurably by those ordeals—and individual histories that even the most transparent historical or chronological narrative shouldn't ignore. (This, I think, is the predicament Levi made clear in his chapter entitled "The Gray Zone"—from his last book, *The Drowned and the Saved*—in which victims were made simultaneously to be perpetrators of acts against their fellow inmates, complicating any blanket assumptions we might make about their motivations.)

Lang's point about historical writing "conveying the features" of the Nazi genocide better than imaginative writing's ability to represent them is equally problematic. If you turn this statement around, you could say that, in spite of historical writing's inevitable reductiveness—it has to compress the events into a narrative that isn't as expansive or contradictory as the events themselves—it nonetheless allows readers to see the events as they occurred. But other forms of writing (maybe imaginative writing like novels, stories, and poetry) may better "convey the features" of the genocide. What's at stake here is the difference between the events and their "features." Lang cites Theodor Adorno's essays on fascism to make the point clearer: "'The impossibility of portraying fascism springs from the fact that in it . . . subjective freedom no longer exists. Total unfreedom can be recognized, but not represented'" (154). If history's job is to represent what happened during the fascist regimes in Germany and other parts of Europe, and in particular the fate of the Jews under fascist Germany's Final Solution, then it succumbs to the same fate as imaginative writing. It is impossible to convey the features of the Nazi genocide as they occurred in a historical narrative any more than we could in a fictional narrative because *no* language is adequate to the task of bearing up under the enormity of the event. It exerted so much pressure upon thought and language, so Lang's argument goes, that any representation of it will inevitably show that pressure on its language, in the same way that we can no longer hear about someone being singled out for "special treatment" without, in some corner of our minds, fearing for the worst. History, Lang insists, should find a way to represent the enormity of the Holocaust that is responsible both to the events of the past, and that provides us in the present with a sense of its enormity. And yet even the transparent writing of history runs the risks of carving out a "figural space" in language, because any reduction of the events to writing resorts to the "reduction" or addition inherent in the medium itself. "It may be true that there are no 'bare'—that is, without means of representation—historical facts; and it may also be true that there is no writing (historical or imaginative) that does not in principle engender what has been referred to here as imaginative space" (156), though Lang goes on to say that we're nonetheless responsible for *trying* to write in such a way as to leave the facts unaltered. But what Lang leaves his readers with at this point is a serious question: just what would such a historical writing look like?

☐ ☐ ☐

History *as* Narrative (Hayden White)

One answer is provided by the historian Hayden White. The historian's job, he argues, isn't so much trying to get what happened right; instead, it is to understand how any historical narrative gives evidence of the problems of writing history. It's more important to understand the obstacles to drawing the outlines of what happened than it is to draw them. Pushed to its logical extreme, such a position "takes seriously [the idea that] 'language [i]s the origin of history'" (Bennington, Attridge, Young 9), that it is *only* through the medium of historical writing that we know anything at all about the past; evidence is mute without the coherence given to it by the historian. Some historians—like Lang and Pierre Vidal-Naquet to name only two—are suspicious of this view. They reach the same conclusion that George Kren does: that there is something in the historical documents and the diaries of those (like Abraham Lewin's) that registers somehow as "sincerity," "honesty" (7). This feeling may not *be* the event; but for Lang and for Vidal-Naquet, there is something in history that resists universalization, abstraction, and the language of narrative (see Lang, *Act and Idea* xv–xix).

Hayden White's revolutionary view of history as narrative was made clear at a conference at UCLA in 1990, entitled "Nazism and the Final Solution." White was responding to the question of whether "there are any limits on the kind of story that can be responsibly told" about the Holocaust and Nazism, and his talk (and the essay that was written to expand on it) amounts to a resounding "no." It is true, he says, that there are any number of ways to "emplot" history—as tragedy, comedy, epic, fable, pastoral—and some seem more plausible than others. One example he cites is Andreas Hilgruber's 1986 book, *Two Kinds of Ruin: The Shattering of the German Reich and the End of European Jewry.* It's one of several histories of the Holocaust written (or "emplotted") as tragedy, the tragedy of the German Army's destruction at the hands of the Russian army during the winter of 1944–45. In Hilgruber's view, the defeat of the Wehrmacht overwhelms and contextualizes the (secondary) tragedy of the acceleration of the Final Solution in the year before the German army was crushed on the eastern front, a defeat that had been foreseen by the German army command during that year. There were two tragedies in the war—the German tragedy and the Jewish tragedy—and the second of these was the result of the first, more profound one. This emplotment of the events of the Holocaust—events we have access to only through documentary evidence and artifacts—flies in the face of what we generally think about the Holocaust, namely that its magnitude dwarfs that of other tragedies. But for White, the fact that what happened and the story of what happened conflict does not rule Hilgruber's account out of court. If we rule out his version of the tragedy as an unacceptable historical narrative, what do we do with Art Spiegelman's *Maus,* about which White speaks approvingly, an account that is (at least on the word of Terrence DesPres, quite literally) comic? Hilgruber's account of the Holocaust as secondary tragedy, like Spiegelman's account of the survival of his father (and his own subsequent "survival") plotted as comedy, is simply one narrative that competes with other narratives of destruction and survival. None of these narratives should be judged on whether they accord with the "facts" of history. Instead, they should be judged by the criterion of whether or not they "violate any of the conventions governing the writing of professionally respectable" narratives of history (42). Analyzing the *success* of the narrative means that we have to decide how its structure—tragedies require heroes who succumb to a flaw, and for Hilgruber the hero is the German army—determines what we can say about the evidence available to the historian and, in turn, the reader. For Hilgruber, European Jewish culture becomes the foil for the hero in the tragic tale of the Wehrmacht, but the reader will find that the substance of the first tragedy (the destruction of Jewish culture in Europe) undermines the substance of the second tragedy (the destruction of the German army). It is this contradiction, suggests White, that signals the ultimate failure of Hilgruber's narrative, not the fact that it is somehow distasteful to canonical historians, or that it violates contemporary mores, and certainly not the fact that it is somehow out of accord with the facts (in White's terms, the "chronicle") of history itself.

The historian Carlo Ginzburg noted that the problem in White's formulation is that it doesn't allow legitimate historians to say that Holocaust revisionists or deniers are lying or are mistaken (White, *The Content of the Form* 77). To know if a person is lying, you have to know whether they are saying that something they know *didn't* happen actually *did* happen. But the "solidity" of the events in White's account isn't in question: what we're interested in is whether any particular story of the events is coherent, not whether the teller of the tale is lying (since, after all, the events in question aren't accessible to the historian). So White is left to assess only the effectiveness of competing accounts. As Ginzburg points out—somewhat unfairly—"we can conclude that if [Robert] Faurisson's narrative [of denial] were ever to prove *effective,* it would be regarded by White"—like Hilgruber's—"as true as well" (93).

To get around this problem White says that the most effective historical writing is what he calls "intransitive writing," a term he adopts from Lang (who in turn attributes it to Roland Barthes; see *Act and Idea* xii, 107–9). We generally think that the language of a narrative is "to be read *through;* it is designed to enable readers to see what they would otherwise see differently or perhaps not at all." Here, the writing isn't as important as what it allows the reader to see. Intransitive writing, on the other hand, "denies the distances among the writer, text, what is written about, and, finally, the reader; they all converge upon a single point," the point of writing. The act of writing becomes the object of history, in a narrative that tells "the story of the genocide as though [the teller herself] had passed through it" (Lang xii). Here, the writing is also important to see, because it's the writing (after all) that presents what the reader sees. This kind of historical writing succeeds, for White, because it brings to the surface of the narrative the gaps that exist between subject and object, literal and figurative language: the distance between what Hans Frank wrote in July 1942 and what Abraham Lewin saw and wrote in August of that year; the distance between what we think the phrase "we shall have to finish with the Jews one way or another" might mean and what it actually meant for those whose children were taken away to the trains. Intransitive writing makes clear that the one and the other aren't reconcilable, and that something else—something beyond any description—is the object of history. The most effective history of the Holocaust isn't the one that is the most effective or persuasive, the narrative that most completely contextualizes the documentary evidence of the event. It's also not the one that lets the reader put himself in the place of the historical actor. The most effective account draws the reader's attention to the *impossibility* of putting himself in the place of the historical actor and saying "I am here," I understand; in later work White suggests that it's just this impossibility that provides evidence of the event, even though it's not something we can represent directly in writing.

Abraham Lewin's account of his ordeal in the Warsaw ghetto, like other such accounts, is not nearly as transparent as historical writing is supposed to be, however. It is "intransitive," rather than transitive, because it draws the reader's attention to aspects of the event that can't be accounted for by the language of the historian. To take one example, though he sometimes makes comparisons between objects or events from radically different contexts (as he does when he compares the liquidation to the worst ordeals of the Jews in the land of Egypt), he more often simply makes lists of events, often tiresomely, gruesomely similar events, and names appear after names. On White's accounting, these lists should lull the reader into understanding that what is being repeated is simply sameness, things we recognize as real. So then take this passage from Lewin's diary: "Today the Germans have surrounded the following streets: Gesia, Smocza, Pawia, Lubiecka, and took away all the occupants. Yesterday the following were taken away: Khanowicz, Rusak, and Jehoszua Zegal's whole family" (Lewin 146). It takes a footnote by the diary's editor to make the reader understand that Jehoszua Zegal was the grandfather of Lewin's wife Luba, and there are no notes to establish the context for the names of the streets that were surrounded, and what events took their toll upon the inhabitants of the houses on those streets bordering the Jewish cemetery on the western side of the ghetto. Instead of being a passage that lulls the reader into thinking "I know this," and that allows us to forget that "I was not there," the writing in this passage draws a reader's attention to the *impossibility* inherent in the description: the repetitive language here, in which street names and family names are run together as a litany of destruction, seem alien to both the writer and to the reader. This language seems unconnected to the network of other words or signs that a reader might use to make sense of it. It's hard to create even an imaginary position from which to see and understand what's going on. This writing is intransitive because it draws attention at least as much to its language—and to the moment the language was set down on the page—as it does to what is being written about.

The disagreement between White and Lang is over what Lang calls the "aestheticization" of the events of the Shoah. White cites a long passage from Lang's *Act and Idea in the Nazi Genocide* that reads, in part, "imaginative representation would personalize even events that are impersonal and corporate; it would dehistoricize and generalize events that occur specifically and contingently. And the unavoidable dissonance here is evident" (144; qtd. in White 45). He notes that Lang suggests that providing individual points of view for "characters" whose individuality was stripped bare by their treatment (as "corporate entities" or automatons) by the Nazi Final Solution misrepresents this depersonalization, an element essential in understanding the Holocaust and its effects. But Lang's assertion of a dissonance between figural and historical representation, between the transitive and the intransitive dimensions of language, and between the occurrence of an event and the narrative of it, isn't limited to "aestheticized" versions of historical events, but to the records themselves. At their best, Lang notes that even historical writing ought to have an "instransitive" dimension. So in the end, it's possible to see both Lang and White as arguing the same thing: that there is an aspect to the Holocaust that may simply be unwritable. The disagreement is over whether some genres are better than others at making this aspect of the Holocaust visible.

□ □ □

HISTORY AND/AS THE UNWRITABLE (JEAN-FRANÇOIS LYOTARD AND MAURICE BLANCHOT)

It's the notion of unwritability that concerns two thinkers who aren't normally associated with histories of the Holocaust. Jean-François Lyotard's book, *The Differend,* is a treatise on what happens when individuals confront an event or a reality that is so extreme as to seem unspeakable. The book describes, in theoretical terms, some instances where there is a damage done to an individual by this unspeakable reality, instances in which the person is damaged because of his *inability* to make a claim against his tormentor. The historical circumstance that surrounds the writing of this book is the wave of anti-Semitism that overtook France in the late 1970s and early 1980s. It culminated in the trial of Klaus Barbie, the person immediately responsible for the deaths of thousands of France's Jews at the hands of the Nazis, and the claims of Robert Faurisson, who claimed that the gas chambers could not possibly have been used for the extermination of Jews. Lyotard's book, in one important sense, is a discussion of how to respond to Holocaust deniers, who would argue that anyone claiming firsthand knowledge of the gas chambers must be a liar, because anyone with such experience, and who is right about the purposes of the gas chambers, would be dead. Maurice Blanchot is an intellectual who was alive during the Holocaust and who remained curiously silent about France's complicity with the transport and killing of its Jews. His book, *The Writing of the Disaster,* takes the Holocaust as an event that seems not only to defy writing at all—any sort of writing, whether it's history or fiction— but also as a historical event that is purposefully forgotten or ignored by those for whom it is simply too painful to remember. Both books are intended to move the reader of history beyond claims about the past, and to see instead how past events, particularly the events of the Holocaust, compel us to confront their effects in the present and, more importantly, in the future.

Lyotard begins his book by defining the *differend* as an instance in which individuals can't agree on the proper language to use when discussing an apparently unspeakable event. A proper history of the Holocaust, one that makes its mark not on the present but on the future, is one that doesn't try to get the past right for the present, but tries instead to get at something that, so far at least, has never been told, an event that is so horrifying or damaging that it has no reality in the present because no language has yet been found to "phrase" it. The *differend* is an event whose "reality" can't be named in part because the parties involved in the discussion—in the case of Auschwitz, the victims and the perpetrators—can't agree on the terms of the discussion. The perpetrators believe the Jews to have been subhuman, and thereby subject to national laws directed at objects rather than at citizens or subjects and thus have no claim to damages. The victims believe that they were "desubjectified" illegitimately. What results is a silence, into which no sensible discussion—in Lyotard's term no "phrase"—can be uttered. In the section of *The Differend* entitled "The Referent, the Name," Lyotard claims that "reality does not result from an experience," but rather from the palpability of utterances, assertions about the real (46). This doesn't mean that "the real" doesn't exist, or that events like the Holocaust didn't happen. It means that what is currently the case (and the utterances that bring the case to others in the present) and the prior case (history, what we believe happened because we have read accounts of it or see evidence of it) are built in language differently. Expressions about what is currently the case, about what's going on in the present, aren't expressed like *x is the case,* but by a phrase like *x is the case and not this other case* (45); not "this is what is happening," but rather "this is happening; these other possibilities are not happening." Lyotard puts it this way: "the thing one sees has a backside which is no longer or not yet seen and which might yet be seen"; any statement about what we see is "simultaneously an allusion to what is not the case," to what we can't see. It isn't just that there are many aspects to what happens, and what has happened, that we don't have access to. More importantly, any statement of what happened leaves out other possible statements—other ways of saying what happened, other descriptions—that are omitted as possibilities. Any statement of affairs—of what happened—ought to allow for the possible, for what we can't imagine in the here and now but which might be the case, but just out of the line of sight, or just out of the realm of what we can imagine. This is all the more pressing a problem in the case of Auschwitz (the Holocaust): these are not simply garden-variety events, but rather events that are so extreme that even extreme language seems to leave out aspects of the event. Even the witness (maybe the witness most of all) can't see all aspects of what happened to her, and as a result cannot testify to all its aspects. Even if the witness could see all aspects of the event, the language she has at her disposal could not bear it.

Lyotard calls history a "fairly stable complex of nominatives," a well-understood and agreed-upon set of terms or names that make reference to equally well-recognized states of affairs in the past, events and objects, all of which have a certain durability (through historical artifacts, documents, and other material). The witness who testifies to what she saw doesn't simply make a statement about those states of affairs that she and she alone saw. She describes a state of affairs in the context of history, and of what other witnesses saw and said. "It suffices that something be shown and named (and thus can be shown as often as desired because it is fixed within nominal networks), . . . and that this something be accepted as proof until there is further information" (53). But in such a system, the traditional distinction between "history" and the actual events breaks down, because the "complex of nominatives"—written history—could just as easily be written in another way, and because of this other possibility, what happened could just as easily be understood differently—and thus *be* different—as well.

"Reality is not a matter of the absolute eyewitness, but a matter of the future" (53), Lyotard writes. What he means by this is that there is no perspective—not even the witnesses'—through which every aspect of a historical event, particularly events like the Holocaust, can be understood. What actually happened matters less than what the narrative of history allows others in the future to see, what effect testimony or narrative has upon the listener. Ideally this effect allows the reader to get a sense of what happened, but not understand it as if it were represented as an image or as something clearly or completely knowable. The effect seems to emerge from the reading or from the reader's "seeing," in which what happened emerges in the present as something altogether new and unprecedented. "For [the event] to become real, it is necessary to be able to name and show referents that do not falsify the accepted definition"—to use a language that isn't inconsistent with language we've become familiar with—but in the case of disasters such as the Holocaust the stable complex of reality has been destroyed, because the event itself was so radically unfamiliar, and the ways in which it distorted language (part of Berel Lang's point) was so unprecedented. This destruction prevents what the witness saw, and what documents tell us about what happened, from being tested against the stable complex—history—and requires something altogether new.

Auschwitz, for Lyotard, is the sign of the limit of what we understand in history, in which "the testimonies which bore the traces of the *here*'s and *now*'s, the documents which indicated the sense or senses of facts," have been destroyed. The witness, as much as the historian, is charged with "breaking the monopoly over history granted to the cognitive regimen of phrases," the narrative of history that is well worn, well understood, and that because of this regularity runs the risk of letting us think we can "know what it was like." Both witness and historian must lend an ear "to what is not presentable under the rules of knowledge" (57), things that seem utterly impossible to know. To write this kind of history requires a writing that allows the impossible to impress itself upon the narrative of history, that seems to work against it. Such writing may require the historian to forge or use a language other than that of history or memory. This kind of historical writing is concerned less about the facticity of history (which is anyway exceedingly difficult to establish in the case of the Holocaust, in which the witnesses are either dead or sentenced to testifying to a world that mistakes narratives and movies about the event for the event itself) and attempts instead to write the impossible, to write that "which [may have not] yet taken place" so far as history and the narrative of memory is concerned (Lyotard 47).

Maurice Blanchot's book, *The Writing of the Disaster,* is less a book "about" the Holocaust than it is about how writing might work in the face of it. Like Lyotard, he's concerned about whether historical knowledge and historical writing leaves out traces of the event, traces that are valuable not because they help us understand chronology but because they give us a sense of the *effects* of the events of history. Blanchot is particularly worried about the effect of the Holocaust because it seems powerful enough to keep people from *wanting* to write about it, or if they want to, keeps them from being able to do so. In order to explore the relation between writing and the "disaster" that seems to defy writing, he investigates the relation between what we know and what we see—the relation between how we make sense of events and the events themselves. He argues that some events—and maybe even *all* events—have effects upon individuals that aren't integrated into knowledge. Experiences are only experiences once they're organized by the human mind; but the occurrence of an event in which a person is implicated precedes experience (Blanchot 24). Events occur to us and we think of them as experiences once we're able to find categories and words to organize them *as* experiences. This process becomes complicated when, as Lyotard suggests, we confront or are implicated in events that are so extreme that they defy the narrative patterns—White's "emplotments"—that are familiar to us. At the moment the witness is subjected to the extreme event, that event is simultaneously lost to her, and created as an experience that can be written as a historical narrative. Once the event occurs, the witness is left with two possibilities: she either does not integrate it into her storehouse of experiences, blocking it out as if it were a trauma so severe as to be completely repressed; or she integrates the event into experience with the language and the categories she has at her disposal. I'll spend some time in the next section of this book discussing what happens to Holocaust witnesses in the first of these possibilities. In the second, the moment the individual recognizes the occurrence of the event as an experience, the event "falls in its turn outside being" (24): she emplots the event (to borrow White's language), even if only to herself, and leaves out all of the other possible ways in which the event might be emplotted or narrated as testimony. This leaves other aspects of the event unnamed, and in Blanchot's terms the experience, whether recollected in memory or written as a narrative, is haunted by its status as an event and by those other unnamed possibilities. "The names [for it are] ravaged by the absence that preceded them"—the event now lost to memory except as a name—and "seem remainders, each one, of another language, both disappeared and never yet pronounced, a language we cannot even attempt to restore without reintroducing these names back into the world" (58).

Blanchot begins *The Writing of the Disaster* with something like the following question: how is it possible to write the events that occurred under the name of Auschwitz? In writing the events that comprise the liquidation of the Warsaw ghetto in the summer of 1942, a man like Abraham Lewin both regularizes the events so that they become narrative, but in it he may also make apparent the uncanny aspect of the events that cannot be written, but can nonetheless be glimpsed in writing. Documents and remnants of history don't speak uninterpreted; they don't make sense on their own. In fact, Blanchot's point is that documents, diaries, and observations by witnesses seem to *resist* speaking. They must be inserted into a historical narrative and made sense of, as the reports of those losing children to the transports to Treblinka, and of work cards never to be used by those waiting in the Umschlagplatz to be herded onto trains, must be understood. To be understood, a writer creates a narrative in which those documents may be integrated. The events, however, of which these documents and records are the remains, are irretrievably past—they have already been passed by the narrative that has been written to speak in their place—and between the events themselves and the narratives that speak them, there is a kind of gap or silence. It is the job of historian to bridge this unbridgeable gap.

Blanchot's point, however, is that in attempting to bridge this gap—in expressing the difficulty of, and the obligation to, write into history this irretrievable series of moments—writing itself leaves a trace of the event, as a mark on the face of the narrative. The immediacy of the moment, which makes itself felt in the silences between the event and its narrative—between the phrases written by Hans Frank in July 1942 and by Abraham Lewin in August of that year—becomes apparent. The historian comes to realize that the relation between the one's words and the other's, the one's phrases and the other's phrases, is at no point perfect: there's no way to connect the phrases with events themselves. At one point Abraham Lewin writes the following:

> What Luba recounted of the children (150) and the women teachers during the blockade. Their packages in their hands, ready to set off—to their deaths. Kon said yesterday, "I am writing a testament about the events." Chmielewski's parents were taken away yesterday and he comes to the factory and is still on his feet. (150)

Any intention that would drive the historian to provide a causal connection between those phrases, and between those phrases and the events that they try to reflect, would be refused by what Blanchot calls the silence of suffering, the destructive aspect of the event. Still, naming is impossible to avoid. Even in silence, he suggests, there is a telling. Writing makes present the intention of naming—of knowing—at the same time that it makes clear just how impossible it is to name certain realities. When you see words on the page, or when you try to write words on the page, implies Blanchot, your attention is drawn to the relation among the words as much as to the presumed relation between words and events, words and things.

Events seem to obliterate history: Blanchot writes that "the disaster is related to forgetfulness—forgetfulness without memory, the motionless retreat of what has not been treated—the immemorial, perhaps" (3). If the immediacy of the experience hurtles inevitably into the past, into the narrative of history once we name it (once we speak it, once we know it), then we lose it. We remember names and knowledge, but the experience itself is, in Blanchot's terms, "immemorial." To "remember" such moments of immediacy, the witness "remembers forgetfully." Events are recalled not *in* the narrative with which they attempt to pin down those events and in some important ways themselves. Instead, events come to the witness as traces of what happened, traces that disrupt and destroy the carefully regulated history into which the person listening, the historian, inserts himself. The disaster can't be remembered for history, exactly, but it can be seen in the attempts to recover it.

□ □ □

THE INTRANSIGENCE OF HISTORY
(PIERRE VIDAL-NAQUET)

In a review of Josef Yerushalmi's book, *Zakhor,* on the relation between Jewish history and Jewish memory, the French historian Pierre Vidal-Naquet makes clear why the argument over history's role in making the Holocaust available to present generations is important. Vidal-Naquet links the biblical command to remember to the difficult situation of Jews since 1945. Connecting Yerushalmi's book to Aharon Megged's novella *Yad Vashem,* he notes that "In Hebrew, 'zakhor' signifies 'remember.' In the Jewish tradition, remembering is a duty for those who are Jewish: 'If I forget thee, O Jerusalem . . .' What exactly must be remembered?" (58). One of the strands of Megged's novel is about the difficulties of an Israeli couple trying to hold fast to the family's history in eastern Europe while trying to make a life for themselves in Israel. The problem is made evident in their attempts to find a name for their child that connects him to Israel and yet doesn't offend one of the child's grandfathers, who is a refugee from eastern Europe. The problem of remembering, suggests Vidal-Naquet, is the problem of putting together the object of remembrance and the name: *yad vashem,* which in Hebrew means "the monument (or place) and the name." We attach names to objects, and see those names as mnemonics for objects and events that are no longer there, which have been lost: like the six million in Europe, or, in the case of Megged's grandfather, the decimated eastern European Jewish culture. But what has been lost, what is absent, also exerts pressure upon the monument and the name. "What exactly must be remembered?" Vidal-Naquet answers: "Aharon Megged's novella clearly shows that one can choose between memories," though one of the main points of Yerushalmi's book is that, in cases where a disaster befalls a people, the historical and religious narratives that are built to frame it are often lost; all that is left is a choice of *how* to tell a story. The choice of which story

to tell comes not from our relation to the past but from our difficulties here in
the present: which story relates best to what's going on right now. Vidal-Naquet
writes that our challenge since 1945, as historians and as writers, is to "set memory in motion," though to do so we must also understand that "writing history
is also a work of art" ("The Historian and the Test of Murder" 140).

Vidal-Naquet is writing about history and memory with the Holocaust revision industry on his mind: much of his work was written in the same historical
context as Lyotard's and Blanchot's. By the late 1970s and early 1980s, in part because of an influx of Islamic immigrants mainly from north Africa and a backlash against them by French-born citizens, and in part because this backlash of
nationalism also had Jewish citizens as its aim, the political and cultural climate
in France became difficult for Jews. The rise in anti-Semitism brought with it a
rise in the number of instances of Holocaust denial. Coming at the same time as
many hard and fast historical tenets were being severely tested by professional
historians in the colleges and universities, many deniers felt as though they had
a chance in such a climate to dismantle, if only a piece at a time, the edifice of
Holocaust history. What happens to an individual in Auschwitz, and what is remembered and written as testimony, tends to be collected together with all other
such remembrances and taken as an amalgam. Through that amalgam historians
are able to tell us that such-and-such happened in Auschwitz. The difficulty, in
the face of Holocaust deniers, is that any discrepancy among the testimonies and
the memories of those who were there is taken as an error or a lie, and is used to
impeach the knowledge we do have of the atrocities. Vidal-Naquet, a historian
as well versed in classical history as in the history of contemporary Europe, writes
that the paradigm for history's flattening of memory is the classical historian
Thucydides's account of the "disappearance" of the Helots at the hands of the con-
quering Spartans in 424 B.C.E. In that account, the Helots' disappearance—very
likely their liquidation—is disposed of in a single line of historical writing. "To
constitute the two thousand helots as a historical whole when each helot had his
own life and his own death," Vidal-Naquet writes, "one obviously must construct
the set 'helots.' To us, this would seem to go without saying; it would seem to be,
as one says, 'obvious,' but in reality it is not so, any more or any less than the set
'Jews' or the set 'National Socialist Germany'" ("The Holocaust's Challenge to
History" 144). The construction of the set doesn't give us a way to describe the
experiences of individuals. There is no room, in other words, in collective memory, for individual memory to intrude or interrupt the narrative. The reality of
the individual experiences do intrude upon Thucydides's text, as Vidal-Naquet tells
us by pointing attention to the word "each" as it refers to the helots: "shortly
thereafter, they were made to disappear, and no one knew in what manner each
of them had been eliminated" (cited in *Assassins of Memory* 100). The attempt by
the historian to write a collective account that eliminates the individual (his manner of death, the quality of suffering, in each instance of "elimination") is foiled

by language's ability to register just that absence: helots as a set includes its members, each of whom suffered and died.

But Vidal-Naquet worries that this isn't enough in the face of efforts by deniers to foreground the narrative over the silence of the victims. And so he points approvingly to Claude Lanzmann's *Shoah*, a documentary film about the Holocaust that foregrounds the individual's recollections of events rather than black-and-white, WWII-era footage, the narrative we all know so well. Lanzmann's film puts the narrative of the Shoah entirely into the background. Vidal-Naquet sees *Shoah* as something almost crazy: it is "a historical work where memory alone, a memory of today, is called upon to bear witness" ("Holocaust's Challenge" 150). Lanzmann's film is an instance in which those who saw and experienced the atrocities are given an opportunity to recall those events and to have a chance to speak. Each produces a language that is both a presentation of the object of memory, and a presentation of the object's loss and of that loss's effect upon the witness and his memory. The film is admirable because it places together, in an almost jarring fashion, *yad vashem,* the monument and the name. There is Simon Srebnik in peaceful fields outside Chelmno, fields where forty years earlier he exhumed and burned bodies. There is Simon Prodchlebnik nonchalantly telling Lanzmann that the trucks that were used to gas members of his town are very like those that deliver cigarettes to stores in his current hometown of Tel Aviv. Vidal-Naquet suggests that Lanzmann managed to create in his film something like Blanchot's disaster: a memory that is not a representation but a moment of seeing without knowing. Lanzmann has made a film that manages to "search for time lost as at once time lost and time rediscovered." He finds the memory of events "[b]etween time lost and time rediscovered," and he finds it there as "the work of art" (150). For Vidal-Naquet, *Shoah* is a work of memory precisely because it navigates between *yad vashem,* the monument and the name. What lies between them is both the destroyer of history and the language that gives events a palpable presence.

Vidal-Naquet sees the cause for this absence in what he calls the intransigence of events. Intransigence exerts itself upon narratives that try to flatten them into collective memory, or render them as things: the Holocaust, the Diaspora, Auschwitz. "A historical discourse is a web of explanations that may give way to an 'other explanation' if the latter is deemed to account for the complexity (or, maybe more precisely, the heterogeneity) of events in a more satisfactory manner" (*Assassins of Memory* 97). It is heterogeneity or the unreasonableness of events, their inability to fit paradigms, that makes it so hard to account for them in historical writing. It is this unreasonableness that compels writing. "The historian writes; he conjures up a place and time, but he himself is situated in a place and time, at the center of a nation, for example, which entails the elimination of other nations. As a writer, he has depended at length solely on written texts, which has simultaneously entailed the elimination of oral or gestural manifestations, the booty of anthropologists" (*Assassins of Memory* 110). The historian has to recognize that "oral and gestural manifestations," as well as the storehouse of rhetorical figure, are *also* elements of the real. If he doesn't, and writes only about the past, then we lose the connection with "what might be called, for lack of a better term, reality," and become immersed "in discourse, but such discourse would no longer be historical" (111). It would just be one of an endless number of stories.

Speaking of Holocaust denial and revisionism, Pierre Vidal-Naquet explains that "a historical discourse is a network of explications that can give way to 'another explication' if the latter is judged to take better account of the facts," but "events are not things, even if an irreducible opacity of the real exists" (318). The opacity of reality is available in the distance between the occurrence of an event and our ability to place ourselves, as speaking subjects, into their midsts through *writing*. It is in writing that we are both disconnected from the object or event to which we'd hoped to have access, and irrevocably tied to it. The philosopher Louis Mink argues that "the unique problem of history is not the explanation of *events* but the understanding of *advents*" (115), not things that happened in the past but literally the "arrival" of those events into the present. It is these advents that make their way to the surface of the historical narratives that historians—or the individuals who find themselves living in the midsts of events—cannot avoid writing.

□ □ □

HISTORY, COUNTERHISTORY, AND MEMORY (AMOS FUNKENSTEIN)

As a historian and philosopher of history, Amos Funkenstein probably was best known as one of the co-founders, with Saul Friedlander, of the journal *History and Memory*, one of the first publications to take serious note of the interest in the vexed relation between the two terms of its title. He was inspired by his mentor, Josef Yerushalmi, to imagine new ways to understand where history ends and memory begins. As a serious historian of the Jewish middle ages himself, Funkenstein devoted many essays and books to the varieties of memory and how a culture's construction of collective memory may be substituted for history, and at what cost. His book *Perceptions of Jewish History* is a collection of essays written on just this topic over the course of almost fifteen years. In one of its first chapters, "Collective Memory and Historical Consciousness," Funkenstein provides a useful distinction on the topic of history's relation to memory as he continues the dialogue that Yerushalmi began seven years earlier.

The distinction Funkenstein provides is the one between individual, personal memories, and memories of a more collective kind. He says that "even the most personal memory cannot be removed from its social context" (4); the relationship between individual memory and the material realities that constrain it is not static but productive: each informs the other, and to some extent changes it. "No memory, not even the most intimate and personal, can be isolated from [its] social context, from the language and symbolic system molded by the society [in which it is embedded] over centuries" (5). Memory as retrieval—as the recuperation of events that had for all other purposes been lost—becomes insinuated in the fabric of history, in the language and symbolic systems of a culture that any individual takes for granted. Funkenstein sees that in the distinction made in *Zakhor* between *mneme* (memory as conscious remembrance or retrieval) and *anamnesis* (memory as almost an involuntary flash of what had previously been thought to be lost), both terms might best be thought of as referring to memories recalled by individuals. (Yerushalmi himself intended the first term to refer to collective memories, memories established by a culture as normative and historical; whereas the second term referred only to memories held by individuals.) Lost events—memories of "even the most personal" kind—indicate something that has fallen outside the sanction of the collective. Funkenstein provides this example: "When I remember (and none too happily) my first day at school, I recall the city, the institution, the teacher—through and through social entities or constructs" (4). But even the memory of the "first day at school" is not the memory of the city, or the teacher, or the institution, but of what falls between those objects. The memory of the first day at school may have only tangentially to do with teacher, institution, and city, and perhaps everything to do with what falls outside those indices. But even those "absences" are palpably present to Amos Funkenstein decades later. *Anamnesis* and *mneme* function in close relation to one another, though the latter does not so much resolve the former and regularize it as it does trouble or complicate it, and reveal something that was otherwise lost to it.

Funkenstein makes another useful distinction in this essay, the one indicated by his title, between "historical consciousness" and "collective memory." Historical consciousness is "the degree of creative freedom in the use of interpretation of the contents" of memory (10), the writer's or historian's sense that the constraints of knowledge and language that sometimes prevent us from recollection might also be seen as tools with which to construct the collective memory. Language and the categories of knowledge provide the way to articulate memory collectively in the first place. This distinction is useful because it sets up a kind of triadic division of memory, history, and recollection. Here history (or historical consciousness) is the critical manipulation of collective memory—presumably to recuperate the events of the past that reside behind it—and which is itself made up by individual memories. One way to understand the distinction is to think of historical consciousness (and the language or tools of historiography) as mediating between collective memory (*mneme*) and individual memory (*anamnesis*). The work of the historian is a work not of retrieval but of construction. In it she has a great deal of freedom to produce a narrative comprised by the testimonies and available recollections of individuals who were there at the occurrence of the event. "The more a culture permits conscious changes and variations of the narrator in the contents, symbols, and structures of collective memory, the more complex and less predictable the narrative of history becomes" (9).

And for Funkenstein—as, certainly, for Hayden White—this is not a disadvantage but an advantage. The work of the historian is the work of the writer. Historical consciousness can be thought of as an act of mediation, and what it mediates are constructions, where individual memories, inscribed or insinuated in the fabric of the language and rhythms of a people, are available to the historian to be woven into the fabric of collective memory and taken as history. It's something like a discontinuity in the simple story of what happened rather than as an object that makes sense on its own without interpretation or context. Like the memory of Funkenstein's first day of school, it is located somewhere *among* descriptions of a city, or of a teacher, or of an institution, but it isn't the same as any one of these descriptions, and may in fact be indicated most clearly by his parenthetical throwaway, "and none too happily." (You wonder just what Funkenstein remembers, through that one phrase, that isn't available in his written account of it.) The historian is free to forge, as collective memory, a written account that makes present something that is altogether discontinuous with the language or system she has at her disposal, and she mediates competing narrative accounts whose effects may or may not make visible to the reader what was present in the memory of the witness or narrator. It's through the historian's critical consciousness, in other words, that she finds a language with which to indicate *anamnesis* as it imprints itself upon, and problematizes, *mneme*.

In the middle ages, Funkenstein suggests that "the writing of history . . . was guided by the implicit assumption that the historical fact is immediately given: it does not need to be *interpreted* in order to be meaningful except at a deeper theological level (*spiritualis intelligentsia*). The eyewitness thus seemed to them the most reliable historian . . ." (14, original emphasis). At least in this period, historical writing is more closely connected to individual eyewitness testimony than it is to collective memory. What happened happened, and we have the authority of the eyewitness to go on. Individual memory (*anamnesis*) and the historical consciousness were closely aligned. So in the medieval historian's view, the writing of history was not meant to provide a collective or *mnemonic* (that is, contextual) understanding of events. Instead, historical writing had as its aim a kind of witnessing, and seemed to work against a collective understanding. Seeing was more important than knowing, and more important than forging the collective consciousnes that would allow its transmissibility. The "none too happily" of Funkenstein's account of school would in this older paradigm be more important than the language of institution or place or person, and the historian's job is to create a language through which seeing—individual memory—was possible for the reader

as much as for the witness. What is important in both distinctions is the elabo-
ration of a "third term," a facet of memory that cuts against the grain of collective memory, and that is associated with certain kinds of writing, though not
necessarily with the kind that we usually think of as the transparently historical.

It is the connection to *writing* that is important in Funkenstein's essay entitled
"Perceptions of Historical Fact." There, he introduces the idea that the writing
of history has an effect upon the individual writer as well as the reader of the account. Like the freedom associated with historical consciousness—a freedom
whose result is often complex and unpredictable—it is understood here that writing intervenes in and mediates memory. Funkenstein is primarily interested in how
the choices historians make—of voice, selection, plot, genre—consciously and
sometimes unconsciously alter historical work and as a result the collective memory of those who read it. The historian "can make and unmake history, can obliterate names, events, identities by not recording them" (30). By writing history,
medieval historical writers "found themselves admitting that by writing, they act
upon history" (31). If we take historical consciousness also as a kind of "freedom" to inscribe what has been seen but not necessarily integrated into the languages of history, then the writing of history can be seen as the creation of
something quite different from the events that are apparently its focus. And if we
go farther, and take *anamnesis* as the nagging suspicion that events that make
themselves apparent to us are quite different from the narratives we may have at
our disposal with which to render them, then the writer of history doesn't write
memory. She writes something else entirely. The goal of the historical writer is to
make visible what lies at the foundation of memory—namely, what has been forgotten or, better still, what is unavailable to memory at all—and to replicate the
effect it has on the individual who recalls it in the reader.

All individual memories are constrained by reality. The real—both the material dimension of the world that affects individual memories and the affective
and sometimes irrational aspect of those individual memories—"escapes our control, [and] forces itself upon us whether or not we welcome it," but it is also "that
which we make relevant, construct, manipulate" (68–9). We write both to make
sense of the impingements of the real—the reality of memory as it forces itself
upon us—and to gain some control over it and (at least insofar as the historian
is able) to make it into something that resembles collective memory and, eventually, history. We write both as a result of the real's violence in the midsts of the
order of knowledge—"the language and symbolic system molded by society over
centuries" ("Collective Memory" 5)—and as a way to produce in the reader a
sense of what was recollected by the original witness. And though the real impinges
itself upon us, it may or may not be narratable, though it is visible as it works its
way against the grain of the narrative of history.

Funkenstein, like Vidal-Naquet and Blanchot, is ultimately concerned that
any questions raised by historians about the solidity of historical facts, particularly

those having to do with the Holocaust, will erode the Holocaust's "reality" and open the door to Holocaust deniers. But it's just this reality—the intransigence of the real—that finally is the greatest safeguard against the deniers and their allies on the lunatic fringe. Funkenstein argues that—in spite of Nazis' "arguing away" of the facts of Jewish citizenship or the fraudulence of the *Protocols of the Elders of Zion*—Holocaust deniers in France, the United States, and elsewhere can't get away from the impingements of the real, such as the reality of the gas chambers, of anti-Semitism, and the historical break of the Shoah. It is these realities that will ultimately disturb the narrative of denial and show the revisionists for the liars they are. Their "arguments" make sense of the crimes of the Final Solution that are otherwise not sensible or rational: "Many of us say that the Nazi crimes were 'incomprehensible,' that the sheer limitless inventiveness in degradation and killing of that regime defy all our historical explanatory schemes. . . . Precisely this incomprehensibility of the crimes makes their denial into a much more rational account of a possible world (better than ours) in which people act out of rational, or at least predictable motivations" (79). But individual memory—that which at its foundation is counterrational—"'shines through'" and affects that rational, collective narrative. The effect of the event prevents it from becoming an arbitrary concoction altogether removed from what happened (79).

It is to the degree that the real makes itself apparent in the narratives that try to bring the events of history into the collective consciousness that the Holocaust is (in Funkenstein's terms) comprehensible (see "The Dialectical Theology of Meaninglessness" 334–7). It is an event that imprints itself into the memories of those who were there and—through writing—on those who weren't, and these memories shape the lives and actions of all involved. That those memories are often inaccessible to the language and context that the historian and the witnesses themselves have at their disposal and that would, for lack of a better term, transmit them doesn't make the Holocaust incomprehensible, or absent from memory. It simply makes whatever we can say or do with those memories susceptible to misreading if we are not very careful to watch for the reality that shines through them but is not represented, and it means that testimonial, historical, or literary accounts that appear seamless or transparent may be the most suspicious of them all. What we say can't be made equivalent to what we know; and what we say can't be made equivalent to what happened. Memories of events like the Holocaust need to be seen, instead, as something like knowledge's "other." "Closeness to reality [in a testimony derived from memory of the catastrophe] can be neither measured nor proven by a waterproof algorithm," writes Funkenstein. "It must be decided from case to case without universal criteria" ("History, Counterhistory, Narrative" 79). The relationship between history and memory is a complicated one; we'll see, in the second section of this book, just how complicated it is in recollections of the Holocaust written by eyewitnesses.

CHAPTER 5

Case Studies: History, Narrative, and the Problems of Evidence

History, as we've seen, is a far more complicated affair than simply reporting the events of the past. Because it requires the historian to both collect the evidence of those events, and to arrange that evidence into a pattern that can be narrated or retold in such a way that members of an audience can understand it, history pulls in two opposite directions. The act of collection assumes that there is a direct relation between events and the detritus of events—between what happens and the traces left by what happens—and the historian's task is to reconstruct, insofar as it's possible, the event from its trace and its effects. The act of narrating the event, however, is not an act of reconstruction—or not only such an act—but also an act of invention, in which the historian, as a writer, has to give a cogency to the event by describing those aspects of it that are not made clear but obscured by its material leavings, and by drawing conclusions about the gaps left in the event by documents, testimonies, and other artefacts that simply aren't available (or are available but are incomplete, or faulty, or whose authenticity is in question). What you have, then, in the writing of history is a built-in tension between what happened, which is forever in the past, and how we report what happened, which requires a language of the here and now, and a logic that can be understood in terms of what we know or have had experience with.

This is made all the more complicated, as we've seen, when dealing with an event like the Holocaust. In addition to the complicating factors we reviewed in the last chapter, historians of the Holocaust also must contend with the political stakes involved in the study of what could easily be called the watershed moment of recent history. There have been many disasters in recent memory: the cultural revolution in China that led to the murder and resettlement of vast proportions of the population; decimation of Cambodia under the Khmer Rouge regime; the ethnic cleansing in the Balkan wars of the 1990s, to name only three. It's not a coincidence that many, if not all, have been compared in one way or another with the Holocaust. The historical events of 1939–45 provide a historical template on which to overlay other instances of genocides. Because of its enormity and our tendency to use it as a yardstick for atrocities, it has also been used as a stick with which to beat proponents of a policy, foreign or domestic, that would replicate the events that led to the Final Solution. Historians must contend, in other words, not just with history but with history's cultural valences, with the role history plays in our contemporary culture.

In this chapter, I outline three controversies of the last decade or so, controversies that lay bare some of the historical problems associated with the Holocaust and its effect in everyday life in the United States, Europe, and elsewhere. The first two involve arguments over the accounts of Holocaust victims and survivors held by Swiss banks for the last fifty years, and the controversy raised by Jan Gross's book about a massacre of Jews in a village in Poland in the early years of the war. Here I provide the outlines of the argument and untangle the strands of historical research that are the main bones of contention in each one. As you'll see, these strands are associated with the arguments over history and the possibility of writing a history of the Holocaust that have been simmering since the end of World War II. Arguments over evidence and its status, the difficulties in making clear the context (both in the present and in the past) in which that evidence makes sense, the problems associated with eyewitness "reliability" and the problems inherent in testimony, and the dangers associated with the emplotment of history are all clearly visible in the first of these controversies. The third—the trial of

Deborah Lipstadt, a historian and scholar of the Holocaust denial movement, for libeling David Irving, a historian notorious for his attempts to discredit mainstream accounts of the Nazi Final Solution—is a more difficult case. In part this is because it has served, in the United States, as a platform on which to question whether Holocaust deniers like Irving shouldn't have their say on the grounds of free speech. It can be used as a test case that, after outlining the first two cases, may serve as a point of departure for further study.

□ □ □

JEDWABNE, POLAND

On the 10th of July 1941, not far from the village square in Jedwabne, Poland, several townspeople forced most of their Jewish fellow residents into Bronislaw Szlezinski's barn, and burned it to the ground. This act preceded the brutality of the Final Solution, but was part of the dynamic of anti-Semitism and xenophobia that existed in much of Poland during the war years. The killing is all the more horrifying in part because it was an act of neighbor against neighbor. And it was an act that, like many during those years, was witnessed by many whose testimonies are troubled by doubt, by forgetfulness, the inevitable passage of years and of regimes, and by the calcification of what we now know as "the Holocaust." The monument put up to commemorate the pogrom memorialized the over one thousand killed simply as Polish victims of Nazi brutality. In May 2000, Jan Gross's book, *Neighbors,* was published. Like earlier accounts of the killing in Jedwabne, it presented eyewitness testimony and other documents to make clear that "the Polish half of [the] town's population murder[ed] its Jewish half." Since that time, and particularly since the book's translation into English that year, the memory of the events in Jedwabne, if not the events themselves, have raised charges of bad faith, shoddy historical work, and—in their most extreme form— Holocaust denial. The book's veracity has been called into doubt, and this in turn has led to charges that the book is an instance, if not a useful tool, of denial. At issue in Gross's book is the possibility that the evidence available, and the eyewitness testimonies of the survivors and perpetrators, can't be understood simply, and that in fact that evidence doesn't provide "history" at all but only its raw materials. The book and the charges against it are an example of the predicament of historical writing in the face of the absence of the event: when confronted with the incredible, witnesses and readers alike reduce the events to what *is* credible, what *is* narratable, and what *is* manageable. Those aspects of the event that seem to resist logic, or that—when put into words—seem outrageous or just plain wrong, are often either left to the side or are seen as irreconcilable details best chalked up to failures of memory or bad record-keeping. And Gross's account of the Jedwabne killings seems to have an aspect of the incredible to it.

The outlines of the story are as follows: between the signing of the nonaggression pact between the Soviet Union and Germany in 1939 and the German invasion of the Soviet Union in 1941, a swath of Poland changed hands three times. For the years between the conclusion of World War I and 1939, it had been in independent Poland; between September 1939 and June 1941, it was occupied by the Red Army; and from 1941 until the last year of the war, it was occupied by the Nazis. Jedwabne, a town in that swath of Polish land, had been on the map for a couple of hundred years by 1941, and had—like many small towns in the "pale of Jewish settlement"—always included a fairly large number of Jewish residents, numbering about 1,400 in that year. It was a rural town, in which a majority of landowners were non-Jewish, and a majority of shopkeepers and other merchants were Jewish (again, much like many small towns in the Polish pale). It had a *cheder*—a Jewish day school—and many residents belonged to Jewish religious and social organizations, including the socialist Bund. While the non-Jewish and Jewish residents of the town generally got along with one another, there was also mutual suspicion and envy, particularly after the signing of the nonaggression pact that placed Jedwabne in the Soviet sphere of influence. Because Jewish residents were rightfully suspicious about the Germans' intentions toward the Jews after 1933, and because some residents were politically sympathetic to socialism, the pact was welcomed by some Jewish residents; some of the more active socialists among them celebrated the erection of a bust of Lenin in the town not long afterward, and one or two Jewish residents were put into positions in the town's governance.

After the Nazi invasion in June 1941, events turned badly very quickly. Within a day of the invasion, witnesses reported a carload of German soldiers riding into town, though the numbers of soldiers in the car (or truck) differ depending on which witness's testimony you read. Included in this number were officers, and a group of them spoke with members of the Jedwabne town council—non-Jews, by this time, since the town government had rid itself of Soviet "sympathizers" before the arrival of the Germans. Almost immediately, a number of non-Jewish townspeople began to take action against several of their Jewish neighbors, in some cases invading their homes and, in one event noted by a large number of eyewitnesses, several Jewish men were forced to topple the statue of Lenin and to carry it on a little wagon out of town while being whipped and struck and forced to sing socialist marching songs. In towns neighboring Jedwabne, similar events were taking place; a number of Jews who managed to escape those towns made their way to Jedwabne to report that the entire Jewish populations of the places were being killed, some by German soldiers and some by non-Jewish residents.

By the beginning of the second week of German occupation, a plan had been hatched by a number of residents. Together, they drove the majority of Jews into the square and from there into a barn. The doors to the barn were closed and locked, and gasoline was poured onto its walls. A fire was lit in the barn, and while townspeople looked on—some with shovels and hoes to beat to death anyone who tried to escape—the barn, with hundreds of people inside, burned to the ground. Those who stayed in their homes, afraid to come out, reported hearing the screams of their neighbors and smelling the burning bodies from miles away.

This is the story that Jan Gross, a sociology professor at New York University, tells in *Neighbors*. He tells it with the aid of testimonies taken from trials of perpetrators held in the decade after the conclusion of the war, from records found in the town's archives (both formal and informal), in Germany, and from *memoribuchen* or *yizkor* books, written remembrances of Jewish townspeople who either escaped or who retell stories they themselves had heard from relatives and friends. In some instances, the testimonies provided at trial and those taken in the years during which Gross conducted his research differed quite a bit. Recent excavations in Jedwabne since the publication of Gross's book have unearthed physical evidence that at once contradicts Gross's account and supports it, depending on how one reads it. And records left by the German military of its actions in Jedwabne and surrounding towns shed light—or no light at all—upon whether the Germans instigated or plotted the murders, or stood by and watched while non-Jewish Poles did it on their own. And the entire episode—both what happened in Jedwabne and what happened after the publication of *Neighbors*—is vastly complicated by the history of Poland just before and during the war and the even more vexed history of Jewish relations with non-Jews in Poland after the war's end. A good deal has been written about the years between 1939 and 1941, during which some non-Jewish citizens had very mixed feelings toward Poland's Jews. They were often seen as aliens, transients, communist-sympathizers, plutocrats, often all at the same time. Non-Jewish Poles in Jedwabne and elsewhere became concerned in 1939 when invading Soviet troops were welcomed by some of their Jewish neighbors, and took minor positions in the soviet bureaucracy.

The four central points of disagreement over the historical "accuracy" of Gross's account (or, maybe more accurately, the historical authenticity of that account) are its use of the evidence found in archives and on the Jedwabne site itself, the "context" in which that evidence can best be understood, the reliability of the memory of those individuals involved in the events, and the "emplotment" of the narrative provided by Gross. In the years since Gross wrote his study, the vicious disagreements over its veracity—mainly in Poland, but also in the United States—have hinged on precisely these questions, and not long after the publication of *Neighbors*, the Polish Institute of National Memory (IPN) undertook what it claimed was an exhaustive study of the massacre in order to settle the matter. That the IPN study upheld, in most matters of substance, Gross's narrative of the event seems not to have settled anything at all for those who see Gross's version of events, like Goldhagen's attempt to tar all Germans as anti-Semites, as a kind of cultural smear campaign. What all this suggests is that though matters of history may be settled, matters of history's narrative may never be settled at all.

The *evidence* in the Jedwabne case falls into two main categories. The physical evidence, in the form of documents and of the detritus of the massacres, forms the first category. The documents on which Gross relies are transcripts taken immediately after the war from survivors across Poland and housed in the Polish National Archives (IPN); transcripts of trials of several of the main actors in Jedwabne taken in 1952 and 1953; and German documents, dated 1941, that record the movements of the Einsatzkommados in the Bialystok region of Poland (in which Jedwabne is located). The physical evidence, mostly brought to light in the IPN investigation, includes the remains—mostly ashes—of those murdered in Szlezinski's barn, and bullets found inside the barn among the remains, presumably from German carbines. The second category of evidence is the eyewitness testimonies, along with those found in the trial transcripts, of those who were present in Jedwabne on July 10, 1941.

Gross reports that the 1,400 Jews in Jedwabne—those that survived the first few days of anti-Semitic violence immediately after the German occupation—were killed together in the barn. The physical evidence uncovered in the barn, however, suggests that maybe a quarter of that number were burned to death there. Several writers, Norman Finkelstein and Tomasz Strzembosz the most vocal among them, note that this grave error on the part of Gross throws his entire study into question. But the fact remains that there are still three-quarters of the Jews of Jedwabne left unaccounted for: there is no evidence whatsoever that they survived either the massacres in July or the remainder of the war. This means that they were either driven out of the town, left of their own accord having seen what their non-Jewish neighbors would do or had done already, or were killed by other means. The matter of the bullets found in the remains of the barn are also seen as evidence that Gross's argument—that the Germans in the town had nothing to do with the massacres except perhaps its planning—fails to account for the Germans' part in the massacre. Strzembosz and others suggest that the presence of two German bullets is evidence that soldiers or police must have prevented the Jews from exiting the barn, and that some of those Germans must have shot into the barn, thereby actively taking part in the massacre. That these bullets may have been in the barn before the burning, or that they may have been fired by residents of Jedwabne, or that they were fired after the massacre at either terribly burned survivors of the fire or at non-Jewish Polish looters by German soldiers, is not accounted for by Gross's antagonists.

Eyewitness testimony given by perpetrators has also been disputed. Gross estimates—by doing the demographic math—that in a town with under a thousand non-Jewish residents, the total non-Jewish adult male population was around 225, and that this number is the baseline from which the number of perpetrators would have to be calculated; Gross eventually puts the number of active perpetrators at 92. The investigation concluded by the IPN put the number of active perpetrators at 40, a number that does not include the possibility of German soldiers or gendarmes. Many of those who dispute Gross's findings argue that his initial number, 225, so inflates the number of potential non-Jewish perpetrators (by a factor of nearly six) is evidence that Gross must have an anti-Polish bias; in fact, though the actual number determined to have been active in Jedwabne is less than half Gross's number, it is hardly evidence of an insidious agenda. Moreover, both Gross's book and the IPN report that a crowd of residents actively took part in rounding up the town's Jews, taunted them as they were driven into the town square, and eventually herded into the barn at the point of shovels, axes, and clubs. Steve Paulsson, arguing against Finkelstein recently, writes, "So we have a crowd, which is standing around, while 40 (or maybe 92) people are taunting and tormenting the Jews, driving them towards the barn, forcing them inside, dousing it with gasoline, and setting it on fire. It doesn't seem that any of them did anything to try to stop the perpetrators or help the victims" (email, 17 July 2002).

Finally, on the point of the German presence in Jedwabne, the documentary evidence is contradictory. German archive documents suggest that Einsatzkommandos had already passed Jedwabne by the time of the massacre; other documents suggest, however, that a Gestapo detachment, following the Einsatzkommand, had established a presence in Jedwabne in early July. Eyewitnesses in Jedwabne remember two or three "taxis" arriving before the massacres, dispatching a lightly armed group of German police, the officers that met with the town council and, according to some, helped plan the massacre. The same eyewitnesses recall some of these Germans taking photographs—none of which, apparently, have survived the war—of the burning of the barn, but that none of them actually participated in either rounding up the Jews that day or driving them into the barn. (They did, however, have a part in forcing several Jews to take down the Lenin statue and be humiliated in the process.)

The problem of historical *context* also complicates matters. While it is impossible to make blanket statements about Jewish and non-Jewish allegiances during those years, some Jewish and Catholic Poles in Jedwabne were often highly suspicious of one anothers' motives. Writing a few months after the publication of Gross's book, Tomasz Strzembosz argues that any Catholic reprisal against the Jewish residents of Jedwabne are perfectly understandable: "Roman Sadowski . . . wrote me on November 10, 2000: 'During the Soviet occupation Jews were the "masters" of this region. They entirely co-operated with the Soviet authorities. According to the accounts of my wife's cousins, it was Jews together with the NKVD [the Russian secret police] that compiled lists of those to be interned (deported).'" Strzembosz goes on to say that one of the participants in an action against collaborationists "called for settling scores with the Bolsheviks and Jews, saying: '. . . [T]he time to settle accounts has come, down with communists; we'll butcher every last Jew.'" Surely the actions of the Jedwabne residents might be understandable when read against a background of Jewish-Bolshevik complicity, he suggests.

Adam Michnik and Leon Wieseltier, writing in *The New Republic* not long after the publication of Gross's book, cite an example from 1942 of what Michnik calls "the paradox of Polish attitudes toward Jews": "Our feelings toward the Jews haven't changed. We still consider them the political, economic, and ideological enemies of Poland. . . . [But] the knowledge of these feelings doesn't relieve us of the duty of condemning the crime." In response, Leon Wieseltier demands a reassessment of the notion of collective responsibility. In fact, Gross's book is an argument for working *against* a collective memory that risks reducing the events of the Shoah to a well-wrought narrative.

> When considering survivors' testimonies, we would be well advised to change the starting premise in appraisal of their evidentiary contribution from a priori critical to in principle affirmative. By accepting what we read in a particular account as fact until we find persuasive arguments to the contrary, we would avoid more mistakes than we are likely to commit by adopting the opposite approach, which calls for cautious skepticism toward any testimony until an independent confirmation of its content has been found. . . . All I am arguing for is the suspension of our incredulity.

It's incredulity that leads a writer in 2001 to take the virulent anti-Semitism of 1942 as the paradigm in which to witness the Jedwabne massacres. But it's that same incredulity that leads Israel Gutman, a survivor and Yad Vashem historian, to say that "Strzembosz's rumors and generalized accusations . . . are the products of fantasy and are not worth discussing. Although he does not say so clearly, these words suggest a certain tit for tat approach to Jedwabne—'you hurt us, so now we'll hurt you!' It is difficult to hold a conversation" in the midsts of hostile antisemitism.

Each *eyewitness*—those of the current generation, like Strzembosz, Wieseltier, and Michnik, who weren't there; or those, like Jakov Piekarz or Szmul Wasersztajn, who were there in Jedwabne—can only remember what has been called to mind *as* a memory. Whether it is the burning of their neighbors and family members alive in a barn, or the horrifying narrative account of it that disturbs their sense of history, or membership in the collective "we" of Polish identity, or simply their own memories, those events have had the effect as of staring into the sun. They've been blotted out from the narrative that would integrate them into history. To bear witness to the possibility that those whom you know might for whatever motive herd you into a barn and set it afire is to look directly into the sun. Antoni Niebrzydowski issued kerosene to his brothers at his warehouse and then they "brought the eight liters of kerosene that I had just issued to them and doused the barn filled with Jews and lit it up; what followed I do not know." Perhaps he doesn't, but he saw. It would be easy to deny what he saw because it is simply too horrible to remember. In fact, what Antoni Niebrzydowski saw may be lost to knowledge altogether, though his testimony ("what followed I do not know") can be corroborated by others who were there and thus be called a lie. But his testimony is not inauthentic. If we, like the witness himself, were to "suspend incredulity," we could only be horrified by what glimpse we catch of the event. Is he denying history or the Holocaust by refusing to see?

This is the crux of the problem: the impasse between what the witness saw and what he can tell us. How firm is the connection between the testimony and the events that are its object? It is a question about the relation between the memory of the witness and the immemorial and irretrievable events that the witness saw as much as it's a question of history. To suggest that the testimony is finally incredible, given all of the evidence that can be marshaled against it, is maybe the most rational answer. But by saying so and then ruling out of court evidence of what the witness saw that doesn't accord with the available historical record would also be hugely problematic. In the case of the Jedwabne massacre, in which the testimonies of eyewitnesses disturb the prevailing histories of Poland just before and during the war, Gross's historical narrative provides a glimpse of something that may not be substantiated in the end by other documents or testimonies. But his book forces readers—the next generation of witnesses with no historical link to the events—to confront aspects of the history and collective memory of the Holocaust that aren't easily integrated into the seamless fabric of narrative.

In his book *Selling the Holocaust,* Tim Coles makes a smart point that's relevant here: that Holocaust denial could only happen if the Holocaust itself were so firmly established as to become altogether intransigent as a historical construct. "In many ways, 'Holocaust denial' has emerged only within the context of the emergence of the myth of the 'Holocaust.' It was not until the 'Holocaust' emerged as an iconic event that it was perceived to be an event which was deemed worth denying." The collective memory of the event has become ossified, and because there are so few survivors with individual recollections of the event, there is nothing left to go on but accretions of other people's stories. We believe we know the events of the Holocaust because we have read them over and over again, against the backdrop of national identity (be in ours in the United States or Jan Gross's in Poland) and whatever personal stakes we have in the event. So we read

Gross, which troubles that collective memory, and may give in to the impulse to deny its implications. What doesn't accord with knowledge is seen as something else, even though we are aware that what the witness saw strains at the boundaries of knowledge and of testimony's ability to contain it. This kind of denial is an attempt to keep what we see in such testimonies at bay—the neighbor's ability to kill his neighbor.

□ □ □

New York City

In the federal courthouse in the Eastern District of New York in Brooklyn in August 1998, the government of Switzerland agreed to settle litigation that had been brought by, among others, the World Jewish Congress (WJC). The WJC had sued to recover assets deposited by Jews before and during the Holocaust and that had remained in Swiss banks ever since. The case was exceptionally complicated and highly controversial: not only were the banks accused of keeping funds deposited by Jews whose survivors could not produce the required documents, including death certificates, receipts of deposit, or statements. They were also accused of knowingly accepting deposits from the Reichs government in the form of gold bars that had been produced by melting down material wealth that had been confiscated from Jews across Europe, including not just silverware and gold coins but also eyeglass frames, rings, and dental fillings removed from Jewish camp inmates from concentration and death camps. The controversy arose from arguments over historical documents and over how those documents were handled in the media. At one time or another, six investigations into the Swiss banks' culpability in the affair were going on during the four years during which the "case" was active, and while only two of them were completed by the time of the 1998 settlement in federal court, none of them made clear whether the Swiss in general, or individual Swiss banks in particular, had violated the principle of neutrality that allowed the country and its banks to function as a safe haven for people and, far more importantly, their money during the years of World War II.

In spite of what the historical record showed, each side in the affair—the WJC and its representatives; individual survivors and their families, along with the families of those who did not survive the Holocaust; lawyers and officers of the banks named in the litigations; representatives of the interests of Holocaust survivors living in the United States and in Europe, most notably Senator Alfonse D'Amato who led the United States Senate Banking Committee—painted their opponents as manipulating that record for their own benefit. In one of the most popular and widely read accounts of the affair, Norman G. Finkelstein makes the case that the litigation against and eventual settlement with the Swiss banks amounted to a "double shakedown." The "Holocaust industry," Finkelstein's name for those who use the event of the Final Solution for personal or professional gain in what Peter Novick called the "olympics of suffering," took the wealthy and partially guilt-ridden Swiss to the cleaners simply because they appeared to have the guilt of history, if not history itself, on their side.

The case of the Swiss reparations litigation, and the way history figures into the controversy, illustrates again just how difficult it is to separate the events of history from the narrative into which those events are woven. Finkelstein's book, among others, paints the WJC and the litigants for survivors and victims' families as hucksters, selling victimhood and profiting handsomely from its sale. Others, including Jean Ziegler's book *The Swiss, the Gold, and the Dead,* written before the settlement, paint the Swiss government and its banks during the war as knowingly participating in the Nazis' looting of Europe's Jews. Here I simply want to trace the history of the settlement affair, and then to tease out of it the ways Finkelstein's account of the affair—like Gross's account of Jedwabne and the various accountings of the Irving libel suit—provides a narrative that is far from a transparent rendering of history and falls hard on the rocks of the event itself.

Most people thought the issue of reparations had been settled forty years earlier. In the years between 1945 and 1952, the allied forces in Europe, along with groups (including the WJC, the American Joint Distribution Committee, and the American Jewish Committee) representing Jewish organizations in Europe, Palestine (later Israel), and abroad, negotiated with the German government(s) terms of an agreement that would eventually be known as the Claims Conference. The Conference on Jewish Material Claims Against Germany, signed in September 1952, took as its aim the material—and, through it, according to West German Chancellor Adenauer, spiritual—expiation of German crimes against the Jews. After the negotiations were completed that year, the conference would eventually transfer over 115 billion Deutschmarks to individual victims and Jewish organizations principally in Israel and the United States by 1967. According to Ronald Zweig, whose book *German Reparations and the Jewish World* lays out the history and the results of the Claims Conference clearly, by the conclusion of the allocation program, "there were few Jewish victims of Nazism whose needs had not been met by one part or another of the reparations process" (197).

But Switzerland was a tough case even in the early 1950s, when the plight of the Jews of Europe—at the time, several of the DP camps were still in operation—was still apparent. Because it was neutral during the war, it claimed that it should reach a separate agreement with the holders of accounts in its banks. After what Zweig calls "fruitless negotiations," the Conference transferred responsibility for negotiating with the Swiss and its banks to the state of Israel in 1950. Very little came of the negotiations from that point onward until Itamar Levin, an Israeli journalist, began to refocus attention on the dormant accounts in the mid-1990s. His articles in the Jewish presses reached a ready audience in the United States, particularly with the families of survivors. Since 1950, the heirs of those who had died during the war and in the Holocaust had presented their claims to Swiss banks, but had been turned away for lack of documentation and identifying codes that would have otherwise compelled the banks to release the funds. In the 1990s, faced not only with renewed claims but now with the bad press from Levin and others, the banks responded with—as Zweig puts it—"vague hints of antisemitic response in Europe if the Jewish organizations did not moderate their attacks" (5).

In 1992, the World Jewish Congress, which had been a more or less moribund organization since the end of reparations payments from the Claims Conference, formed the World Jewish Restitution Organization (WJRO). It was this organization that spearheaded the claims laid by the families of survivors and victims of the Holocaust, and took legal jurisdiction of some of the cases that would eventually be filed in U.S. federal court. Led by Edgar Bronfman, the heir to the Seagrams organization and known by that time as a leading philanthropist for Jewish and other charities and organizations, the WJRO met with representatives of Swiss banks in 1995 to talk about how to resolve the affair. The Swiss offered a sum of $32 million. There were, in the lists of accounts combed by the banks and their accountants, 775 dormant accounts that could be traced to victims of the Holocaust, and the sum offered was the total—along with interest accrued since the time of deposit—of those dormant accounts. In part because the banks refused to allow the WJRO to oversee the audit that turned up these dormant accounts, and in part because of mutual accusations of arrogance and manipulation, the WJRO refused to continue negotiating directly with the banks. Bronfman met at the end of the year with Senator D'Amato, who chaired the Senate's Banking Committee. In 1996, the committee agreed to hold hearings on the question of the accounts in part because a fair number of U.S. citizens—refugees from Europe or their descendants—were directly affected by the banks' actions.

Those hearings became the backbone of the case. They functioned as a public courtroom, giving faces to those victims whose assets presumably rested in vaults in Switzerland. The hearings also functioned as an investigative forum, through which congress could have access to intelligence reports from the war years and those immediately afterward that would shed light on both the total assets held in the accounts and the total number of those affected by their failure to be paid out. In what would become part of the Report of Dormant Accounts published a year after the settlement in 1998, 54,000 accounts in Switzerland were identified as having a "probable or possible relationship with victims of Nazi persecution." In evidence that would find its way into what was known as the

Gribetz Plan, which made recommendations about how the settlement monies would be paid out, the number of Jewish victims of "Nazi persecution" still alive in 1999 was put at between 832,000 and 960,000, though one of the lawyers familiar with the settlement put the number at closer to 130,000. What became clear during the hearings, in other words, was that the historical record was unclear both about the numbers of survivors who would benefit from a settlement with the Swiss, and the total of the funds that were deposited by the victims themselves. And as we'll see, this disagreement had as much to do with who was doing the counting as it did with the math.

In May 1996, Paul Volcker—who had until recently been the chairman of the United States Federal Reserve—began an independent commission whose task was to determine both how much in unrecovered assets still resided in Swiss banks and how culpable those banks were (in withholding information about the source of the funds and failing to disclose the receipt of funds from Germany during the war). Late in the same year the Swiss banks themselves set up an independent commission to do precisely what the Volcker commission was doing. As a result of that latter commission, the Swiss government established a fund of $200 million, the "Special Fund for Needy Victims of the Holocaust." By the fall of 1996, three class-action lawsuits had been filed with the federal court in New York, which were consolidated into a single class-action suit in January 1997. Partly because the lawyers had a hard time agreeing how to negotiate working together, and partly because the judge in the case wanted to wait until the Volcker commission, at least, could recommend how best to proceed, he delayed ruling. The hearings in the U.S. Senate Banking committee had been joined by parallel hearings in the U.S. House of Representatives' Banking Committee. By 1997 several organizations— including several U.S. cities whose pension funds included investments in Swiss banks—threatened to boycott Swiss banking concerns.

In the summer of 1998, the Swiss independent commission released its report, which focused primarily on the question of whether Switzerland had accepted gold from Nazi Germany during the war whose origin was Jewish confiscation. Much was already known about the confiscation of Jewish assets during the early part of the National Socialist regime through documents available to Raul Hilberg, which he published in the *Destruction of the European Jews* in the early 1960s. The report found that Swiss banks accepted gold from the Nazis that they had good reason to believe had been confiscated from central European banks. But the commission was not able to state clearly whether individual accounts deposited by Jews had been kept illegally, or through the unreasonable demands for certification or identification. The Volcker commission report, which was not released until December 1999, was clearer. It noted that there was "no evidence of systematic destruction of records of victim accounts, organized discrimination against the accounts of victims of Nazi persecution to improper purposes. [. . .] There is ample evidence of many cases in which banks actively sought out missing account holders of their heirs, including Holocaust victims, and paid account balances of dormant accounts to the proper parties." But the report also found that the banks had behaved badly in many cases when dealing with both the unclaimed accounts and those who wished to claim them. There were about 26,000 accounts that "probably" had belonged, or still belonged, to Holocaust victims, a number far in excess of the initial number of over 700 identified by the Swiss. Of those accounts, many had been charged fees that brought their balances to zero; safe deposit boxes had been opened and raided to pay the fees on them; exorbitant fees had been charged to search for heirs of the funds, and some of these searches were done laxly or not at all; and even after the report was released, the banks refused to release a database that listed the names of 4.1 million Nazi-era accounts, which included over 275,000 that matched names of Holocaust victims.

A $1.25 billion figure was decided upon by the parties involved in the litigation; the organizations charged with disbursing the monies then had to settle on a number of persons to whom the funds should be released. Again, the records and calculations provided by archival figures and by estimations based on the survival rate of slave laborers and others who made their way out of the camps proved unreliable. At the end of the war, the figures used by the Claims Conference included estimates that between 135,000 and just under 200,000 Jewish displaced persons survived the Final Solution. Henry Friedlander estimated that at most 500,000 camp survivors remained at the end of 1945; Leonard Dinnerstein estimated that only 40,000 remained by the end of that year. And yet the Gribetz Plan puts the number at closer to a million, though its definition of "survivors" or "Jewish Nazi victims" alive today is far broader and includes those who escaped to the Soviet Union and who survived the war in exile. So there was even some real question as to how best to divide payment, and whether to release funds to individual victims or in larger amounts to Jewish organizations around the world.

This is the outline of the events that took place on several fronts—in New York, in Zurich and Bern, and in other cities—between 1994 and 1998. But entangled in this outline are other events (the concentration and liquidation of Jews, life in the Displaced Persons camps, emigration out of Europe), and other locations (Berlin, Kovno, Auschwitz, the DP camps) whose facticity, and whose documentary evidence, make matters more complicated than they already are. Jean Ziegler's *The Swiss, the Gold, and the Dead* is the most comprehensive account of just how "useful" that documentary evidence could be in making a case that the Swiss were "Hitler's fences," laundering funds pillaged from European banks. Her evidence comes, in large measure, from documents obtained from the Swiss National Archive, and from those obtained from "confidential" informants who currently and formerly worked in the Swiss banking industry. The years 1939 to

1945 began with informal contacts between Goering and several officers in a number of different banks in Basel, Zurich, and Bern, and the contacts became formalized in 1942, during the turning point of the war for Germany, when the Nazi war machine became stalled for lack of equipment and—more crucially— money. It was at that point that Germany, short of cash, began systematically melting gold from the occupied countries—either in Berlin or in Switzerland itself—and depositing it into accounts it had established in Switzerland as early as 1940. Rudolf Hoess, camp commandant at Auschwitz, testified at the Nuremburg War Crimes trials that "special trucks were employed to transport [victims' jewelry and other valuables], and we packed the rings, watches, and bracelets separately. Exceptionally valuable pieces were later sold in Switzerland" (Ziegler 115). Gold from victims' dental work was melted into bars and sent to the Reichsbank in Berlin, where it was remelted and transferred to Switzerland, to be exchanged for foreign currency. The Swiss National Bank had primary responsibility for the central European loot, and three bank officers—Ernst Weber, Alfred Hirs, and Paul Rossy—"presided over" the German deposits, knowing full well where they came from (Ziegler 75). It was this information—this historical knowledge— that played a part later on during the class-action suits and the Senate Banking Committee hearings in the 1990s.

So maybe even more than the Jedwabne affair or the *Irving v. Lipstadt* trial, the case of the Swiss accounts is fraught with intersecting histories and historical memories—of the years during the war and of the contemporary scene; of Swiss complicity in 1942 and perceived Swiss "arrogance" in 1995; of the acts of bankers who were seen as safekeepers of Jewish assets before and during the war, and those of bankers who kept the heirs of those assets at bay for fifty years; of Swiss guilt and of Jewish anger during both periods. The fact that there are at least two historical chronologies to attend to means that rectifying them requires carefully disentangling the motivations of those who would write history, who understand the contexts in which the protagonists—Swiss bankers and Jewish litigants alike— act, and who make use of that history to understand the implications of the Holocaust today.

One writer who has attempted to make sense of the affair is Norman Finkelstein. His *The Holocaust Industry* (1998) devotes a chapter to the events of 1995–1999, and in a revised and expanded edition of the book published two years later, he adds an additional chapter to the Swiss banking "scandal" and its aftermath. Finkelstein's account of the matter is interesting in part because of its treatment of history and the evidence of history and in part because of the argument which that history serves. Like Gross's book on the Jedwabne massacre and the intersection of histories that text bring to the surface, Finkelstein's account calls into question a number of the components of historical work that contribute to our understanding of the Holocaust and its after-effects. Finkelstein's thesis is that on the evidence presented during the dormant accounts trials, those acting on behalf of the plaintiffs wildly distorted what happened in Switzerland during the war years, and vastly inflated the number of camp survivors. They did so in the hopes of squeezing billions of dollars out of the Swiss as a way of gaining reparation for their actions and, more, for their guilt. Finkelstein cites accounts provided by the lawyers and actors on both sides that give credence to his argument that there were often base motives at work. More damning is Finkelstein's assertion that during the negotiations over repayment, the representatives of the WJRO invented survivors in order to raise the amount of money, and perhaps guilt, required as repayment by the Swiss banks and, later, Germany through insurance payments. In the latter case, Stuart Eizenstadt of the U.S. State Department put the number of Jewish and non-Jewish slave laborers alive in 1999 at between 70,000 and 90,000. Given the widely accepted ratio of non-Jewish to Jewish slave laborers put to work in the Reich during the war at 4 to 1, that would mean between 14,000 and 18,000 Jewish survivors would have been alive in 1999. Finkelstein writes that "as it entered into negotiations with Germany" after the WJRO had won its settlement with the Swiss, "the Holocaust industry demanded compensation for 135,000 still living former Jewish slave laborers" (126).

To make his argument, Finkelstein's work is best examined in light of the four large categories I've outlined throughout this chapter: the question of evidence, the context in which that evidence is laid out, the memories of those involved—the writers', the witnesses', and the readers'—and the narrative through which the historical event is emplotted. In Finkelstein's case, there are two broad categories of *evidence* used to make his case: the different numbers of victims adduced by those on either side of the debate, and the various commissions' reports of the actions of the Swiss during and immediately after the war. The first of these is a tenuous matter. For a long time, the figure of six million was used to describe the number of Jewish victims during the Holocaust. This figure was based on census figures of Jews just prior to the war, the figures used by various countries to count the number of Jewish refugees who arrived through their borders from 1933 until emigration was effectively halted in 1938, and the deportation and liquidations records left (undestroyed) by camp personnel and the occupied countries during the war. Raul Hilberg's exhaustive account of the Nazi apparatus of the Final Solution cites a slightly reduced figure of 5.1 million victims. Using that number—along with the number of those who were rounded up for extermination but who survived the final push by the Nazis to complete the Final Solution in 1944–45—as a baseline, and combining it with information from censuses taken after the war in the DP camps and elsewhere, leaves several competing accounts of the number of Jewish (and non-Jewish) survivors of forced labor, concentration, and death camps, from a low of 70,000 to a high of 200,000 (with Henry Friedlander's 135,000 the most widely cited). Finkelstein rightly takes issue with the greatly inflated number of survivors used in some cases by those working on behalf of the WJRO in order to seek compensation from the Swiss banks. (The Gribetz plan cites a figure of 800,000 surviving in 1999; taking into account the mortality rates immediately after the liberation of the camps, along with normal mortality rates and the ages of those who survived at the time of the liberation, that figure is preposterously high.) In citing the higher figures, however, Finkelstein errs on the other side, estimating that 40,000 survivors were alive at the end of 1945, a figure cited by only one scholar and then just in passing.

As for the evidence cited by the Volcker, Independent, and other commissions on the culpability of the Swiss, Finkelstein argues that none of them directly link the banks to any systematic scheme to defraud Holocaust survivors or their families. He cites the Gribetz Plan: "it admits that 'very few if any' direct links—let alone direct *profitable* or *knowingly* profitable links—could be established between the Swiss, on the one hand, and looted Jewish assets and Jewish slave labor on the other" (157). Citing the Volcker commission, Finkelstein notes that it reads, in part:

> [F]or victims of Nazi persecution there was no evidence of systematic discrimination, obstruction of access, misappropriation, or violation of document retention requirements of Swiss law. . . . [T]he criticized actions refer mainly to those of specific banks in their handling of individual accounts of victims of Nazi persecution in the context of an investigation of 254 banks covering a period of about 60 years. (cited in Finkelstein 111)

This, he suggests, gets the Swiss off the hook, and he notes that the *New York Times* misreads the Volcker Commission when it reports that the Committee "found no conclusive evidence" of mishandling of dormant accounts. ("Inconclusive" means no conclusions could be drawn from the evidence of mishandling of accounts; there was evidence of that mishandling.)

The difficulty with these reports, however, is that they are contradicted by other evidence, some of which is provided in Jean Ziegler's and in John Authers's and Richard Wolffe's accounts of the affair. Zielger's book in particular makes use of evidence not available or not sought by the commissions, some of which included members of the boards of the very Swiss banks that were being investigated. In a footnote, Finkelstein cites Ziegler, along with Itamar Levin's book (and three others), and says that they contain much useful information, "although [they suffer] from a pronounced anti-Swiss bias" (89, note 14). For a reader seeking to understand the matter of reparations paid by the Swiss, Finkelstein's book seems authoritative on the evidence—it does, after all, cite the figures and make use of the scholarship cited in his footnotes—but he interestingly only makes use of the evidence that he himself finds useful in making a case against the "Holocaust industry."

The matter of *context* is also informative in understanding the historical import of Finkelstein's book and of the Swiss reparations debate more broadly. Finkelstein is writing in the wake of Peter Novick's exceptional but—by some accounts, anyway—cranky and cynical reading of how the Holocaust is used in contemporary cultural representations. Because Novick's case is so powerfully convincing, Finkelstein cites it (sometimes approvingly, sometimes not) in the first chapter of his book. Novick's case is as powerful as it is because, like it or not, the Holocaust has become a flexible and omnipresent symbol for Americans' role, Jewish and non-Jewish alike, as the world's protectors of the oppressed. Finkelstein turns this symbol upside down (as does Novick) to suggest that its symbolism has become more powerful than the facts, and it is that symbolism that is deployed by those who wish to profit from the suffering of others. It's a cynical move, but it's not without substance. The other contextual issue in play is a clearly rising wave of anti-Semitism in the United States and Europe during the 1990s. Some of it is simply the repetition of centuries'-old hatreds, but some of it is a backlash against what Finkelstein sees as the omnipresence of the Holocaust and the guilt that it inspires in Germans and in Americans (who largely stood by), and in those other individuals and governments who profited from suffering (including, in this argument, the Swiss). Part of Finkelstein's motive is to suggest that the WJRO and the plaintiffs for survivors are providing ammunition to anti-Semites and Holocaust deniers by supplying inflated figures for survivors, and by acting as caricatures of themselves by pursuing profit at the expense of others. He writes, "As the Holocaust industry plays with numbers to boost its compensation claims, anti-Smites gleefully mock the 'Jew liars' who even 'huckster' their dead" (127).

But Finkelstein leaves out a consideration of the supposed "anti-Swiss" bias in the books he cites (and by implication in the books he doesn't). Ziegler notes that in the early 1990s, heirs to victims who had deposited accounts in Switzerland were met with two types of response by Swiss tellers. The first is a question: "Can you produce a death certificate for the alleged account holder?" The second is a statement: "Kindly produce proof that you're the deceased's sole heir." She goes on: "Swiss bank clerks seem unaware that no death certificates were issued for their victims by the commanders of SS death squads, the Gestapo thugs who operated in the torture chambers . . . , the men and women who ran [the extermination camps] . . . , the SS troops who liquidated the ghettos" (91). This may appear to be "anti-Swiss bias," though Ziegler documents these and other instances of what looked very much like insensitivity on the part of the banks' representatives—and, in many cases, bank officers who had records of the account holders and were obliged by law to notify surviving relatives of the existence of dormant accounts. The point is that while there were apparently base motives on the part of some of those who wished to retrieve accounts, there were equally base motives on the part of some of the Swiss who wished to keep those accounts from being claimed, for whatever reasons.

The matter of *memory* is complicated in the Swiss reparations argument, not so much because of what the reader remembers but what the author himself does. Clearly the bias that Finkelstein talks about is simply unavoidable: what's bias for one writer is a clear vision for another. What's notable is the unacknowledged perspective that Finkelstein nonetheless mentions several times in his chapter on the events surrounding the Swiss reparations, as if it did not also play a part in the direction in which his historical narrative proceeds. Speaking of the claims conference, and of the fund meant to compensate victims who were not already part of other reparations agreements, he writes the following:

> [My mother,] a survivor of the Warsaw Ghetto, Majdanek concentration camp and slave labor camps at Czestochowa and Skarszysko-Kamiena, she received only $3500 in compensation from the German government. Other Jewish victims (and many who in fact were not victims), however, received lifetime pensions from Germany eventually totaling hundreds of thousands of dollars. (85)

Later on, he writes, "although my late mother received only $3500 in compensation, others involved in the reparations process have made out quite well" (87). Finkelstein goes on to note the salaries of officers of the Claims Conference, the rates charged by lawyers and plaintiffs for the WJRO, and other principals in the claims against the Swiss, noting finally that the Executive Secretary of the Claims conference "rings up in 12 days . . . what my mother received for suffering six years of Nazi persecution" (88). Clearly the memory of his mother's experience during the war years, told to him later on (or perhaps not told but reconstructed through his own research; I simply don't know), has become woven into his narrative of the injustice not of the Swiss, but of the "Holocaust industry," which profits in spite of—or, worse in his eyes, because of—the suffering of those like his mother. The insinuation of memory here is obviously understandable; that it should motivate the direction of the narrative of the claims against Swiss banks or, worse yet, provide a pretext for omitting historical facts that are obviously relevant to Finkelstein's thesis, seems more problematic.

Finally, the emplotment of the *narrative* of the Swiss accounts is worth taking a look at, since it too seems to problematize the history of the culpability of the Swiss during and after the war. The argument about the culpability of the banks is part of a broader argument about the manipulation of history for profit on the part of Finkelstein's omnipresent but undefined "Holocaust industry." Part of this argument requires that Finkelstein, while not absolving the banks of some complicity in the affair, nonetheless makes the plaintiffs and their representatives guilty of their own crimes of bad faith and greed. At one point, he writes that the WJC "leapt at this new opportunity to flex its muscle. Early on it was understood that Switzerland was easy prey. Few would sympathize with rich Swiss bankers as against 'needy Holocaust survivors'" (89–90). Later on he writes that, "in what has become a mantra of the Holocaust restitution racket, [the dormant accounts] constituted 'the greatest robbery in the history of mankind.' For the Holocaust industry, all matters Jewish belong in a separate, superlative category— *the* worst, *the* greatest. . . ." (94). Finkelstein's own narrative account of the affair places the historical facts, and the words of the primary actors, against a backdrop of racketeering, Jewish hucksterism, and a game of blame-the-victim, where no one comes off looking good at all.

But there's another issue here. Parallel to Finkelstein's story about the Swiss is another story about the Americans: while the Swiss banks were knowingly stowing away large caches of European and Jewish assets and gold, the Americans were quietly doing exactly the same thing. Now, while the Swiss are getting all the negative press, the American Jewish community, knowing full well that the U.S. government was also squirreling away large quantities of gold and funds that had been emptied from the banks of the conquered countries of Europe, was trying to divert attention from what it knew had been going on under their noses all along. Like Andreas Hilgruber, whose depiction of the Final Solution, in *Two Kinds of Ruin,* was placed alongside the decimation of the Nazi Wehrmacht so as to play down the former in favor of the latter, Finkelstein essentially writes of two kinds of extortion. One set of parallel extortions (one by the Swiss, the other by the WJC), and another, more horrifying one for American readers of his book (the Swiss laundering of money and the American laundering operation). But even the evidence Finkelstein himself adduces doesn't quite make the case. At the most, $6 million in dormant accounts rested in American banks after the war (though, to its shame, the U.S. Congress released only $500,000 of that amount for restitution). The remainder of Finkelstein's parallel case against the Americans depends on the U.S. record of failing to allow entry to most Jewish refugees from Europe, suggesting that the U.S. representatives of the European survivors pressing their case with the Swiss should themselves repay the survivors of those on the St. Louis who were refused entry to United States ports. In a bait-and-switch of his own, Finkelstein cites the U.S. failure to recompense survivors of war in Cambodia, Vietnam, and the Balkans to suggest that the Americans ought to clean house first before accusing the Swiss of "perfidy."

□ □ □

LONDON, ENGLAND

In 1996, David Irving—the intellectual front man for Holocaust denial—sued Deborah Lipstadt. Lipstadt had written in her 1993 book *Denying the Holocaust: The Growing Assault on Truth and Memory* that Irving was (in the words of Martin Broszat) a "Hitler partisan wearing blinkers," and who thought of himself as "carrying on Hitler's legacy" (Lipstadt 161). Irving claimed that she had libeled him, ruined his reputation, and distorted the facts. He sued not in the United States, where Lipstadt wrote and worked, and where the vast majority of her books sold, but in England, where the standard of proof is somewhat lower than in U.S. courts. American courts put the burden of proof on the plaintiff to make clear beyond a doubt that the defendant had knowingly printed false statements about the plaintiff. British courts only required that the plaintiff prove that the statements themselves were false, and put the burden of proof on the defendant. At issue were Lipstadt's claims that, as suggested by her title, Irving wasn't only a bad historian, but that he—like those she catalogs in her book—was a Holocaust denier. This was too much for Lipstadt, and she launched a strong defense. For almost a year, during the process of discovery, Lipstadt's lawyers combed through Irving's research, making their way through the archives that he himself had visited during his researches on the calendar of the Final Solution and on Hitler's subordinates' connections to the evolution of that policy. They also went through his travel records to determine whether his association with the Institute for Historical Review, the deniers' pseudo-historical think-tank, also included contacts with obviously anti-Semitic groups. Irving served as his own lawyer in spite of the court's strenuous objections. He spent much of his time in court outlining Lipstadt's purportedly false statements about him, calling a number of witnesses whose testimony purportedly corroborated his claims, and pointing to the integrity of his research. Much of that research attempted to prove that the gas chambers at Auschwitz were not used for the liquidation of Jews but for the delousing of their clothes, and that the crematoria were designed to dispose of the bodies of those who died by disease and starvation, not systematic execution.

The case for the defense, unlike that of the plaintiff, took several months, and was founded on two premises. First, Irving's work as a historian was not only in error but was knowingly so. Second, the reason his work was shoddy wasn't that he was a bad historian—though at times she seemed to prove that he was—but that he was sympathetic to the anti-Semitic groups that lauded his work and that he was very likely anti-Semitic himself. She called a number of historians whose work was on subjects parallel to Irving's own. In one case, she called Robert Jan van Pelt, who went so far as to conduct his own research into the question of just what the Auschwitz gas chambers were used for and how they were engineered for the purpose of killing large numbers of people. She called these witnesses to make clear where Irving's work was wrong, sometimes egregiously so, and she confronted Irving with his own statements and calendars to suggest that he had met with members of anti-Semitic groups and spoke with and about them and their agenda in favorable terms. In short, Lipstadt's case was based on the idea that not only was Irving an anti-Semite, which motivated his research—leading him to "find" in the historical record that which would support his view of the history of the Final Solution—but also that the record of the event left by camp commandants, Nazi officials, and the physical remains of the camps and gas chambers and crematoria, all "shone through" his (fictional) narrative to render it as the lie that it was.

It's worth noting that Lipstadt's defense against Irving has little to do with the truth of the Holocaust. It had instead to do with the evidence that Irving and other historians have adduced about it. In one instance, Lipstadt's lawyer brings Irving's attention to a memo written by Himmler, which Irving says is part of the evidence that exonerates Hitler from any part in the Final Solution. In the memo that records the conversation—Himmler provides notes for a phone conversation with the general in charge of the concentration camp system—Irving writes that the phone call amounted to an order to prevent Jews from being liquidated in December 1941. The order, according to Irving, was, "Jews are to stay where they are" (qtd. in Evans 208–9). But the memo actually reads "the administrative leaders of the SS are to stay where they are," and Irving's arguments about Himmler's bad handwriting were unsubstantiated (his handwriting is indeed legible). So we do not have an argument over the matter of historical truth here; what we have instead is the manufacture of evidence, evidence that says what it says and around which contexts of whatever nature can be built to provide whatever historically pertinent account of the Final Solution one wants to build. But Irving has tried, and at countless other points in the trial where he is caught in the same sorts of blatant lies about evidence, to simply make something up out of thin air.

There are other instances in the Lipstadt case like this one. One piece of evidence brought to the court's attention late in the trial was the question of Irving's association with racist groups in the United States. In a written interrogatory, Irving denied—as he has done in the past—that he'd had any association with a white-supremacist group called the National Alliance, and denied in particular that he'd attended any meetings of the group. After the defense produced a letter of invitation to Irving from the Alliance and an entry from Irving's diary describing the meeting, Irving became angry, saying, "There is not the slightest reference either in that diary entry or in any other diary entry to the NA or the National Alliance which confirms what I said about having had no knowledge of them" (Guttenplan 250). The defense attorney then read a further entry in the diary:

"Drove all day to Tampa, phoned Key West, etc. Etc. Etc. Arrived at the Hotel Best Western at 4:00 PM. Sinister gent with pony tail was the organizer. Turned out the meeting here is also organized by the National Alliance and the National Vanguard Bookshop. Well attended." Now, Mr. Irving, do you want to revise the answers you have just been giving me? (Guttenplan 250)

There are multiple narratives that might account for the evidence left of the Final Solution, the countless memos, lists, speeches, and other documents produced by the SS, the Wehrmacht, and the Order Police. There are multiple narratives, too, that might account for the evidence left of Irving's work in archives, his meetings with racist groups, and his travels and phone conversations. That evidence has a materiality to it. It's the evidence's materiality, the fact that it simply cannot speak for itself, that is so problematic and that leads us to try to draw lessons from that evidence, to construct narratives that make sense at some level. The Final Solution and the destruction of Jewish culture in Europe seems to make no sense, and this makes the job of historians of the Holocaust that much harder. The evidence leads to a narrative of utter unreality and so contrary to human reason that the denial of those events on the grounds that they are too unreasonable to contemplate—how, paraphrasing Yehuda Bauer's question, could the most civilized nation in Europe contrive to eliminate an entire people in a systemic and scientific way?—might in the end seem easier than accepting them (see Bauer 14).

But it's the evidence's materiality that seems to exert a pressure on the narratives that would seek to explain them. If it's true that the work of the historian is "the combined product of past events and the discovery and description of past events" (Shermer and Grobman 21), then "[a]ccording to this language, events exert a pressure on their own discovery and co-operate, in a way that remains unspecified, with the task of describing themselves" (Fish 509). The real—both the material dimension of the world that affects individual memories and the affective and counterrational element of the individual memories themselves—"escapes our control, [and] forces itself upon us whether or not we welcome it," but it is also "that which we make relevant, construct, manipulate" (35).

Oddly, individual memory seemed to be entirely missing from the court's proceedings during the Lipstadt trial. In summing up the trial, D. D. Guttenplan writes:

And so we take refuge in history, in documents, in facts—cool, detached, silent, precise. [. . .]

But witnesses, memories, testimony—all that was left outside the courtroom. And that seems to me cause for regret.

Witnesses are always partial. Memory is by definition selective. And testimony—not the sworn responses of expert witnesses, but the still-vivid responses of people whose history is lived, not studied—can be treacherous. (307–8)

While it's possible to disagree with Guttenplan's sense of facts as "cool" or "detached," it is finally the witnesses who were there. Historians do their work "by telling a story that fits with the stories we already know to be true and telling it in ways that corresponds to our by now intuitive and internalized sense of how one connects the dots between observations on the way to a conclusion" (Fish 510). This "fit" is achieved by hewing closely to the practices and protocols established by historians whose work is more or less conventional. The argument that Irving was unjustly prevented from selling his version of events in the Nazi Reich because, as an academic, he was simply doing what academics do is corrupt. He was justly prevented from purveying that version because he was not hewing to those conventional methods of inquiry that makes a historian a historian.

But what about witnesses, real people, like those survivors in Skokie who would be harmed by a neo-Nazi march through the city, or like those who saw what they saw in hiding and in the camps but whose reality is impugned by those like Irving whose academic credentials are in shreds but who nonetheless tell a certain tale and have a ready audience? Individual witnesses have a real stake in *Irving v. Lipstadt* and the phenomenon of denial. And the deniers themselves, particularly those unlike Irving who have no claim on history and who have no other stake in denying the Shoah except their racism and anti-Semitism, must also be accounted for.

Holocaust denial isn't only about history and about how one responds—through law, or through discourse, or through other rational, political means—to false claims. "Denial hurts people," Raul Hilberg told Guttenplan before the trial (302), and therein lies an aspect of Irving's pronouncements about Hitler. Guttenplan is right: "Irving does represent a real danger" (298), whether or not he's been rendered toothless (and certainly now penniless) by the British courts. Deniers assault memory as is implied in Lipstadt's title. During a *Donahue* show taped in 1994, the deniers David Cole and Bradley Smith share a stage with Michael Shermer and a camp survivor. At one point, the producers show a clip of Dachau, and in what Shermer hopes will be a rational discussion of the relation of what we know about the Holocaust to what we have heard, he refers to the claim (now known to be, in all likelihood, untrue) that soap was mass produced from the remains of dead Jewish inmates. The survivor, Judith Berg, insists, "It was true. They made lampshades and they cooked soap. It's true" (Shermer and Grobman 113). In response Shermer tries to explain the difference between reassessment of facts and the wholesale denial of history, but Smith quickly accuses the survivor of lying. From this point things get ugly, and Berg shouts, "I was seven months there. If you are blind someone else can see it. I was seven months there—," to which Smith replies, "What does that have to do with soap? No soap, no lampshades. The professor [Shermer] says you're wrong, that's all." The eyewitness's very real suffering, and her confusion of her own memories and others', become conflated: it doesn't matter at all that she was there, and that what she has to offer by way of evidence is both heartfelt and unquestionably verifiable. Her "mistake" is enough for Smith to discount her testimony altogether, regardless of the event which that testimony clearly indicates (though perhaps fails to represent clearly), and the historian's explanation is seen as the hair-splitting of the base casuist.

It is finally memory on which denial has its most profound and damaging effect: not history, not the truth, but the events of the Shoah that reside in the memories of those who were there and, more and more through the projections of history, and of fiction, and of images, of those who weren't. It hurts them by filling the silence that inevitably comes from the "damage" of denial with the deniers' false but apparently plausible explanation of the destruction of central European Jewish culture. Lyotard tells us that the Holocaust is a limit case in which the testimonies that bore the traces of the *here*'s and *now*'s, the documents that indicated the sense or senses of facts have been destroyed. The witness, as much as the historian, is charged with "breaking the monopoly over history granted to" so-called transparent language and must lend an ear "to what is not presentable under the rules of knowledge" (Lyotard 57). Our job is to find a way to write that allows what is impressed in memory but lost to language and to "evidence" to have an effect on history. We'll see, in the next section, just how difficult this, too, may be.

DISCUSSION QUESTIONS, Part II

1. What is history? What obstacles are there in the historian's way? What specific challenges does the Holocaust present to history?

2. What is the relation between the story a historian tells about events and the event itself? Does the Holocaut, as an event, complicate this equation?

3. What does it mean that history is "constrained by reality" (Amos Funkenstein)? How does this become complicated by the reality of the Holocaust?

4. Does a "good story" work better to give you a sense of what happened in history than an accurately written historical account? Why or why not?

5. Is there any moral responsibility attached to writing history? To writing a history of the Holocaust?

6. Write, as clearly as you can, what you can remember about where you were and what you thought when you became aware of the terrorist attacks on 9/11. Would you say that this is an accurate account? A good story? What audience were you writing for, and did that audience change what you'd say about the event?

7. Clearly Adolf Hitler was a perpetrator, and someone like Primo Levi was a victim. But what about people who didn't know, or didn't *want* to know, about what was happening? Are they simply bystanders, or could they also be considered victims, or perpetrators? Were Jewish camp inmates who beat their fellows for a piece of bread perpetrators? What about members of the Jewish councils who helped the Nazis transport members of the ghetto to the camps?

8. Consider that fifteen million people died in World War II, that more than half of them were Russian soldiers, and that more than twenty percent of them were German soldiers. How would you respond to the argument that, by the sheer numbers of history, the Holocaust is a secondary tragedy to the destruction of the war?

9. Is it possible to say that if the memories of the witnesses are fallible, then the history written on the basis of those memories is also fallible?

10. What is the relation between history and memory?

III | MEMORY

CHAPTER 6 | # Memory, Witness, and Testimony

When analyzing Holocaust history, historians and writers have three elements of that history in mind. First, there are its material leavings, the objects left behind that form traces of the event, objects like the camps abandoned by the Nazis just before the Soviet army swept into the eastern territories in late 1944 and early 1945, and like the piles of shoes and jewelry found in camp after camp that had been taken from Jews sent to their deaths in the gas chambers. Second, there are the documents and other records left behind that provide a glimpse into what passes for the logic of the Final Solution, documents like the Nuremburg Laws that dispossessed Jews gradually over several years during the 1930s, and like the memos passed between Himmler and Eichmann on train schedules, and timing, and how and where to do the killing. And then there are the testimonies, forged from memory, of those who were there—survivors, perpetrators, and bystanders alike.

While the interpretive framework into which each of these strands of history may be shifted and forged by the historian trying to make a coherent narrative of the horrible incoherence of the Holocaust, it is only the living memory of those who saw with their own eyes that is shifted and forged by the witness him- or herself. While the words of the eyewitness are often the most powerful instruments of history, they are in the eyes of many historians the most imperfect. Memories fade over time, and the events that intervene between what the witness saw and the time of the testimony subtly (and in some instances not very subtly) change the nature and substance of what the witness believes about what she saw. Most troublingly, the extremity of the events recounted, what has been called by some people working on the Holocaust its *traumatic* nature, makes these testimonial accounts imperfect and fallible by nature, because they have literally been blotted out by the horrors of the Holocaust as a kind of protective mechanism of the body. It's this last claim that, over the last decade or so, has become important for those who are interested in the events of the Holocaust, because it seems to undermine the evidentiary power of eyewitness testimonies that we have for decades taken to be more or less accurate records of what happened.

In this chapter, and the two that follow, I want to lay out some of the debates over the memories and the testimonies of those eyewitnesses to the Holocaust. These debates revolve around just how close a witness's testimony is related to the event she saw. By "close," I have in mind temporal distance: is the witness writing about the events as they occur (as in a diary, like Abraham Lewin's account of life in the Warsaw ghetto, or like Anne Frank's account of her life in hiding in Amsterdam), or immediately after they occur (as in Etty Hillesum's letters, or Primo Levi's narrative accounts written after the war), or well after the event (as in video testimonies, taken thirty to fifty years after the event)? What about the events told by children and grandchildren of survivors, who recall their parents' and grandparents' stories of life in hiding, or in the camps (like Art Spiegelman's record of his father's testimony in *Maus,* and Helen Epstein's search for her mother's stories of life before the camps)? How does that distance affect the accuracy, or the authenticity, of those testimonies? But I also have in mind what could be called epistemological distance: because the events were intensely brutal or traumatic, the witness's capacity to recollect those experiences come into direct conflict with her inability to reconcile those aspects of her past with her survival in the present. What Cynthia Ozick's character Rosa, in a story of the same title, says of herself is also true of the eyewitness: there was the time before, and there is the time now; between them there was Hitler. It is that time during the Holocaust that seems, to many eyewitnesses, to drive a wedge between the victim's or perpetrator's past and her ability to tell the story in the present. It's also worth exploring the problem of Holocaust memory, and suggest some of the ways that problem manifests itself in testimonial accounts of the events.

THE PROBLEM OF MEMORY

At the heart of the question about the uses of memory in any understanding of history is the difference between history and memory. History, as we saw in the previous chapters, is an attempt to recover the past, tenuous as that recovery may be; memory is what is created by the mind to represent to ourselves and to others our understanding of the past. While the two terms are inseparable, Yerushalmi's point in *Zakhor* is that at least in Jewish culture, the terms have worked against one another, and that it is only recently that, after a long period of avoiding history in favor of collective memory, history is taking pride of place again. The recosideration of history—as "what happened"—is even more urgent in the wake of the Holocaust, since it's important for the next generations to remember the events in Europe so that something like it can't recur. But the relation between the two, between history and memory, is a troubled one. Yerushalmi writes that "perhaps the time has come to look more closely at ruptures, breaches, breaks, to identify them more precisely, to see how Jews endured them, to undertstand that not everything of value that existed before a break was either salvaged or metamorphosed, but was lost, and that often some of what fell by the wayside became, through our retrieval, meaningful to us" (*Zakhor* 101). Writing at the conclusion of a century that was to witness one of the most profound breaks in all of history let alone Jewish history, this is an understandable desire. It is not just the desire to understand the ways in which what has been lost to memory affects the writing both of testimony and of the histories that make use of it as its raw material. It is also a desire to understand the ways in which that effort at retrieval—sometimes exceedingly selective, sometimes careless or mightily subjective—creates something something new, something perhaps tenuously related to what took place. Most conventionally, the relation between history and memory has been seen as a relation between what we know happened, and what can be recalled of that same event by individuals who were there, with the understanding that memory is incomplete and selective, recycled through what the witness knows already, and in its raw and undigested form is an incomplete record of what happened.

David Roskies is a professor of Jewish literature at the Jewish Theological Seminary and the author and editor of a number of books on the subject of memory and historical catastrophe. His work examines the relation between cultural memory of the Holocaust and the individual memories—and those aspects of memory that seem to fall out of narrative—from which it is forged. In the introduction to the book that established him as perhaps the best historian of Jewish memory and disaster, he writes the following:

> When Jews now mourn in public, . . . they preserve the collective memory of the collective disaster, but in doing so fall back on symbolic constructs and ritual acts that necessarily blur the specificity and the implacable contradiction of the event. (*Against the Apocalypse* 4)

During the *yizkor* services in synagogues around the world, and when Jews say *kaddish* for their family members, the liturgical recollections and the prayers that accompany them are attempts to weave together the strands of individual memory to form a collective. But those memories don't take as their object the destruction or deaths. They are specific to a name, or perhaps a face and a set of images from life, that have little or nothing to do with the language of the liturgy. The events called to mind can't be directly connected to the language meant to present it. Though they are related, the effect of the prayer and the memory it is meant to conjure are disparate and extremely hard to connect. Roskies opens *Against the Apocalypse* with a story of Moroccan Jews, who have "kept the keys to their ancestral homes in fifteenth-century Spain and Portugal," and who, when they were dispersed again to France, Quebec, and Israel, carried with them "their most tangible link to their great Sephardic past" (1). The keys, like the prayers recited at services, are specific and to the representations of memory that are uttered collectively as prayers or, for that matter, as historical narratives. They have nothing to do with those homes, and everything to do with a remembrance of "home" that is now far in the past and utterly irretrievable.

Roskies writes that "to approach the event as closely as possible and to reach back over it in search of meaning, language, and song is a much more promising endeavor than to profess blind faith or apocalyptic despair." The focus on "the Event"—to look at memories and testimonies as if they had something profound to tell us about the Holocaust—is to "rob the dead of the fullness of their lives and invite the asbraction of . . . the Holocaust into Everything" (9). He suggests that maybe we shouldn't try to create a collective memory or come up with a name for the event, because to do so risks that we substitute that memory, and that name, for other events and other names (the Inquisition, the Egyptian or the Babylonian Exiles, or, perhaps more banally, the "Holocaust" of abortion). The better option is to see the memory of the event as unnameable. That memory has its effect on the witness or the reader, and at the point we try to name it or identify it or describe it, it becomes part of our knowledge of the event, and it stops having its effect. Roskies, like Yerushalmi, sees the act of memory as something that works at cross-purposes with knowledge, particularly memories of the disaster of the Holocaust. Though we may find contexts through which to construct a collective memory—the *yizkor* or *Yom ha Shoah* service, or at the U.S. Holocaust Memorial Museum, or through reading a memoir or testimony of the Holocaust—individual memories of survivors and of secondhand witnesses (readers, veiwers) cut against its grain.

The event taken as a whole is not available to recollection, any more than its details are available to knowledge. But the act of "reach[ing] back over [the abyss] in search of meaning, language" is, as far as Roskies is concerned, a compulsion. In his analysis of the members of the Oneg Shabbas organization and other diarists and chroniclers of ghetto life, he suggests that the initial impulse of these writers was to record the events as clearly as possible, and to embed them into the larger chronicle of other disasters. The ghetto writers saw their travails as of a piece with earlier ones. "After 1940 everyone became a historian, from forty-year-old [founder of the organization Emmanuel] Ringelblum to fourteen-year-old Yitskhok Rudashevski of Vilna, both of whom recognized the ghetto as a 'return to the middle ages'" (202). Part of this sense was due to Nazi calculation, to be sure: their coordination of violence with the Jewish calendar had its precedents in imperial Rome, and its internal government of the ghettos through the *judenrat* was taken out of historical accounts of Jewish ghettos from hundreds of years earlier (Roskies 202–4). But it was also due to the long tradition of Jewish historical writing that took individual trials and worked to integrate them into a larger collective memory.

But Roskies argued that this sense of *déjà vu* only came to be truly realized once the diarists and pamphleteers tried to write in older traditional forms. The older forms of writing began to break down where the intrusions of the real, the incomparable sufferings that were only impoverished and made incredible by comparing them to sufferings understood by many only through stories and the recollections of the seder table, intruded upon it. Before this recognition, many Jews in the ghettos fell into a sense of resignation or precedent, in which the collective memory—Judaism's traditional way of dealing with disaster—was a default position. The primitive conditions in the ghetto, they may well have reasoned, are like the primitive conditions experienced during World War I, in older ghettos, and in ealier pogroms against Jews from as far back as the middle ages. Once the conditions worsened, and there appeared to be no redemption at the end of the road, writers had no choice but to record suffering as individual rather than as collective. As Roskies puts it, what became the focus of writing in 1942 was "the use or abuse of those archetypes [of memory] by individual writers as they stood facing the void" (220–1), and the result was testimonies of seeing but not knowing: they wrote what they could remember of the terror and hunger, but there was no collective memorial context in which to make sense of them. "The people . . . had to be recreated before a memorial could be built in its memory. 'I have imagined you!' [the poet] exclaimed from his last and temporary refuge" (224). There is no way to integrate into collective memory the individual instances and memories of suffering. They are not the reader's (she was not there) or the writer's (the event is past and unavailable at the time of the writing). The writer's only choice is not to remember but to create an event out of the void of memory, and also to create the context and a community in which that memory makes sense.

Yerushalmi ends his book with the following rumination: "Though modern historiography may give the illusion of both *mneme* and *anamnesis,* it is really neither collective memory nor recollection in any of their prior senses, but a radically new venture" (114). What lies between the two is neither a retrieval or a construction but an *indication,* whose vehicle isn't the language of history or the flat and repetitive rhythms of testimony or diary, but the language of literature. But this is a controversial point: how could it be that the language of literature (which, after all, includes fiction) is the language of memory? This thesis seems to contradict the idea that reality, after all, must shine through the language of history and of memory. It suggests that we should give up on the idea of memory as a kind of representation. David Krell, a philosopher and literary theorist, tells us that memory is "indexical": it's a convergence of collected, collective memories, and of histories, that provide a way to know a memory's *environs*, but not the object of memory itself.

Yerushalmi provides a couple of good illustrations for this in *Zakhor*. As he enjoins writers to examine the break of the Holocaust, he comes back to the inevitable relationship between memory and forgetting. In biblical and early Jewish texts, injunctions to remember are frequent: they show up in Deuteronomy ("Remember the days of old"), Isaiah ("Remember these things, O Jacob, for you O Israel, are my servant . . . O never forget me"), Exodus ("Inscribe this as a memory, blot out the name of Amalek"), Micah ("O my people remember now that Balak plotted against you), and the ever-present "remember that you were slaves in Egypt." These injunctions establish the almost anxious demand that neither God, nor God's covenant, be forgotten. But because the historical is only as good as the memories and the testimonies of those who bear it, there will come a time when the children of several generations removed will wonder about the memorials, divorced as they are by distance and time, and ask how they are connected to the events they were designed to call to mind. This is precisely the problem now faced by the second and third generations after the Shoah, who have only the most tenuous connection to the historical circumstances to the Shoah, let alone the individuals in their families who survived (or who didn't), and whose living memories are now failing or do not exist at all. Yerushalmi's response, following Joshua, is that it is "not the stone, but the memory transmitted by the fathers, [that] is decisive if the memory embedded in the stone is to be conjured out of it to live again for subsequent generations" (10). Hence the testimony—the narrative of history—is a sign of the lost event, not a representation or simulation of it. Memory itself is not "in" the sign but independent of it. In this defense of memory and history there are two senses of memory: the one transmitted by the fathers and the one to be conjured from the stone. But neither the stone nor the story—neither the indication or mark of events that takes the form of a pile of stones or a vast museum nor the story of the exile to Egypt and return to Canaan or the tale of destruction in Europe and redemption in Palestine—contains the memory. Between the two lies the void that is only filled by language. Whether this memory belongs to the person narrating the story or to the person who hears the story is not clear. What is clear, though, is that Yerushalmi means for the memory to belong to the person who is at the receiving end of the language or testimony.

These injunctions to remember transmit memory in a way that seems unrelated to the historical writing we're used to. It makes sense to insist, like Amos Funkenstein or Pierre Vidal-Naquet, that the narrative freedom borne by historical consciousness is constrained by reality, by what really happened, so we don't open the door to preposterous versions of what happened. But it is this poetical dimension of testimony that seems to give the memory its power, and seems to most clearly connect it with the event itself.

> Oral poetry preceded and sometimes accompanied the prose of the chroniclers. For the Hebrew reader even now such survivals as the Song of the Sea or the Song of Deborah seem possessed of a curious power to evoke, through the sheer force of their archaic rhythms and images, distant but strangely moving intimations of an experience of primal events whose factual details are perhaps irrevocably lost. (11)

Its poetry is neither archaic nor primal but "evocative": it marks the disconnect between the narrative force of history and the affective force of the song. Placed together, they call to mind something other than what is represented in the story. It marks a moment in the present where the coordinates of narrative understanding and aesthetic pleasure meet and collide.

There is a disconnection between the object of memory and remembrance itself, Yerushalmi insists; the past isn't made clear in a moment of remembrance. Instead, memory involves a collapse of time and space, and testimony doesn't provide a description of what is remembered but, oddly, indicates what *isn't* remembered. The antiphony of the lament from the Tish'ba Av prayer, which is recited on the date held to coincide with the destruction of the temple in Jerusalem and that ushered in ages of Jewish exile from Zion, is a case in point:

> A fire kindles within me as I recall—when I left Egypt,
> But I raise laments as I remember—when I left Jerusalem.
>
> Moses sang a song that would never be forgotten—when I left Egypt,
> Jeremiah mourned and cried out in grief—when I left Jerusalem.

Yerushalmi tells us that the memory of exile here is not a memory at all—the departure from Egypt and from Jerusalem are now part of a narrative of prayer and of history that is recognized as much by American Jews as it is by members of the Knesset negotiating the case of Palestinian sovereignty. Between the narrative of exile and the rhythmic repetition of Egypt and Jerusalem is a "there"—not temporal or spatial but certainly palpable—that is produced by the language of the prayer itself. In other words, the prayer doesn't call up a memory of either the locations noted in the prayer or the memory of exile, but something else, something purely individual to each member of the congregation that recites it. So, while it may be an odd claim to say that memory, particularly memory of the

Holocaust, is produced through poetry or literature, Yerushalmi sees it as uncontroversial: in poetic language as in prayer, what is remembered is a "departure" (44), a break or crux in memory indicated by breaks in the narrative (those located in the Tish b'Av prayer, in the repetition of the first-person "I": "I left Jerusalem," "I left Egypt").

WITNESS AND TESTIMONY

Lawrence Langer, in his book *Holocaust Testimonies,* is interested in how survivor and bystander testimonies of the Holocaust function as instances of indicative— or maybe "forgetful"—memory. Langer, who has been writing about Holocaust representation since the late 1970s, is one of the pioneers in the field of Holocaust studies. *Holocaust Testimonies* was written after Langer spent nearly a year in the Fortunoff Archive at Yale University, which contains thousands of hours of video-taped testimonies collected from hundreds of Holocaust witnesses. His book is a rich and disturbing collection of the anguished memories of Holocaust survivors. It also works as a meditation on the difficulty of seeing these testimonies as a record of human behavior recognizable in the "normal" world outside the camps and the ghettos. In the preface to his book, Langer writes that one of the first tapes he watched in the Fortunoff archive was of a Mr. and Mrs. B., who tell their stories in sequence. Afterwards, the interviewer asks one of their daughters, who was born after the Shoah, one of the same questions she'd asked the couple. Immediately after that response—in which the daughter talks about her connection to Judaism through the experiences of her parents—the tape abruptly stops, leaving Langer, expecting to see more, to think, "'Wait a minute! Something's wrong here! Either someone's not listening, or someone's not telling the truth!" (x). The horrific stories told by the parents and the tale of strength and connection told by the daughter just don't seem to add up. Langer concludes that the division between the witness's presence in the historical circumstances that she tries to narrate, and the moment of testimony itself, is a division between a moment that lies outside of our ability to understand it, and the witness's struggle to narrate that moment in a "now" that seems completely divorced from it.

Langer draws a number of conclusions from his viewing of the testimonies in the Fortunoff archive, which are extremely valuable when considering the role of memory and its relation to testimony. One is that the two "selves" involved in all of the narratives of survival and life after the Shoah vie for prominence in the narratives. He complicates this idea in the chapter on "deep memory," suggesting that "the two kinds of memory [of the pre-camp and post-camp selves]," rather than remaining mutually exclusive, "intrude on each other, disrupting the smooth flow of their narratives" (Langer 6). Another of Langer's conclusions is that the testimonies of these witnesses are disrupted because they are oral, unvarnished and unrehearsed, and that it is oral testimony that confirms the "vast imaginative space separating what he or she has endured from our capacity to absorb it." Written testimonies and memoirs, on the other hand, "eas[e] us into their unfamiliar world through familiar (and hence comforting?) literary devices. The impulse [in written testimonies] is to *portray*" reality (19).

These are important points: the first implies that survivor testimonies are difficult tools through which to understand the Holocaust because there is no clear position from which even the witness can understand his experiences. Because his self is "divided," the disruption involved in the conflict between them renders the testimonies incoherent in places, unclear in others. The second point implies that testimonies are at their most "authentic" when they are unrehearsed and "unliterary." Even though they most clearly indicate the conflict of selves, and do so through a kind of inner inconsistency, they are better than literary or fictional testimonies, since these latter testimonies tend to varnish over those inconsistencies through literary devices, devices with which we have become familiar and through which the horrors of the Holocaust become "domesticated." It's worth looking carefully at these premises, because the extent to which they hold true is the extent to which memories depicted through testimony can be seen as windows on what happened during the Holocaust.

Let's turn to some examples from recorded oral testimonies. The tape of William R. offers an example of the difficulty of finding coherence between the act of witness and the testimony that presumably opens that act up for another to understand. Langer sees the following testimony as an example of the heroic act turning tragic, a turn that the witness has to come to terms with, but which makes no sense in either the logic of the present or of "Hitler."

> I'll never forgive myself. Even if I want it, I can't. I had a brother, he was 16 or 17 years old. He was taller than I, he was bigger than I, and I said to him, "Son, brother, you haven't got no working papers, and I am afraid that you will not be able to survive. Come on, take a chance with me, let's go together." Why did I take him with me? Because I had the working papers, and I thought maybe because I gonna go to the right, I knew people who had their working papers, they gonna go to the right, because the Germans need people in the ghetto, to finish the job, whatever they had to do. He agreed with me. At the same time I said he is built tall, then maybe he gonna have a chance.
>
> When I came to the gate where the selection was, then the Gestapo said to me (I showed him my papers), "You go to the right." I said, "This is my brother." He whipped me over my head, he said: "He goes to the left." And from this time I didn't see any more my brother. . . . I know it's not my fault, but my conscience is bothering me. I have nightmares, and I think all the time, that the young man, maybe he wouldn't go with me, maybe he would survive. It's a terrible thing: it's almost forty years, and it's still bothering me. I still got my brother on my conscience. God forgive me! (FVA tape T–9)

In Langer's terms, there are two selves and two memories at work here that do battle for control over the narrative. There is the "self who 'does' and [the] self who is 'done to,'" but these selves can't be reconciled by William G.'s narrative (47). The two selves "interact and intersect continually" (7). But in what context—in what temporal or geographical location—does this memory make sense? The moment in which the brother goes to the left and is lost, and the moment in which the witness testifies to the act, collapse into the moment of the memory— "I'll never forgive myself. Even if I want it I can't"—that is told in words that can't do it justice, and that can't represent what the witness sees now or saw then.

The language of the testimony is evidence of the inaccessibility of the historical moment of witnessing, and of the rupture of the testimony in the face of the moment's absence. It's worth asking what, precisely, is the act witnessed here by the survivor. Is it the moment of his separation from his brother? Is it the moment of his decision to take his brother with him, in spite (or because) of his failure to have papers that might otherwise have kept him alive a little longer? Neither of these circumstances is made available by the testimony, though both of these moments are part of the narrative, told without words—"And from this time I didn't see any more my brother." The decision to take his brother with him is provided as litany: "Because I thought I had the working papers, and I thought maybe because I gonna go to the right, I knew people who had their working papers, they gonna go to the right . . . ." This is language that reports a series of events, but it's also language that describes or indicates a rupture of a normal sequence of events. You could say that this language indicates the *absence* of the event witnessed rather than the event itself. William's conclusion—"I still got my brother on my conscience. God forgive me!"—is not so much an appeal to the divine in the present (the moment of the interview) as it is a recognition of the failure of his testimony to recover, and certainly its failure to purge or even work through, the palpable existence, even now, of his unnamed seventeen-year-old brother. William G.'s exclamation provides the viewer of the videotape a glimpse of what has been lost: not just a brother, but also the language with which to do justice to the horrible act that remains on William's conscience every moment of every day.

What Langer calls an "inner coherence" of these testimonies is the context in which the loss or rupture being described can be seen. What is coherent or consistent is the pattern visible in each witness's testimony, in which the event that causes the witness so much pain shows up almost in spite of the telling of what happened. Listen to the description of Moses S.:

> Two boys having one bunk. One said to the other, "Will you watch after my piece of bread? I'm going to the bathroom." He said, "OK." When he come back, was no bread. Where was the bread?
> "I'm sorry. I ate it up."
> So he reported to the Kapo. Kapo comes along, he said, "What happened?"

"Look, I ask him to look after my piece of bread, and he ate it up."
The Kapo said, "You took away his life, right?"
He said, "Well, I'll give it back this afternoon, the ration."
He said, "No, come outside." He took the fellow outside. "Lie on the floor." He put a piece of *brett* [board] on his neck, and with his boots—bang! On his neck. *Fertig* [finished]! (FVA tape T–511)

What is perhaps most horrifying about this tape is what can't be placed into the narrative: the cracking of the board against the child's neck, the quick, almost frantic walk outside the barracks to the yard, the look of panic in the boy's eyes just before the Kapo sentences him to death. They are nowhere to be found in the language of narrative, but they do have a place in the testimony of Moses S. through his gestures. The self caught up in the time during the killing—"'This was Hitler'" (Ozick, "Rosa" 58)—wins the battle over the present, so sickening the interviewer and Moses's wife that they both urge him to stop the interview. The witness is seeing an event that disrupts his present circumstances—the interview—and the event and those circumstances become inseparable. Moses's language becomes submerged by his gestures, and he actually, with a motion of his hands and his feet, becomes the Kapo and finishes the memory with the violence that killed the other little boy forty-five years earlier.

Langer's point that there is a significant difference between oral testimonies and written ones is also important. "When a witness in an oral testimony leans forward toward the camera . . . that witness confirms the vast imaginative space separating what he or she has endured from our capacity to absorb it. Written memoirs . . . strive to narrow this space, easing us into their unfamiliar world through familiar (hence comforting?) literary devices" (19). As the writer experiences the space "separating words from the events they seek to animate[, t]he writer strives to narrow that abyss. At a more fundamental level, driven by anguished memory, witnesses in oral testimonies plunge deeper into it even as they venture to escape" (42). Langer then points to the middle chapter of Primo Levi's *Survival in Auschwitz,* in which the author tells the story of his encounter with Jean, the pikolo of the "chemical command," a young man who spoke no Italian, though he was fluent in German and his native French. As they carry water, Levi tries to find a common language through which they may communicate, and what flashes through Levi's mind is Dante's *Divine Comedy.* If he can only teach Jean phrases from this work, one of Levi's favorites, then they may be able to engage in a connection that was prohibited by the SS. Langer points to Levi's hesitation, his inability to recall the Italian, and says "it is not Auschwitz he is forgetting; it is literature, Dante, poetry, the *Commedia.*" He goes on:

I think the irony of this passage, whose content [i.e., lines from the *Divine Comedy*] contrasts so visibly with the setting and the scene, is explicit. For a

moment, both Levi and Jean, under the compelling sway of Dante's art, forget who and where they are. And this is precisely the point: when literary
form, allusion, and style intrude on the surviving victim's account, we risk
forgetting where we are and imagine deceptive continuities. It is a dramatic
interval in Levi's own text, as Dante's lines seize him with a fervor and transport him for an instant into the literary reality of the poem. . . . But his fervor quickly abates and . . . he escapes unscathed from the confusion of genres.
(Langer, *Holocaust Testimonies* 45)

But this section of Levi's story is highly self-conscious about the difficulty—
if not the utter impossibility—of translating what the witness sees into a memory, and finding the words, in testimony, to make that memory available to
another person.

Here, listen Pikolo, open your ears and your mind, you have to understand,
for my sake: "Think of your breed; for brutish ignorance/Your mettle was not
made; you were made men,/ to follow after knowledge and excellence." As
if I was hearing it for the first time: like the blast of a trumpet, like the voice
of God. For a moment I forget who I am and where I am. (Levi 113)

In *Survival in Auschwitz,* Levi says that he is quite ambivalent about the line that
separates "the facts" of the camps from "documentation . . . of certain aspects of
the human mind" (10, 9). The urgency of bearing witness is worth paying attention to in that book, because it suggests that Levi is trying hard to translate
the events in Auschwitz for readers who were not there and who have no context
or set of experiences to which they can refer in order to understand them. Levi
seems to be trying to speak memory in a way that shows us what he remembers
precisely at the point where the language of the testimony breaks down. Just as
with oral testimonies, written testimonies like Levi's attest to the difficulties—if
not the impossibility—of recuperating those events that seem to defy memory.

TESTIMONY AND TRAUMA

Holocaust testimony is hard to work with for many reasons: the failure of survivors'
memories, the present's insinuation into their remembrance of the past, the problems inherent in putting something as horrifying as the death of one's family by
starvation or the loss of one's property or one's dignity in a ghetto or a camp. All
of these things stand in the way of seeing testimony as a window onto the events
of the Holocaust. Moreover, there is an inherent divide between what the witness saw and the witness's memory of the event, and there is a divide between
that memory and the language and conventions of narrative into which the event

may be translated. But perhaps more troubling than any other single aspect of memory or testimony is the fact that the events experienced by Holocaust survivors are often traumatic. The enormity of the events is simply too much for the witness to remember, let alone retell, with any reasonableness or order. As we saw with William G., Moses S., and Primo Levi, there is an inherent gap between the moment witnessed and the moment of testimony, and what emerges from that gap— "forgetful memory"—is often something only tangentially related to the object of memory. We might best think of the events of the Holocaust, and their effect upon its victims, as so horrible that they affect those victims every day of their lives in ways the victims themselves simply can't explain. For this reason it's easy enough to suggest that the Holocaust—either in its effects upon victims one at a time, or as a collection of events taken as a whole—functions as a historical trauma.

Over the last dozen and a half years, but particularly since the middle 1990s, a good deal of the work on the Holocaust has been done under the rubric of "trauma studies." With its foundation is psychoanalysis and psychotherapy, the analysis of trauma focuses on its physical causes, the period of latency between the occurrence of the trauma and the emergence of symptoms, and the nature of those symptoms. The study of trauma seems to have had its contemporary origins in the immediate aftermath of the United States' involvement in Vietnam, after which thousands of men and women returning from the military exhibited symptoms of what used to be called "shell shock": horrible nightmares and waking dreams, sudden panic attacks, moments during which they felt they were back in the war, and instances of severe depression, all of which frequently led to bouts of alcoholism and drug abuse. It was during this period that the disorder was renamed posttraumatic stress disorder (PTSD). While a good deal of analysis has been done on the psychosocial symptoms of trauma visible in Holocaust survivors since the 1960s and 1970s (including the work of Bettelheim), much of the work done in Holocaust studies itself is less interested in diagnosis and cure than it has been in understanding the effect of trauma upon representations of the Holocaust in testimonies, histories, memoirs, and fiction, poetry, and drama. Some groundbreaking work has been done at Yale University, where the Fortunoff Archives are housed, by Dori Laub, a professor of medicine and psychiatry and the author (and a coauthor, with Shoshana Felman) of a number of papers on Holocaust testimony. Among other exceptional work on testimony is that of Dominick La Capra, a professor of Humanities at Cornell University, and Cathy Caruth, a professor of comparative literature at Emory University.

Cathy Caruth's theoretical explorations of trauma are heavily indebted to Freud's lectures on psychoanalysis, particularly *Beyond the Pleasure Principle* and *Moses and Monotheism*. In her book *Unclaimed Experience,* she writes that "the notion of trauma" allows for a "rethinking of reference [that] is aimed . . . at resituating it in our understanding, that is, at precisely permitting *history* to arise where *immediate understanding* is not" (11). Historical memory is always a distortion—and this point is, to a greater or lesser degree, supported by much of the historiographical work done over the last thirty years—because historical events make their mark upon the mind of the eyewitness in substantially the same way that a trauma makes itself apparent to the victim. Citing Freud, Caruth writes that "the victim of the [terrible event] was never fully conscious during the accident itself: the person gets away, Freud says, 'apparently unharmed.' The experience of trauma, the fact of latency, would thus seem to consist, not in the forgetting of a reality that can hence never be fully known, but an inherent latency within the experience itself" (17). "A history can be grasped [by the witness] only in the very inaccessibility of its occurrence" (18). For Caruth, the eyewitness doesn't remember the traumatic event so much as she forgets it. She "take[s] leave of it," in Caruth's terms, though it leaves an indelible mark on everything she says including the subject of the narrative of the event. Asked to describe the death of her mother in the Lodz ghetto, a survivor named Mary R. lapses into a recitation with which she is familiar as docent at a Holocaust museum: "very difficult; I don't even like to think about it. In all eleven million civilian people killed in the concentration camps . . ." (Stanovick 1–2). Once an experience, but particularly a traumatic experience, occurs it is forever lost to understanding. It is at this point—"upon losing what we have to say" (Blanchot 21), the point of forgetfulness—that writing begins. To put it another way, it may be that forgetfulness, not memory, is the source of testimony.

As Caruth understands it, the witness saw, but *only* saw, the deed or the circumstance that presented itself as trauma. Forgetting is a way of explaining the structure of witness and of narrating the event, because the traumatic circumstance was never fully known, and so could not be remembered, at all. What follows after the "in-experience" or forgetting is a profusion of language that erupts after a period of latency, during which the witness is silent. This theoretical view is consistent with the experience of many Holocaust survivors, who found that the only way to deal with their experiences in camps and in hiding was silence, either because no one wanted to hear what they had to tell or, more frequently, because they couldn't find words to make sense of what they'd seen. What we read in survivor testimonies that were spoken after that period of latency, as in the brief example of the septuagenarian Mary R., is the displacement of the traumatic event by the language of testimony. That testimony is the sometimes broken, sometimes contradictory set of stories of the camps, or of hiding, or of the aftermath.

Caruth's point about testimonies is that they don't disclose events as much as they disclose the *effect* of events upon witnesses. As we'll see in the next chapter, memoirs and diaries as different as Ann Frank's and Abraham Lewin's may be seen to function as instances of traumatic memory. Their language doesn't easily follow the patterns that correspond to the general rules of historical narratives and by themselves don't give us a way to adjudicate the competing claims and differences in details one finds from one diary or memoir to another. In the testimonies' depictions of events, their gaps and variances can't be said simply to represent inaccuracies. As Caruth suggests, they represent and "preserve history precisely within this gap in his text" (190). History as the event is the unspoken traumatic kernel inside memory and testimony, and it's that history-as-trauma that intervenes in and interrupts history-as-testimony.

Shoshana Felman's understanding of trauma parallels Caruth's. In a much-cited essay entitled "Education in Crisis; or, The Vicissitudes of Teaching," Felman describes a class she taught at Yale University on testimony. The course involved the reading of poetry, fiction, and other narratives that could be called "testimonial" or "confessional," and near the conclusion of the course she and her students viewed several hours of videotaped testimonies from the Fortunoff Archive. The pattern that Felman observed in all the testimony, but particularly the Holocaust testimonies—both written and oral—was similar to that observed by Caruth. Each witness spoke "in advance of the control of consciousness, his testimony is delivered in 'breathless gasps': in essence it is a *precocious testimony* . . . that speak[s] beyond its means," that testifies to the event "whose origin cannot be precisely located but whose repercussions, in their very uncontrollable and unanticipated nature, still continue to evolve even in the very process of testimony" (Felman 29, 30; original emphasis). Like Caruth, Felman insists that the memory of the event, particularly the traumatic one, "evolves" in the process of the telling, and that its language is uncontrollable and unanticipated.

Felman complicates the matter of the eyewitness and her testimony by taking into account what happens to the secondhand witness, the one who reads or sees a witness to the Holocaust tell her story. Just as the witness feels compelled to talk, to give testimony, so also the secondhand witness feels a compulsion to talk. As Felman puts it, the trauma that pursues the witness also pursues witnesses to the witnessing. In her seminar at Yale, students experienced what she calls a "crisis" of witnessing, in which they became profoundly ill at ease with what they were seeing, and broke into an "endless and relentless talking" about the class. They also had horrible nightmares. The accident, the "disaster," whose representations had been read and viewed by the class had, according to Felman, "*happened* in the class, happened *to* the class. The accident had *passed through* the class" (52, original emphasis).

Felman argues that texts that bear witness to an event that has been blotted from memory keep the reader from making sense of the narrative, and what results is a break or a crisis, resulting in talk, the testimony of the secondhand witness. Felman's students found a need to fill the abyss of the event, what has been forgotten and irretrievably lost to history, with language. In most cases, though, the language these students used wasn't their own. In one case, the student used language of a parent whose narrative of his experiences succumb to the same discursive problems as any other testimony. In another, a student saw in the language of literature the closest corresponding "trauma" to the one she had experienced but simply couldn't find a way to describe.

In a book on the relation between events, their images, and history, Edith Wyschogrod refers to an archival photograph of a child—neatly dressed and well fed, apparently unaware of his surroundings—walking on a road in the woods past corpses strewn outside what the caption tells us is Bergen-Belsen. Of the photo she says, "so long as the boy in his uncanny flight is permitted to break into the narrative of what is depicted"—and, presumably what is depicted is the destruction of the Holocaust—"the child's face becomes the escape route for an unsayability that seeps into the . . . image and contests any narrative articulation of what the camera captures, a world where death and life are virtually indistinguishable" (142). The language of testimony, like the facets of the photograph, is fragmentary and incomplete. The dilemma faced by readers of testimony is that even if they match fragment to fragment, or incident to incident, you still get only an incomplete tapestry of destruction. The individual pieces themselves, when looked at one at a time, or in succession apart from the tapestry, seem to fall apart. There is something behind them that resists telling. Individual descriptions "break into the narrative of what is depicted" and contest any reasonable sequence of events that we may wish to attribute to it.

TESTIMONY AND THE SUBLIME

In the *Critique of Judgment,* the eighteenth-century philosopher Immanuel Kant attempted to work out the relation between what we are able to perceive and to think, and our *capacity* to perceive and to think. In the aesthetic moment, we are able to bring into accord rational capacity (our ability to know), that which makes us human, and the physical world that surrounds us. He also examined what he called the sublime. Whereas the apprehension of the beautiful has to do with form of and our ability to make sense of the objects and events around us in terms of it, the sublime is the "exhibition of an indeterminate concept" that is "unbounded" (II.§23.244). Kant goes on: "what is sublime . . . cannot be contained in any sensible form . . . which, though [it] cannot be exhibited adequately, [is] aroused and called to mind by this very inadequacy" (II.§23.245), and "carries with it, as its character, a mental agitation" (II.§24.247), an agitation that isn't harmonious but is instead irritating, troubling, traumatic. In moments of the sublime, the mind is forced to deal with something completely boundless. In the feeling of the sublime, "our imagination strives to progress toward infinity": as Russian and American troops entered the camps in Poland and central Germany in early 1945, they were confronted with the most unimaginable sense data— walking corpses, bodies piled upon bodies, the smells of decay and defecation and the sounds of suffering, and of death, and of birds, and breezes, and the feeling of warmth that comes with impending spring. In comparison to what these soldiers may have seen in their travels toward the camps—in wartime, with the atrocities associated with the belligerence of nations—these "data" were infinitely more difficult to organize, because they were unassociated with the war. Whose enemies were these, and by what combination are the chills of typhus and the warmth of earliest spring to be unified as knowledge?

Kant also described the sublime as a "simultaneity," a feeling of both pain and pleasure, revulsion and attraction. It is also a simultaneity that annihilates time. "Comprehending a multiplicity in a unity (of intuition rather than of thought), and hence comprehending in one instant what is apprehended successively, is a regression that in turn cancels the condition of time in the imagination's progression and makes simultaneity intuitable" (II.§27.258–9). It is the moment of pleasure and pain that characterizes the feeling of sublimity that seems to be the source of Adorno's admonishment to poets (and writers in general) to avoid the pleasure afforded by works of art that represent the immeasurable suffering of the victims and survivors of the Shoah. In Kant's *Critique of Judgment,* the sublime is a key moment in a theory of knowledge. In the apprehension of the sublime, the witness is presented with the limit of her capabilities to judge, to reason, to understand.

The sublime works negatively. To put this in the words of Irving Howe, who has written on the Holocaust, "it leaves us intellectually disarmed, staring helplessly at the reality or, if you prefer, the mystery of mass extermination. There is little likelihood of finding a rational structure of explanation for the Holocaust" (cited in Lang, *Writing the Holocaust* 175). In the face of such a vastness, the witness's inability to produce an image of the event "is the awakening of a feeling . . . within us . . . not of an object of sense [but of something] absolutely great" (Kant §25, 97). That which beggars the imagination, to cite the words General Eisenhower used describing the camps he liberated, is beyond what the mind can express, and its object is the source of feeling in the sublime.

There are at least two risks associating sublimity to the Holocaust: the risk of silence and the risk of dissolving the particular horror into the ether of a broadly defined "discursivity," in which—with reference to Lyotard—"the Shoah is transcoded into postmodernism" (LaCapra, *Representing* 98). In an analysis of Lyotard's *The Differend* and *Heidegger and 'the Jews,'* Dominick LaCapra notes that Lyotard's view "of the 'excess' of the Holocaust whereby one is recurrently confronted by the need to put into language what cannot as yet be acceptably 'phrased'" is convincing (97). He goes on, however, to suggest that this same confrontation leads ultimately to a sublime silence, whereby one "'trope[s]' away from specificity and evacuate[s] history by construing the caesura of the Holocaust as a total trauma that is un(re)presentable and reduces everyone (victims, witnesses, perpetrators, revisionists, those born later) to an ultimately homogenizing yet sublime silence" (97). In later work, LaCapra wonders whether the sublime doesn't also give us a way to name the horror, making the Shoah a divinity in whose presence we dare not speak, or whose negative presence calls forth silence, or flight, or pleasure.

Sublimity doesn't call forth "'appropriate' response[s]" (LaCapra, *Representing the Holocaust* 106) because it is experienced uniquely, with each individual responding to the event or object differently from every other individual. The "silences" Lyotard describes in *The Differend* are the silences of Blanchot's disaster, which "interrupt the chain [of discourse] that goes from them" (Lyotard 106). La Capra is right to worry about the ethical consequences of understanding the Shoah and representations of it as sublime. But it's not at all clear whether a witness's words could ever call up "appropriate" reactions. One of the reasons the discussion of *Schindler's List* as a representation of the Holocaust (an example I'll come back to) sheds so much heat but such little light is that participants in the debate failed to distinguish between considering the film as a representation—a testimony—and considering moments of sublimity—of witnessing—that may have been experienced by (some, a few, all) viewers of that film. The complaints leveled against Spielberg's film—that it was not accurate enough, that it was too accurate, that it focused too much attention on non-Jews, that it relied too heavily on conventions of filmic representation—say very little about the dynamics of the sublime that are encountered by viewers at certain points throughout the film. In judging the film, or any work, we create knowledge about it and its subject based on what we already understand (for example) about film, about narrative, about Hollywood convention, about how characters in films or plays or stories behave. But such knowledge cannot be equated with what the film is "about," or the event that lies beyond the representation.

Kant tells us that the feeling of the sublime is the feeling one gets at the edge of a precipice, "an abyss in which the imagination is afraid to lose itself." It's not quite right to say that the feeling of the sublime—whether it is encountered in the deeds or creations of humans or in the natural world—embodies the truth, that it indicates in a fleeting moment a sense of all there is beyond our limited abilities to sense it. To suggest this of the sublime is also to suggest of witnessing that in the act of piecing together the bits of what we know, that we can experience or see what the witness saw or experienced. It is to say that we bring into being the horror of the seen by forging together testimonies and narratives until, taken together, they stand in for the events themselves.

The sublime moment is that in which the witness knows that she is seeing, but can't say what it is, and yet must say what it is. Adorno is right: it is barbaric to create poetry after Auschwitz. There is a certain barbarism, a certain horror, involved in representations of the Holocaust, or involved in any representations at all in a world that made the Holocaust possible. But this is not a barbarism that can be avoided by ruling such representations out of court, either by banning graven images or by insisting on a "modernist" rendering of the events of the Shoah.

CHAPTER 7

The Language of the Witness: Diaries, Testimonies, and First-Person Narratives

One of the most fundamental problems in understanding the Holocaust through testimony is the numbers. By some estimates, there were eight hundred thousand survivors of the camps upon liberation in 1945; many of those died in the months immediately following the end of the war. Of between six and seven million Jews who had direct experience with the Holocaust, something under fewer than ten percent of those capable of testifying to what happened did so. Now, six decades after the event, far fewer remain alive and capable of telling their stories. There are other issues to be accounted for when considering individual testimonies. For one thing, memories fade over time. It stands to reason that those accounts of the Holocaust written after the events have taken place would be less accurate, and perhaps less rich in detail, than those written at the time of the event's occurrence. One could conclude that diaries written as events took place would be more accurate than testimonies written after the event, or memoirs written years later.

This conclusion is one reason why the diary written by Anne Frank, a young German girl whose family fled the Reich to Holland, and who spent a good part of the war in hiding, has taken such a prominent place in the canon of Holocaust literature. In addition to the remarkable clarity of its observations and the richness of its voice, it presents a record of the eventful and the commonplace occurrences that fill the days and the mind of a witness. She is not only a witness to the Holocaust, but also to the minutiae that comprise it. Frank's memory, like the memories of others who wrote diaries (two of the most notable being Avraham Lewin's Warsaw ghetto diary and Avram Tory's diary of life in the Kovno ghetto) didn't fade because it was recorded on the spot. And yet that conclusion is put in doubt when one examines the language of diaries and letters. That language is often curt, abbreviated, and sometimes not particularly thoughtful. In the haste of recording what one saw, the diarist may have had no time to consider the implications of what she saw, and was unable to fully understand the context inside of which her readers might make sense of the horrifying details she writes about life and death in the ghetto. Contrary to one of Lawrence Langer's conclusions, it may be that those accounts written later—after some time in which to consider the language that would most clearly render the event—are more useful for us than diaries and letters that are written without access to long-term, cultural, or historical memory.

Alongside the problem of memory—a problem of what one might call the temporal proximity of the event—are problems of language. The first has to do with whether the language of the diarist, memoirist, or other witness is adequate to the task of recording the events she has seen. For many of the writers considered here, and for many of those whose testimonies have been recorded on audio- or videotape, one phrase recurs consistently: "I simply can't describe it." Words seem to fail them in the face of what they saw, though the witness is compelled nonetheless to do her best. Primo Levi, Elie Wiesel, and others have attempted to describe a world that has "deformed language": the language of the camp and the ghettos was not only an amalgam of Yiddish, German, Polish, French, Hungarian, and the myriad other languages of Europe. That language also took on a shape of its own, a shape that poorly reflects the objects and events described but suggests the terrible deformity of reality of the ghettos and the camps. *Stücke* (literally "pieces") referred to corpse, *fressen* (which Primo Levi tells us describes, in proper German, the action of farm animals) referred to eating, and the ominous and bureaucratic "special treatment" referred to the gassing of Jews and others. To testify to a reality that seems out of all proportion to life before and after the Holocaust is to look for language in the storehouse of words and phrases and to come up empty time after time.

The other discursive problem is one of translation: each writer has a language, and a set of expressions, all his own, and those languages run the gamut. Unless the reader is fluent in prewar Europe's several languages, it is difficult if not impossible to read and to hear testimonies as they were written and spoken by their authors. They must be translated into our own language (in the case of those in the United States and Britain, English, a language unknown to the vast majority of European Jews). We are not only at the mercy of the speaker's or writer's storehouse of language. We are also at the mercy of a translator who himself may or may not have been there to witness a version of what the writer of the testimony saw.

Finally, how does one account for the traumatic effect of the events upon the language and narrative descriptions provided by the witness? If Cathy Caruth, Shoshana Felman, and others are right, then we have to be just as mindful of what isn't said as of what is. There can't be a direct correspondence between the testimony of a witness—regardless of whether his words were written on the spot, as in a diary, or years later, as in a videotaped testimony or a memoir—because what the victim saw wasn't experienced as a memory at all. Research on the memory of those who witness crimes has suggested that eyewitness testimonies can be unrealiable (see, for instance, some of the very good essays in Gruneberg and Morris, and in Radstone), though the general contours of what they saw is a good indicator that *something* terrible happened. But it's possible that in the most extreme cases the witness's testimony is *unrelated* to what they saw. This matters only a little to the historian, who is trained to consider different types of testimony; it matters a great deal to the Holocaust denier, who sees in any discrepancy bad faith and base motives.

Taken together, these problems make the matter of testimonies and first-person narratives of the Holocaust difficult to navigate. Nonetheless, it is important to keep in mind that we have learned a great deal from the diaries, letters, and oral and written testimonies provided by those who were there on the spot. It remains the task of this chapter to outline some of them, and to suggest how they might be understood.

□ □ □

DIARIES

There are dozens of diaries written by victims of the Holocaust, by bystanders, and a few by perpetrators, in print and translated into English. Many of them are published by small presses with funds provided by the author or the author's family or a trust; a few of them have been picked up by university presses in the last

ten to fifteen years, primarily because of their value as documents of life under the
Nazi occupation of Europe. A few, including Anne Frank's *Diary of a Young Girl,*
have taken on a life of their own, having gained canonical status as "Holocaust literature" through their widespread publication and dissemination in the United
States and abroad. Though written under different circumstances, diaries generally have several factors in common. They were written by witnesses immediately
or not long after the events they describe; many were kept informally and were not
meant for publication, but were instead a way of "working through" the circumstances of ghettoization and concentration (see, for example, Victor Klemperer's
recently published *I Will Bear Witness*); in some circumstances they were meant to
serve as a record of the events described for posterity, as in those kept by the Oneg
Shabbas organization in the Warsaw ghetto, and in those written by other Jewish,
Zionist, or quasi-religious groups sanctioned or marginally sanctioned by the Judenrat in other ghettos. In all the diaries that I know of, the entries ceased once
the writer was taken from his or her home and transported either to transit or to
extermination camps, since the wherewithal to write—pencil, paper, and time—
would have been confiscated. Taken together, they don't form a unified picture of
life under concentration or in hiding, since they were written in various locations
and from various cultural, religious, and national perspectives. But they do provide, one by one, a glimpse of individuals' circumstances, circumstances that sometimes work across the broad strokes of history and cultural memory.

Anne Frank

Perhaps the best known diary, at least in the United States and Britain, is Anne
Frank's. It was published in Holland originally as *The Secret Annex* in 1947, and
in the United States as *The Diary of a Young Girl* in 1952. It was begun two days
after Anne's thirteenth birthday, and it ends a month after her fifteenth, which
was also two days before the annex of the house in Amsterdam in which she and
her family were in hiding was raided. The diary is an unusually astute accounting of the circumstances of those two years, including not only the travails of the
family in the political context of those years, but also the sometimes intimate details of a young teenage girl's attempts to come to terms with her family, her
growth into adolescence, and her life of the mind. As Peter Novick (117–20)
notes, it was one of the very few accounts of the Holocaust willingly read by
Americans in the decade immediately after the war, and it became popularized
through a Broadway adaptation in 1955 and a film in 1959. Part of the reason
it was so widely accepted, in spite of its subject matter, is that it seemed not to
depict a particularly European, and certainly not particularly Jewish, life, but the
life of "a young girl" that might have been at home in most any suburban or
urban community. Meyer Levin, the novelist whose screen adaptation of the diary

was rejected by Anne's father, Otto Frank—who had retrieved the diary from Miep Gies, the person largely responsible for keeping the family safe for so long—describes the language of the diary as "wondrously alive," language that allows one to "feel overwhelmingly the universalities of human nature. These people might be living next door; . . . This wise and wonderful young girl brings back a poignant delight in the infinite human spirit" (Levin 1).

What few realized at the time was that, as published, the diary had been edited by Otto Frank. In fact he eliminated nearly thirty percent of his daughter's text, including some passages on sexuality and unflattering remarks on her Annex inmates, now victims of the Holocaust. It was also not widely known until fairly recently that Anne Frank herself edited her diary. She understood it might become public, and her language thus reflects her attempts to reshape individual entries for an audience. The 1986 Critical Edition of the diary published by the Dutch Department of War Documentation establishes the three versions we know now to exist: the first is the unedited diary, to date never published intact and by itself; the second is Frank's own edited version, begun four months before her arrest; the third, drawn from the first two, is Otto Frank's editing, the text that has been translated into 55 languages. With the understandable impulse to distance his daughter from the Shoah that stole her life, Otto Frank expressed his desire for the published diary to accentuate what he termed "Anne's idealism and spirit." He wanted to create an image of a girl struggling with mundane adolescent problems rather than a Jew struggling with her identity in Nazi-occupied Amsterdam. Thus the more familiar version deletes explorations of religious faith and a reference to Yom Kippur to ensure that Anne Frank isn't rendered too Jewish. Even Eleanor Roosevelt's introduction to the first American edition in 1952—which spotlights the diary's coverage of "the crucial years from thirteen to fifteen in which change is so swift and so difficult for every young girl" (ix)—leaves out any reference to Frank's status as a Jewish victim of the Holocaust. Instead, she concludes that "her diary tells us much about ourselves and about our own children. . . . I felt how close we all are to Anne's experience, how very much involved we are in her short life and in the entire world" (x).

Anne began rewriting her diary upon hearing a 1944 London radio broadcast calling for eyewitness accounts of the suffering of the Dutch under German occupation. Frank's revisions consisted of omitting passages and adding others from memory, a kind of "testimony" where the partial memories of present and past mingle. A stand-alone publication of Anne's unedited diary does not exist. This fact suggests the difficulty of coming by an unmediated testimony of any sort, even of this most famous diary, and even in a genre that at first glance seems to be written in the midsts of events. It also works against the orthodox understanding that a diary is a transparent reflection of an individual's intimate reflections. The Critical Edition of the diary gives visual form to competing notions of constructing traumatic history and of voicing consciousness within contexts that seek to stifle that very consciousness.

It's also worth considering the diary's interlocutor, "Kitty," to whom Anne addresses its entries. The rhetorical strategy of conjuring an audience allows readers to engage in what Susan Bernstein calls "promiscuous identification," something especially visible in Frank's diary but also visible in others. Bernstein writes, "on the one hand, this address ['Dear Kitty' and the closing, 'Yours, Anne'], along with the confiding tones that inflect what Frank imparts, signifies Frank's desire for an audience, not a detached other but an intimate friend. On the other hand, Frank constructs Kitty as outside the reality of Frank's own experience, as a naive listener who must be informed about the atrocity of war, the barely imaginable terrors of the programmatic annihilation of European Jews" (156). In 1943, Anne writes that "Since you've never been through a war, Kitty, and since you know very little about life in hiding, in spite of my letters, let me tell you, just for fun, what we each want to do first when we're able to go outside again" [July 23, 1943, p. 115]. As Bernstein notes, this telling "just for fun" "jars against historical contingency, the unfolding of the chain of catastrophic events once Frank and her family do 'go outside again'" (157). What Frank's diary shows is the limits of crossing the divide between the writing self and the other (the reader, the audience, which is most often unidentified or, at best, only vaguely recognized in the moment of writing). In effect, Anne—in writing her diary to "Kitty"—acts both as the witness and the one who hears the testimony (in the person of Kitty), making explicit a version of the "divided self" of which Lawrence Langer speaks, one marked by trauma.

It may be that it's this same divided self that marks Frank's ambivalence about her Jewishness (see Brenner 123). In the Critical Edition, one passage that illustrates this problem reads:

> Our thoughts are subject to as little change as we are. They're like a merry-go-round, turning from the Jews to food, from food to politics. By the way, speaking of Jews, I saw two yesterday when I was peeking through the curtains. I felt as though I were gazing at one of the Seven Wonders of the World. It gave me such a funny feeling, as if I'd denounced them to the authorities and was now spying on their misfortune. (80)

Frank's distinction between "the Jews" of "misfortune" and informants, with whom she (ironically) identifies, reveals a kind of double consciousness, the sense that one sees oneself through the eyes of another. Frank's uncanny feeling of seeing Jews "as if gazing at one of the Seven Wonders of the World" exposes the limits of this kind of doubling of selves. For Frank to identify as a Jew also means to imagine her own destruction based on a politics of identification: Jew, Slav, non-Jew, Aryan.

Etty Hillesum

Unlike Frank's diary, the diaries of Etty Hillesum have no audience at all except, perhaps, the writer herself. She realized that, on her departure for the Dutch transit camp at Westerbork as a cultural affairs worker, she might not return. But the diaries and letters were her attempt to maintain control over the events that swirled around her. She writes, in the first diary entry written in March 1941, when she was still living in Deventer in eastern Holland, "Here goes, then. This is a painful and well-nigh insuperable step for me: yielding up so much that has been suppressed on a blank sheet of lined paper. The thoughts in my head are sometimes so clear and so sharp and my feelings so deep, but writing about them comes hard" (*An Interrupted Life* 1). Hillesum makes clear here, to herself if no one else, that writing even the most mundane moments of her life is difficult to do because those moments seem to resist writing. In 1941, not long after the Nazi occupation of Holland, Hillesum was made a member of the Jewish council in Deventer. Though her position exempted her from transport to Westerbork, Holland's "last stop before Auschwitz," she volunteered to work there in July 1942. By June 1943, between two and three trainloads of Jews were leaving Westerbork for the east, each carrying 1,000 Jews from Holland and refugees from other parts of Europe who, like the Frank family, thought they'd be safe there.

On 14 March 1942, Hillesum writes:

> And now on Thursday evening the war raged once again outside my window and I lay there watching it all from my bed. Bernard was playing a Bach record next door. [. . .] What a bizarre new landscape [there is in recently bombed Rotterdam], so full of eerie fascination, yet one we might also come to love again. We human beings cause monstrous conditions, but precisely because we cause them we soon learn to adapt ourselves to them. Only if we become such that we can no longer adapt ourselves, only if, deep inside, we rebel against every kind of evil, will we be able to put a stop to it. Aeroplanes, streaking down in flames, still have a weird fascination for us—even aesthetically—though we know, deep down, that human beings are being burned alive. (*An Interrupted Life* 80–81).

The passage is remarkable for several reasons. It displays a complexity of observation that is rare in such reports. Perhaps because she is older and more mature than Anne Frank—she was 28 when she wrote this entry—her understanding of the circumstances of the destruction is far more complicated. Though clearly aware of the horror visited upon Rotterdam, perhaps seventy miles away, and of the individual lives that are being destroyed by the destruction, she is also fascinated by the attraction that such destruction exerts: why would she note, in the same stroke of the pen across the page, the noise of the bombs ("there were planes, ack-ack fire, shooting, bombs—much noisier than they have been for a long time" [80]) and the "powerful and glowing" Bach record, if she did not admit to a certain fascination with the combination of pleasure and pain herself? As she says later on in that same entry, she would like to be able to say "Yes life is beautiful, and I value it anew at the end of every day, even though I know that the sons of mothers, and you are one such mother, are being murdered in concentration camps" (81). In Hillesum's diary and letters her act of witnessing seems to take in what she calls an alternative to "textbook history": " 'It's probably worth quite a bit being personally involved in the writing of history. You can really tell then what the history books leave out" ' (109). The complexity of observation in the diary is almost an aesthetic one, where the didactic function of Anne Frank's diary—which she rewrote in order to preserve her observations of suffering— seems to be, at least for a time, subsumed to its purely observational, and very consciously *written,* mode. Hillesum seems very aware of the limits of writing.

In a letter dated 22 August 1943, only a little more than two weeks before she would be transported to Auschwitz, she writes to her family about the children waiting for the transports at Westerbork:

> I met a slightly built, undernourished twelve-year-old girl in the hospital barracks. In the same chatty and confiding manner in which another child might talk about her sums at school, she said to me, "I was sent here from the punishment block; I am a criminal case." [. . .]
>
> What children here say to each other is appalling. I heard one little boy say to another, "You know, the 120,000 stamp [in one's identification papers, signifying 'pure Jew'] isn't really any good; it's much better to be half-Aryan and half-Portuguese [i.e., a sephardic Jew]." And this is what Anne-Marie heard one mother say to her children on the heath: "If you don't eat your pudding straightaway, then Mummy won't be with you on the transport!" (*Letters from Westerbork* 121)

In July, writing from Deventer and just prior to her volunteering to go to the camp, Hillesum has something of an epiphany: "Very well then, this new certainty, that what they are after is our total destruction, I accept it" (*An Interrupted Life* 130). You could argue that the clarity and distance of the passages from the letters and diary entries from Westerbork are a result of this change of heart, since she understood by this point that the diaries are not meant to record the details of everyday life but, like Frank's, were meant to tell of the destruction that was surely coming.

But it's also possible to suggest something else at work here. In a letter dated only two days later, on 24 August 1943, Hillesum writes of those who would be on one of the last transports from Westerbork. In a note to her dearest friend and intimate companion Han Wegerif, she tells him, "One always has the feeling here of being the ears and eyes of a piece of Jewish history, but there is also the need sometimes to be a still, small voice" (124). Using words from a prayer traditionally said on Yom Kippur, the Jewish day of atonement (the "still small voice" of the penitent), Hillesum seems intent not on writing Jewish history so much as recording individual history, her own "little piece of stone to the great mosaic that will take shape once the war is over" (124). Though Hillesum's understanding of her fate, and of her fellows' fates, has changed by mid-1942, her strategy of writing has not: it remains to provide a sense of those moments that seem to drop out of history. But maybe it *has* changed, if only slightly. It may be that in these last letters, written as the Westerbork camp is being emptied, Hillesum sees herself writing Jewish history *through* the writing of individual histories, as if the litany of destruction itself risks being taken for history unless small moments—the still, small voice—that seem to drop out of it are also heard. One way to read Hillesum's diaries and letters, then, might be as a record of the tension between the individual witness and the witness-for-history.

Abraham Lewin

A small number of diaries written during the war had the expressed purpose of providing a record of history that obeyed broad sweep of chronology and the drive for completeness. Unlike the diaries of Frank and Hillesum, which form an uncanny mix of the mundane events of everyday life and the exceptional circumstances of the Holocaust, these diaries focus their attention squarely on the atrocities of the Holocaust, sometimes minute by minute, killing by killing. Emmanuel Ringelblum, a leader in the Warsaw ghetto and founder of the Oneg Shabbas organization (which took as its mission "to record the martyrology of the Jews of Warsaw"), encouraged members of his organization to keep diaries. The idea was that they'd be recovered after the war. Abraham Lewin became a member of that organization after the establishment of the ghetto in Warsaw in 1941. His diary, along with others, was buried in milk cans in a basement in Warsaw, and was recovered after the war. The first of two caches of papers recovered after the war contained a series of notebooks, written in Yiddish between May and August 1942, that provided a detailed record of what Lewin saw, sometimes contextualized by his sense of Jewish history or of the broader life of the Warsaw in which he grew up, but most often in a listlike fashion, with little transition between events and abrupt additions, as though Lewin would write something down when it occurred to him.

On 20 May, Lewin writes the following:

> Yesterday afternoon, at half past two in the afternoon, two officers drove a 17-year old Jewish girl out from the Pawiak Prison. They took her as far as 11 Pawia Street, led her into the entrance-way, let her walk a few steps in front and shot her several times from behind with a revolver. They had found that the girl was living on the Aryan side [of the ghetto wall]. Yesterday morning

she was arrested in her flat, not fully dressed, wearing slippers. She was taken
away as she was and after several hours in the Pawiak she was executed without further ado. . . . The level of Nazi brutality quite simply lies beyond our
power to comprehend. It is inconceivable to us and will seem quite incredible to future generations, the product of our imagination, over-excited by
misery and hunger. . . . I'm not making this story up, God forbid. It happened
today . . . (Lewin 80, 81)

Lewin admits that there is no language with which to record the events reported
to him or which he has seen himself with his own eyes, a distinction he makes a
number of times in his entries. Still, he dutifully writes those events in a transparent prose, taking care to include details. The girl did not expect to be found,
as she apparently had just gotten out of bed; she walked a few steps ahead of the
authorities, not directly in front of them, and was allowed to put some distance
between them before they took aim at her back. Five days later, Lewin heard reports of the conditions in the ghetto at Lodz, in which young children were being
indiscriminately killed. After two paragraphs wondering how these murders could
be placed into the cycle of atrocity and vengeance in both secular poetry and the
Torah, he writes, "Words are beyond us now. Our hearts are empty and made of
stone." Then, after a paragraph break, he continues: "My sister who lives at 17
Dzielna Street came to me deeply agitated and upset. She has witnessed two incidents," which he goes on to record. Knowing full well that the language at his
disposal is unable to bear the weight of the events he tries to write for others, he
nonetheless dives back into that impoverished language and represents for an absent reader what he's seen and heard. Faced with trying to testify to that which
he's witnessed, and knowing that the events in which he finds himself mired seem
to occur outside the precedent of history, the events for which "there is no name
in our impoverished tongue" are nonetheless written.

Writing on 30 May, Lewin—exhausted by what he has seen—lists the victims
of a roundup of Jews for reasons he does not disclose ("one opinion I heard was
that they were all racketeers"). He complains about the complicity of the Jewish
police in the action, and summarizes a conversation he'd heard among community officials about the conditions in Lvov and the province of Galicia (106–8).
Then he writes:

The details of these events are so devastating that they are not for the pages
of a diary. This must all be told in full. I hope and believe that this one day
will happen, that the world's conscience will be taken by storm and that vile
beast that is at the throat of the peoples of Europe and choking them to
death will be bound and shackled once and for all. . . . When the lawyer had
finished his account of these horrors and Mr G. had thanked him, many of
us had tears in our eyes.

Those two hours belong to the darkest of my life. (108)

What is remarkable about this passage is that Lewin does not in fact record the events, aside from numbers and locations. Though Lewin is privy to the details, and though he is a witness to the events surrounding the roundup of the "racketeers" and a secondhand witness to the reports of the destruction of the Jews of Lvov, the event *as* an event stands in the way of Lewin's ability to testify to it, to provide a language that might represent the devastating events. "The details of these events are so devastating that they are not for the pages of the diary. . . . Those two hours belong to the darkest of my life." This intrusion upon testimony—typical of many written and videotaped survivor testimonies—is a mark of the event that troubles history.

TESTIMONIES

In the years immediately after the war, a small number of survivors turned to writing. Several of them, including Elie Wiesel, Filip Mueller, and Primo Levi, sought to publish their work, though the publishers were at first hesitant to get too close to an event that the world seemed to want to make a break with. In part because they became public during a time when relatively few survivors were willing to do so, these three writers in particular have come to be canonized as representative of three different sorts of testimonies, and of experiences, of the Holocaust. Perhaps the most visible—and for that reason, the most controversial—writer of testimonies is Wiesel, whose book *Night* is a brief and horrifying account of the months he spent, with his father, in Auschwitz-Birkenau between the spring of 1944 and mid-winter 1945. His book has become the gold standard both in written testimonies and fictional renderings of the event. In part because of its sparse language, lately critics have paid a great deal of attention to its use of "novelistic discourse," a convention that seems to make it less "testimonial" and more "aesthetic," and so less near to history. Mueller's book, *Auschwitz Inferno,* is far less "novelistically" rendered. It is a chronological tale of his arrival at Auschwitz and his entry into the world of the *sonderkommandos,* the special squads of Jewish prisoners charged with clearing the bodies out of the gas chambers and cremating them. This is a world that was never meant to be revealed, as the *sonderkommandos* were executed periodically so that their testimony would never see the light of day. His book is a version of a story he has repeated in print (and orally in Lanzmann's *Shoah*) a number of times, and so it provides an interesting case of a testimony whose rhythms belie the experiences that reside behind the words. Levi was also at Auschwitz, though he was at the Monowitz work camp, attached to the Buna chemical plant. He began writing almost as soon as he returned from the camps. One could argue, then, that his language is the most unadulterated of the three. And yet it is Levi whose testimony seems most suspect—precisely because of its "writtenness"—as a historically accurate document about what happened in the camp.

Filip Mueller and Elie Wiesel

Mueller's *Auschwitz Inferno,* taken together with *Eyewitness Auschwitz* (both were published in the same year: the former in Britain and the latter in the United States, in 1979) are stark accounts of the brutality of the camps as seen from the perspective of someone charged with making them run efficiently. The second chapter of *Auschwitz Inferno* begins this way:

> In my terror I heard neither the ringing of the bell nor the door being un-
> locked. It was only when Schlage shouted: "Get out of here, you fucking
> thieves!" that Maurice and I raced out into the yard where an SS guard was
> waiting for us. He hustled us to the main gate where he handed us over to
> two SS men who took us to the right behind the Blockfuhrer's room, their
> pistols at the ready. At any moment I expected a bullet through the base of
> my skull. (11)

Typical of the testimony, it seems to replicate the unbearably quick pace and the chaos of the unexpected that is common in nearly all of the reports from those who survived the camps. Mueller's account is also remarkably candid about the brutality of the language used by those in charge and by those who were victimized by them. In an episode that Mueller recounts to Claude Lanzmann in *Shoah,* he tells of the first time he was made to work in the crematoria where corpses from the gas chambers were burned. At this point he was only used to undressing the corpses that had been removed from the gas chambers prior to their being burned, and Mueller expresses his incredulity at the task he is asked to perform: to "stir" the bodies. He tells Lanzmann, with wide eyes and a matter-of-fact voice, that he failed to grasp what the man had wanted him to do, and so he ran—as he puts it, "instinctively"—into the cremation room where he says he looked around, completely at a loss. There were, he says, bluish crystals on the floor that came into sharper focus as his eyes got used to the darkness. And then, he says, he saw Fischl, who walked up to one of the ovens and, lifting a flap in the lower half of the oven door, proceeded to poke around inside the oven with what looked like a long fork. Mueller tells Lanzmann that Fischl called to him to grab hold of the poker, and that he whispered to him to poke the fork in and rattle it about, and that doing so would make the bodies burn better. So, continued Mueller, he grabbed the diabolical tool and used it as Fischl had shown him, poking the burning, disintegrating bodies as though, he says, he was poking at a coal fire with a poker. Mueller moved on from this incident to others without comment, and the remainder of the testimony in this segment of Lanzmann's film seems primarily designed to provide a record of the dehumanization associated with the tasks of the *sonderkommand.*

Mueller's account seems mainly chronological and mainly "nonredemptive": he survived, but only by chance; he survived, but he was responsible for keeping the Nazi death machine relatively well oiled; he survived, but better people than he did not. Still, several writers have noted the constructed nature of the testimony. Mueller reports that a rabbinical student, on learning that he and members of his cohort in the *sonderkommand* would be killed, speaks to his comrades. He says, "it is God's unfathomable will that we are to lay down our lives. . . . Let us now go to meet death bravely and with dignity"; in doing so we "did nothing shameful" (161–2). The student speaks to his cohort after calling on the *oberscharfuhrer* in charge to be quiet "with sublime courage" (161). Inga Clendinnen takes note of portions of the text that seem out of character with the rest of it, which is by and large chronological and well-substantiated by other testimonies, particularly those by other (rare) surviving members of the *sonderkommand* (see Vrba, *I Cannot Forgive*). She writes, "Time and again, after gruelling descriptions of gaschamber killings—descriptions which can be broadly authenticated from other sources—the reader is comforted by notably less well-authenticated scenes of defiance and/or faith" (28). One such scene concludes the book's second chapter, where Mueller describes his anguish at his father's death: the father's body winds up in the crematorium in which Mueller is stationed. "In front of the blazing ovens a team-mate recited the Kaddish. . . . As the flames busily devoured the mortal remains of my father, the words of the traditional prayer gave me solace in this hour of sorrow" (48). This is one of the very few times the unobservant Mueller discusses his own implication in a religious ritual. As Clendinnen and others suggest, it is moments such as these—moments in which witnesses try to put the language of destruction into the language of redemption—that reveal the "novelistic" impulse of the testimony, and suggest that its conventions are those of fiction rather than history.

Given the traumatic nature of the events, though, it could just as easily be the case that it is precisely these conventions, and the need for the redemptive moments in which the horror of the event is "saved," that evidences the moments that cannot be told—or their effect—that reside in the narrative. The book's tendencies toward a redemptive narrative mask the writer's incredulity at the fact that he, among so many others, was saved. The relative success of Mueller's narrative has partly to do with its unflinching realism. Mueller's hints at redemption suggest that something else is going on in the testimony: that what the writer has seen can't be matched by what he says, and so must contrive another narrative with which to make sense of what he witnessed.

Sue Vice, in her analysis of narratives of the Holocaust, agrees with David Roskies when he says that the original version of *Night* included a palpable note of reproach: Eliezar, the book's narrator, angrily accuses the world around him of disbelieving the warnings of the coming catastrophe, and is much harder on his fellows in the camps for their failure to resist. (*And the World Remained Silent*, Wiesel's original account in Yiddish, didn't find a publisher until it was greatly reduced and rendered into French.) She notes that, in the English language version of the book, that reproach is displaced onto members of Eliezar's community and his family: "The Germans were already in the town, the fascists were already in power, the verdict had already been pronounced, yet the Jews of Sighet continued to smile" (19). As the train onto which the Jews of the town had been loaded pulls closer to Auschwitz, Madame Schachter screams, terrified, about fire. Because she'd been hysterically shouting throughout the journey, most paid no attention to her as the train remained stopped near the ramp at Birkenau— "she must be very thirsty, poor thing; that's why she keeps talking about a fire devouring her" (35). Continually the auguries of disaster make themselves plain to Wiesel and the others; continually they seem to ignore them. In part, the strain of anger and guilt that runs throughout *Night* turns the book from a testimony of the horrors of Auschwitz-Birkenau to an account of a son's break from his father's tradition, culture, and family bond.

The section of Wiesel's testimony that has gained the most attention from critics is that which falls nearly in the center of the book. Two adults and a young boy—a *pipel,* essentially a gopher and procurer of illicit material—are accused of an act of sabotage and are taken to be hanged. The entire population of the camp is arranged in rank and file in front of the gallows to witness the execution before the distribution of the evening's soup ration. While the two adults die quickly, the younger boy remains alive while he hangs from the rope. The narrator and all of those in the camp had witnessed executions like these before, and so the custom of removing their caps and replacing their caps before and after the ceremony, as Wiesel writes, was quite regular in its dehumanization. Just before the chairs are kicked out from under the three, a man mumbles "Where is God? Where is He?" During the march past the gallows, which takes half an hour, the young boy struggled in the noose, and as he passes the boy and looks him full in the face, the narrator hears the same voice ask, "Where is God now?" The answer, as it wells up in the narrator's mind, is " 'Where is He? Here He is—He is hanging here on this gallows. . . .' That night the soup tasted of corpses" (75–6).

This seems an odd mix of testimony and self-reflection: we learn of the cruelty and, oddly, the strange guilt of the camp officials (they seem "preoccupied" and "disturbed" at this particular execution) who hang the child along with the adults. But we also seem to hear, in this one episode, the voice of the narrator renouncing God. It is here where readers find the calamity of the Holocaust at its most brutal. This is the point where the narrator, who has up to this moment hung onto his traditions and his faith, now ceases to believe. It is from this point onward that he seems defiant both to his faith and, at times, to his father. And yet this is not testimony of what the eyewitness saw; this is, instead, a testimony of the *effects* of what the eyewitness saw. As Inga Clendinnen asks about the plausibility of the redemptive scenes that seem to punctuate Filip Mueller's testimony about the *sonderkommand,* it's possible to ask whether, in the memory of Elie Wiesel, the revocation of belief that is uttered silently by his narrator here and throughout the book's second half is a kind of "precocious testimony." Maybe it's language that stands in—as it does in cases of trauma, according to Shoshana Felman—for an event so horrible that it simply remains unspeakable, though its effects are nonetheless visible in the lines of the narrative.

The most terrifying words on the testimony may be those that close the eighth and penultimate chapter of the book. Dying of dysentery, his father goes to sleep in a bunk just above his son's; when the son awakes the next morning, there is someone else in the bunk in place of his father. "They must have taken him away," he writes, "before dawn and carried him to the crematory." Wiesel concludes the chapter this way: "In the depths of my being, in the recesses of my weakened conscience, could I have searched it, I might perhaps have found something like—free at last!" (124). These words are horrifying not because of their inhumanity, the words of a son finally freed of his father's corpse. It is because they seem to indicate something far worse, far more morally ambiguous and historically problematic. The only language Wiesel seems to be able to find is the language of renunciation, the language of the death of God. This would seem to be the only vehicle for a child dedicated to his father and to his father's traditions to describe the rupture caused by the events of the camp. The events as they are described are horrible enough.

The language of narrative—the novelist's ability to follow the contours of a story from innocence, to discovery, to the tragic low point of the loss of one's father, to the liberation that seems, tragically, not to be a liberation at all—allows the destruction's effect to be seen, and then only obliquely.

Primo Levi

Along with Wiesel's, one of the most widely read testimonies of the Holocaust is Primo Levi's *Survival in Auschwitz,* originally published in Italy as *Se questo e un uomo (If This is a Man).* Levi himself says that he is conscious of the difficulty of sutaining the line between telling what happened and remembering what happened. Levi writes in the testimony's preface that it "goes without saying" that the events he writes about are true. What takes precedence for him is the urgency of bearing witness, of making sure that the registers of the language provide the reader access to its object. Levi's purpose is to provide a translation of the events in Auschwitz to readers who were not there and who have no point of departure or set of experiences to which they can refer in order to do so. The point, in other words, isn't to say what happened, but to translate what happened into a language understandable to readers who have very little point of contact with which to make sense of the events.

The book moves roughly chronologically from the time Levi was captured by the German regular army in Italy in 1943, to his transportation to Auschwitz shortly thereafter, to his efforts to become part of the "chemical command" at the Buna rubber factory adjacent to the huge camp, and finally to his eventual liberation by the Russian army in early 1945. Like Wiesel's testimony, it begins with the capture and ends with the liberation, the typical trajectory of testimonies of those who survived. What makes Levi's testimony stand out—and the reason it poses some problems for readers of testimonies generally—is its aesthetic quality. As a testimony its langauge surpasses the language of the diary, the daily recording of events, and manages to capture in what some have called a "literary language" something of the horror of events.

Levi seems to know that no language can do justice to the language of the camps, the *univers concentrationnaire* in which only a certain kind of sense was allowed but that left an impression that made no sense at all. And he also knows nonetheless that beyond the language of the camps as well as the language into which he must translate it, there lies something perhaps inaccessible, the abyss of the event as it precedes experience and discourse. Knowing as we do the historical context of the events taking place in Auschwitz in 1944–45, and knowing the parts played by the SS, and the kapos, and the *haeftlinge,* we're able to construct a narrative into which we may place Levi's stories, and those stories then become understandable as episodes in a life lived in unbearable circumstances, episodes that perhaps brought a moment of clarity. Levi writes at one point about trying to make contact with a fellow prisoner who doesn't understand Italian. He says, "I must tell [the pikolo]," he says, "something gigantic that I myself have only just seen, in a flash of intuition, perhaps the reason for our fate, for our being here today . . ." (115). It makes a great deal of sense if we think of *Survival in Auschwitz* as the story of Primo Levi, *haeftlinge* number 174517, chronicler of the *univers concentrationnaire,* rounded up in Italy and transported to Auschwitz in 1944, and freed by the Red Army at the end of January 1945. But there's more to it than this, because the language of the book writes something beyond that simple story. The urgent, fragmented, and out-of-place words and phrases are attempts to describe a moment so utterly alien that they jar the writer and the reader out of the narrative of history. If so, we can see it as providing access to the act of witness. This language doesn't quite make visible the world of Auschwitz in 1944, or a life or series of lives of those who lived and died at the hands of the Nazis. Instead it suggests something of the events that we simply cannot know, and through that opening comes a confrontation with what the human mind can and cannot do. The central chapter of Levi's *Survival in Auschwitz* ends this way:

> We are now in the soup queue, among the sordid, ragged crowd of soup-carriers from other kommandos. Those just arrived press at our backs. "Kraut

und Ruben? Kraut und Ruben. [Cabbage and turnips? Cabbage and turnips.]
. . . Choux et navets. Kaposzta es repak."
"And above our heads the hollow seas closed up." (115)

In what Levi cannot say we glimpse the traumatic event as it affects him and as it destroys the narratives we created to contain what we think we understand about the Holocaust.

ORAL AND VIDEO TESTIMONY

Over the last fifteen to twenty years, there is a greater urgency to collect the oral testimonies of those who can give us their firsthand accounts of what happened during the Holocaust. That urgency is borne of simple mortality: those who were old enough to remember the events—older than six or seven years old—are now in their seventies and eighties, and most of those who were older at the time of the policy of Final Solution have by now died. Recognizing that there is little time remaining to gather these stories—this evidence—of the Holocaust, several organizations have taken responsibility for seeking out those who are willing to tell their stories. Yad Vashem, Israel's "Heroes' and Martyr's Remembrance Authority" (Israel's Holocaust memorial and museum), has recently accelerated its program of "cataloguing" survivors by name, country, and even physical appearance. They are asking visitors and friends of the organization to fill out a form with their recollections of those who, in their hometowns or in neighboring communities, lived during the Shoah. The Fortunoff Video Archive at Yale University has for nearly two decades trained and dispatched interviewers to collect video testimonies from those who have contacted the university. After the release of *Schindler's List,* Stephen Spielberg founded the Survivors of the Shoah Foundation, which has also begun to train and dispatch interviewers for the same purpose. In addition to these large-scale efforts, many Jewish organizations across the country and abroad (many of which are indexed at the United States Holocaust Memorial Museum) have collected videotaped testimonies from members and nonmembers, and individuals and their families have also begun to record their relatives' and their own recollections.

Like the videotaped testimonies found in the Fortunoff Archives and in the ongoing collection of testimony undertaken by the Survivors of the Shoah Foundation, Claude Lanzmann's interviews of survivors, bystanders, and perpetrators in *Shoah* reveal the complexity of the characters who were involved in the destruction. It also clearly demonstrates the travails of the witness in trying to come to terms not just with memory but with the words that would make the memory available. Time after time, when viewing tapes at the Fortunoff and elsewhere, I am surprised by the fact that many of the survivors are, despite what they say, apparently just like the fathers, mothers, grandfathers, and grandmothers I know, and whose stories come off as remarkable for their unremarkability as often as not. They tell their stories as if their lives in the Warsaw ghetto before the deportations were not unlike their lives prior to the ghetto's establishment. In the case of the Poles interviewed by Lanzmann over thirty years after the removal of the Jews from the villages of Grabow and Chelmno, they speak in remarkably candid ways about what happened to their former neighbors. They do so with a nonchalance surprising even for the virulent anti-Semite one encounters from time to time in the interviews. Another way to put this would be to say that in videotaped testimonies, there are long stretches of language and of narrative that seem oddly distant from what we think of as the horror of the Holocaust, and there are times when it takes real prodding from the interviewer to get the witness to talk about what she saw. If Felman is right, and there is a kind of precociousness to the language of the eyewitness, that precociousness is as often as not mundane as it is horrifying.

Lanzmann insisted that *Shoah* would document the events of the Holocaust without using archival film. Lanzmann relies entirely upon what the witnesses saw, sometimes through translators. He superimposes what the witnesses saw—their memories, conveyed by words, of the events that occurred now more than fifty years ago—upon their present locations by bringing them back to the earlier physical landscapes. All that's missing from those landscapes now is the one thing that linked the witnesses to them then: the horror. Unlike the videotapes of witnesses from the Fortunoff and the Survivors of the Shoah, these testimonies bear the locations, the physical space, of the memories themselves.

The Poles whose fields abutted the camp perimeter at Treblinka are perhaps fifty when interviewed by Lanzmann. They were in their teens in the early to mid-1940s. They describe working those fields just the other side of the fence from where thousands of Jews were being unloaded and almost immediately gassed. Asked if they could see what was happening in the camp, one of the two thin farmers says (in Polish), "Sure, we could see," while the other one seems not so sure, suggesting that it was dangerous to be too obvious about looking at what was happening. That second farmer then gets a big smile on his face, and makes a gesture as if he's shooting a pistol in the air. Because they're speaking in a language with which Lanzmann is unfamiliar, he has to wait for the translator to tell him in French what they said (in the English-language version of the interviews, subtitles appear when the French-speaking translator tells Lanzmann what is said). They are describing what the Ukrainian militiamen might do if they were caught peering across the fields and into the camp. We hear from the two of them that, despite the risks, they looked nonetheless, though carefully. Lanzmann, upon hearing this, rephrases what they've told him, asking if they looked with "sidelong glances," to which they answer, again in amused tones, "yes, side-long glances."

One of the striking things about this exchange is the ease with which these Polish farmers can describe looking at the annihilation, day after day, month after month, of Jews from across western and central Europe. In fact, they seem almost pleased about it. Another man in Grabow, not far from Chelmno, when asked if he misses the Jews who were killed forty years earlier, says "no" quite matter-of-factly. What one could obviously say about these testimonies is that they are quite unvarnished, quite transparent instances of an anti-Semitic disdain for Jews that has continued unabated over the decades since the Holocaust. Far from functioning as a transparent screen through which we can see what the eyewitnesses saw through their testimony, Lanzmann and his film act more like a prism or a catalyst, through which the testimony is filtered so that we catch a glimpse of what impels it. In the case of these Polish villagers, who initially told Lanzmann that they were rueful about the absence of the Jews and not pleased with the fact that they were transported and eventually killed, their nonchalance and their descriptions of the risks they overcame to take "sidelong glances" as the Jews were brought to Treblinka to be killed suggest something else—anti-Semitism; hate; murderousness; one could even say glee—that compels these stories.

The driver of the train responsible for bringing trainloads of Jews to Treblinka provides an example of how the location of the interview blocks testimony. In a long following shot, Lanzmann keeps his camera focused on the driver of the train as he looks backwards and forwards, up and down the track, as he pulls into the Polish station of Treblinka. Later standing next to the engine of his train, the driver gazes down at the ground at his feet almost emotionless. Lanzmann asks him, through the translator, why he looks so sad. The driver responds, "Because so many people went to their deaths." Clearly the driver saw, in bringing the train into the station, what he had seen thirty-five years earlier, through the prism of memory. Asked by Lanzmann to describe the reason for his sadness on the spot, all he can muster is a detached statement about the hundreds of thousands of Jews killed there, some of whom he had transported into the camp himself. What this shows, among other things, is the manipulation of memory and some of that manipulation's effects: in some instances it provokes testimony, though testimony of a precocious sort. At other times, it stops testimony dead in its tracks. It may also be that the questions and the setting of the interviewer him- or herself may be instruments in the creation of memory and testimony, rather than an instrument through which memory and testimony is retrieved. We'll see if this hypothesis can be borne out in one of the case studies that follows in the next chapter.

MEMOIRS

There is a very fine line between the testimony and the memoir. The memoir, more than testimony, tends to be self-conscious about the intersection of the present and the past, and of the results of the witness's travels through time and location from the site of the event—Auschwitz, Belsen, Warsaw, France—to the site of writing. What distinguishes the memoir from the testimony is that the memoir focuses on the memory-making process itself, and the way that memory-work creates something other than a memory of the past on the one hand, and a recitation of the work taking place in the present on the other hand.

In the past twenty years, the writing of memoir has been something like a growth industry in the United States. What marks this period of memoir writing is the degree to which writers have used the techniques of fiction—and, some have argued, used fictional events in place of real ones—to render the past. The memoir growth industry has not passed by writers taking the Holocaust as the location of their autobiographies. A number of them have been published in both the United States and Israel (among other countries) in the last twenty years, in particular over the last seven or eight years. An example of the most typical might be *Shoah: Journey from the Ashes,* the recollections of Cantor Leo Fetterman as he made his way from a small town in Hungary, to Auschwitz, through the DP camps, and eventually—via Madison, Wisconsin—to a congregation in Nebraska. It is a well-written memoir, and takes account of the years of the Holocaust as formative of the author's later life and vocation. That this memoir is published by a small press (Six Points, in Omaha, Nebraska) is also more or less typical, since there seem to be a greater number of Holocaust memoirs, and memoir writers, willing to make their stories available than there are trade (or even university) presses willing to publish them. Most Holocaust memoirs, like Fetterman's, are aware of the problems inherent in memory, and foreground them from time to time, but are less likely to take them into account than some, like those by Saul Friedlander and Peter Gay, whose object in the memoir is as much to inquire about the nature of memory as it is to inquire about the events that swept them into the Shoah.

Peter Gay

Gay's *My German Question* is not a memoir of the Holocaust as such: Gay's family, living in Berlin in the 1930s, managed to leave the country by 1939 and spent two years in Cuba before arriving in the United States in 1941. For Gay, the years of the Final Solution were spent listening to the radio, hearing from relatives who remained in Europe, and trying desperately to "become American" as a teenager while the United States went to war against his country. What sets this particular memoir apart is its frame of reference: a professor of history at Yale for decades, Gay took Sigmund Freud and psychoanalysis as his academic focus, and tried to understand the historical and cultural context in which Freud worked. That is to say, Gay's focus was Freud's "German question" (or, perhaps better, his "German Jewish question"), and it is Gay's residual Germanness that forms the central question of the book. He asks how it is possible to maintain a connection with Germany when the country was responsible for his expulsion and the deaths of millions of Jews. Gay tells us his family, while Jewish, was secular and politically liberal. So Gay also wonders how it was possible that their nationality, their politics, and their status in the economic and cultural hierarchy mattered for nothing while their residual Jewish identity was a matter of life and death.

Gay begins his book this way: "On June 27, 1961, we crossed the Rhine Bridge from Strasbourg to Kehl, and I was subjected to the most disconcerting anti-Semitic display I had endured since I left Germany twenty-two years earlier" (1).

> Getting out of the car on the German side to buy marks for dollars in a little kiosk, I had faced a young woman clerk behind a grille ready to serve me. She had looked at me coldly, her eyes registering pure hatred as I handed her my passport. A glance at her had left no doubt in my mind: murderous anti-Semitism was alive and flourishing in my native land. (5)

"What had happened? Nothing." The hatred Gay saw in his opposite was in fact his own: "I did not know the word *projection* then, nor would it have helped me to thaw out antagonisms so long frozen in my mind" (6); in fact, the entirety of the memoir could be said to be an analysis of the mutual antipathy experienced between Gay, the contemporary author who escaped from the destruction his country was bent upon inflicting on him, and the anti-Semitic but perhaps less personal hatred Germany held for Jews. The irony was that, as Gay himself describes, Germany since the war had become exceptionally well aware of its transgressions against Jews and the world, and had gone to great lengths to squeeze whatever anti-Semitism still resided there completely out of its system. Gay rightly describes his memoir as the memoir of a "trauma" that "survives everything—the passage of years, the rewards of work, the soothing touch of love, even psychoanalysis" (21).

I think a case could be made that Gay's memoir is an artful attempt to get at the central absence of trauma. It does so by working backward from the present (his visits to Germany in 1961 and afterward; his career as a historian, writer, and academic; his full participation in an American life) and forward from the past (his early years in school; his family's life; the aspects of the everyday in Berlin, which included the typical teenage complications that accompany the onset of adolescence) to the core of the traumatic event. In this case, it is the trauma of loss or of departure. Gay writes with a distance about the turn his life took in the immediate aftermath of Hitler's rise to power. He says this about an incident at his school:

> [My French teacher] had asked Landsberg to translate a passage in which the word *pluie* occurred, and Landsberg rendered it *Wolkenbruch*— cloudburst. This is admittedly rather strong for *rain,* but I was baffled when our teacher responded with a cloudburst of his own: "The Jews always ex- aggerate!" he shouted. This was news to me, and I found the accusation trou- bling. Was hyperbole one of those Jewish defects that the Nazi authorities kept denouncing?. . . Perhaps loading down a casual explosion with heavy sig- nificance, I have sometimes wondered whether my unremitting search for precision in my writing was in part fueled by this outburst. (65)

The qualifiers "perhaps" and "sometimes," along with his bafflement, seem to downplay the extent to which this incident had an effect upon the hatred Gay ex- presses at the border bridge.

And yet he shows his hand more than he might wish when he wonders whether this anti-Semitic cavil—"Jews always exaggerate"—isn't one reason why his writ- ing is so qualified in the first place. In other words, what is most interesting about this passage, and this memoir, is what it tells us about the complexity of mem- ory when placed under the burden of both a physical and a psychological depar- ture: his family's brutal removal from Germany and his exile in Cuba and the United States, and his estrangement from German culture and history. The mem- oir, as a genre, is for Gay an instrument of history, because it both acknowledges history and it avoids an obsession with history. "[H]ave I been obsessed with an effort to recoil from [the Holocaust]?" he wonders (203). Perhaps he has; but his memoir, as do most memoirs, seems to move back and forth between the events of the present and the void of the past.

Saul Friedlander

Saul Friedlander, speaking of his recollections of life as a child in Prague, says that "for each of us who lived through the events of this period . . . there is an impassable line of cleavage somewhere in our memories: what is on this side, close to our time, remains dark, and what is on the other side still has the intense brightness of a happy dawn—even if our powers of reason and our knowledge point to obvious links between the two periods. When one looks back to the other side of the line, an irrepressible nostalgia remains" (*When Memory Comes* 33–4). How one deals with that nostalgia—that yearning for and willingness to create an event that was, perhaps, never there in the first place—is the key prob- lem in memoirs of the Holocaust. In part this is because those events are so fraught, and because their occurrence is an element of history that most of us agree shouldn't be forgotten. Friedlander's memoir is unusual in that it describes not only the loss of a country (as in the case of Gay's reminiscences) but also the loss of parents and identity. Friedlander's parents left Czechoslovakia in 1939 and settled in France; after the occupation of France a little over a year later, Friedlander's parents managed to have him taken in at a Catholic seminary before they attempted to emigrate to Switzerland, which was dangerous and from which they were eventually turned away and were never heard from again. While at the seminary, Pavel Friedlander became Paul-Henri Ferland; the Jew became Catholic; the Czech became French. And from the years after the war when he discovered his past to his journey to Israel at a time of war, he wrestled with the chaos of memories that constantly interrupted his sense of who he was.

When Memory Comes, more self-consciously than many memoirs, moves back and forth between Friedlander's coming of age and his experiences, in the 1970s, in Israel. He attempts to make Jewish cultural heritage, a heritage that had been stripped from him earlier, his own. The book ends with the author's arrival in Israel (which had been proclaimed as a state one month earlier) in 1948, on the heels of being told of his parents' deaths in Auschwitz and a hasty departure from the seminary. There are three memorial "nodes" in the book: 1942, 1948, and 1977 (which roughly coincide with Friedlander's parents' departure, his own departure for Israel, and his diary of the six months he spent in Israel). They consistently intersect, mimicking—in almost novelistic fashion—the constant intrusions of memory Friedlander experiences. One of the central moments illustrates the difficulty of understanding just what the object of memory is in a memoir, let alone a memoir of the Holocaust years. Friedlander recalls being placed by his parents in a Jewish children's home near La Souterraine. After a short time the proprietors of the home were ordered by the police to send away its children, and they all spent an evening in the woods before returning, when Friedlander was retrieved and brought back to his family. A diary entry in 1977 begins: "What became of the children of La Souterraine? Thus far, I have never tried to find out" (75). This is followed by the author's recollection of listening on the radio in Israel to a commemoration of the Warsaw ghetto uprising. A survivor recounted a story: it is after curfew, he is upstairs in his room, and he hears the cry of a child on the streets below. *A shtikl broit* ("A piece of bread"), he cries, and the child is suddenly directly below the window of the storyteller. He throws a piece of bread from the window. The child, by now lying on the pavement, does not see that the bread has landed just beside him, and the storyteller calls out, "Reach out your hand, to the right! . . . Look, lift your head, there's bread right next to you!" The child, now motionless, is dead. Discussing this story with a friend and his wife the next day, she says:

> "Is it possible [. . .] That twenty-five years later, the narrator still has no notion of what he should have done? The strange thing is that none of those who heard the story here in Israel seems to have understood."

"What do you mean?" [Friedlander asks.]

"Don't you see either? Instead of throwing the bread down and calling out directions from his window, the narrator should have gone downstairs, opened the door, and taken the child in his arms . . ." (75–6)

This recollection is then followed, without comment, by a recollection of his parents packing suitcases on his return home from La Souterraine.

One question to ask is this: to what does this recollection, now ten years after Friedlander writes it down and thirty-five years after his parents' departure, refer? It's like Gay's moment of transferrence twenty-two years after his departure from Germany, in which he sees in an exchange teller's efficiency an anti-Semitism that is in fact his own complex reaction of hate aimed at the country that expelled him. Here Friedlander's memory seems also to be an oblique reference to some other event—the loss of his parents, or the loss of his identity—which is experienced not at the time but only years later, and *only* obliquely to the initial loss. Memories and memoirs of the Holocaust could be said, like Friedlander's and Gay's, to work by indirection, in which the events that caused the authors so much pain are like infections of memory. What has happened is irrevocably lost; what is happening now, as a result of that lost event, is visible in their infected memories, as they are layered one on top of another. The writer himself bores through those layers in an attempt to make visible, for himself and for his reader, their complexity.

THE SECOND AND THIRD GENERATION

Survivors of the Holocaust began to cobble together new lives in the United States, Israel, and other countries in the years after the war, and in so doing began, or restarted, families. Survivors occasionally reunited with spouses who also survived, but more typically they met one another in DP camps or their new communities. Sometimes furtively, sometimes with a sense of urgency that seemed borne by a need to prevent Hitler from gaining what Emil Fackenheim called a "posthumous victory," they had children, children who in many cases had only vague hints of what their parents went through. Many of these children, some now in their fifties and with children (and some with grandchildren) of their own, grew up in a house filled with silence, a silence borne of horror and shame. The horror came from the memories of their parents, and the shame came from the sense that no one wanted to hear about the desperate conditions through which they lived and the desperate acts they often took to stay alive. These children sometimes had only a vague sense that their family lives were different from those of the other children, immigrant and nonimmigrant alike, with whom they went to school.

Ellen Fine has written about the phenomenon of "absent memory," a term originally coined by Henri Raczymow to refer to the second- and third-generation's temporal disconnection from the event, though they have a palpable connection to it through their parents. Absent memory (Raczymow's term, *mémoire trouée,* literally "breached memory") is a "lack of memory" of the event, accompanied by "a sense of regret for not having been *there*" (Fine 187). Many of the testimonies and memoirs written by the children and grandchildren of survivors exhibit symptoms of absent memory. They feel guilty for not having been able to save their parents from the torment they suffer, and feel a sense of inadequacy because their troubles look puny in comparison to those of their parents during the war. Many of these second- and third-generation survivors, and many individuals born since the war who have no family connection to the events, also display what Marianne Hirsch has called "postmemory." Postmemory is an effect of the repetition of images of atrocities and of other aspects of life during the years between 1933 and 1945 as they are "adopted" by members of these younger generations. Images tend to conjure memories that are both traumatic but also not their own. But these secondhand memories have an effect that disrupts the collective memory that they have forged to deal with their parents' and their own distress.

Helen Epstein

Helen Epstein was a freelance journalist in 1979 when she wrote *Children of the Holocaust.* She was one of the first writers to pay attention to the unique circumstances of the children of Holocaust survivors. Recognizing that her childhood was different from her schoolmates', and guessing that other survivors' families might look like hers, she set out to collect the reminiscences of fellow "children of the Holocaust." One of the recurring themes in Epstein's book is that there is history, and there are memories, but that a wall separates the two. The events themselves belong to their parents, while the family memories belong only to the children. Epstein writes: "The facts were these" (11), and then moves on to recount a brief history of the Holocaust. Then, there is the iron box, in which she placed her memories: "The iron box contained a special room for my mother and father, warm and moist as a greenhouse. . . . The box became a vault, collecting in darkness, always collecting pictures, words, my parents' glances, becoming loaded with weight. . . . [Eventually] I needed tricks to get near it, stragegies to cut through the belt of numbness that formed each time I made a move toward it" (12–13).

Epstein spent two years collecting stories from people like her, who also had iron vaults in which they kept their memories, and within two years had heard stories from over a hundred people, from the United States, from Israel, from

Canada, and from other parts of the world. Their surroundings and the trajectories of their lives were sometimes vastly different from Epstein's own, but their memories were often exactly the same. Those memories were literally breached (*mémoire trouée*), broken off from those of both their parents and their friends. In Israel, Epstein located Sara and Aviva (many of the names, like these two, are changed from the actual names of those interviewed for anonymity's sake). One sister was self-possessed and confident, while the other was uncertain, untrusting, and extremely reticent about the interview. What both of them said in common, though, was that their parents were distant.

> There was never a happy moment that I can remember at home. Never a period of time when you could put your guard down and relax. My mother didn't teach me to be proud of myself. She didn't teach me how to take care of a household, she never told me about my body, she never talked to me, can you understand that? We were not a family that touched. I never felt that we were loved: I felt we were there to be used. I think that they used on their kids the techniques for survival that they had learned in the forest. The order of normal life was so confused for them during the war that abnormalities became normalities. . . . Their needs became the center of their universe. (117)

The memories of their parents, in other words, could not be shaken after the disaster, and their "acting out" of these memories desperately affected the lives of their children. Of course, these memories did not become their children's memories. Those other memories were closely associated with the Holocaust, and yet they were memories of other facts. Sara said, "I remember one time we went to the beach and my mother saw, a very long distance away, an apple that must have fallen from a boat. She swam all the way out for this apple and when she got there she discovered the apple was rotten inside. I remember her telling my brother and me: *This is what life is. Everything looks so beautiful, so nice on the outside and you touch it and see how rotten it is inside.* I was about eight years old then but I still remember that" (116). What becomes evident in Epstein's book is that the memories of the children are not (or not only) memories of the Holocaust. They're memories of having to live with the effects of the Holocaust day in and day out. More to the point, the breach between the parents' memories of the event and the children's memories of their effects upon their families' lives is not bridged. As in Sara's recollection of her mother's and father's stories on the heels of her own recollection of an incident from her childhood, the memories associated with one inevitably lead to the other.

Epstein's most recent book tries to piece together her mother's history (*Where She Came From*). In it she writes the following:

> In most families, there are multiple versions of the family story; the larger the family, the more various the versions. In my family, as in many families of

> Holocaust survivors, it is difficult to construct even one. There are too few
> relatives. They possess few document. Disaster has dispersed them. Moreover,
> each has designed his or her own strategy for coping with the destruction of
> the world into which they were born. One forgets, another attenuates, an-
> other denies key parts of the narrative. (146)

Epstein works from the surviving family members, and the few documents remain in her own family archive along with those that reside in Czechoslovakia
and elsewhere. She constructs a narrative from them that makes sense not only
of her mother's story but also her own. There are two sets of memories here,
both of which are fragmented, both of which involve tremendous loss, and both
of which provide blind spots—moments of forgetting—that present problems for
those who would want to understand the relation between the survivors and
their families.

Art Spiegelman

Art Spiegelman's two-volume *Maus: A Survivor's Tale,* is just such a hybrid text.
It combines the testimony of Vladek, whose family was deported from the cities
of Czestochowa and Sosnowiec in Poland and destroyed at Auschwitz and other
death camps, and the memories of Artie, the son conceived after the war who is
haunted by the memories of his father, his mother's suicide after the war, and the
evanescent but always palpable sense that he cannot take the place of Vladek's
son Richieu, who was born before, and died during, the war. Like Epstein's books,
it is hybrid in another sense: it is a historical document (in this case comprised
by the tape-recorded testimonies of Vladek in the presence of Artie); it is a second-
generation memoir of Artie's efforts to recover the history of his family and of
his distinctly troubled relationship with his father and his family, and an analysis of the problems of representing lost memory through two languages and
worlds, the languages of the survivor (built of Europe and the war) and the languages of the survivor's child (built in the United States and through a prism of
the parents' incomprehensible losses). *Maus* ultimately fails to reconcile the anguished memory of the son and the memories of the father, but it does makes
clear how, in the relation between the memories of first and second generation,
something else is produced.

 As testimony, Spiegelman's account of his father's experience defines the author's
own struggle with understanding, ultimately representing whether it's even possible to produce knowledge of the Holocaust from his father's memories. This does
not mean that *Maus,* as a second-generation testimony, provides a better record
of the events of the Shoah from a survivor's perspective. The narrative focuses on
the problems of knowing the event from the perspective of the second generation

by overlapping present and past narratives, which is—in fact—visible in every representation of the Holocaust. Spiegelman, as the second-generation survivor, shows just how hard it is to know the survivor's memories, since they overlap and interfere with the child's memories of his own anguished childhood and his present circumstances. He balances the telling of his father's witnessing with his own act of witnessing, moving back and forth between what his father is telling of the past and his own perception of his father's experience.

The very opening sequence in *Maus* (volume I) sets up just such an interaction, showing a memory of Artie's childhood and the reaction of Vladek when Artie comes to him after being teased by friends: "Friends? Your friends? . . . If you lock them together in a room with no food for a week . . . then you see what it is friends!" (5–6). The first volume's third chapter begins with an argument at dinner over Artie not eating his food, followed by Vladek's recollection of Artie doing the same thing as a child (40–45). This sequence is immediately followed by Vladek continuing his narrative of serving in the Polish army when the Germans invaded. Overlapping the dinner and the recollection is Vladek's disagreement with his wife Mala, an argument from which Artie tries to distance himself. It is through the overlapping of the first story with the remembered event—the insertion of Vladek's past into Artie's present—that Spiegelman points at what is, for him, the real disaster. It's not the Holocaust; it's his present circumstances and his life with his family.

Art Spiegelman's subtitle for the second volume of *Maus* is "And here my troubles began." One is almost tempted to ask, "where?" and "for whom?" It makes sense to think of the troubles beginning in 1933, or at the point when Vladek's textile business was appropriated by the Polish General Government, or at any number of other temporal locations in the Spiegelman family history. But it's also possible that the troubles begin where Vladek's story ends and Artie's begins. *Maus* is the son's story, not the father's. In the last panels of the book, Vladek's final illness is getting the best of him, and his son knows that he is racing time to allow his father to finish his story. Earlier, Vladek had pulled out a box of photos, many of relatives who survived the war, but a few of them were left from before the maelstrom, including one or two of Vladek, his wife Anja, and their son Richieu. As Vladek welcomes his son into his room, he continues with the story. Barely noticeable, above Vladek's bed, is a portrait of Richieu, the only surviving photo of his first son, in overalls and a white shirt, and at the conclusion of his narrative, Vladek rolls over and asks Artie if it's all right to stop for now. "That's enough for now, Richieu, enough stories" (136). This error, this mistake of identities, is the core of Artie's troubles. Every caricature he has drawn of the Spiegelman family before the war that includes Richieu, at whatever age—even as an infant—is drawn exactly the same: dark overalls and a white shirt. And this is precisely the photo we see of Richieu that appears in the front matter of the second volume of Maus. Artie's second-generation memories have at their core this absence, his "ghost brother's" memory, which is only available in a photo, and which has been rendered indelible in his own memories of after the war.

The place both Vladek and Art Spiegelman's troubles begin is the moment of the destruction of the family, of Richieu, and eventually of his wife Anja as well. Those specific instances of destruction are instances we can't know through the universal narrative of the Holocaust, or through a recitation of the events of a life, or of a series of lives. We know them only through the recitation of the break in the second generation. The memories are rendered, in the case of Epstein and Spiegelman, imaginatively. The line between eyewitness testimony and fiction, between the language of those who were there and the language of those who weren't, is hard to make out. What Spiegelman's second-generation memoir may suggest is that it's only through the language, and the images, of fiction, that we are able to catch a glimpse of the Shoah's effects.

CHAPTER 8

Case Studies: Testimony and the Problem of Authenticity

We live in an age when those who survived the Holocaust are succumbing to the frailties of old age; a great many others have already died. Though we live in an "age of testimony," it won't be long before the testimonies we have can't be verified by others who were also there. We'll be left to take them on faith, or to place them against the backdrop of what we already know about the Holocaust, or to go back to the historical record and either confirm the eyewitness accounts or allow the content of the testimonies—their facts—to change what we think we know about the event. In the last chapter we examined different kinds of testimonial accounts of the Holocaust, and described how their different genres yield different kinds of "information," and different species of problems, to the reader or the viewer (the "secondhand witness"). Each testimony—written during the events, or recollected afterward—gives us the words of the victim (or bystander, or perpetrator) and we quite literally take them at their word: we take seriously their descriptions of events, even at times when what they have to say boggles the imagination and works against what we think of as normal human behavior.

But there's another possibility. As is sometimes the case with those skeptical of the events of the Holocaust, or with those who refuse to believe for whatever

reasons that it happened at all, what the eyewitness says he saw is simply too preposterous, or too horrifying, or too far beyond the pale of reason, to be believed.
Particularly now that fewer and fewer eyewitnesses are alive to tell us their stories, and when those who can tell them have been separated from the events
themselves by nearly six decades, it becomes more difficult to authenticate these
memories and these narratives of destruction by finding others who remember the
same events in the same ways. The historical record presents other problems—
as we saw in the first section of this book—because its narratives, too, seem to present very different versions of the same events, and sometimes even the evidence
on which we might verify testimony seems to contradict itself, let alone the testimonies. To put it plainly, it has recently become possible to seriously question
the authenticity of nearly every Holocaust narrative, even those written or told
by those who were there.

I think it'd be too much to say that we're at a point of crisis in authenticity. There
are too many accounts of atrocity to suggest, as early Holocaust deniers did, that
they were all fabricated from whole cloth. Still, in the last few years a number of
Holocaust testimonies and narratives have been called into question, enough so
that even those who have spent their lives studying the Holocaust have been shaken
by these questions and, in some cases, their answers. As we saw in the case of Jedwabne, Poland, Jan Gross was taken to task by Poles, intellectuals from around the
world, and historians for his "falsification" of documentary evidence and his un-
warranted conclusions about Polish anti-Semitism. No one questioned that an act
of genocide had taken place in the town of Jedwabne, and no one questioned that
it had been precipitated by the Nazi invasion of the country. But because the testimonial accounts of the survivors and eyewitnesses were in some cases contradictory, the *narrative* was called into question, and the credentials of the author were
trashed. Though a Polish national committee formed to investigate what happened
in Jedwabne has since confirmed Gross's account of events, the name "Jedwabne"
will stand for some as an inauthentic episode in the Holocaust.

In this chapter, I present two instances of testimonial accounts of the Holocaust in three different genres and in three competing—and in part mutually exclusive—"registers" of authenticity. (The idea of authenticity is itself often unclear
and confused, but it has an important role in both ordinary discourse and in certain kinds of critical work, including work on Holocaust and other testimonies
and accounts.) The first, Claude Lanzmann's film *Shoah,* is a ten-hour, multipart
documentary in which Lanzmann films his discussions with victims, perpetrators,
and bystanders from several countries. In some instances Lanzmann brings the
survivors back to the location of the events they describe. It is Lanzmann's technique of bringing together the speakers' memories of past events with the speakers' present—and, at times, locations and circumstances that the speaker would
prefer not to revisit at all—that makes the film so effective. We see, or think we

can see, the events described through the looks of pain, or disbelief, or (in the cases of bystanders or perpetrators), joy on the faces of the witnesses, even though Lanzmann doesn't show us the object of the testimonies at all. How is it possible that this film, which shows us almost nothing of the Holocaust itself, can provide an authentic account of what happened? The case of Binjamin Wilkomirski's *Fragments: Memories of a Wartime Childhood* complicates matters even further. The memoir, published by a child survivor of the Holocaust now living in Switzerland, captivated the reading public and the vast majority of scholars and historians who spent a lifetime examining testimonies and documents from the events of the Final Solution. Within a few years of its publication, *Fragments* was revealed to be a fabrication, not a memoir, and yet its author staunchly stands by his story. He was a survivor, he still insists, and these horrible things did happen, and he was in fact traumatized. Is it possible, some have begun to ask, that while the "testimony" itself is false, the events that serve as the testimony's origin—if not the events of the Holocaust that serve as the story's object—may have happened? Taken together, all three instances—the documentary, the novels, and the false memoir—raise questions about how testimonies may be considered "authentic," and about what kinds of questions must be asked of Holocaust testimonies and memories even if we cannot ask them of the storytellers themselves.

THE AUTHENTICITY OF TESTIMONY: *SHOAH*

Claude Lanzmann's *Shoah* is considered by many to be the best film ever made about the Holocaust. One reason is that he successfully steered between the realism of fiction—in which what the viewer sees on screen is deemed "authentic" because it looks like what we might imagine the Holocaust to look like, or because it mirrors documentary and other footage of the events—and the documentary. Lanzmann himself has said that he did not want to use documentary footage. Nor did he want to tell a fictional narrative, a coherent story that might be elevated to the place of a singular rendition of the Holocaust. Instead, *Shoah* was created of new material, evidence consisting almost entirely of witness testimony taken not in the immediate aftermath of the war, but at an interval of twenty or thirty years and sometimes on the spot of the events. While the witness's memories are thirty years old, the location of the events was in many cases almost entirely unchanged over that time. By bringing the witnesses to those locations, Lanzmann seems almost to have created a new criterion of authenticity.

The film begins with Simon Srebnik revisiting the death camp at Chelmno, where as a young boy he sang folk songs to the Nazis, ran errands for them, and helped burn the remains of those gassed in vans. Lanzmann shows us the face of

Srebnik, and of all of the other witnesses, as they speak about what they saw. Often the most revealing moments involve no words at all. They involve instead images, such as those of a survivor staring (as when Srebnik stands, alone in a field, in the very place where thirty years earlier he exhumed bodies for burning); or a Pole sorrowfully thinking about lost friends; or a historian contemplating the medieval roots of Hitler's Final Solution. Lanzmann's camera captures the remembrances of witnesses. "Capture," though, might not be the best term, since he is an active film editor, and he punctuates the moments and stretches of remembrance with his own interventions. It's these interventions that connect survivor recollections and Nazi officials describing the way a camp functioned. It's these interventions that connect the testimony of Polish farmers who watched the deportation trains go by their fields with the recollections of those who were on those very trains. In linking these pieces together—the words and faces of survivors, bystanders, perpetrators—Lanzmann juxtaposes past and present, and different versions of the very same past and the very same present. He doesn't show us the atrocity, or the act of survival, itself.

In at least two scenes, Lanzmann is not giving us "authentic" remembrances: no one watching this film actually sees the acts the witness remembers. The focus here is not on (or is not exclusively on) those acts; its focus is at least as much upon the present—the witness's present, the viewer's present—as it is upon the past. And unlike the videotaped testimony at the Fortunoff Archive, the acts of remembrance in Shoah are visibly, sometimes artfully edited: we don't so much get the survivors' recollections as we get Lanzmann's construction of a version of the survivors' recollections. Lanzmann produces a palpable tension between the horror's presence in the present moment and its point of origin in history.

If such a technique doesn't give us properly "authentic" testimonies, it nonetheless follows a consistent logic. It's worth investigating this logic, because it provides an authenticity that the testimonies' connection with history might not. Whether Lanzmann interviews survivors, bystanders, or perpetrators, he generally begins a scene in the midst of a testimony, after he has already started his questioning. Sometimes the speaker of the testimony is all we hear and see; at other times we also see Lanzmann as he prods the witness for more information. When Lanzmann interviews Mrs. Michelsohn, the German wife of a Nazi schoolteacher at Chelmno, he weaves together her testimony with that of Polish witnesses and of the two survivors of Chelmno, Simon Srebnik and Mordechai Podchlebnik. Shifting from witness to witness, Lanzmann presents a scene where Michelsohn tells about what she saw, and she also tells about her present understanding of what she saw. The scene is interesting because in connecting the past and present in her memory, something is revealed to the viewer about her need to distance herself from the past. In telling a story that is, in many ways, "inauthentic," she nonetheless points to an aspect of memory that is so authentic, and so painful, that she resists it. The scene begins with Michelsohn detailing the arrival of Jews at Chelmno.

First she describes their mode of arrival, in trucks. Later, she goes on, they came in railway cars pulled on a narrow-gauge railway line that came through the town. They were packed in tightly. There were many women and children, but there were men too, though most of them were old. The strongest of the men were put into work details, she goes on, and for that reason they had chains on their legs. In her matter-of-fact tone, Mrs. Michelsohn relates that these men weren't killed right away, but were executed later, though it's unclear just how Mrs. Michelsohn knows this. And anyway, she goes on, she doesn't know what became of them. She only knows they didn't survive.

Lanzmann, at this point, breaks into her narrative, and says simply that two of the men did survive. Not quite incredulous, but also not registering any kind of emotion, Mrs. Michelson says, rather than asks, only two. When Lanzmann asks her whether the Jews she saw were in chains, she says yes, and when asked if Mrs. Michelsohn or anyone else could speak to them, she tells him that no one dared try, that it was far too dangerous. And it's at this point that there's a demonstrable change in her tone. She tells him that there were guards, and goes on to say that people wanted nothing to do with "all that." "Do you see?" she says. It "gets on your nerves, seeing that every day. You can't force a whole village to watch such distress!" she tells him sharply. She tells Lanzmann that when the Jews arrived, when they were being held, first in the town's church and then later in an old ruined castle, there was interminable screaming. Day after day, the same spectacle, she says. And she uses that word—"spectacle."

When Lanzmann asks Mrs. Michelsohn whether she knows how many Jews were exterminated in Chelmno, she answers in a way that makes one wonder whether she'd memorized the figure at some point: four something, she says, or maybe four hundred thousand. Lanzmann provides the correct number—four hundred thousand Jews were murdered in Mrs. Michelsohn's adopted town—and with resignation, she gives a tiny shrug and says, yes, four hundred thousand. She concludes by restating what she'd said before, as if the horror of the numbers now replaces the horror of the screams: "sad, sad, sad."

Lanzmann's intrusion into Michelsohn's narrative (when he tells her that two of the men survived) refers to Srebnik and Podchlebnik, who viewers have seen just prior to this clip. That intrusion tears apart the seamless fabric that her testimony attempts to create: Lanzmann reveals to her that there are two survivors, moving her from the past that makes her uncomfortable, to the present in which what she says can be questioned. Lanzmann also pushes Mrs. Michelsohn to speak about the public nature of the treatment of Jews in Chelmno, drawing her into places where her narrative doesn't cohere: "there were guards. Anyway, people wanted nothing to do with all that. Do you see? Gets on your nerves, seeing that every day." Between her statement about not being allowed to speak to the work details (she tells him that no one dared) and her statement about not *wanting* to speak to them ("gets on your nerves") there is a switch in Mrs. Michelsohn's "position," from simple onlooker to someone intimately involved in what she saw.

The tension between being present and seeing Jews marching through town chained ("Gets on your nerves, seeing that every day") and a disavowal of seeing ("no one dared") presents Lanzmann, and his viewers, with a problem of authenticity. Here is a witness quite certain about what she saw, but unable to find a stable position—guiltless observer? guilty bystander? some combination of the two?—from which to tell it. It's possible to say that what the viewer sees, in this scene, is the impossibility of grounding history securely in the story of this one witness. The eyewitness isn't enough to render an authentic account of what happened. It takes an editor (of memories, or of film?) like Lanzmann, who cuts the film and puts it back together to create the memory by marking it with its inherent tensions, to make it authentic.

Another example of the tension between what the witness can say about what happened and the actuality of the event is visible in Lanzmann's secretly taped interview with Franz Suchomel, an SS Unterscharführer who guarded prisoners at Treblinka. Sitting at a table, with Lanzmann next to him and an easel with an architectural plan of the camp propped upon it, he's asked to describe, in as precise a fashion as possible, his first impressions of Treblinka. Lanzmann makes very clear that—consistent with his stated purpose in the film—what he is after is the most precise of answers. He wants the facts. Suchomel replies that, not only his impression, but the impression of his men was that the place was "catastrophic." They hadn't been told, according to the Unterscharführer, what the conditions would be like, or that people would be murdered there, en masse. Lanzmann, in what comes off as mock disbelief, asks him if he seriously didn't know and when Suchomel affirms his point, Lanzmann responds with true incredulity. But Suchomel goes on, undeterred: He was told there would be workshops, there would be shoemakers and tailors at the camp, and his job and the job of the soldiers that accompanied him would be to guard those in the camp. The Führer, he goes on, had ordered a re-settlement program. No one ever spoke of killing, he says. At this point, as if to press his point about preciseness home, but also to reassure him, Lanzmann interjects that he understands. We're not discussing you, he tells Suchomel, only Treblinka. He flatters Suchomel by telling him that he is a very important eyewitness, and that only he can explain what Treblinka was like. The Unterscharführer demurs—he asks Lanzmann not to use his name—and Lanzmann, again to reassure him, promises not to and asks Suchomel to go on to describe his arrival at Treblinka.

This exchange involves two deceptions: the implicit one, in which Lanzmann, toward the end of the segment, tells Suchomel that they're discussing Treblinka, not Suchomel himself; and the more explicit one, in his promise not to use Suchomel's name. What the viewer knows, but which Suchomel does not, is that this whole scene is filmed with a hidden camera. We know this because Lanzmann frequently cuts from his interview to the technicians in the van outside Suchomel's apartment trying to maintain a clear signal. So part of what Lanzmann shows, in addition to Suchomel's testimony, are the lengths to which he goes to get it. The testimony of the Unterscharführer is open to question: was it Jews or German soldiers and officers who removed the pile of corpses? Did he or didn't he know what his charge would be at Treblinka? Suchomel himself, like Mrs. Michelsohn, seems unwilling to answer, as if the answer would make him complicit. And like the interview with Mrs. Michelsohn, Lanzmann keeps the present (and the presence of) the memory in question, both in his own interrogations and by keeping the process of testifying open to serious questioning.

Perhaps the most controversial segment of Lanzmann's film is his interview with a survivor living in Tel Aviv. Abraham Bomba was moved to a work detail by the Nazis because he said he could cut hair. He was immedaitely placed inside the anteroom of one of Treblinka's gas chambers and, along with other barbers, was told to remove the hair of those about to be gassed. In what some have called an act of cruelty, Lanzmann conducts the interview with Bomba in a Tel Aviv storefront barber shop, as if to replicate the conditions of horror he experienced at Treblinka. We see customers and barbers move about in the background as Bomba cuts the hair of a middle-aged man who seems not to know that a charade is playing out in front of him. As the interview goes on, Lanzmann's questions become more and more aggressive, and Bomba tries to distract Lanzmann's attention by talking about other, more abstract issues. As he did with Unterscharführer Suchomel at the latter's apartment, Lanzmann wants precise and direct responses to his questions: What was Bomba's first impression the very first time he saw naked women arriving in the gas chamber with their children, waiting to be shaved? Bomba, who is being interviewed by Lanzmann in English—the barber had spoken Yiddish but has spent the years after the war in the United States—replies without answering Lanzmann: that it was hard to feel anything at all. He tells the story of a friend of his, a barber in Bomba's hometown, who was also put to work by the Nazis at his trade in the camp. He begins to tell Lanzmann about this man's reaction, but can't. He can barely contain his emotion. It's too terrible, he says.

But Lanzmann is insistent. He tells Bomba that they have to do it, almost accusing him. It's very hard, he acknowledges, and he even goes so far as to apologize. Bomba again demurs, and as we watch, we realize that he's having a hard time keeping something—though we don't know quite what it is—from his memory at bay. This section of the testimony is full more of silence than of sound. This is all the more arresting because it's also clear that Lanzmann and Bomba have spoken about what today's testimony would be like—he tells the interviewer at one point that he told him it would be very hard to tell the story—but even with a dress rehearsal, something is getting in the way of Bomba's story. As the silence in Bomba's testimony goes on and on, and as he circles around the barber chair, he mutters something barely audible under his breath as he tries desperately to regain his composure.

Lanzmann tries one more time—please, we must go on, he says—and still he is met with silence. Finally, after what seems like an interminably tense period, Bomba resumes his story. When his friend's wife and sister came in they tried to talk to the men, but that knowing they couldn't tell them what was about to happen—and that the two women were probably doomed to die—the men simply tried to do their best for them by showing them affection with hugs and kisses because they knew they would never see them again.

It would be hard to say that Bomba's testimony isn't authentic: it's so authentic, both for him and for viewers of this segment of *Shoah,* that one can almost see, or imagine seeing, what Bomba remembers. But the memory itself isn't the focus of the scene. The memory's impact in the present is much more horrifying, and it's the manipulation of the present in the hands of Lanzmann that seems most palpable. What you see in the ferocious battle over Bomba's memories in this section of the film is not the disintegration of the present in the face of the past (since it's only partly the horrifying memory of his friend's encounter with his sister and wife that brings the barber to tears). More horrifying, and more visible, is the memory's disruption of the present: Bomba's present, and Lanzmann's, but perhaps more importantly, the viewer's. But what does the viewer see? The terrible scene that passed before the barber's eyes? The eyes of his friend? The persistence of the traumatic kernel whose object is lost? Bomba insists, "Don't make me go on." Lanzmann shows how the events comprising the Shoah persist. He shows how the feelings of the wife of a Nazi schoolteacher at Chelmno still reflect Nazi racial attitudes. He shows how some Poles think their lives are better without Jews. He shows the anxiety and fear a survivor feels upon coming back to Berlin. The events persist in the viewer's unease, at the end of the film's first part, when the viewer realizes that the truck the camera has been following bears the insignia of the company whose vans were used to destroy the Jews of Chelmno. Though Lanzmann makes use of live eyewitnesses, the result is not history. The language of the witnesses reinvokes the events of history in the present. Each of these individual eyewitnesses experiences—and sees—something that is more than a memory, more than what happened.

There are times in *Shoah* when Lanzmann does use previous testimony. When introducing the deportation of the Jews of Grabow to the camp at Chelmno, Lanzmann reads a letter written by the rabbi of the Grabow synagogue to friends in Lodz. Lanzmann stands in front of what remains of the Grabow synagogue and reads the letter from Rabbi Jacob Schulmann, who explains that he has just heard of the gassing and shooting of Jews in Chelmno. Lanzmann concludes by telling us that three weeks after sending this letter Rabbi Schulmann and all the other Jews in Grabow were sent to Chelmno and immediately gassed. On the surface, the use of Schulmann's letter seems no different from the testimony of those who Lanzmann interviews; in fact one could say that because it was written on the spot, in the midst of the Final Solution, it has more historical authenticity than the testimonies of those who are recollecting the events from a distance. In fact, its authenticity is

open to question, because the letter functions as a tool for Lanzmann's own interrogations. As in other interviews, the scene begins and ends with Lanzmann's presence. As evidence, the letter is clearly an authentic document of suffering and
cruelty. But Lanzmann's use of the words of witnesses does not offer more authenticity than the words themselves offer. It may in fact provide a different sort of authenticity altogether. Very soon, all of the interviewees will be dead, and their
recorded words and experiences will have the same limits, the same distance from
the event, as Schulmann's letter has. Put another way, at this moment in *Shoah*
Lanzmann places himself in the position to offer testimony, offering himself in the
place of Rabbi Schulmann. We are not witnesses to Schulmann's testimony. We
see Lanzmann's represention of Schulmann. This is not a criticism of Lanzmann's
use of the letter; but it does problematize the question of authenticity. Are the words
themselves available as authentic evidence of the murder of Rabbi Schulmann, or
do the words require a speaker—in this case, a speaker in the present of the film—
to make them authentic for a viewer who can't imagine the murder otherwise?

    Shoah is not a film about testimony, if we think of testimony as offering a win-
dow on what happened. Its presentation of witnesses doesn't even try to be historically authentic: the "now" matters more than the "then." But *Shoah* may well
propose a different kind of authenticity, one that depends on the effect of history
on the present. The voices of the people whose stories we hear have more to do
with the effects of history upon the present than they do about verifying the
events of history themselves. It could be that *Shoah* foregrounds the notion of
"space." While Lanzmann provides images and situations that are palpably

Figure 8–1   Henrik Gawkowski, who drove the trains to Treblinka. From *Shoah*.

present—the fields into which Simon Srebnik walks, or the pathways on which the gas vans traveled fifty years ago; the gas vans whose similarity to cigarette trucks in Israel gives Michael Podchlebnik barely a pause—they indicate a location that is impossible to find on any map of the camps. The philosopher Michel de Certeau says that space is "produced by the operations that orient it, situate it, . . . and make it function in a polyvalent way" by "actions of historical subjects." If so, *Shoah* is saturated not so much by actual places (the fields, the forests, the interiors of buildings and the architecture of the camps and ghettos, and the constant, noisy presence of the trains) as it is by a no-place. It's a terrain of horrifying experience that even Lanzmann's most persistent questioning of witnesses—and even Lanzmann's testimonial position itself—can only scratch the surface of.

Simon Srebnik's words punctuate the beginning and end of the film's first half. Walking through the fields outside Chelmno where bodies were burned by the thousands, he says that no one can recreate what happened here, that it's impossible. He goes on to declare that not only can what happened not be understood, but that he himself can't understand it, and that he can't believe he's here, in the very place where the Nazis burned two thousand people—two thousand Jews— every day. Even then, he says, it was just as peaceful as it is now. In part, it was because everyone went about his work. That's why it was silent. He concludes by describing to Lanzmann a dream: that if he survived, that he'd be the only person left in the world. Just him, just one. All the viewer sees is testimony. Impossible, he says, just him. Just one. You could argue that Lanzmann's film is, finally, inauthentic, that he has produced a film that implicates the viewer, that makes us a part of his own story to find out what happened, to see a survivor's return to Poland, to watch his face as he points to where the bodies were buried at Chelmno only to be dug up and burned later. But it doesn't present the Holocaust as such. This doesn't mean that it's ineffective; in fact, just the opposite may be the case. Maybe it's the film's constructed nature—the way Lanzmann weaves past and present together, rather than relying on a kind of realism in which the past, or an image of the past—that is most important, what makes the film work so well. But how can a film that is less about the Holocaust and about testimony than about the Holocaust's effects be less "authentic" but more effective, than a film or a medium (a testimony) whose focus is on what happened?

TESTIMONY AND THE "LIE": THE WILKOMIRSKI AFFAIR

Binjamin Wilkomirksi's *Fragments*, a "memoir" whose main character survived the Holocaust as a child, was originally published in Germany in 1995. By 1996 it had been translated into a dozen languages and become an international sensation, in part because it was a lucid, excruciating tale that resembled others in the genre, but which was remarkable in its own right. The child, whose ordeal "escap[ed] the laws of logic" (4), was presumably no more than four or five years old when the narrative begins. The story takes place in the years between the German occupation of the Baltic countries and the immediate aftermath of the war through the early 1950s. It alternates between two main narrative strands: the author's experiences in two camps (Majdanek and an unnamed camp that was identified later as Auschwitz), and his later life in orphanages immediately after the war. In the afterword to the book Wilkomirski writes that he had "received a new identity, another name, another date and place of birth," but that none of it has to do "with either the history of this century or my personal history" (154). The book seemed to attest to the radical division between history and memory, between the fragmentary images of a past the author couldn't shake and the historical circumstances into which those images were fit.

In late 1998, Daniel Ganzfried, an Israeli-born Swiss writer, began to investigate who the author was and to learn about his memory. What he found was that *Fragments* was written by Bruno Doesseker, a clarinet-maker whose adoption papers record his birth in Switzerland in early 1941 to Yvonne Grosjean, an unmarried woman who was herself, along with her brother, separated from impoverished parents. He was placed with foster parents, Kurt and Martha Doesseker, in 1945 and was eventually adopted by them legally in late 1957. Doesseker's current house is full of archival material, including oral testimonies, films, photographs, and historical accounts of the events that comprised the Final Solution and its aftermath. Doesseker claims that the research helped to place into context the flashes of memory that result from a child's perspective on events, and that it offered "the calming 'possibility' of finding 'the historical center' of [my] own past" (Gourevitch 56–7). Israel Gutman, a historian who was himself a survivor of Majdanek, says that though very few children survived, there were an extraordinary few who did: "Look . . . we know that during the Holocaust extraordinary things happened, which did not correspond to the general rules" (Lappin 46). Doesseker's current companion, Verena Piller, and a psychiatrist with whom he has traveled and spoken at conferences, Elitsur Bernstein, both say that his emotional condition and physical infirmities are consistent with a man who has suffered a severe trauma or set of traumatic experiences. Lappin suggests that as a child Bruno Doesseker constantly tinkered with the story of his origins—one friend recalls that "'he used to say that his adoptive parents wanted him as a medical experiment,'" and a couple says he told them in the 1960s that "'he had been in the Warsaw ghetto and was saved from the Holocaust by a Swiss nanny'"—as a way of dealing with the trauma of a forcible separation from his mother, Yvonne Grosjean. She found that Doesseker's mother was separated from her parents as *verdingkind* ("earning child") under a seventeenth-century system of child welfare, which was not abolished until the 1950s, in which poor or unmarried parents sent their children away to work for other families in exchange for food and shelter. "Beatings and sexual abuse were often part of their childhood"; Bruno himself may have been separated from his mother under similar circumstances (Lappin 63).

The most straightforward interpretation of the "Wilkomirski affair" is that *Fragments* is a fabrication, a hoax, or a delusion. The first question to ask is whether or not there is a kernel of truth that lies at the heart of the book. The second is whether this kernel of truth means that the book can function as an authentic testimonial account, even if it doesn't qualify as a testimony to the Holocaust. This raises another, perhaps harder, question: can (or should) fiction serve as a vehicle for memory? Any testimony would have to agree with or at least corroborate a good deal of other eyewitness testimony of the Holocaust in order to tell a certain truth. It would have to represent a reality to which other witnesses have testified and which is internally coherent. Yet Holocaust testimony is often both incredible—the events to which the witness testifies seem impossible, unreal—and incoherent—exhibiting gaps, silences, and disjunctions. Potentially corroborating eyewitnessses and other documentary evidence may have been destroyed.

As we've seen, the French writer Jean-Francois Lyotard, in his book *The Differend,* makes a point about limit events like Adorno's "Auschwitz": it isn't enough for an eyewitness to testify to the reality of an event to give it authenticity or establish its veracity. He writes that "[r]eality is not a matter of the absolute eyewitness, but a matter of the future" (53). The job of the writer is to "name and show referents that do not falsify the accepted definitions," and to write in a language that "obey[s] heterogenous regimens and/or genres" (55). In other words, the language has to be both consistent with what we know of events, and allow for imaginative possibilities beyond what we think of as rational or probable. The language of fiction may be just such a language. To qualify as testimony, literature must also be mapped onto "the signification that learning establishes"—the tapestry of historical evidence, other testimonies that verify and corroborate the witness's—while it "lends an ear to what is not presentable under the rules of knowledge" (57). Under this definition, does *Fragments* function as testimony? Can it, even if what the reader sees may not match what's in the narrative, let alone what Bruno Doesseker saw?

Earlier Cathy Caruth made the point in "Unclaimed Experience" that history and trauma bear a close connection with one another. We consider history as what can be preserved as a memory and written, but the event that serves as the object of history, what happens, is erased or blotted out. The traumatic circumstance was never fully known—and so couldn't be remembered—at all. What we read in survivor testimonies is the displacement of the traumatic event—the historical event, lost to memory—by the language of the testimony. Is the language of Wilkomirski's book this sort of language? It isn't a narrative that reconciles two lives (the life lived during the Holocaust and the writer's life in the present) so much as it is a series of tableaux, in which one set of experiences of orphanages, homes, and schools is connected to another set of experiences of the camps.

One such pair of images involves the young Binjamin hiding near a pile of corpses, one of which—a woman's—begins to move. As its belly bulges and writhes, Binjamin watches in horror as a rat emerges, slick and blood-covered, and he wonders what this birth-scene suggests of his own origins. Then:

> Many years later, I went with my wife for the birth of our first son. . . . The first thing that slowly became visible was the half-round of the baby's head. As a first-time father, I didn't know how much dark hair a newborn baby can have. I wasn't ready for this little half-head of hair. All I could do was stand still and stare at it, once again, like an echo from before, I heard the ringing and crackling noise in my chest. (88)

Between the horrible memory of the corpse that Binjamin can't seem to shake and the image of his son's birth into which that memory intrudes unbidden is something unavailable to knowledge. Whatever it is, it can't be presented as a narrative: it's seen but not recognized by Bruno Doesseker and—in different terms—by the witness to the text: the reader.

What can't be placed into the narrative—what the boy Doesseker saw that became coded in the language of the Holocaust and that makes its way to the surface of the text as Binjamin Wilkomirski's memory—finds no place in the language of narrative. But it may have a place, of sorts, in testimony. "There are no feelings left. . . . I'm just an eye, taking in what it sees, giving nothing back" (87). Maybe the moment of witness is here: in losing what he has to say, the testimony begins, a testimony that refers to what has been blotted out as much as to what has been fixed as a memory. Here, in the no-place of the narrative, is the gaping, open wound, the trauma experienced by the writer (who may or may not be the boy Binjamin, we may never know). It's witnessed only in terms of the absence of Doesseker's place in the historical circumstances he narrates.

As a memoir, the language of *Fragments* doesn't easily follow the patterns that correspond to the general rules of historical narratives and by itself doesn't give us a way to adjudicate the competing claims of Bruno Doesseker and Daniel Ganzfried. As for the narrative itself, and its depiction of events, its gaps cannot be said simply to represent inaccuracies; rather—as Caruth suggests, speaking of Freud—they represent and "preserve history precisely within this gap in his text" (190). But this doesn't mean that *Fragments* (like testimonies, written memoirs, or fictions) can't be disproved as an inaccurate account of the events it purports to narrate. It means that whatever the book's significance, it can't be attributed to its worth as "authentic" history, but must be connected to events unrecorded (or unwritable) as history. Pursued by the obligation to speak, the witness is not

necessarily pursued by the obligation to provide a historically accurate accounting of the event, because the event as such has disappeared.

Philip Gourevitch reported that while he was interviewing Bruno Doesseker for
an essay in the *New Yorker,* he read an article on memory by Alan Baddeley. Baddeley reports that memories can be "coded" differently depending on the context
in which one does the remembering (66). Gourevitch goes on to suggest, as Lappin did earlier, that Doesseker's attempts to address the forgotten events of his
own life with a narrative were biased by the reaction he received as he "encoded"
them with the context of the Holocaust. As the public reception of the Holocaust
changed gradually from shameful taboo to hallowed icon, the reaction to the stories Doesseker told about his own experiences as a "survivor" changed as well.

> When [Doesseker] said "nightmare" and [the reaction] came back "Holo-
> caust," he could both resist and creep up on the possibility, in a hypnotic,
> semiconscious manner, which not only seemed like memory but felt like it,
> too. . . . Wilkomirski [said], "By the time I started my historical research I
> slowly got used to the idea that a part of my memory is in a part of
> Auschwitz." (66)

Whatever Doesseker's motives, if his aim was to produce a document through
which readers would experience the shock at the horrors of the Shoah,
it shouldn't come as a great surprise that research that involved looking at photographs of the camps and of their destruction of Jewish central Europe would
have provided him with a vocabulary of horror. And if Doesseker himself was
shocked, if not traumatized, by what he read and saw in his research, then it's perfectly plausible that he would have experienced a kind of correlative horror. If
Elena Lappin is right, and Bruno Doesseker was forcibly separated from his
mother and was subject to experiences to which he still cannot put a name and
which have had a hold on his imagination since that time, it isn't surprising that
he testifies to those experiences through the language of the most significant horror of the twentieth century. As Lappin has said, "Wilkomirski often refers to his
memories as being film-like. They are, I believe, more than that: they are, I believe,
derived from films. . . . I cannot believe that *Fragments* is anything other than fiction. And yet, . . . anguish like [his] seemed impossible to fabricate" (Lappin 61).

If a witness's participation in the events of history—particularly traumatic events—
can't be recuperated except through the fragmented and troubled narratives that fail
to contain them, then the connection between the event and the resulting testimony
may be more tenuous than we'd like to think. These narratives may well serve as evidence of the events comprising the day-to-day litany of destruction. The historical
circumstances of these written accounts—some of which were found buried amidst
the rubble of ghettos, some of which are corroborated detail by detail in other

accounts—would also seem to bear out and confirm their status as evidence. But when those historical circumstances—corroborating witnesses, documents, place names recollected—can't be recovered, the best we can do is rely upon the effect of the writing itself. Hayden White would argue that its status as evidence depends in part upon its effect, and that effect—produced metonymically either by design or by circumstance—in the case of the Wilkomirski book, is a disturbing one.

Wilkomirski may be a liar, after all. No one would say the same of Primo Levi. So what if the uncertainty over Wilkomirski's narrative leads, as Philip Blom has suggested, to an "ero[sion of] the very ground on which remembrance can be built" (Blom)? What if it leads to "a new revisionism that no longer attacks the truth of the Holocaust but only individual claims of survival" (Peskin)? If we can undermine the authority of the writer of a Holocaust testimony, and say with certainty that he was never there and that he did not see what he claims to have seen, then we have eliminated one piece of evidence that we can use to argue that the atrocities of the Shoah occurred. Such testimonies—in the form of eyewitness accounts, documentary evidence, trial transcripts, and diaries—taken together form the tapestry of suffering that we have inherited as the narrative of the Holocaust. But such testimonies may be as inaccessible to those who survived as they are to those who created them.

In the case of the Wilkomirski "memoir," we may well be able to undermine the authority of the writer if we take him to be trying to establish a narrative of the circumstances of the Holocaust that will settle the matter, either of history or of biography. The converse is also true: his lack of credibility seems to throw open to question the veracity of testimonies of other survivors. But this is not to say that it lessens the disastrous effect of the testimony, or the testimony's ability to indicate something about the nature of the event, though that disaster may not be the historical object whose "content" we take to be coequal with the narrative's shape. Elena Lappin suggests that the author of *Fragments* may have suffered some shocking accident in the events surrounding his separation from his mother, or the years in which he lived in orphanages or foster care or in the care of adoptive parents. Such an event might mean that the book's fragmented language indicates an event that is not only inaccessible to its readers but inaccessible to its author as well.

This is a troubling place to be left. As some have said of the Wilkomirski affair, to suggest that false testimony may nonetheless be an effective instrument through which we may bear witness to the Shoah is to provide Holocaust deniers with one more way to doubt all testimonial evidence about what happened in Europe between 1933 and 1945. So to conclude that there is, in the Wilkomirski "fraud," a kernel that may be connected somehow to the horrors inflicted on the victims of the Final Solution would seem to fly in the face not only of good taste but of human decency as well. Common sense tells us that testimony undoubtedly bears some relation with the events it depicts, and once we find divergent accounts of those events, we generally think of the testimony as erroneous, flawed, or patently false. But what was seen and what a witness can say about it inevitably diverge. The effect of the seen gets in the way of the fabric of testimony, leaving the witness to find some other language to stand in its place. So while we may want to banish false testimonies like Wilkomirski's from what one writer has called the "Holocaust archive" so as not to taint what remains, knowing how to draw the line between unbelievable and beyond belief may be very difficult to do.

DISCUSSION QUESTIONS, Part III

1. In the case of witnesses to the Holocaust, how does the time that has intervened between the events they lived through and their experiences since then help preserve memory? Does it interfere with, or get in the way of, memory?

2. Berel Lang has argued that the most appropriate accounts of the Holocaust are chronicles, because they don't "add anything to" what really happened. Would you agree? Why or why not?

3. Lawrence Langer argues that oral Holocaust testimonies are a better vehicle for memory and history than written ones because of their spontaneous nature; he argues that written testimonies give the witness a chance to consider what language she'll use to tell the story. Do you agree? Why or why not?

4. In what way might diaries, testimonies, and letters function as evidence? Evidence of what?

5. Can you think of an instance in which forgetting is a prompt for, or something that initiates, writing? In such a case, what event or object is that writing evidence of?

6. Maurice Blanchot speaks of the "immemorial" aspect of memory. What might this be? What, in histories or testimonies of the Holocaust, have you seen or read that might be considered an instance of the immemorial?

7. How can we tell whether the testimony of a witness to the Holocaust is true? How can we tell whether it's accurate? What's the difference between a testimony's "truth" and its accuracy?

8. Is it possible that a narrative of events that's completely fabricated can act as a vehicle for memory?

9. What would it take for a testimony—or any historical artifact, for that matter—to be considered "authentic"?

10. If the effect of a testimony or other piece of evidence is what matters, and not its fidelity to what really happened, is it possible to say that a "fabricated" testimony is more valuable as a representation of the Holocaust than an actual testimony? (If so, what are the implications of your answer, and what dangers—if any—do they carry?)

IV | REPRESENTATION

CHAPTER 9 | # The Problem of Representation

Aharon Appelfeld, one of the best-known writers of Holocaust fiction, says that we should "keep literature out of the fire zone." Though there's something legitimate about the survivors' desire to tell their stories, there seems to be something illegitimate for those who were not there to tell stories as if they were. James Young has suggested that in order to fend off this criticism, novelists from the generations after Auschwitz make use of the "trope of the document" by mimicking the historical and documentary prose of the eyewitness (see Chapter 3, *Writing and Rewriting the Holocaust*). But as we saw in the previous chapter, there are some real questions as to whether or not such a "trope of the eyewitness" doesn't backfire on the author.

The ring of fire that Appelfeld describes has roots that go beyond the question of Holocaust representation. Gertrud Koch, a prominent film scholar, and Miriam Hansen, a scholar of film and the humanities, both connect the problem of representing the Holocaust in fictional terms to what has come to be known as the *bilderverbot,* the German term for the ban on mimetic representations, which itself comes from the biblical commandment against graven images. The *bilderverbot* has formed a focus in the last hundred years as to just whether, or how, literary and other arts can realistically represent objects and events, and whether there aren't some objects and events that are better left unrepresented. In her essay entitled "Mimesis and Bilderverbot," Koch points out that the *bilderverbot* may require a kind of representation that at once obeys the injunction against slavish copying while also making visible a trace of the object. Through "unsensuous likeness," the fragmented image calls to mind objects that couldn't otherwise be thought. (Koch points to hybrid beings from Jewish art with human bodies and animal heads.) The hybrid artistic object provides, through indirection, a figure that both obeys the second commandment injunction and also manages to imitate the object perhaps better than direct or realistic representation. In an essay on Lanzmann's film *Shoah,* Koch writes that the kind of representation heralded by the ban on graven images is an "autonomous art" that works by "expression rather than illustration" ("The Aesthetic Transformation . . ." 18). But while hybrid, nonrepresentational modes of writing may well obey the injunction against representing the unrepresentable, they may also go beyond what humans can or wish to see at all.

Miriam Hansen links this problem of the *bilderverbot* directly to the problem of Holocaust representation. In an essay on Steven Spielberg's *Schindler's List,* Hansen rightly criticizes those who complained that the film breached the limits of decorum by showing scenes it had no business showing. It was too realistic, these critics argued, and "by offering us an 'authentic' reconstruction of events of the Shoah, the film enhances the fallacy of an immediate and unmediated access to the past . . .—by posing as the 'real thing,' the film usurps the place of the actual event" ("*Schindler's List* is not *Shoah*" 300–01). The problem with such complaints, however, is that they rest on the assumption that the Holocaust has a status beyond that of other events or objects. Claude Lanzmann, one of those most loudly denouncing Spielberg's film, calls the event "unique in that it erects a ring of fire around itself, a borderline that cannot be crossed because there is a certain ultimate degree of horror that cannot be transmitted" (quoted in Hansen 301). But Lanzmann ignores, according to Hansen, the degree to which Spielberg manages to obey the second-commandment injunction while representing the Holocaust's horror. Hansen, Koch, and others have begun to forge a notion of representation that doesn't rely on realism (mimesis) or the tropes of the eyewitness, but instead relies upon indirection, hybrid forms, and the fact of absence rather than presence: the absence of the writer and the eyewitness, and the absence of direct representation itself.

A version of Lanzmann's position appears in Berel Lang's book, *Act and Idea in the Nazi Genocide.* The aim of the Final Solution was to desubjectify its victims, to render them without the ability to act or to think themselves as individuals. The problem with literary representations of the Holocaust, then, is that they present to the imagination characters in situations over which they have at least some degree of control. Literary and poetic representations tempt us to imagine Jews as individuals in the context of the Holocaust, when in fact the Nazi genocide was horrifying precisely because such an individuality of personhood was prohibited.

Theodor Adorno was originally concerned with representations that provided a realist sense of events, particularly horrifying events like the Holocaust or the de-

struction of the war. He was concerned that they would provide the reader a spec-
tatorial position from which to experience the horrors of Auschwitz from a distance, a distance that in turn allowed a certain appreciation and pleasure. The
event would disappear behind the image. In an aesthetic bait-and-switch, the representation becomes the image, and the realist novel becomes the Holocaust. But
Lang seems more wary of those representations that seem patently different from
historically or realistically transparent ones. What is forbidden, in Lang's aesthetic
canon, are those works that "focus attention on a subject by distancing it from its
context, at once singling it out and bracketing its singularity" (143–4). In a different kind of bait-and-switch, what is held up by the artist is a work that doesn't
try to stand in for the event or object, but that diverts the reader's attention from
the horror by putting in its place a "universal" version of the event. The novel, or
the poem, or the play can't present the horror because its language adds to the spare
detail of the historical or testimonial account. It presents a *version* of horror, not
the Holocaust or facet of the Holocaust but something else entirely.

What concerns Lang is what Cynthia Ozick calls the "idol." In an essay entitled "Metaphor and Memory" published in *Harper's* magazine in 1986, she argued
that the injunction often heard about literature, that the poem should not *mean*
but *be,* is connected to the Greeks' understanding of the irrational aspect of art.
It's this irrational aspect of art—the way in which the poem itself seems somehow
disparate from the national or social realm—that seems always to be pressed into
service of the rational or moral, with sometimes disastrous results. If there is a
moral lesson to be learned from the example of the Greek oracles or playwrights,
it is that representation either forges a link between the illogical and the logical—
between the play that seems to function on its own and the moral realm in which
lessons can be learned and lives lived—or it indicates that any link between art and
life is doomed to fail. Art is either purely didactic or purely useless.

This view of art is "idolatrous." In terms of Holocaust representations, it survives in the argument over how fictions of the Holocaust (narratives, poems,
plays, movies) may or may not be created. They must function purely as cau-
tionary tales whose lessons must be learned through careful observation of the
form and the content of the work or by following the traditional recipes for their
interpretation; or they are idols, works that stand on their own, are historically
or morally unconnected to the event, and may serve as a way to begin understanding the event but are evocative rather than representative.

There's another way to see the stakes, however. Metaphor connects aesthetics—
the illogical or chaotic element of history; that which happens in spite of our inability to make sense of it—to history. It connects, in other words, what we take
as experience and that which is apparently outside experience. For Ozick,
metaphor had its birth in the Jewish world, in the injunction to treat the stranger
as one would wish to be treated. Leviticus (19:4)—"The stranger that sojourns

with you shall be unto you as the homeborn among you, and you shall love him as yourself; because you were strangers in the land of Egypt"—connects poetry and moral precept: the other becomes the same, the stranger becomes the homeborn, "because you were strangers in the land of Egypt." Metaphor forces the unfamiliar to be spoken in terms that we know but in doing so provides the unfamiliar (the impossible) with a moral force. In order for art, but particularly art of the Holocaust, to have a moral function, that art must be understood to work metaphorically. It has to bind together the everyday and the strange. More to the point, it must do so in a way that doesn't try too hard to "get it right"—to be historically accurate, or to be so transparent as to let the reader believe that she knew what it was like to be there—or to present the work as if it were able to stand on its own autonomously.

The *bilderverbot* is an injunction against idolatry in the sense that it rules out of court works that attempt to provide moral lessons or works that attempt to void themselves of any connection to history or to morality whatsoever, but instead attempt to "be." In terms of literature of the Holocaust, it cautions against a story or novel that stands on its own: that has its own beauty, or its own internal coherence, or that creates an effect that doesn't depend on its connection to the suffering of the victims or the culpability of the perpetrators; that can be judged as a work independent of its historical, or moral, claims. When the event of the Holocaust is put into a category of its own, it is elevated to the status of the divine, and this is precisely what the second commandment prohibits. We violate the *bilderverbot* by making an idol of the event. But to understand the event of the Holocaust as demanding representation that is at once moral and aesthetically coherent—as demanding, essentially, the impossible—is, according to Ozick, to take the demands of representation seriously.

The injunction to represent the event is inevitably bound by historical circumstance, and what we'll see in this chapter and those that follow is that those circumstances—that vary radically from region to region, and from historical period to historical period—bind writers as much as (if not more than) their talents and their own assumptions about what can and cannot be represented. In addition, the generations in which the writers are born also make a difference as to how much, or how little, each is able to say about "the Holocaust" as they tell their stories, invent their characters, and follow them through imagined histories. In Israel, for instance, the Holocaust and its aftermath is inevitably bound to the historical circumstances of the withdrawal of the British from Mandatory Palestine and the war for independence in 1948. The real of the Holocaust was early on bound to the imaginary of the state, not quite a political reality immediately after 1948 so much as a promissory note for things to come. It is that connection between the current political reality and the past destruction that weighs, sometimes quite heavily (as responsibility or guilt) on writers as diverse as Aharon

Appelfeld and Shulamit Hareven. The problem of attempting to understand the role of the Holocaust for both Israeli and for Jewish national and cultural identity also weighs heavily on these writers.

In Europe, by contrast, and particularly in Germany and Poland, the Holocaust sometimes seems to exert a pressure on writers after the event more as an absence than as a presence. It goes without saying that it was the Germans, in cooperation with anti-Semites and nationalists of central and western Europe, who were responsible for the conflagration; the fact of the Holocaust sometimes finds its way into the narratives and poems of those like Bernhard Schlink as a kind of totem. The ground on which the war was fought in Europe, particularly that between the Rhine river in the west and the Bug river in the east, is a reminder everyday to those who live there now of the atrocities that were committed. The stories that are contrived to explain the atrocities and their effects on those who make their homes on that ground must deal with what no longer exists there—the camps, the barracks, the actions of soldiers and citizens, Jews—but which exerts a pressure on memory nonetheless. Many political changes have taken place since the war: the division of the continent and of the nation of Germany; the parallel but very different development of the communist east and the capitalist west, with its different treatment of the legacy of "fascism"; the reunification of the continent, and the country, and its cultural and economic aftereffects. Each one carries traces of the abbreviated Thousand-Year Reich, and these traces find their way into the representations that have been written since.

Much of the work that has come out of North America, and the United States in particular, deals with what Marianne Hirsch has called "post-memory." Many writers, particularly Jewish writers, either were not alive during the time of the Holocaust (though in some cases their parents were), or were alive but lived through the events at a distance through radio or the newspapers. Their "memories" of the Holocaust are not properly their own. Their representations of the event, according to Geoffrey Hartman and others who study post-memory, contain evidence of what might be called memory envy, a compulsion to create representations of the event that "make up for" their absence. This is, of course, certainly not true of all American writers: no one would accuse Cynthia Ozick or Lore Segal of wishing to have authentic memories of the horrors of Auschwitz. Nonetheless, America resides at some distance—both geographically and culturally—from the event, and that distance has allowed some writers from the United States to write with a great deal of aesthetic freedom, and with a great deal of collective "survivor's guilt" over having escaped unharmed. The United States, like Israel, is a refuge for many of those who escaped the Holocaust, and though it was a promising refuge, it also came with a price: silence. Many writers from the United States and Canada have had to imagine the circumstances their parents refuse to talk about, resulting in narratives that are sometimes surreal, sometimes inaccurate, and oftentimes anguishing in their inability to make sense of an event that causes so much pain as well as so little discussion.

REALIST FICTION

For decades after the war, those who had experienced the privations of the camps and of exile firsthand often remained silent in the face of incredulity on the part of those who, for one reason or another, weren't interested in stories of what happened. Those who did write immediately afterward often wrote, as Primo Levi has said, "as an interior liberation" (*Survival in Auschwitz* 9), as a way to obey the urgent and sometimes violent impulse to purge the experience. As a result, there exists a body of literature—which includes Levi's *Survival in Auschwitz,* the earliest French- and Yiddish-language drafts of Elie Wiesel's *Night,* and some of the fiction described below—that recounts the events of the Holocaust in excruciating and realistic detail. It is as if, by staring down the Holocaust they would win a victory over it. That victory, such as it was, sometimes comes at a price: Jean Amery, whose *At the Mind's Limits* chronicles and meditates on the torture he underwent in concentration camps as a political prisoner, committed suicide in 1978; Primo Levi, according to biographers and friends, committed suicide in 1987 after the publication of *The Drowned and the Saved;* Tadeusz Borowski, who was a political prisoner in Auschwitz, also killed himself after writing the brilliant collection of stories entitled *This Way for the Gas, Ladies and Gentlemen.* The list goes on, a list that includes authors who fought depression and other mental illness, and who fought to publish work that few people, early on anyway, wanted to publish. These works are detailed and to a certain extent "documentary." Their language obeys the tropes of realism and of history, attempting even through the use of fictional narrators and characters to tell what happened and, as Levi puts it, "to furnish a documentation for a quiet study of certain aspects of the human mind" (9).

Borowski

Tadeusz Borowski was twenty-two years old when he was arrested in Warsaw in the late winter of 1943 for his part in publishing an anti-Nazi underground newspaper. He was eventually sent to Auschwitz, where he worked at various "jobs." After the war, he continued to write fiction, poetry, and for newspapers. When, in 1951, Borowski died by suicide (he turned on a gas valve in his apartment and waited), it was a surprise to those who knew him; he was seen as a bright light in Polish literary circles.

   A posthumously published five-volume edition of his collected works includes a small group of stories, titled *This Way for the Gas, Ladies and Gentlemen.* Those stories provide a very good example of the realist impulse in fiction that followed immediately on the heels of the war. Its first story, from which the collection takes its name, begins innocuously: "A cheerful little station, very much like any other provincial railway stop: a small square framed by tall chestnuts and paved with yellow gravel. Not far off, beside the road, squats a tiny wooden shed, uglier and more flimsy than the ugliest and flimsiest railway shack" (33). But as the passage continues, the reader finds that she is in a different place than she'd presumed:

> Farther along lie stacks of old rails, heaps of wooden beams, barracks parts, bricks, paving stones. This is where they load freight for Birkenau: supplies for the construction of the camp, and people for the gas chambers. Trucks drive around, load up lumber, cement, people—a regular daily routine. (33–4)

Slowly the accumulation of details begins to add up—there is a series of equivalents here. Jay Cantor, a writer on many topics including the Holocaust, says that the accumulation of detail presents impossible equivalents (freight = humans = death; railway station = unloading station for the gas chamber = death) and destroys the reader's sense of the commonplace. "This is like that: metaphor, the trope which gives value, that makes a world, here destroys it by yoking our present with the kingdom of death" (Cantor 182). For Lawrence Langer, Borowski presented the *univers concentrationnaire* quite perfectly, whereby the reader is lulled into believing, if only for an instant, that there is in fact a ring of fire surrounding the events described, but that in that instant it was possible for him to be transported into it.

As if trying to obey Ozick's demand that one find a language between the known and the unknown, Borowski compares what he knows to the absurd without letting it seem so. As Andrej Wirth said once of Borowski, he felt as if he had no choice: "who in the world will believe a writer using an unknown language? It's like trying to persuade trees or stones" (Wirth 52). Borowski occasionally breaks the pattern as if to ensure that the reader doesn't mistake the work for the thing itself. In "This Way for the Gas," for example, Tadek (Borowski's narrator) is unable to rest between unloading one trainload of Jewish victims at Auschwitz and another, they're rolling in so quickly. Train after train, victim after victim. But then:

> Here is a woman—she walks quickly, but tries to appear calm. A small child with a cherub's face runs after her and, unable to keep up, stretches out his little arms and cries:
> "Mama! Mama!"
> "Pick up your child, woman!"

"It's not mine, sir, not mine!" she shouts hysterically and runs on cover-
ing her face with her hands. (43)

A Russian prisoner, disgusted, hits her, knocks her down, picks her up with one
hand, throws her onto the truck taking the unloaded Jews to the gas, and throws
the child into the truck at her feet. The description ends this way:

> From under a pile of rags [Andrej, the Russian] pulls out a canteen, un-
> screws the cork, takes a few deep swallows, passes it to me. The strong vodka
> burns my throat. My head swims, my legs are shaky, again I feel like throw-
> ing up. (43)

This passage, and others like it, seems almost to remind that the self-enclosed
world, the *univers concentrationnaire,* with what passes for its own perverse logic,
cannot be circumscribed by logic at all. There's something at the limits of description that also limits our ability to impose order upon these or other circumstances.

Nomberg-Przytyk

Other fiction writers who survived the war engaged in a strategy similar to that
used by Borowski: regardless of the "fictionality" of the stories, they look directly
into the horror of the events, and unflinchingly use a language that is both the
most mundane of language and that comprises the most horrifying of images. Sara
Nomberg-Przytyk was originally from Poland. Because she came from a Hasidic
Jewish background, she was ensnared in the net of the Final Solution and was deported from the Bialystok ghetto and eventually brought to Auschwitz. Nomberg-
Przytyk's fiction took nearly twenty years to see print, and even now a good part
of it remains untranslated into English. (*The Pillars of Samson* was published in
Polish in 1966, before she emigrated to Israel in 1968.)

Her work would not be known in English at all had it not been for the chance
discovery of the manuscript of *Auschwitz: True Tales from a Grotesque Land* in the
Yad Vashem archives. The stories are detailed vignettes of everyday life in the
camp and, in some cases, life just before concentration. Like Borowski's stories,
the matter-of-factness of the descriptions works repetitively. It provides images of
things unimaginable yet in language reminiscent of descriptions of other, far
more mundane things. In one story, the narrator Orli tells of "friendly get-
togethers" in the camp among the young women who occasionally organized
themselves in order to avoid the destruction all around them. Nomberg-Przytyk
describes briefly the change that overcame the story's narrator, who was happy to
laugh and joke when she had the chance, but who earlier had not been able to
avoid the corpses, the pain, and the mud. Looking outside from the infirmary,
where this particular gathering was taking place, we have this description:

>Now the unloading of the people was starting again, but quietly, without the usual screaming. Nude men came out, so skinny that it was difficult to believe that those people were moving on their own power. . . .
>
>"Those are Russian prisoners," Orli whispered. "They were working someplace, and now, since they are incapable of working any more, they are being sent to the gas chambers." . . .
>
>"Let's not tell the girls anything. Let's not spoil their fun," Orli said quietly. We did not return to the infirmary. To sing and joke now was beyond our strength. After all, you could not get used to everything.

It is the tension between the descriptions of what could only be called joy in the gathering in the infirmary that precedes this description, and the efficiency with which the Russian prisoners and their fate is written here, that makes the story, as most of Nomberg-Przytyk's narratives, so brutally clear.

"The Verdict," a story of several pages, is the reported speech of a Mrs. Helena, who reports the deaths of over 150 young women at the hands of Dr. Mengele, which she witnessed. The details of the story, and the moral quandary that is presented in its last lines—" 'I still don't know whether we should have told the women about the death that was waiting for them. What do you think?'"—makes a reader wonder: to what purpose was this incident fictionalized? Nomberg-Przytyk's stories seem to suggest—ironically—that the only way to obey the *bilderverbot* is to circumvent it entirely through the genre of fiction. The stories Borowski and Nomberg-Przytyk tell are horrifyingly like the stories told by Levi, Wiesel, Abraham Lewin, and others who were there on the spot and who used the language of history and of testimony to describe what they saw. They act as firsthand witnesses to, as far as they were able, directly represent the event. And yet the work of Levi and Wiesel present, as one could argue, odd test cases. They don't present events that are imaginative, but that take place against the backdrop of actual events and in language that mimics the historical and testimonial. Instead these authors present events that occurred, but they use the genre, and mimick the language, of fiction.

Delbo and Eliach

Charlotte Delbo, a Frenchwoman imprisoned in 1942 for her husband's (and her own) activity in the resistance, wrote a beautiful collection of vignettes and episodes that realistically depict her experiences in Auschwitz and its aftermath. Like Borowski and Nomberg-Przytyk, her prose is clearly intended to convey a sense of the terror felt by inmates in the camps and the filth of the barracks, yet its stylized language of figure, of metaphor in Ozick's terms, makes the reader wonder just where the line is between the actual and the imaginary. *Auschwitz*

and After, Delbo's trilogy, continually causes grief for literary critics, who can't decide whether to place it into the category of fiction, since its language is highly
evocative and figurally rich, or of autobiography, since it's clear that the events
depicted, however richly, are Delbo's own. Sue Vice, who in *Holocaust Fiction*
pushes against the lines that divide these categories, suggests that Delbo is aware—
as, I would add, are Borowski and Nomberg-Przytyk—of the line that separates
"truth" from "accuracy" (191 n. 75), a distinction that might be usefully connected to the question of authenticity (as in, is authenticity more closely linked
to truth or to accuracy?). These authors' control over their medium allows them
to create patterns of language that produce effects akin to the effect of witnessing events that are out of the ordinary. It is worth asking: does their approach to
the *bilderverbot* prevent them from succumbing to the "sin" of idolatry by allowing them to report "the truth" at the expense of "what happened"? Are they
able to manage the difficult task of writing so that the reader sees the tension between the two categories?

Yaffa Eliach's *Hasidic Tales From the Holocaust* is an interesting and problematic case. James Young has made clear that the collection of nearly ninety tales collected from Holocaust survivors between 1974 and 1981 in nearly all the
languages of central European Jewish life is not a collection but the creation of a
mystical religious understanding of the Holocaust built through the collaboration
of the storytellers and Eliach and her Brooklyn College students. But as Alan
Rosen points out, it is written in English, when the tales themselves were told in
Yiddish, Hebrew, German, Polish, Russian, and other languages. The muted multilingualism of the book throws into relief the difficulty of reducing the events of
the Holocaust—through the prism of a single language, let alone from the perspective of a monolithic religious understanding—into a manageable image.
Rosen cites the final tale in Eliach's collection, "God Does Not Live Here Anymore," to make the point that the question of language is also a question of appropriateness. It's Tisha B'av, the day mourning for the destruction of the Temples
in Jerusalem, and Miles Lerman is with a contingent from the United States
Holocaust Memorial Commission visiting Kracow; during the ceremony, Lerman—in English—interrupts and proposed to put God on trial for the destruction rendered during the Holocaust. Taking up the rhythm from the book of
Lamentations—"how is it possible"—he goes on, with none of the locals from
Kracow able to understand. After he is finished, a Pole asks Eliach, who was also
on the Commission, "What did your American friend say in the language of dollars?" (Eliach 213). For Rosen, this episode makes clear just how difficult it is to
find a language to describe what in historical terms is barely imaginable. The
Pole who leans over to Eliach seems to point her attention to a case of idolatry—
how, after all, can the Holocaust be understood by an American, in English, on
the ground, in Poland, on which the atrocity against European Jews took place?

In fact, it may be that Eliach's "translation" of these tales is the most appropriate approach to the *bilderverbot:* rather than trying to replicate the language of the events, told from the perspective of those who were there, Eliach chose instead to retain the details of the story, but to refract them through the prism of a language that doesn't properly "belong" to the Holocaust at all.

ANTIREALIST FICTION

Berel Lang reports that he once heard Aharon Appelfeld, responding to a question about the "obliqueness" of his novels' representations of the Holocaust, say that "one does not look directly at the sun." Looking directly at the sun—the Holocaust itself—blinds the writer and the reader alike. Lawrence Langer wrote that Appelfeld has a way of writing about before, and about after, but not during: this is forbidden territory. For him as for a number of other Israeli writers who emigrated to Palestine (later Israel) after the war, the Holocaust's effect upon the *writer* registers as absence, but one that has a profound effect upon the present.

Appelfeld

Appelfeld was born in northern Romania in 1932, and when he was eight he was separated from his parents during the German push toward Russia. His mother was killed immediately; his father was sent to a forced-labor camp. Appelfeld himself was sent to a camp, but he escaped and spent the next three years hiding in forests before he was found by Soviet army troops and began work as a cook's helper. After the war, he spent time in a DP camp in Italy before leaving for Palestine, through funding of a Jewish aid society, in 1946. He discovered his father, alive and living in Israel, fourteen years later.

Appelfeld writes exclusively in Hebrew, his adopted language, so it was not until *Badenheim 1939* was translated into English in 1980 that he became well known in the United States and Britain. That novel depicts a collection of characters, most of them Jewish, whose vacation in a German spa town of Badenheim becomes forced confinement. They are prevented from returning home, and their actions are eventually restricted until, at the end of the novel, they are required to be transported by train to an unknown destination in the east. The novel won acclaim in part because of its allusive quality. It did not forecast the fate of the characters directly. Instead, Appelfeld used language that had little, if anything, to do with the Holocaust. He sprinkles the narrative with words or phrases used by characters in complete innocence but that to our ears ring in a sinister and deadly way. Though the characters in that novel have a sense of what might become of them, their attention is diverted by the details of everyday life, a life that becomes increasingly shabbier and more limited as the end of the novel—and the moment of deportation—approaches.

To the Land of the Cattails, published in English six years after *Badenheim,* is similar to the earlier novel in its use of language and its avoidance of the horrors normally associated with the Holocaust. The book's principal characters—Toni, a poorly educated single mother originally from a small town on the Czech–Hungarian border who has lived most of her life in Vienna, and her son Rudi, well educated and urban—travel by carriage from the relative safety of Vienna around 1938 toward the east. They're going "back home" but also directly into the area that would be emptied of its Jewish population by the *einsatzgruppen* three years later. Throughout the journey east, only partially aware of instances of anti-Semitism and the hardships of travel, Toni tries to impart lessons to her son about her dimly remembered connection to Judaism, and her reasons (having to do with what she believes more than what she actually knows) for returning home. Speaking of a Ruthenian woman's enthusiasm for Jews, Toni explains: "the Jews mixed them up a little, spoiled them a little, but in a year or two they will forget the Jews" (17).

Given the historical context of central and eastern Europe in the years between 1938 and 1941, language like the passage I've just cited both avoids and doesn't avoid the Holocaust. As Berel Lang has written, it "demand[s] that the reader provide a supporting ground and literary frame of fact and expression—detailing the face and aura of horror—that more usually . . . the writer himself would accept responsibility for enacting" (*Act and Idea* 106). The historical reality of what would occur means that the Jews were not "forgotten" but were murdered. The reader knows that the near-total annihilation of the Jews will lead to their culture being forgotten. But the historical circumstances are never present in Appelfeld's novel. They are always evoked, supplied by the reader. Appelfeld is a realist, in the sense that he depicts a world whose detail is utterly imaginable; but it is antihistorical in the sense that the "Appelfeld world" (as the critic Alan Mintz calls it) seems at times hermetically sealed off from the events the reader knows full well are going to occur.

Alan Mintz has written of Aharon Appelfeld that his struggle—and the reason for avoiding a direct representation of the Holocaust—was to find a language that will render the *univers concentrationnaire* without destroying the writer. Appelfeld is "so confident of [his] reader's familiarity with descriptions of Nazi bestialities that [he] never needs to mention them at all in order to have their specter loom in the interstices of every scene and dialogue" (206). His strategy instead, suggests Michael Andre Bernstein, is to focus on the characters' "limited selfawareness" of the catastrophe going on around them, a catastrophe about which his readers are fully aware, and that myopic focus itself becomes an object of horror.

ISRAELI FICTION

A number of Israeli writers have attempted to take account of the Holocaust not by focusing attention on its horrors but by discerning its imaginative or memorial effects. (A very good anthology, *Facing the Holocaust,* edited by Gila Ramras-Rauch and Joseph Michman-Melkman, includes a dozen stories by some of Israel's best writers.) Israelis have had to forge a national (and Jewish) identity in the wake of the events of the Holocaust, and one theme through which they do so is that of "return," whereby those whose communities have been destroyed in Europe "come home" to Palestine/Israel after the war. It is an odd sort of homecoming—it is, after all, not a geographical return—that relies on tropes of redemption rather than actual, physical reoccupation of place or space. Yehuda Amichai's first novel, *Not of This Time, Not of This Place,* contrives two narratives—one in which the protagonist remains in Israel, one in which he returns to his childhood home in Germany—that become constantly intertwined. It's as if Amichai suggests that to return is impossible since to do so requires a point of origin, which is, for Israelis anyway, also not quite home. Shulamith Hareven—who was born in Palestine and lived there during the war—writes in "Twilight" of what amounts to the horror of return. The narrator dreams—though readers only realize it's a dream at the end of the story—that she has returned to the city of her birth, though it looks oddly unfamiliar to her. She makes her way to the opera house, where—at the intermission of the performance—she and all the others in attendance are rounded up, shoved into trucks, and taken away. Finding that the entire series of events repeats itself night after night, she escapes with a man who becomes her husband and with whom she has a child who grows up within a few days and goes to the opera house only to be caught in the repeating tragedy. In the closing paragraphs of the story, the narrator awakes, in her home in Jerusalem, surrounded by the voices of her children and her husband. When the surreal dream of horror and the return come to an end, what takes its place is an awakening in the present, but it's a present that seems to exert a horror of its own. The story closes with the words, "my heart [was] beating very hard." The reader seems left to wonder whether the events of the past—the city to which the narrator returned in her dream—will, in their absence, have a horrifying effect upon the narrator's present.

Amichai was born in Germany and emigrated to Palestine just before the war. He also seems more concerned with the Holocaust's effects—as an absence—than with its presence in the lives of his characters. His story "The Times My Father Died"—from a wonderful collection of stories entitled *The World is a Room*—is not so much about the Holocaust as it is about the irrational kernel lodged inside our attempts to describe events. Like Appelfeld's novels and Hareven's stories, Amichai's narrative depicts by avoidance the effects of events as they take their toll—in this case—on the narrator's father, who dies by inches through the degradations of anti-Semitism and exile from Germany. "The Times my Father Died" is about a survivor's attempt to find a place in life when, around him, are the effects of the mass murder of millions of Jews. The father is a devout Jew who nevertheless identifies himself as German first; he is forced out of Germany by anti-Semitism, in spite of his service, on behalf of the fatherland, in World War I. His Germanness, and his Judaism, take the form of an abiding humanism, though the degradations he experiences don't alter it much. On his deathbed he tells his son, "There's a cat mewing on the neighbor's roof. Maybe it's shut in and wants to get out." But life itself seems to him like a series of deaths:

> He died when they came to arrest him for throwing into the garbage the Nazi pin I had found. The black uniforms came to our door. The black uniforms broke it down. And the boots tramped in. It was terrible for me to see that my father was no longer able to defend our house and withstand the enemy's onslaught. That was childhood's end. How could they just burst into our house like that, against Father's wishes! . . .
>
> He died when they stationed bullies outside his shop to keep people from buying there because it was a Jewish shop. He died when we left Germany to emigrate to Palestine, and all the years that had been died with him.

The son is left to understand that real death through all the previous, smaller deaths: the events that the son doesn't know except through what he saw of his father. The Holocaust is an absence, one that makes itself felt upon the imagination of the writer, whose refusal to represent the events directly leaves him to write in a language that is both an everyday language of the beauty of the natural world, and of faith, and of hunger, and of degradation.

ANTIHISTORICAL FICTION

Many writers who were witnesses to the Holocaust write either in what could be called a "language of presence" or in a "language of absence." Writers who were not there, or who were born after the event, are at an impasse. Do they write as if they were there, creating a language that replicates the rhythms of eyewitness testimony, thereby (as some might say) breaking the faith with their readers, allowing them to believe that what they are reading is real? Or do they create a language that is eminently fictional, thus risking that their readers will take pleasure in the prose and the event they're attempting to fictionalize (namely, the Holocaust)? This is the risk Michael Andre Bernstein writes about in *Foregone Conclusions:* Does the writer speak for the survivors, and thus risk substituting her voice for theirs, or does she allow the survivors to speak for themselves, risking the silence that comes with reticence, or trauma, or death (42–52)?

Ozick

Cynthia Ozick is among writers who weren't there but who take the Holocaust as their subject. In what is perhaps the most anthologized story of the Holocaust, "The Shawl" fictionalizes the death of a child in a concentration camp. Its companion piece, "Rosa," depicts the child's mother dealing with her child's absence decades later in the United States (the two stories were published together as a novella in 1989). In these stories Ozick creates what could be called a poetics of unspeakability: the reader not only senses the presence of the unspeakable, but sees that unspeakable event (the death of a child witnessed by the child's mother) presented as an absence, decades later as the mother attempts to work through that death in a language that can't make sense of it.

Ozick's story begins by describing the child being carried by her mother, Rosa, in a shawl to an unnamed camp, accompanied by Rosa's niece. The shawl is what gives the child Magda life: she suckles it, and as she does so, she remains silent; it's this silence that keeps the child alive. At one point in the story, Rosa notices that the child is screaming in the yard of the camp, and realizes that the shawl is missing. Finding that her niece has taken the shawl to keep warm, Rosa tears the shawl away and runs toward the child with it. The child, however, has been picked up by a camp guard and thrown into the electrified fence, too late to be saved by Rosa. As the SS guard raises the child on his shoulder and runs toward the fence, "the electric voices began to chatter wildly. 'Maamaa, maaamaaa,' they all hummed together" (9). The poetic language continues—"the steel voices [going] mad in the growling;" Magda "swimming through the air" in "loftiness," "like a butterfly touching a silver vine"—until the child falls: "Magda had fallen from her flight against the electrified fence" (10). The story is less about the event of the Holocaust than it is about the intricacies of its effect. To show this effect, Ozick weaves together contradictions—the horrifying and the poetic—to allow the reader to see something that's otherwise invisible.

It's the invisible effect that Ozick works toward in "Rosa." Set in Miami Beach thirty-five years after the events depicted in "The Shawl," the cast of characters is the same: Rosa has sold her secondhand store in New York and moved south; her niece—now a doctor in the New York suburbs—sends her money and the occasional letter. Magda, long dead, occupies Rosa's thoughts and is the receiver of many letters composed in thought and, in some cases, in reality. Without Magda, and outside of her home in Warsaw, Rosa is a refugee in every sense of the word: she is at a distance from her daughter, from her place of birth, and from her language. She is cut off from everything that comprised her life in Poland before the war, and is ill at ease in the language of both her current home (English) and of her suitor Persky (English as well as Yiddish). The only person with whom she feels comfortable is Magda, and she can only communicate in letters:

> A lock removed from the tongue. Otherwise the tongue is chained to the teeth and the palate. An immersion into the living language [Polish]: all at once this cleanliness, this capacity, this power to make a history, to tell to explain. To retrieve, to reprieve!
>   To lie. ("Rosa" 44)

Even the language with which Rosa is most familiar is a lie since it can't grasp hold of what she wants to say, even to her daughter. She is, like her daughter with the shawl, mute. She tells Persky, the buffoonish senior citizen who tries to flirt with Rosa, that there is "the life before, the life during, and the life after. . . . The life after is now. The life before is our real life, at home where we was born." "And during?" Persky asks. "This was Hitler," she replies. "Before is a dream. After is a joke. Only during stays. And to call it a life is a lie" (58).

There are two voids in the story that Ozick points out to the reader, voids created by the Holocaust. The first is a void of language. The language Rosa uses to communicate to her daughter is a literary Polish she learned from her father and to which she no longer has access in the United States. But it is simply not enough to convey her experience of loss to her niece by phone, or to Persky, who is also from Warsaw but from a very different class and upbringing. The second void is a geographic and temporal one: Rosa's Warsaw is not Persky's Warsaw, her Miami Beach is not her home, and her daughter was killed in Europe while she resides in the United States. Ozick has created, in this pair of stories, a kind of imagined yet impossible world, in which the poetry of literary Polish and the pidgin English of east European Holocaust survivors exists side by side. The story concludes with the words, "Magda was away" (70), though Rosa, too, is away, separate, the victim of a terrible absence. In Ozick's story, the Holocaust is both there and not there, visible in its effects upon her characters—and upon her reader—generations later.

Bellow

It's this strategy of making plain the effect of the Holocaust, without focusing attention upon its horrors, that Saul Bellow has taken in many of his novels. None of Bellow's novels are "about" the Holocaust. Many of them, however, find their characters confronting the historical event of the Holocaust at a geographical remove from it: they are American Jews who either wish to avoid the stigma attached to their Jewishness and to the Holocaust, or who have a tremendous amount of guilt over their own survival. Four of Bellow's novels dwell on the subject of the Holocaust: *Dangling Man* and *The Victim* were both written in the immediate aftermath of the event (published in the 1940s); the title character of *Mr. Sammler's*

Planet (1970) was a Polish Jewish refugee from the Nazis trying to feign British-
ness; and *The Bellarosa Connection* (1989) is about the Broadway producer Billy
Rose's attempts to save Harry Fonstein from the Nazis. More typical, however, is
Humboldt's Gift, an novel whose two principal characters—Citrine and Von Humboldt Fleisher—only make reference to the Holocaust through their troubled
and sometimes neurotic musings about their places in the university. Like Ozick's
fiction, Bellow's allows the history of the Holocaust and its effects to enter through
the back door: the event and its effects make themselves evident to the reader as
absences more than as direct representations.

   There are two ways in which to see *Humboldt's Gift* as usefully indicative of a
fictional approach to the Holocaust. The first is in the characters' attempt to contain the horror through dark comedy. Bellow is a writer who has captured—or,
depending on which critic you read, caricatured—dark Jewish kitsch comedy
well. Citrine's memories of his family, for example, are quite friendly and rich,
while his brother Ulick's are marked by forgetfulness and absence: "Our grandfather was one of ten guys in the Jewish Pale who knew the Babylonian Talmud
by heart. . . . I don't even know what it is" (236). Ulick reproaches his brother at
one point not to talk to the Ukrainian gardener: "He was a concentration camp
guard and still insanely anti-Semitic" (239); Citrine's long-time friend George
Sweibel says admiringly of Citrine's silver Mercedes-Benz, "Murder Jews and
make machines, that's what those Germans really know how to do." (33). The
critic and scholar Elizabeth Bellamy has written that these remarks, and these
memories, offer "a salutary, protective transcendence to history's traumas" (167),
and that Bellow, through his characters, "seeks to contain the horrors of the Holocaust within the parameters of comedic 'bad taste'. . ." (168).

   Second, Von Humboldt Fleisher's downward spiral toward self-destruction
and death takes place against the backdrop of his residence at Princeton University, a university that, in the 1950s, was still gentile and anti-Semitic. His decision to take a one-year teaching appointment at Princeton and to turn down a
year's visiting position at the Berlin Free University indicates not only his ambivalence about his Jewishness, but his concern with the Holocaust. Fleisher tells
Citrine at one point that the two of them will never be accepted at Princeton: here
"you and I are Moe and Joe, a Yid Vaudeville act. We're a joke—Abie Kabibble
and Company. Unthinkable as members of the Princeton community" (120).
The reason Fleisher declined the invitation to go to Berlin is that "'I don't feel quite
ready'. . . . He was afraid that he would be kidnapped by former Nazis" (32). It's
one thing to be an outcast in Princeton; it'd be another entirely to be a Jew in the
midst of the country that tried to eradicate Jews entirely. What Bellow finally
does is to cast the demise of his character against the backdrop of an event that
is never depicted clearly, but which nonetheless is palpably present in the character's greatest fears and most harrowing visions.

David Grossman

What Bellow does realistically, David Grossman does fantastically. Grossman, an Israeli, confronts the Holocaust far more directly than Bellow. But because of his characters' inability to understand it, that historical reality becomes submerged in the literary language of a writer trying to come to terms with tales told to him, and learned by him, both as a child and as an adult. Grossman's novel, *See Under: Love,* begins as Momik, the nine-year-old child of Holocaust survivors, copies the tales told to him by his parents and neighbors into a notebook. As an adult, this writerly obsession with tales of the past and of survivors working through that past becomes a profession. As a child, the character Momik is unable to understand the historical referents for terms such as "over there," or "the beast," or "children of the heart"; this inability becomes refracted through fantasy as the author Shlomo, as an adult, essentially channels the German writer Bruno Schultz and his great-uncle Anshel Wasserman, who was the author of popular children's stories.

In the section of the novel entitled "Bruno," the novelist Bruno Schultz provides a vehicle for the writer Shlomo to imagine himself in the historical circumstances of the Holocaust. He imagines himself escaping from the Drohobycz ghetto and going to the Danzig art gallery to see Edvard Munch's "The Scream." At that point, he goes into the sea to join a shoal of salmon, where he is literally submerged in the surrealism of the tale. Though odd, this section of the novel seems to point to the impossibility of finding a way to write about the destruction in the language of the known. Shlomo, as Schultz, writes that "the Messiah would never come in writing, would never be invoked in a language suffering from elephantiasis. A new grammar and a new calligraphy had first to be invented" (Grossman 89).

The new calligraphy allows Shlomo to "invent" Wasserman, whose children's stories are transformed into fantastic tales told to SS officers each night during his captivity. The writer becomes, essentially, immortal, though this makes his time in the camp a living death. This living death gives way to the creature Kazik, an eternal Jew whose entire life as an inmate in the camp lasts twenty-four hours. Kazik is a new Adam, who engenders a new dictionary that redefines humanity and reality after the Nazi destruction (both of Jewish Europe and of language). As the title of the novel suggests, he reintroduces the entry that had been erased from other Holocaust dictionaries and encyclopedias: "love." Grossman, through the fantasy of the characters and the stark reality of the child trying desperately to decipher his parents' repressed memories of their terror, creates a new grammar and a new calligraphy of the Holocaust.

Poetry and Poetics

It's possible to think of Holocaust poetry as the severest abrogation of the *bilderverbot.* To represent the event in fictional form requires the writer to understand the forms of narrative, forms that history, testimony, and fiction have in common. But poetry's conventions are by definition an estrangement of garden-variety language, a condensation of images, of rhythm, and of figure that in most cases prevent any confusion. Poetry's aim is to provide an image of what could be or what is generally the case, not to provide an image of what is or was. Poetry seems to stand in and substitute itself for the event. But poets have attempted to find a language with which to point to, if not represent, the incoherence of the event. In fact many find it impossible to write poetry about the events without also writing about the difficulty of writing it. Some of the writers discussed here began writing poetry before the Holocaust, and continued to do so afterward; their experiences in the camps, or in hiding, changed the way they saw writing itself. Others did not write before the event and, like Primo Levi, attempted to come to terms with the experiences later on through writing.

Celan

Paul Celan's "Death Fugue" is one of the two most anthologized Holocaust poems. Written in German, though Celan lived most of his life after the war in France, it is an evocation, rather than a representation, of images that fail to pass the historical test. Celan (originally Ancel) was born in the same northern province of Romania as Aharon Appelfeld was, to a Jewish household. His parents spoke German, but he was also exposed to Yiddish through his friends, and to Hebrew through religious education. Confined in the Czernowitz ghetto, he was eventually transported to a forced labor camp, from which he escaped to join the Soviet army. After several years moving around central Europe after the war, he eventually settled in Paris, where he published several volumes of poetry, most of which engage with the problem of the Holocaust's ruinous effects on Europe and on its languages.

The poem is, as its title suggests, a fugue, in which themes and phrases are repeated and combined to form a kind of tapestry of death images. Its first stanza contains all its principal elements:

> Black milk of daybreak we drink it at sundown
> we drink it at noon in the morning we drink it at night
> we drink and we drink it
> we dig a grave in the breezes there one lies unconfined
> A man lives in the house he plays with the serpents he writes
> he writes when dusk falls to Germany your golden hair Margarete
> he writes it and steps out of doors and the stars are flashing he whistles
> his pack out
> he whistles his Jews out in the earth has them dig for a grave
> he commands us strike up for the dance
>   (in Lawrence Langer's *Art from the Ashes,* 601)

The images of confinement, of the golden-haired girl Margarete (later contrasted with the ashen-haired Shulamith, providing an ironic contrast between the German ideal and the Jewish caricature), of serpents and the digging of graves, continue throughout the poem, in a litany. The line that is as famous in English as it is in German—"death is a master from Germany" ("der Tod ist ein Meister aus Deutschland")—also recurs throughout the poem, and provides it with a kind of thematic unity. It is a German master that "calls out" to the Jews to "stroke your strings then as smoke you will rise into the air/ then a grave you will have in the clouds there one lies unconfined." There is a kind of dark, brooding quality to the poem, but there is also a great deal of irony, connecting the confinement of concentration and death with the unconfined moment in which the dead, as smoke, rise through the chimneys of the crematorium.

In fact, one of the qualities of Celan's poetry is that it refuses to represent, but only evokes, the horrifying images that we've come to associate with the Holocaust. A poem like "Alchemical," for example—which takes its title from the mystical "science," popular in the middle ages, that took as its aim the transformation of worthless elements into precious ones—is essentially absent images of the Holocaust, and could be classified as something other than a poem of the Shoah. The repetitive use of the terms "cinders," "charred," and "ash," however, invoke the burning of corpses in the crematoria. It's possible to read it as an attempt to see the Final Solution as a perverse reversal of the alchemical process. The poem's first stanzas reads:

> Silence, cooked like gold, in
> charred
> hands.
> Great, grey
> sisterly shape
> near like all that is lost.
>
> All the names, all those
> names
> burnt with the rest. So much
> Ash to be blessed, so much
> land won
> above
> the weightless, so weightless
> rings
> of souls
>
> Great, grey one. Cinder-less.
>   (Langer, *Art* 609)

It's not clear here whether the ash is being transformed into gold, or whether the gold is being transformed into ash; in fact, the poem seems to suggest the latter, that it is the names, the individuals burned, which have value, and that they are being transformed into ash. On the principle of alchemy, it is the element being transformed that has the least value; on this reading, it is silence, ash, and the death of the millions upon millions, that has been rendered valuable. By the end of the poem, in other words, Celan seems to suggest that it is only through a coherence that places God in the position of the "Great, grey one," a God of death and of ash, that such alchemy could make any sense at all. Celan's poems seem to operate on the principle that the stable context of the Holocaust provided by the reader must be overturned through a mixing and matching of the images. The intention is to confound the reader's understanding of how words are connected to reality or—as in "Alchemical"—proposing a horrifying reversal in which what we know of the destruction makes a (perverse) sense.

Sachs

Like Celan, Nelly Sachs's poetry is also highly evocative, and like Celan's it seems at pains to avoid images of destruction. Sachs was born in Germany in 1891, and received an education in music, dance, and literature, among other things. She began writing poetry at an early age, and through her literary work made contact with a Swedish novelist who, in 1940, arranged to have Sachs and her mother emigrate to Sweden, where Sachs spent the rest of her life. It was only after the war that Sachs began writing about the fate of the Jews in Nazi-occupied Europe. (Karen Gershon, who also wrote poetry on behalf of those who suffered, rather than from her own experiences, is the author of poetry and prose collected as *We Came as Children*. It is a far more detailed depiction of the destruction itself, though its poetry bears some stylistic similarities to Sachs's.) Some critics have pointed to Sachs's faith in words: it's as if she was attempting, in her poetry, to salvage some sense of meaning from a language that had been ruined by the calamity of the war and of the Shoah. Whereas Celan did not foreground the discursive problem inherent in writing in a world after Auschwitz, Sachs—in several of her poems—does.

In Sachs's poem, "If I Only Knew," the first-person "I" wonders what a victim saw just before death. It begins, "If I only knew/On what your last look rested./Was it a stone that had drunk/So many last looks that they fell/Blindly upon its blindness?" and continues through three stanzas much like the first. There is an evocation of great sadness here, but there is also a kind of faith in *things,* a faith in objects like the stone in this stanza, or the earth that fills a shoe in the second, or a road in the third, or a belt buckle in the fourth (Langer, *Art* 642). Sachs builds images not of death and destruction, but the moment prior to that death, in which there is a firm link between the world and the individual. In the last stanza, things change: "Or did this earth,/Which lets no one depart unloved,/Send you a bird-sign through the air,/Reminding your soul that it quivered/In the torment of its burnt body?" Here, in much more explicit form, is an image that the reader knows perhaps too well: the burnt corpse. There is, in addition to the horrifying image, a glimpse of something else: the possibility of love. But that love is only available through the suffering, the "bird's" quivering—the sign of love—visible only in the "torment of [the] burnt body." The question to ask here is whether the last stanza, in its simultaneous evocation of both suffering and of love, undermines the previous four stanzas, with their establishment of a link between the world and the living, or whether it provides a sense of hope—through love—that reinforces that link.

Pagis and Glatstein

If Celan's and Sachs's poetry is primarily evocative, the poetry of Dan Pagis and Jacob Glatstein provides a stark contrast. Taken together, these four poets (Celan and Sachs on the one hand, Pagis and Glatstein on the other) reveal the range of possibilities in poetry of the Holocaust. Pagis and Glatstein in particular seem not to hold out the kind of hopeful (or redemptive) vision provided by Celan and Sachs, and their language reveals glimpses of the profound sadness and anger that lingers in some survivors (and some who were born generations after the events). Like Celan and Appelfeld, Pagis was born in the Bukovina region of Romania; his father emigrated to Palestine when he was four and his mother died shortly thereafter, leaving him to be raised by grandparents. During the war, he was interned in concentration camps in the Transnistria region; afterward he emigrated to Palestine to join his father. He began writing poetry nearly upon his arrival in Palestine, mainly in Hebrew, and became an accomplished poet and scholar of Hebrew literature. What marks Pagis's poetry, like Sachs's, is its concentration of image; like Sachs it provides words and phrases that are linked, in the mind of the reader, with the destruction, though without being primarily representational. His most famous poem is "Written in Pencil in a Sealed Railway-Car," which reads in its entirety:

> here in this carload
> i am eve
> with abel my son
> if you see my other son
> cain son of man
> tell him that i
>   (Langer, *Art* 588)

The poem operates on many levels. At its most obvious, it is meant to represent the pleading of a mother, trapped inside a transport, separated from one of her sons; at another, Biblical level, it evokes a community of humankind riven with violence in spite of its kinship. It is Abel inside the railway car, the brother who was slain by Cain; it would be easy to put Abel in the place of the Jew, and Cain in the place of the Nazi, who also—by dint of his status as the "son of man"—might stand in for bystanders or those who commit murder or atrocity regardless of religious or national affiliation.

But it's also hard to miss the fact that this poem doesn't stray far from the natural rhythms of speech. "Written in Pencil" sounds as if it was written (with the sole exception of the phrase "son of man") by someone in haste. And so the reader, caught up in the language of pleading that might not be at too distant a remove from the pleading that a mother trapped inside a railway car might do, stops short at the incomplete sentence that ends the poem. "[T]ell him that [I]" . . . what? The obvious possibilities are "love him" or "forgive him" or "am here." But the possibilities are cut short by the ending of the line, and the reader is left wondering not only what could possibly follow the first-person pronoun but what stopped the writer from continuing. The answer to that question—debarkation from the train to a camp, or death—is what makes the poem so stark: while it doesn't represent these possibilities, it presents for the reader the *effect* of those possibilities (death or arrival at a camp where death was all but certain) through its abrupt conclusion.

That abruptness—the effect of what is represented rather than its image—is what characterizes Pagis's other poems. In a poem entitled "Testimony," (Langer, *Art* 590) the poet again replicates the language of testimony as if to draw the reader in. It begins *in medias res,* as if the speaker had been interrupted: "No no: they definitely were/human beings: uniforms, boots,/How to explain? They were created in the image." But speaking of himself, rather than (apparently) his tormentors, he goes on: "I was a shade./A different creator made me." In the move from the first to this second stanza, we move from the language of testimony to the language of poetry almost unnoticed. In his attempt to say precisely what it was about the Nazis that was so beastly, and what it was about himself that distinguished him from them, Pagis's speaker has to resort to the rhythms of everyday language—like "if you see my other son"—but uses terms that are, to the reader, uncomfortable in such rhythms. The poem concludes even more uncomfortably, in a reversal like Celan's in "Alchemical":

> And he in his mercy left nothing of me that would die.
> And I fled to him, floated up weightless, blue,
> forgiving—I would even say: apologizing—
> smoke to omnipotent smoke
> that has no face or image.
>   (590)

The nonhuman in Nazi racial ideology—the Jewish corpse burned and floating upward as smoke—is distinct from the cruelly human ("uniforms, boots"), and

through its connection with God with no face or image, superior. But this is a horrifying reversal: the victim is created differently, and by a different creator, from
the human, and this creator is the creator of smoke, destruction, and the non- or
in-human. By the last stanza, in other words, the reader is left wondering just what
sort of theology might see the corpse as having divine origin, and why the Jew
killed by the Nazi would be forced to apologize (and just what, one would ask,
he should apologize *for*).

Of the many poets who have written on subjects related to the Holocaust, it is
perhaps Jacob Glatstein whose anger and sadness at the events is most clearly visible in individual poems. Glatstein was a poet before the war years; born in Poland,
he emigrated to the United States in 1914 and began writing stories in Yiddish almost upon his arrival. He joined a group of poets whose primary objective was to
write "from the self," and eventually began work as a journalist, during which time
he continued to write poetry, poetry that eventually won him great acclaim. What's
obvious in the poems is Glatstein's thorough immerson in Jewish culture, religious
ideas, and Yiddish language, along with his ambivalence toward those themes.

"Good Night World," dated 1938, is something like an elegy on the theme of
Jewish culture, one whose last line reads "I kiss you, tangled strands of Jewish
life./Within me weeps the joy of coming home" (Langer, *Art* 655). These tears
may be of joy, but they also may well be bitter ones, since the Jewish world in the
poem is marked by "kerose, tallowed shadows" from the synagogue, "eternal October," the days of repentance (between Rosh Hashana and Yom Kippur) on the
Jewish calendar, "warped streets and hunchbacked lanters,/my worn-out pages of
the Prophets," and the Talmud; it is also marked by the "hate-filled Pole;/Jew-
killers" and "flabby democracies." The last stanza of the poem is hopeful, but by
1938, the situation of Jews in Europe had become fairly clear even to someone
like Glatstein who was a visitor rather than a resident.

The sadness and anger are compressed in "Smoke" and especially "Cloud-
Jew." "Smoke", in its entirety, reads as follows:

> Through crematorium chimneys
> a Jew curls toward the God of his fathers.
> As soon as the smoke is gone,
> upward cluster his wife and son.
>
> Upward, toward the heavens,
> sacred smoke weeps, yearns.
> God—where You are—
> we all disappear.
>   (660)

The mix of the horror of immolation and the return to God is almost reminiscent of some of the Biblical sacrifices, described in Deuteronomy and Leviticus,

in which offerings are made by fire. It is a perverse, though oddly accurate, rendering of the term "Holocaust," though that term would not come into common usage until the 1960s.

"Cloud-Jew" repeats the theme in "Smoke:" while there is no necessary connection between the cloud of smoke in the one poem and the "cloud" in the second, there is nonetheless an ethereal, deathly implication in the latter poem. "The cloud-Jew writes in Yiddish letters/on an alien sky./I want to read them,/interpret them, explain them./They run like tears,/threads of tears,/before I can make out their meanings." Once again, written into the poem is the difficulty of interpretation and of writing. It's as if what the writer, in the person of the first-person "I" in the poem, has a hard time making out the significance of the destruction. There is "An overwhelming, burning, ancient sadness—/pages falling from a village ledger—/sinks deep in my mind." Eventually, "The letters start to merge" and "I read the scroll of fire." It reads:

> "Even before my body
> was torn apart limb by limb,
> I was no longer a special seed,
> only a flicker of Jewish sanctity.
> That's how you should; render me in your poem,
> you—son of the eternal cloud-Jew."
>   (661)

Is this depiction—an image commanded by another image, writing commanded by writing—of the Holocaust, of the death of Jewish culture, and of writing itself, self-contained and self-sufficient, an instance of abrogating the *bilderverbot?* Is Glatstein's poem—like Celan's, or Sachs's, or Pagis's—an instance of idolatry? One provisional answer might be that such poems obey the commandment so long as they are not confused—either the image they create, or the effect that they have upon readers—with the event, and the event's effect on its witnesses. This is not the Holocaust, this poem is not the event, these images and these words are not the same as the things they depict. Soon enough, within the next twenty years certainly, those who were there on the spot will be gone, and the only medium of representation available to us who weren't there—either because we were too young to have lived through World War II, or because we were separated from them by the good fortune of geography—is by "fictional" or imaginative means, rather than by historical ones. The question, then, of the criteria by which such works can be said to be "authentic" becomes even more pressing.

CHAPTER 10

Picturing Atrocity

If the primary purpose of visual media—drama, film, and photography—is to make the viewer see an object or event, how is this purpose complicated by the Holocaust? Just what is it that the viewer ought to see? Should the viewer act as a witness, and if so, witness to what? In the case of those dramatists and artists who were themselves witnesses and who were there on the spot, how does the artist allow the viewer to see what happened without completely repulsing the viewer? In the case of the artist who wasn't there, the problem is compounded because that firsthand experience must be recast from someone else's memory—the historians', the witnesses', the criminals'—and by the fact that the artist must always face the problem of authenticity. How, in other words, does he provide a picture of what happened, or what might have happened, that is both true to the actual events but also imaginatively full and consistent with the artist's medium? A medium that replicates atrocities—film and photography are meant to provide a picture of what lies before the lens, and the theater and the visual arts, though using different media, are meant to give the viewer a visual representation of something more or less real—risks making the viewer a passive receiver of the horror, or risks giving shape to the event that makes it palatable for that viewer.

Cynthia Ozick wrote an essay in a 1997 issue of the *New Yorker Magazine* that provides a frame for the problem of the visual arts. In "Who Owns Anne Frank?" she complains that in the years since Miep Gies found Anne's diary in Amsterdam, those who've come into contact with it have taken its vision of the girl's two years in hiding and bent it out of recognizable shape. It began, Ozick writes, with Otto Frank's decision to excise passages from the diary before its publication, and has culminated most recently with a Broadway musical production based on the diary. Since Anne stopped writing in her diary in early August 1944, what she saw has been utterly transformed. What secondhand witnesses see when they view the play, or go to the musical, or see the movie, is very different (in Ozick's terms, a "bowdlerization") from what Anne saw, experienced, and wrote about. Ozick concludes her essay by implying that it would have been better for Gies to burn the diary than to have it become so misshapen over the last sixty years.

While it's easy to sympathize with Ozick's complaint, what she may fail to realize is that any act of witnessing is transformed once it is told as a testimony or reproduced as an image. The question isn't whether what the witness sees will be transformed but *how* it will, or should, be transformed. In dramatic reproductions, for example, what the viewer sees is constrained by the stage, by the physical presence of actors (one actor can play only one character at a time), and by time (what the audience can comfortably sit through). The playwright must take what she sees— either the vision that drives the play or the text that forms its core—and manipulate the stage, the actors, and their words and actions so that the audience sees what the playwright has seen. The audience of a play and its actors are both co-present in the space of the theater. They co-produce the act of witness, since the actors are an immediate presence in the lives of the audience. Sometimes the playwright is most effective when he directly affects the members of his audience *not* through what they see but through what the actors *do* to and through their audience.

Sometimes this works through realism, by replicating (in the case of the Holocaust) the squalor of the camps directly or indirectly, given the constraints of the stage or screen. Sometimes this works through abstraction or surrealism, whereby what appears on stage and what is represented appear starkly divergent, forcing the audience to draw the (sometimes uncomfortable) connection by themselves. In the case of Anne Frank's diary, Ozick complains less that the diary has been inevitably transformed and more that it has been transformed badly. Playwrights and film producers have failed to manipulate the medium of the stage and screen in such a way as to help the members of the audience see—or to be affected in such a way that they believe that they have seen—what Anne saw.

In film and photograph, the problem is no different: the question is how the director, the actor, and the photographer produce an image so that its viewers may not see what the witness saw, but so that the effect on them, when they see the image, can be likened to the effect upon the witness. This question of "how" is a question of method: *how* does the playwright, or the producer, or the actor, or the photographer, or the collage artist, produce a composition so that its effect might be likened to the effect of the event that forms the object of the representation? In this chapter, representative examples of plays, films, and visual art of the Holocaust may help answer this question: how do these media produce in their viewers what might be called an act of secondhand witnessing?

DRAMA

In 1980, Susan Sontag wrote, "To simulate atrocities convincingly is to risk making the audience passive, reinforcing witless stereotypes, confirming distance, and creating meretricious fascination. . . . Like its simulation as fiction, the display of atrocity in the form of photographic evidence" and, I would add, film and drama "risks being tacitly pornographic" (36). Theatrical and visual representations of the Holocaust involve the problem of looking, and looking always involves a generic problem and a moral one. "How real does one make visual representations" is a question that begs the question of reality: just what is the reality that one wants to see, and how does one go about making that reality visible to its secondhand witnesses? But it is also a moral question, since putting the audience in the position of the spectator to the horrors of the Holocaust is, potentially, to make them complicit in those horrors. This is what Sontag means by pornography. Looking doesn't just mean passively seeing. It also means taking pleasure in the seeing, and so if we take pleasure in seeing the horrors of the Holocaust visually represented, we're not just witnesses. We become bystanders, or worse.

It's this connection of moral and generic problems that occupy some of the most thoughtful critics and theorists of Holocaust drama. The person who has paid the most systematic attention to the intersection of the moral and generic issues confronting the Holocaust playwright is Robert Skloot. He has compiled two anthologies of Holocaust plays, some of which have been only rarely produced in the English-speaking world, and a critical analysis of their dramatic contours. He writes that "the plays that succeed in both realms [the moral and theatrical], in vision and practice, are the ones I believe should be counted among the major artistic achievements of Holocaust drama or, indeed, of twentieth-century drama in general" (*The Darkness we Carry* xiii). Skloot sets out five objectives of these playwrights that he says are often simultaneously pursued:

> (1) to pay homage to the victims, if not as individuals then as a group; (2) to educate audiences to the facts of history; (3) to produce an emotional response to those facts; (4) to raise certain moral questions for audiences to discuss and reflect upon; and (5) to draw a lesson from the events re-created. (*Theatre of the Holocaust* 1, 14).

To these he adds a sixth objective: "the ways in which playwrights can achieve these specific objectives through new approaches to their subject at a time when cultural and political understandings have become less monolithic or universal than a generation ago" (9). But if there's anything to be learned from the theatrical productions of Anne Frank's diary, as Ozick tries to show in her essay, it's that *any* lesson a playwright or director wishes to derive from the diary will be different from the one that Anne might have drawn. Ozick argues that by paying homage to Frank, the producers of its various productions and renditions have done just the opposite. They have prostituted the witness/victim in the name of entertainment.

Marking a point of departure from Skloot's approach is Vivian Patraka, whose book *Spectacular Suffering* takes on not just the question of what can be seen in Holocaust performances but what "performance" might mean when talking about atrocity. In an examination of many of the same plays that occupy Skloot's attention, Patraka is concerned with the difficulties of representing fascism aesthetically. She works through several issues: playwrights often use the same tropes (violence, race, the denigration of women) that the Nazis used in their reign of terror, and gender and political issues become intertwined with issues of violence against Jews and the nature of totalitarianism. Whatever a theory of Holocaust performance looks like, Patraka argues that it should examine the limits of representations of fascism, the Final Solution, and especially the desubjectification of the victims. Aesthetic theories, which have tended to be totalizing, shouldn't lead to the very same totalizations that led us to the destruction of the Shoah in the first place.

One important aspect of Patraka's work is her consideration of the effect of performance on the body. She frankly asks why we should want to see representations on the stage of the body in pain at all, and wonders how the spaces of performance implicate spectators in atrocity. Taking her lead from Elaine Scarry, author of the groundbreaking work entitled *The Body in Pain*, Patraka argues that testimony isn't easily translatable into theater—in fact, she seems to argue that it isn't translatable at all. Physical pain, particularly the pain of torture and death, reduces and finally voids the subjectivity of the tortured body altogether, thereby "prov[ing Jean-Francois] Lyotard's notion that death 'proves [for the killer] that what ought not to live cannot live'" (93). The sick pleasure derived from the pain associated with some forms of sadomasochism is derived from its ability to apparently hide the desubjectification of the victim by "troping" the victim away. The irony is that attempting to perform atrocity so it lays bare the attempt to varnish over the discursivity of violence "makes pain both too real and too artificial— pain is so excessively real as to dissolve the neat border of imitation, and it is necessarily sustained in representation by considerable artifice" (101). Patraka goes on to suggest that language, not performance, is perhaps the best means of "revealing the conflation of pains in genocide under a single rubric as well as exposing how even one term can convey both so much and so little" (105).

Rolf Hochhuth, Christopher Hampton

Rolf Hochhuth's play, *The Deputy*, which had its first performance in 1963 in Germany, is not about language but about complicity. The problem that confronts the playwright is how to make this complicity visible to audiences and, in the case of German audiences, to implicate them in it. The play is more or less realistic, though its five acts are written in very different styles. Its main character was modeled on historical figures, Father Maximillian Kolbe and Provost Lichtenberg of the cathedral at Berlin, both of whom spoke out against the treatment of Jews; and SS officer Kurt Gerstein, who tried to save Jews through the instrument of the Nazi bureaucracy.

In order to make the question of complicity more immediately available to audiences (in particular to German ones), the main characters are also not Jewish but Christian. The thematic center of the play is Pope Pius XII's refusal to take more concerted action to save the Jews of Rome or, for that matter, the Jews of Europe (which was largely Christian and, in the cases of France, Italy, and Poland, predominantly Catholic). Hochhuth has in mind to make visible the ultimate outcome of the disaster, namely the death of six million Jews and millions of others. But how does a playwright make such a fact visible when what he has at his disposal is a small group of actors? The answer was to make visible a murder, in this case the murder of Father Riccardo, the pope's political deputy (but also, in Skloot's terms, the audience's moral deputy) at the hands of the SS doctor with whom he has been arguing at Auschwitz. It's as if Father Riccardo, who has put himself in the position of Jews, is metonymically murdered in their place in part because his superior, the pope, has figuratively and literally washed his hands of the Jews in Act 4. As the play proceeds, Father Riccardo becomes more and more responsible for the fate of the Jews who are being systematically murdered. He seems to identify with them, and in so doing, the (Christian) theatergoers, with whose outrage they strongly identify from the position of hindsight, identify with Riccardo. When Riccardo—who in the fourth act has pinned a yellow star on his cassock—is murdered, the audience is both complicit in the murder and also (because of Riccardo's identification with the Jews) itself murdered. So while the Jewish characters are unformed and one-dimensional, essentially marginal to the play, they nonetheless figure importantly for the audience as an object of identification. The audience, in this case, not only sees the pope's outrageous unwillingness to act on behalf of the murdered, as Riccardo attempts to do, but sees that its result is Riccardo's demise.

If Hochhuth takes actual history as his point of departure in his play, Christopher Hampton takes imagined history as his: his adaptation of George Steiner's novella, *The Portage to San Cristobal of A.H.,* imagines the capture and transportation of a 90-year-old Adolf Hitler, who has spent nearly thirty-five years in hiding in the jungles of Brazil. In his play of the same title, Hampton—like Steiner—uses the historical ambiguity of Hitler's end at the conclusion of the war and couples it with the fact that many other Nazi officials managed to escape to South America after 1945. (Until the opening of Soviet archives in the late 1980s and early 1990s, there was no conclusive proof that the charred corpse found outside the Fuhrer's bunker by Soviet troops was Hitler's, a fact that Stalin was happy to keep under wraps for his own ends before the beginning of the cold war.) The play itself traces the journey down river of Hitler and his captors, while those accompanying him—each with his own background and motives—wonder what will become of him. The character Lieber, who remains offstage but whose voice is a constant presence on the search-party's short-wave radio, functions like the moral center of the play, continually accusing A.H. from a distance, forcing him and the search party to remember the atrocities Hitler ordered.

There are two dramatic strategies used in *Portage* that cut against one another, and that prevent the play from coming to any kind of formal or moral closure. The first is the disembodied voice of Lieber. It constantly reminds those who accompany A.H., and Hitler himself, of the atrocities and of the names of those who were killed. He recites, in the ninth scene of the play:

> At Maidanek ten thousand a day, unimaginable because innumerable, in one corner of Treblinka seven hundred thousand bodies.
> I will count them now.
> Aaron, Aaronowitch, Aaronson, Abilech, Abraham . . .
> The one being Belin the tanner whose face they sprinkled with acid and who was dragged through the streets of Kershon behind a dung cart but sang
> The one being Georges Walter who when they called him from supper in the rue Marot spoke to his family of an administrative error and refused to pack more than one shirt . . .

There is no ambiguity in these accusations, and what happened—the facts of the destruction—is meant to hit both A.H. and audience members in the face. Here is history, inescapable even in the dramatic imaginary.

The other strategy is the monologue of A.H. himself, who—until the play's final scene—has uttered only a dozen words, usually in untranslated German. If Lieber's voice in the jungle is the voice of history-as-events, A.H.'s voice at the play's conclusion is the voice of history-as-narrative. To put it more bluntly, Lieber is the voice of the past, and A.H.'s is the voice of the (imagined) future. Much of the commentary on the play since its first performances has focused on A.H.'s final monologue, and a great deal of negative energy on the part of critics noted that to conclude the play with the exculpatory voice of history's worst criminal— "Would Palestine have become Israel . . . had it not been for the Holocaust?"— was essentially to give the perpetrator the last word. And it's true that the final Hitler monologue is chilling, giving voice to the worst kind of anti-Semitism of rationalization: if it weren't for the Jews, none of this would have happened. But if they are the play's last words, they are not how the play ends. It ends instead with the sound of helicopters, which have come to take the party, and A.H., away, presumably to a tribunal in the United States. Hampton's stage directions give a hint of what audiences are meant to see here: the helicopters approach at first with a "feathery stuttering" that becomes "a deafening roar," and the stage is "raked by fire and wind." If this sounds a bit like the biblical God—cloud of smoke and pillar of fire—it's meant to. What is important here, more than history's accusation of A.H. (in the form of Lieber's voice), is what the audience is left with: here before the final tribunal—of humankind and of God—it is less important what Hitler finally does, or what is done with or to him in the tribunal that is beyond the margins of the stage. What is important is what happens to the audience, how *it* will react, and what *it* will do once the play is concluded with Hitler's horrifying words. How will it imagine *its* future?

George Tabori, Charlotte Delbo

Hampton's and Hocchuth's plays—like many of those written in the immediate aftermath of the events themselves—were meant to provide a simulation of reality. Even a play like Erwin Sylvanus's *Korczak and the Children,* which takes its events directly from history but which is staged in faux-Pirandello self-consciousnesss, is derived from events. There are other plays, like George Tabori's *The Cannibals* (1968), that are surreal through and through, mirroring the effect of the Holocaust, not its events. Tabori's play takes the form of a "conversation" during a dinner party, though the party is hardly that. It takes place in an improvised replica of the concentration camp where the playwright's father (Cornelius Tabori) was gassed. Each member of the "party," sons of the fathers who were killed and two others playing the parts of two men who survived but had no sons, relives the moral dilemma he confronted when one of them, Puffi, dies and they all must decide whether to engage in an act of cannibalism in order to survive. The moral problem is complicated by Tabori's strategy of having all but two of the characters in the play act not only the parts of the sons but, occasionally, occupy the personalities of their dead fathers. This strategy is meant to force upon the second generation the moral complexity of the first, and to face the audience with the same confusion. What the audience sees, in effect, is the second generation—in whose midst the audience itself lives—moving through their own histories as it was determined in part for them in the camps.

Part of the dramatic action of the play comes from the tensions between the two generations. We find out a number of hidden details of the fathers' lives in the revelations of the sons. Haas's father is gay, Uncle cannot understand his father nor his father's actions in the camp, Glatz's father betrayed friends. The audience sees aspects of lives that have been lost, aspects only visible through the wrenching discussions of food, replicated before the audience, that the characters' fathers engaged in as a substitute for eating itself. But the other part of the dramatic action takes place near the conclusion of the play, when—after deciding not to consume the boiled body of Puffi—Schrekinger (the SS man named "the Angel of Death" in the cast of characters) orders the men to do so or be immediately gassed. What has to this point been humorous bantering about food becomes far from irreverent: they must consume their "brother" or must themselves be consumed by the fire. It is an impossible situation, made all the more horrible because the audience knows the outcome: those who play their own parts, Heltai and Hirschler, survived because they consumed; those who don't (and who play their fathers' parts in the characters of their sons) died because they refused. Scene 14, in which those who refuse to eat are sent to the "showers," ends with Heltai saying, "I've always found it difficult to decline an invitation."

The play ends, however, not with the immediate horror but with a future one. Heltai and Hirschler play the psychiatrist and the patient, and Hirschler describes a dream:

> I dreamt I saw this child in a rice paddy. Had a gaping hole in one eye, a nose burnt off, his tongue cut out, but [. . .] and that's where the fascinating part comes in [. . .] I was happy. [. . .] I was happy because I realized that everybody is a murderer, not only me, everybody, d'you hear?

In the midst of the Vietnam war, when the play was first performed, it becomes clear that the cannibalism the audience has witnessed has at least one historical correlative, and perhaps two. Hirschler is happy because he has, to some extent, been let off the hook. He's not the only one who is a murderer, someone who consumes others; those who are engaging in history in the moment are just as complicit. But there's another ending to the play, piped in through the loudspeakers that just a scene earlier had been part of the camp: "[S]ome savages eagerly desire the body of a murdered man/ So that his ghost may not trouble them." It is better, in other words, to consume the evidence of murder so that the act itself won't haunt the future. It's better to eradicate evidence of the Holocaust lest the audience's present be haunted by images of burning children. Tabori may be after a great deal more than a collapse between the past and the present, between the acts of the fathers and the legacy left to the sons. Like Hampton's *Portage,* Tabori's *The Cannibals* seems more interested in forcing the members of the audience to confront their own futures, to confront—in a word—the consequences of consuming the past so that the future won't be haunted by it. The play forces the audience to confront the denial of history that consuming it (in the form of bodies or words) might entail.

It's words, quite literally, that one of Charlotte Delbo's plays is concerned with as well. Unlike Tabori's play, which—though surrealistically—represents the consumption of the body of a camp inmate directly on stage, Delbo's *Who Will Carry the Word?* depicts no atrocities at all. But the play is quite specifically *about* atrocity and the ways it may be communicated across generations. The characters in Delbo's play, all women, recount their determination, as French political prisoners, to survive in the death camp. All but one of the characters are essentially corpses, and they speak the memories of the one who survives to give them actual voice. The title of the play is both literal and figural: at the play's composition, in 1966, the survivors were aging; by the time of its first performance in 1974 they were older still. So the question of who will carry the words of the survivors and those who were killed is a highly urgent one, since in fifteen years nearly every survivor will have passed away. The problem is urgent in another way, as we've seen with testimonies in the face of Holocaust denial. In an exchange at the end of the fifth scene of the play, Francoise asks Reine, "Would you be able to tell Claire's mother how she died?" Reine replies, "I will do it; I will because it has to be done, because it is in order that the truth be known that we want to return. We will have had the strength to live it, why would the others not have the strength to hear it?" Francoise, doubtful, replies, "I wonder if we will have the strength to tell it. And they won't believe us. They'll think that since we have returned, it was not as terrible as we say. By returning we will deny our own story." Any attempt to cast the events of history into the language of the everyday would seem to put the lie to it, to domesticate the events so that they are understandable, and in that way draining them of their horror.

Delbo, well aware of this conundrum, puts it on stage front and center. Like Tabori, whose act of cannibalism makes the characters' moral dilemma horrifically visible on stage, Delbo reveals the tension between the bodies of those who were killed and the words describing their torture. She enacts the question of who will carry the words, suggesting that the bodies of victims cannot carry them because they're not strong enough. Bodies in pain—the actual bodies of those who have been tortured and killed—are invisible to the audience; there is an unbridgeable gap between the disembodied voice of the prisoners and the actor's bodies, which seem unaffected by the events. Delbo's introductory note to the play makes explicit that "the faces do not count," "the costumes do not count": what counts is the force of their words. As Vivian Patraka writes of this play, "Seeing can never be believing, because the stories that the cadavers have to tell are too horrific, too seemingly unreal. . . . But hearing these stories emerge from the healthy body of the actor exposes the constructedness of any representation of genocide and engages the audience in an active process of imagining the material human consequences" to which the construction refers (104). The audience doesn't see the atrocity, nor does it only hear testimony: it is bearing witness to the failure of language—who, after all, *will* carry the word?—in the face of a violence that can't be replicated upon the bodies of actors on any stage.

FILM

The camera lens is not constrained by the space of the theater. In either documentary or imaginative film, the most significant constraints are what the camera can capture, the willingness of the filmmaker to sustain her (and her camera's) gaze upon the object, and the deftness with which what the camera captures is edited, blocked, lighted, and dubbed. Like the stage, film is a medium that has its own conventions and its own moral quandaries: how much atrocity can you show an audience before they turn away or walk out of the theater? Is the direct approach (realism, documentary) or the indirect approach (fantasy, fable, comedy) the most appropriate for a depiction of the Holocaust and its atrocities? Does the baggage that comes with certain genres of film (noir, documentary, farce, romantic comedy, melodrama) stand in the way of or facilitate the telling of stories that were generated by the Holocaust? And there is the question of voyeurism: more so even than the theater, in which one is never able to escape the fact that these are live actors engaging a live audience in which the events are clearly staged, films create a more passive spectator. What is projected on the screen, with whatever artfulness and whatever technical sophistication, is meant to *create* spectators. If what they're watching is a horror show, how does the filmmaker justify the pleasure the audience takes from watching?

These are the kinds of questions that have been asked by two generations of film critics and scholars about film since the Holocaust. In an encyclopedic collection of criticism and summaries of nearly a hundred films, Annette Insdorf's *Indelible Shadows* essentially paved the way for other film scholars who followed her. Originally published in 1983, her book was reprinted in 1990 and again in 2002, and in the book's introduction Insdorf notes that in the years between its initial publication and its first rerelease, over a hundred films had been made, both imaginative and documentary, about the Holocaust or using the Holocaust as its principal thematic strand. Insdorf, like Skloot, is interested in the connection between moral and formal criticism: how, in her words, does one find a filmic language with which to tell the story of the Holocaust? Does this language bear any resemblance at all to the language of previous films, and if so, do those old forms bear up under the weight of the moral complexity of the Holocaust?

Dozens of other serious scholars have devoted a great deal of attention to Holocaust film. Among the most intelligent have been Geoffrey Hartman (including his essay entitled "The Cinema Animal"), Gertrud Koch, Miriam Hansen, Jeffrey Shandler, and Jay Cantor (especially his essay "Death and the Image"). (An entire volume, edited by Yosefa Loshitsky—*Spielberg's Holocaust*—has been published on *Schindler's List* alone.) Hartman in particular is interested in the relation between documentary films, including videotaped survivor testimonies, and fictional and imaginative renderings on film. He worries, among other things, about a kind of "memory envy." If the object of the film seems real, and the viewer is convinced that what he sees is his and his alone, he puts himself in the place of the camera and claims that what he sees in the film is what he saw in reality. The problem comes when we can no longer distinguish between the realism of film and the reality of the documentary. Once that line is blurred, Hartman worries, then the deniers are liable to make the charge—and make it stick—that there's no way to determine what is and what isn't a "faked" memory, a faked event.

Miriam Hansen and Gertrud Koch have similar worries, but they're more hopeful that the current language of film is capable of representing the unrepresentable. Both of these critics take their point of departure from Kant, whose distinction between what can be shown and what can be replicated through mimesis has been much called upon over the last twenty years. In an essay on Lanzmann's film *Shoah* entitled "The Aesthetic Transformation of the Image of the Unimaginable," Koch writes that Lanzmann successfully "marks the boundary between what is aesthetically and humanly imaginable and the unimaginable dimension of the annihilation" (21). He does so by refusing to show the annihilation and instead films what the survivors now retain in their memories, what for them is now imaginable.

Night and Fog

Alain Resnais's 1956 documentary *Night and Fog* offers one the most widely available, and earliest, depictions of the Shoah. In it, Resnais brings together black and white file footage documenting the evolution of the Final Solution, with contemporary color film surveying the ruins of the death camps as they fell into decay at the time of his filming. The movement back and forth between the black and white and color film, between the past and the present, seems to provide the viewer a glimpse of the distance between "then" (Final Solution) and "now" (the safety of, for Resnais, contemporary France). This movement also creates a narrative tension the film goes on to explore: how do the actions of the past, captured on grainy documentary footage, intrude into the ruins of the present? How do these decaying symbols of horror intrude backwards into a past that already seems distant, a black and white past that cannot be well integrated with the color of the present? Although Resnais and the writer of the narration, Jean Cayrol, never once mention the death camps as a tool for the annihilation of the Jews—referring instead to all victims of the death camps as "deportees"—the film's movement between past and present still makes an important statement about the Shoah.

Early in the film, the camera establishes the movement back in time by following the now-overgrown rails toward a concentration camp. The camera moves slowly along the tracks while we hear a narrator explain:

> Today, along the same track, the sun shines. Go slowly along it, looking
> for . . . what? For a trace of the corpses that fell out of the cars when the

doors were opened? Or the footprints of those first arrivals, driven toward camp
at gunpoint while dogs barked, searchlights wheeled, and the incinerator flamed
in the distance in one of those nocturnal settings so beloved by the Nazis?

Night and Fog makes clear that when we look toward the past and what we construct of it, we see something that comes not only from the material remains but
from what the viewer also brings to it.

In fact, what the film seems to imply is that it's impossible to witness what happened there at all. One feature of the film is that it does not rely on the position
of the eyewitness. No one speaks for the living or the dead. No one leads us back
through memory to reconstruct the horrors of the past. Instead, Resnais reminds
viewers that they are the ones who are burdened to construct what happened
there, follow "the same track." In so doing he reminds us that the narrative we
build to take the place of what actually happened becomes, troublingly, our own.

Through contemporary footage, *Night and Fog* shows that the Shoah cannot
be fully present within the remnants of the past. The file footage might capture
a moment of something we might call the Holocaust, but given what we know
and see now, it is not enough to give form to what happened. For Resnais, evidence can't really account for those who suffered, nor represent the trauma of
the event except as a "shadow" of the surroundings. The contemporary visions of
the material remains of the Final Solution mark a place of memory, but the contents of that memory can only be hinted at. In fact, the content of memory cuts
two ways in this film. Inasmuch as the contemporary footage of the gas chambers may press an ethical urgency on the viewer ("remember"), they may also
present the opportunity for voyeurism ("look here! enjoy!"). The narrator tells us,
over contemporary glimpses of the remains of the gas chambers, that "nothing distinguished [them] from an ordinary block. . . . The only sign—but you have to
know—is the ceiling scored by fingernails." But over contemporary glimpses of
crematoria, he tells us "an incinerator can be made to look like a picture postcard.
Later—today—tourists have themselves photographed in them." The present is
built of what we must know, and what we refuse to know. The comfortable, col-
orful present is our own to do with what we will; what any spectator builds in that
present is not history, not the event.

Night and Fog does, however, allow the viewer to see something important. The
film begins with statements documenting the sources for the black and white
images, setting up a factuality on which the film's structure depends. The implication is that without the images of the atrocities that took place in the concentration camps, how would we read what we find there now? The images of the
present work, conversely, to bring the footage from the past into some form of
accessibility. For example, the camera's movement along the line of bunks in one
barracks connects to footage of haunting faces peering out from the wooden
racks. As the film's narrator makes clear, this linking of the remainders of the past

with the experiences of the camps does not offer a concrete or coherent account of the individual traumas that these pieces of footage point toward. It points toward a different space altogether, a space that is neither present nor past that allows past and present to become commingled. *Night and Fog* shows that present and past are inseparable. Although the film tells us that all we have access to is the "shell" of the Holocaust, its remains, it still maintains a connection between the shell and what's inside, what we call the Holocaust. The event is at the center of, and troubles, history. The film shows us what remains, tells us what happened here, while insisting that the real trauma of the event and the witnesses to particular atrocities are absent, that there is no ground on which a knowledge of the event can be laid. Although these are two contrary notions of history and knowledge, Resnais's film holds both to be true simultaneously. We must remember, and can't remember, at the same time.

Schindler's List

The passionate debates surrounding Spielberg's *Schindler's List,* a hugely successful and popular film, has polarized much of the thinking on Holocaust representation, especially when considered in conjunction with Lanzmann's more "historically" driven, more "factual" *Shoah*. Critics have attacked *Schindler's List* for the way it manipulates history to "please" its audience. Sara Horowitz argues that people's positive reaction to *Schindler's List* is tantamount to a disregard for the truth, that acclaim for *Schindler's List* is "an acceptance of the film's truth claims, indeed an acceptance of the film as a discourse of the real" (Loshitsky 119). By linking historical fact with truth or with a "discourse of the real," Horowitz forces us out of the realm of representation permanently: film and literature—any rendering whatsoever of trauma—must be read only as testimony.

But film, at its best, blurs the line between what the witness (from the perspective of the camera) sees and what actually happens. A moment in *Schindler's List* when a fictional rendering of witness occurs is when Itzhak Stern recognizes that Schindler is buying each prisoner on the list from camp commandant Amon Goeth. When Stern recognizes that Schindler is paying for each name, he pauses and says: "The list is an absolute good. The list is life. All around its margins lies the gulf." At this moment, Stern makes clear one of the most important points the film makes: we are hearing the story of those who are named, those whose names are connected with faces and are seen in the film, as distinguished from the infinite list—the list of 1,100 Schindlerjuden, or of the six million who weren't saved—that surrounds the fixed one at the center. Put another way, the list compiled by Schindler and Stern identifies those for whom there is a narrative, those who will survive to testify to the gulf on the outer edges of the list, where those who are not named reside. This moment in the film shows an awareness of the relation between the gulf and the list, the unnamed and the named, those who can't bear witness (and whom the viewer only sees at the margins of the film) and those who can. If this is true, then it's a mistake to consider the film solely in terms of the names on the list, as a group with definition in the face of the rest that lack definition.

Schindler's List as a film often works to make a distinction between witnessing and testimony. Many critics of the film have difficulty with its narrative, particularly the fact that its story foregrounds an ambiguous Christian savior, a sadistic Nazi perpetrator, and likeable survivors. But this is to think of the film solely in terms of testimony, that it provides an accurate (or an inaccurate) picture of what happened. Because the film falsifies aspects of what really happened, it's seen as historically dangerous. But one way to look at the film is to think of it as marking the distinction, the line, between what the witness sees (and what the viewer sees) and what the witness and the viewer knows about the Holocaust. *Schindler's List* is more than a film that only constructs a narrative that follows Schindler and Goeth, Stern, and the 1,100 Schindler Jews. While telling this one story, the film is marked by moments that go beyond the story.

Perhaps the most obvious example of a moment of witnessing within the act of narration occurs when Schindler observes the purging of the Krakow ghetto. In this scene, Spielberg's camera focuses on a little girl as she makes her way through the rounding up and killing of Jewish families. The girl's coat is colorized a reddish pink until she hides under a bed and the color is gone and the camera shifts to a wider view of the destruction. This mark of color, a stain on the black and white narrative of the ghetto's destruction, marks a breach in the narrative of the film. This cinematic insertion puts the viewer in the position of seeing. You see both Schindler's seeing and the coat, but neither you nor Schindler knows anything about the girl. This moment of seeing is invoked again when the film repeats the colorization of the girl's coat as her body is exhumed for burning as the Nazis attempt to erase the evidence of the ghetto's extermination. It is only in the repetition of the colorization that the image is completed, that we recognize what we see and what we saw earlier as we recognize Schindler's recognition. But what precisely have we recognized? The film itself doesn't say. It demands that the viewer provides coherence; Spielberg doesn't do it for us.

The film's concluding sequence begins with Schindler's departure from the camp (filmed in black and white) and ends with the placing of stones on Schindler's tombstone in a cemetery in Jerusalem (filmed in color). Many critics take Spielberg to task for this scene because of its overindulgence and because it brings narrative closure to a series of events that seem to defy it. Those who react positively to this scene suggest, among other things, that seeing the surviving Schindlerjuden paired with the actors who portrayed them gives viewers a way to identify historical events with their representation, effectively linking what

Liquidation of the Kracow ghetto, from *Schindler's List.* Copyright© Universal. Courtesy Everett.

they saw on the screen with historical truth. But another way to look at the film's conclusion is to see that it works against this impulse at closure, because it puts the viewer in the position of seeing the remnant—what occupies the gulf and remains unnamed—when what the viewer may want is a representation of the named (Schindler, Israel, or the descendants of Schindlerjuden living in diaspora who outnumber the Jews who remain in Poland).

The final scene of the film, in fact, is not the laying of the rose upon Schindler's tomb. It is a silent panning shot in black and white of fragments of tombstones laid as pavingstones on the road leading from the Plaszow camp. The film seems to end with testimony, the memory-making of the survivors, and the seamless transition from Czechoslovakia in 1945 to independent Israel in the 1990s (with "Jerusalem the Golden" sung in Hebrew in the American version of the film). It seems to end with the names that can be connected to individual lives in a series. But in fact the film concludes with what can't be named, only seen: the marker of those who didn't survive, the devastated trace of a European Jewish civilization that has literally been trod underfoot. This is what the viewer sees to close the film, the sign of the remainder, and it has the effect of voiding the names we might provide for the film in the name of memory by drawing our attention to that which exceeds the name: those whose names have been lost. Like the sigh of relief we feel as the women from Schindler's factory have been snatched from the maw of Auschwitz at the last minute, it catches in our throats as the camera pulls away and briefly shows us the stream of those who have been unloaded from trains (probably from Hungary) and moved directly down into the gas chambers never to be seen again.

Life is Beautiful

Roberto Benigni's *Life is Beautiful,* even more than Speilberg's *Schindler's List,* brings into question the accepted relationship between what witnesses and viewers see, and what each can say about what they've seen. It's the narrative of a father trying desperately to keep his child from seeing the horror of the camp by enacting a "game," the object of which is to survive. But in creating that narrative, a space that contains the testimonies that build the historical matter of the film (in the form of the story of Guido and Giosué), Benigni has also opened up a space through which the viewer herself witnesses the underside of history and of representation.

Life is Beautiful doesn't at first make clear whose story we are hearing and see-ing. At the beginning of the film, a narrator introduces what is to follow: "This is a simple story . . . /but not an easy one to tell. / Like a fable, there is sorrow . . . / and, like a fable, it is full of wonder and happiness." The narrator's simile, that his story is "like a fable," a phrase he repeats in separating sorrow from happiness, gets at the difficulty of telling this "simple" story. The narrator returns one more time, at the very end of the film, where we find out that he is Giosué, and that what we have seen is his story: "This is my story. / This is the sacrifice my father made. / This was his gift to me." Once we know the name of the speaker, the dif-ficulty of the story disappears, witness and testimony are seemingly bound together by the narrative position of the child survivor. Begnini's addition of the final voiceover allows the film to rest upon what Giosué saw.

The movie's final voiceover only suggests one reading of the film, though. In fact, you could say that there's a contradiction between the two voiceovers: ini-tially, in terms it acknowledges are inadequate: "This is a simple story . . . /but not an easy one to tell"; and finally as an equation between testimony and wit-ness: "This is my story." Benigni's connection of witness with testimony contin-ually breaks down as his opening remarks prefigure: this is "not an easy one to tell."

We get a sense of why when we see Guido, carrying his sleeping son, walking in the mist, having "taken a wrong turn" in the concentration camp trying to find his barracks. In the fog, he comes across a distorted pile of corpses. He stops in the fog before the bodies can become distinct and then slowly backs away, deliberately keeping Giosué's back to the scene. The moment when Guido sees has no witness. The sleeping child's back is to the bodies and there is no evidence that the game-fiction is broken for him the next day. In fact, this scene punctuates the film retroac-tively. As the film begins and the first voiceover is heard ("This is a difficult story to tell . . ."), we see a man holding a child walking through fog, the same scene lead-ing up to the corpses. At that point—the film's opening—we have no context for this scene, just the initial voiceover. The opening voiceover and its images puts the focus of the film on the difficulty of telling a story at the outset, and it punctuates the then unknown narrator's own comments about how difficult it is to tell this story with a clear tie to the one real moment of seeing in the film. It is this one moment of seeing that the fabular form of the film cannot bear: the image of corpses, corpses among whose number Guido and Giosué are likely to be counted.

Throughout the majority of the film, there's no narrator presence—no voiceover, no sense of who's telling the story. We don't even know that Guido is a Jew until about a third of the way through the film when he remarks about painting "Jewish Waiter" on his chest in response to his uncle's fear of rising anti-Semitism after his horse has been defaced with Nazi symbols and the words "Jewish Horse." In fact, even when Guido is giving his "lecture" on the new race laws in the guise of a fascist official at his wife's school, pointing out his ears, belly button, and "mus-

Guido looking for his son, Giosue, from *Life is Beautiful.* Sergio Strizzi | Melampo Cinematografica | The Kobal Collection|

cular" features, we still don't know he's Jewish. There's a dissonance between Guido's obliviousness to his own Jewishness and the constant reminders of Jewish perse-cution that Benigni invokes: the anti-Semitic graffiti, the store signs forbidding Jews from entering, the harassment by officials. But in order for the romance of the story to develop, Guido and his immediate family cannot actually see it. All we see of what Guido or his son or even Dora sees is wrapped in the one scene in the fog. And at the very end of the film, when there is a chance to remark about Guido's murder or even the Holocaust more broadly, Benigni chooses not to show it. The film closes emphasizing not a moment of witness (which we never see in the eyes of the child) but with a denial of witnessing, an identification with the constructed narrative as a means of survival. We don't see Giosué find out about his father's mur-der, to recognize the limits of the fiction that his father had preserved for him. In-stead, after the voiceover finishes, the camera remains focused on Dora and her son embracing, with Giosué telling her about winning the contest: "A thousand points to laugh like crazy about! We came in first! We're taking the tank home! We won!" What makes *Life is Beautiful* so palatable is the way in which it "reintegrates" the crisis of the Holocaust within a "transformed frame of meaning," a family narra-tive that binds the child together with a loss that is seemingly forever deferred.

PHOTOGRAPHY AND OTHER IMAGES

In her book *Remembering to Forget,* which describes the photographs of the lib-eration of the camps at the end of World War II, Barbie Zelizer argues that pho-tos are important instruments of memory, and yet like all such instruments they fall prey to the context in which they are used. These images may have as much to do with a domestication of their object as with a memorialization of it. Other critics, including not only Zelizer but also Marianne Hirsch, have written exten-sively on how the photograph, like the documentary film, both does and doesn't fix the image, and the knowledge, of the Holocaust for future generations. By freezing the event, it becomes an object in itself, and those who see it are either affected by it, or aren't. But what they see and what they create from that image are distinct. The problem with the photographic image, like that of the document and documentary film, is how to reconcile what each witness sees and what they can know about what they see.

There are, as with documentary and other films, different kinds of, and purposes for, photography. Zelizer is mainly interested in the photographs that were taken toward the end of World War II, its immediate aftermath, what she calls atrocity photos. There are archives full of such photos, including the United States' National Archive along with those located at the U.S. Holocaust Memorial Museum, Yad Vashem in Israel, the British Museum in London, and at other locations. Taken by members of the U.S. and British Signal Corps as well as by photographers from press agencies, newspapers and magazines in Britain and the United States, these photographs were meant to force readers and viewers in the United States and abroad to see the most extreme result of fascism. Other photographs, taken before the destruction, form a tapestry of what was lost: photographs, like those taken of the Warsaw Ghetto by photographers from Propaganda-Kompanie 689, a propaganda unit attached to the German army, portray various aspects of ghetto life. These photographs, over a third of which are collected in Keller's *The Warsaw Ghetto in Photographs,* are used in museum exhibits, photographic anthologies, and history texts to document life in the ghettos. Keller divides the collection thematically, including sections on "Ghetto Labor," "Amusements of the Ghetto Elite," "Street Scenes," Beggars," "Children," and "Burials." Included as part of the collection are a few photographs of the Lodz ghetto. There are other photos, like those included in the U.S. Holocaust Memorial Museum's "wall of faces." This is an installation of images collected by Yaffa Eliach that depict those who lived in the Lithuanian village of Eiszysky in the decades before it was destroyed in the wake of the Nazi invasion of the Soviet Union, and it depicts the everyday-ness of Jewish life. Roman Vishniac took hundreds of photos of eastern European Jews in the 1930s as part of a campaign to raise money from Jews in the United States for impoverished communities in Europe. These images show an eerie prescience of the horrors to come, but as many have pointed out his work also captures something of the particularity of his subjects: individual men and women working, faces of children playing or studying, families living in squalid conditions, windowless basements, alleyways, roofless countryside shacks draped with snow. All these images speak to a daily life that even at the time was far removed from those who were to be the eventual audience of such images, western Jews who would be asked to send money to help those in the east. Finally, in a project begun by Serge Klarsfeld and his wife decades ago, a group of thousands of photographs was assembled to depict the Jewish children of France who were deported to Auschwitz after the occupation of that country. These photos are mostly portraits taken well before the deportations. Some are taken from identification cards, and still fewer are group or unposed shots.

All these photographs, either of atrocity or of everyday life, both capture a moment in time, and insert that moment into the context we know as "the Holocaust." It's the tension that exists between these two poles—what was seen by the photographer and what we can say about what we've seen in the photograph—that is worth examining.

Take, for example, a photograph of a young boy, well fed and well dressed in a sweater and short pants, walking down a road whose distant curve enters a forest. (This much-reproduced image was originally taken by a member of the U.S. Signal Corps but purchased by Time-Life for inclusion in its magazines in the mid-

Sieg Mandaag outside Bergen Belsen, 1945; from *Honnef and Brenmeyer.* George Rodger | Time Life Pictures | Getty Images.

1940s.) The boy's attention is focused on something outside the frame, to his right; behind him, barely visible and a good hundred paces away, are two women. What makes the photo horrifying is that just to the boy's left, strewn along the road's embankment and in the woods beyond, are over a hundred corpses, anonymous bodies dressed not in rags or blankets but in ordinary clothes. Zelizer includes the photo as one of several that depict German children who refuse to bear witness to atrocity; the photo's caption—it's unclear whether it was supplied by the photographer or by editors of the magazine (*Life*) by which it was purchased—explains that this is a Jewish boy outside the concentration camp at Bergen-Belsen. The boy is identified by the curators of the German Historical Museum, where the photo now resides, as a Belgian Jew, Sieg Mandaag, "[who] survived the dying after the liberation of the camp by the British Army" (Honnef and Brenmeyer 202).

What do we make of this photo, the confusion over its object, and the part it plays in the construction of memories of the Holocaust? We could integrate it into a narrative of witness, and place it alongside other archival photos of witnessing and refusals to bear witness. But this would simply place it into a collective memory that we have already learned to accommodate. As Zelizer and others have made clear, photos like these are also the medium of a collective amnesia. Sieg Mandaag stands in for us: we've seen these images again and again, as the young Belgian child must have seen corpse after corpse; and that accommodation, like the child's, allows our attention to be diverted from the atrocity. But there is, in the image of this child, something that goes beyond this collective memory we have built for ourselves of the Holocaust.

So how do images from the Shoah both fix and work against memory? To begin to answer this question, it's worth spending some time with photographic images currently collected in the Photo Archive of the Prussian Cultural Trust, which was opened in what was West Berlin in 1966 and now includes over seven million images. We can also look at the collection of images of Jewish children deported to the east from France from 1942 to 1944 collected by Serge Klarsfeld. These two collections contain photographs whose images at times do not speak directly to the disaster, and whose contexts only partly account for the disruptive capacity of the images.

The photographs from the Prussian Photo Archive appear to be the most susceptible to being stripped from their connection to a specific time and place, because the captions that connect them to that context are so brief. Some of the photos in the Prussian Archive depicting life in the Warsaw ghetto, or the liquidation of the Jews of the Russian pale of settlement, are familiar to many people who have a passing knowledge of the Holocaust. There are also photographs that, without caption or the context of their place in an archive that documents the destruction associated with the Final Solution, would not seem out of place in a chest full of photos from the old country. There are no yellow stars to give the story away. Photos such as these would seem to indicate nothing of the disaster at all. It's only their location in the Archive itself that gives them a double life as a marker of destruction.

There are also photos that, to second- or third-generation eyes, create a knowledge and a memory of the events in Europe in the years between 1933 and 1945. And yet these photos also indicate—at their margins, or in what can't be captured by the camera but that is just off to one side—something lost, forgotten, and yet which troubles the memory conjured by them. In a photograph taken in what the caption tells us is late 1940 in Warsaw, the center of the frame is taken up by an open wood-panelled door to a nondescript gray building. The building itself is institutional, probably built in the very late part of the nineteenth century, pillared and made of sandstone. On either side of the door stand three men, each in military-style peaked cap, one in a dark uniform, and two others, to the door's left, in light coats. The caption on the photo tells us that this is the Jewish Council office, so we can guess that these two men, in ill-fitting uniforms and badly made shoes, are Jewish police, and they seem to be each looking at the individuals who are coming out of the door of the building. Just inside the open door stands a short man in bowler hat, buttoning his coat. He is following a couple, a man in full-length coat and a woman beside him in a frock coat, a leather purse slung over one arm. The man seems to be saying something to her, and her left hand, reaching for her head, seems to be in gesticulation, perhaps in response. Under her right arm is either a book or a set of documents.

Out of the line of sight of any of the pictured individuals, but very much in the viewer's, is the man in the photo's lower left. Sitting on the second step of the entryway to the office, and either asleep, passed out from hunger, or dead, he wears a rumpled dark coat and hat. His head is bent sideways and is just barely propped up on the elbow of his left arm. His legs are sprawled out in front of him in no particular direction. As he lies there, his mouth hangs open. Unlike the others in the photo, he is not well fed, or well dressed, and he is unable to return a glance. On the margins of the photo in more ways than one, he is neither en-

Entrance to the Jewish Council office with Jewish Police at the door, Warsaw, late 1940. From the *Preussicher Bildarchiv.*

gaged in the drama of departure from the building, nor is he a central figure in
the composition of the photo.

This isn't an image of atrocity. It's just one of several hundred photos of "Poland
under German Conquest," one of a number of images of ghetto "street scenes"
taken in 1940 and 1941. It accompanies other photographs of life on the streets
of Warsaw. The bustle of activity in front of the door of that building, like the
bustle of activity in each of the other street scenes from these years, seems less to
create a memory of the Final Solution than to build a memory connected to a collective sense of a European past. It depicts a fast-paced urban engagement with
bureaucracy and barely concealed commerce whose inhabitants apparently express the full range of human emotions we might expect. Barely visible—if visible at all—in many of these images are the armbands with the Star of David that
identifies their wearers as Jews.

Just to the edge of the frame is the one who undermines this well-wrought
narrative, and this well-founded memory, of the urban bureaucracy of the ghetto:
who is this man, and how did he come to be here? More importantly, what
calamity is it that no one, not a single person pictured here, seems to notice that
he's there? This one man, without a clearly marked role and without an identity
at all inside the frame of the photo, troubles the image whose caption seems to
provide it a coherence in the context of the officialdom of the Final Solution,
and opens the door to what will be painfully evident less than a year later, when
the starving, anonymous, and barely visible inhabitants of the ghetto move from
the margins of the photographs to the center. It works against the memory that
would allow us to keep the date and place of the photo—"Warsaw, late 1940"—
sealed from the dates and places and memories of atrocity we know too well—
"Auschwitz, late summer 1944;" "Dachau, summer 1945." In other words, this
marginal image intervenes in the memory that we would otherwise construct. It
calls to mind something otherwise forgotten, and stands in the way of the name
of the image ("the Holocaust").

Serge Klarsfeld's attention is mainly focused on children outside the contexts
of their destruction. If the Prussian Archive focuses its attention on the calamity
of the Shoah by forming a mosaic of images in a metaphorical association, Klarsfeld's photos of children transported from detention camps in France to death
camps in Poland are largely repetitive and with few exceptions simply full-on
shots of individual children. Klarsfeld's aim is made clear in the preface of his
book: after putting together a huge book that simply listed the names, dates, and
places of birth, nationalities, and the convoys on which 76,000 Jews were transported from France to Auschwitz, he became "gripped with an obsession. . . . To
know their faces," particularly the faces of the children (xi). The book is essentially
a photo album, comprised of single photographs—many of them posed formal
and informal snapshots outside the context of destruction—that captures the chil-

dren as they might have appeared in well-worn pages of albums that they them-selves might have kept for their children as remembrances had they survived.

One image that is particularly arresting is the photo of Irene Simon, standing casually in a clearing in a park. She smiles into the camera while she holds the hand of an unseen individual who remains outside the photo's frame. It takes a mo-ment—particularly if you focus on her hand—for you to recognize that the blotch on her dress, just over her heart, is the yellow star emblazoned with the word "juif" (French for "Jew"). Another arresting image is the cluster of photos of the Rozenblum family, set into an oval that contains head-and-shoulders shots of the unnamed mother's four children. The oval is set inside a grave marker, whose partial Hebrew is unreadable outside the frame of the photo except for the word *l'zakhor* ("in memory") inscribed just above the oval, and whose French is partly readable just below, *memoire de ma chere* ("in memory of my dear one").

Each of these photos seems to produce a glimpse of something that escapes memory. That something is unmappable, unforseeable, and destructive of the narrative that the photos—in Klarsfeld's telos or anyone else's—desperately try

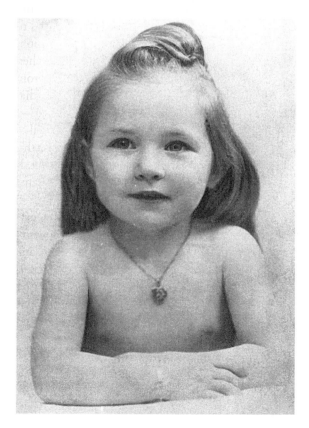

Aline Korenbajzer. From Klarsfeld, *French Children of the Holocaust*. Dr. Jonathan Hunt, PhD.

to forge. Outside the series—taking each photo on its own—the images taken as substitutes for a memory that cannot possibly be ours can be inserted into a collective memory. The collective includes images of face upon face of individuals destroyed by the Final Solution that attempted to eradicate individuals in the name of the collective. But even as they form a series, something at the margins of the photos seems to carry with it an unspoken past. Maybe it's only that past invoked by the opening and closing of the shutter of the camera, the moments in whose midst the image is taken and that are lost except as traces that reside in the curious faces of the children. Perhaps it's the past marked by the names of detention camps stamped across the faces of the children in identity cards, places and names whose histories seem incongruous with the histories of children that appear so happy. These incongruities of time and place, of a collective memory and memories lost and marginal to the greater narrative, interrupt any history we may think is "fixed" by a photographic image.

CHAPTER 11

Making Memory: Case Studies in Holocaust Art and Architecture

The children and grandchildren of Holocaust survivors comprise two generations whose memories of the Holocaust are not direct. These children and grandchildren are left to wrestle with the aftereffects of the events that affected their parents' and grandparents' lives. How do these second and third generations, born well after the events of the Holocaust but still living in their midst, deal with and represent those events? The question is urgent in the case of the children and grandchildren of survivors, because it is they who now deal with those events every day.

The question is equally if not more urgent in the case of those who have no historical or cultural connection to the event at all. How is the event to be represented so that they may come to either remember it or learn from it? Do the modes of representation available to the second and third generations stand in the way of memory or make remembering possible? Do sculptures, images, monuments, and memorials inculcate memory, or do they make the horror of the Holocaust safe, holding it at arm's length, and making that horror somehow less horrible?

In this chapter I consider how two types of Holocaust representation, the visual and the spatial arts (specifically the architecture of Holocaust memorials), might help us answer some of these questions and to understand the stakes of creating memory in the generations that come after Auschwitz. Some pathbreaking work on Holocaust memorials and museums has been done by a number of scholars over the last fifteen years. Primary among them has been James Young: since the publication of his *Reading and Rereading the Holocaust* in 1988, but especially in his more recent books (*The Texture of Memory*, on memorials and museums in the United States and Europe, and *At Memory's Edge*, on art and architecture), he has paid sustained and serious attention to memorials and museums in the United States, Europe, and elsewhere. He has also focused on how European and particularly Jewish artists have confronted absent memory—the memories of their parents' and grandparents' generations, and their effect on their own—in government-funded and nationally sponsored buildings and in privately funded shows in galleries and museums. Edward Linenthal, in the year after the opening of the United States Holocaust Memorial Museum, wrote what is still the most comprehensive account of the establishment of the museum and the very complicated and politically fraught process of building it. His *Preserving Memory* outlines how the U.S. Holocaust Memorial Council, headed for a time by Elie Wiesel, negotiated the competing claims on Holocaust memory from groups that represented Armenians, Roma and Sinti (gypsies), victims of the famines and liquidations of the Stalinist purges, and others in an attempt both to maintain the specificity of the Holocaust in the museum's design and permanent exhibit as well as to maintain the Holocaust as a paradigm for other atrocities. Other important work has been done by Andrea Liss on Holocaust art and photography (in *Indelible Shadows*) and by Efraim Sicher, who has collected essays on the second- and third generations of artists and writers in Israel who have confronted the Holocaust directly and in innovative ways (in *Breaking Crystal*).

The central questions to bear in mind in this chapter are two. The first is whether the historical distance from the Holocaust gives artists a certain license to deviate from the "actuality" of events. Because artists and architects born since 1945 are presumably not tied to the reality of events biographically or historically (though this, too, is debatable), they may not bear the same moral responsibility to tie themselves to what happened in their representations as do those who were there on the spot. If this is true, it may or may not follow that they are also not beholden to tell a certain "truth" about the events of the Holocaust. It is also difficult to say just what this truth is for those in the generations that came after Auschwitz: the reality of the camps is quite different from the reality of living with a parent who survived the camps; it is one thing to have experienced the logic of the Final Solution, and it may be another quite different (though related) matter to see a version of that logic play itself out in contemporary events. How much freedom do artists have in exploring the relation between past and present, and by what means can they do so? This is a question of decorum and taste as much as it is a question of form.

The second question is how "the Holocaust," as a representation rather than as a historical fact, can best be made visible to those who were not there. This is a question of artistic and architectural form. Particularly in the case of museums and memorials, whose first aim is, in Linenthal's phrase, to "preserve memory," how does one do so when "ownership" of memory is itself an open question? It may be that the memory of the Holocaust "belongs" to the survivors, though most survivors aren't architects or artists. How do artists and architects, who don't "own" the memories, make others' memories visible for those who have no experience to match the survivors'?

VISUAL ART

In her discussion of the second and third post-Holocaust generations, Marianne Hirsch defines post-memory as the memories created rather than retrieved in art and writing by members of the second generation. Unlike the first generation, for which representations induce a memory of the event, the second generation—those who weren't there—sees and creates not representations of their own memories but of others', created as they imagine them and not as they were. Post-memory is a projection of memory rather than a recreation of it. Such texts and images impress on the viewer a trace of the event that is lost to the creator. It is this "memory effect"—the effect of the forgotten and immemorial event—that a number of visual artists aim to produce by integrating photography into their work. The margins of the photographs in collections like the Prussian Photo Archive and Klarsfeld's memorial seem to undo the collective memory of what is at the center of the photo. Visual artists have also begun to focus their attention on what is marginal to photographic and other images.

Bracha Ettinger, Samuel Bak

The artist Bracha Litchenberg Ettinger is a good example of how the second generation attempts to deal with what Hirsch calls post-memory. Her paintings are explicitly about the aftereffects of the Shoah. In what Griselda Pollock calls "after painting," Ettinger uses the "found photograph" as the anchor for a collage that "prevents a fall back into a fixed image" and "keeps to the margins and thresholds where another process of meaning is glimpsed" (Pollock 143–4). The work "makes possible another kind of vanishing point—beyond appearance—that is not located" in the object of memory (144). Ettinger's images speak as much about the trauma of what lingers at the back of memory as they do about the atrocity itself. Her collection of collage paintings is entitled *Autiswork,* connoting, vaguely, a sort of autistic inner space of the mind that inhabits neither the "here" of the image's origin (the Holocaust) nor the conscious representation of the image in word or narrative or visual representation. It includes realistic images, text, and what Alain Kleinmann calls the "annulled image," in which the object of representation is scratched out or disfigured by the artist in such a way that the blot itself becomes the object of memory (Feinstein 233–6). It also includes vaguely recognizable photographs seen through a pointillist or impressionist screen of paints and washes.

Ettinger is a child of survivors who was born in Israel. She wrote, "My parents are proud of their silence. . . . But in this silence all was transmitted except the narrative" (cited in Pollock 137). It's as if in her paintings she wants to indicate the trauma of a memory that transmitted itself silently. Several of the photographic images Ettinger uses in her paintings are from collections widely available, including one or two from the Prussian Archives and Klarsfeld's book. They are integrated into the impressionist-like images recast in the paintings as ghostly afterimages that reside just out of reach of collective memory.

One image, repeated again and again in *Autiswork,* depicts four figures, probably female, in purples, blues, and whites. One of the women is clearly cradling what appears to be a child, and seems to suggest something beyond what it portrays: the child, it seems, is being clutched not cradled. In fact, this image is a repetition of one of the photos in the Prussian Archive, one that has been reproduced in the U.S. Holocaust Museum's permanent exhibit as part of its narrative of the *einsatzgruppen* but that in fact depicts events in Poland in 1943: two dozen women, naked and huddled together in a line, stand at the bottom of a low grassy rise. In front of them, partly occluded from view, are two uniformed soldiers, and just beyond are strewn the clothes the women have just been ordered to remove. In the line are also two children: one of perhaps four in one woman's arms, and the smaller child of perhaps two that appears in Ettinger's image. The caption tells us that the women are lined up for execution in Mizocz in 1943.

Speaking of other images of execution, Marianne Hirsch says that images like these don't allow us to see a point before and a point after the photo was taken in which we might imagine another life, another existence, other possibilities. There is something uncanny about the image because the moment reimagined in the painting is unmoored: the women and children in the photo now dead, whereas in the painting they live. Because it is unmoored from memory—this artist, born a good ten years after the event and a child of its silence—its reproduction has the effect "of cutting and shocking in the ways that fragmented and congealed traumatic memory reenacts the traumatic encounter" (Zelizer 237).

Samuel Bak also uses photographic images in his paintings for the purpose of memory work. Unlike Ettinger, Bak was born in Vilna prior to the Holocaust, and was seven years old when he and his family experienced the Nazi occupation of Poland, in 1940. He lived in the Vilna ghetto, and after a short time in a work camp, he took refuge in a monastery, the image of which figures in many of his paintings. After the war, Bak studied painting in Munich, and in 1948 emigrated to Israel. He has been painting since the early 1950s, and has shown his works across Europe, in Israel, and in the United States. As might be imagined for someone who as a youth experienced the deprivations of the ghetto firsthand, images of the Holocaust are important in Bak's work. But those deprivations don't appear immediately in the paintings. When they appear at all, they do so as representations of photographic images, sometimes highly stylized ones. More often than not, the "Holocaust" appears only obliquely or quite symbolically, as if Bak's intent is to render something like an allegory of the effect of the Holocaust on more or less traditional Jewish life.

Bak's work seems heavily influenced by the paintings of Salvador Dali, but there is nothing so surreal in Bak's paintings, though, as the images of the destruction of the years during the war. In Dali's paintings, there is no material correlative to the images: at best, they are a person's more sinister nighttime imaginings. With Bak, what we see is tightly tied to facts captured in photographs. One series of images is derived from the famous photograph—also found, among many collections, at the Prussian Photo Archive—of a youngster of about ten years old surrendering at the end of the Warsaw ghetto uprising. Wearing a peaked cap and a thigh-length wool coat, he has his hands raised in abjection, looking (as one would expect) distressed at his situation, including the fact that those German soldiers with guns at his side will undoubtedly kill him. In the paintings (all entitled "Study" followed by a letter of the alphabet), the child has become an image: in one, his head and two hands appear in stone— as if carved, or maybe formed naturally—in a low cliff face, with the child's features weatherworn but very clearly visible. In another, the image of the child appears to have been painted on thin sheets of metal and cut out, in pieces, and nailed to a rough wooden frame. The child on the frame, in the foreground, is raised high above a hilly townscape, painted in blues and grays below the figure's feet. In this image, the child's face is invisible behind a crude target with five or six holes shot into it; the child's raised hands each have a bullet hole shot through the palm. In a third painting, the child appears as part of a ruined house's wall, on which the brick is partially exposed underneath a thin and deteriorating layer of plaster. The child's hands and head are still clearly visible above the portion of the home (and the child's figure) that seems at best propped up by wooden support beams. The wall/figure itself is in the midst of a decaying forest, whose trees grow up around it as they themselves are only stumps and volunteers, the remnants of a sturdier wood as the house and the figure seem remnants of a livelier place.

All of these images work from the photograph that acts as its anchor, and yet all produce something quite different from it. This isn't a memory of defeat and resistance so much as a series of images that understand the boy and what he represents as (in the first and third painting) a creation, or as a part, of the natural world, or (in the case of the second image) an image, the image of an image related to the crucifixion rather than to any particularly Jewish memory. Are we meant to see a roughly hewn manmade image that has been weathered and beaten into the natural landscape (as the child's hands and face are etched into the cliff outcropping) that figures the human's (and Jew's) defeat at the hands of the natural world? Or are we meant to understand the remnant, even the desecrated image of the now-faceless child on a makeshift crucifix, as a victory over the process that would attempt to destroy it? And how are visitors to the galleries in which these paintings are displayed to take the vision of the crucified Jewish child, except with an ironic glance? (Or are they meant to see, in this crossover of Jewish and Christian iconography, a kind of universalist appeal, a sense that the Holocaust, as the destruction of the innocent, can be integrated into a secularist or Christian tradition that gave us Salvador Dali?)

But Bak's images are not all photographic correlatives. In fact, many of them depart quite clearly from the realistic image altogether, and are meant to be integrated with a much more specific Jewish cultural memory. A great number of his paintings are filled with Jewish icons: the tablets of the commandments; the

Aftermath of the Warsaw Ghetto uprising. National Archives and Records Administration.

star of David that functions both as a symbol of the Jewish people and as the badge that marked them for extermination during the Final Solution; Shabbat (sabbath) candles. In nearly all of Bak's paintings, there appears a ruin: of a person, of a village, of a train or a ship. In fact, it could be argued that Bak's repeated theme is the ruin of memory. Not only is the memory of the twentieth century ruined by the events of the Final Solution and the destruction of the Jewish people in Europe; future memory is also ruined: what can be imagined for future Jewish generations in a landscape filled with the distorted images of the past?

In "Exercise of Memory" and "Public Space," two paintings from 1998, the iconography of the Shoah is implied rather than made (photographically) plain. In both paintings, a ragged string quartet serves as the central image on the canvas; in the former painting, the quartet is seated around a stylized heap of ruined violins, violas, and cellos, and the members of the quartet hold twigs in their right hands while the left hands are raised in the position of the instrument though they are empty; in the latter, the quartet is figurally absent, replaced instead with larger-than-life hands holding instruments made of stone or painted on makeshift wooden boards, while in the background amidst and behind ruins of a town, a dozen or more individuals, all of whom appear beaten down or at the very least unhealthy, stand while their eyes appear to be focusing at a point

Samuel Bak, "Quartet II", mixed media on paper, 19 3/4 x 25 1/2". Image courtesy of Pucker Gallery, Boston, MA.

at the viewer's midsection. As implied by the title, the public space in the latter painting is occupied both by a present and a past. The present is a ruined one, while the past is evoked by the presence of the musicians' images. What was this music that filled the public space now filled with sadness? And what has happened in the interim that has produced this discontinuity? What the viewer sees here is absence, marked quite clearly in the faces of the individuals residing in the painting. In "Exercise of Memory," the "exercise" is both a musical exercise—played, at one time perhaps, by the musicians in the painting's margins—as well as an exertion on the part of the viewer. Like the piles of shoes, eyeglasses, and suitcases left from the liquidations and deportations to the camps, the pile of musical instruments at the center of the painting is a representation of a ruin of the past, though that ruin is not only visible as a remnant but as a painful presence for the musicians themselves. They are left to "play" only on their memory; their realities have been destroyed and any future that might be imagined is, like that of "Public Space," a barren one.

Markiewicz, Kupperman, Tiecholz

A number of Israeli and American artists born after the events of the Shoah explore their effects on the current generation. Among these artists—and I'll mention only three here: Lily Markiewicz, Wendy Kupperman, and Deborah Tiecholz—there is a preoccupation with the realistic image. These aren't images of atrocity or even memory, though, so much as images of the present as they are affected by the very real, palpable presence of the Holocaust in their contemporary realities. It is as if they wish to examine the individuals behind the ruined village in Bak's "Public Space" and not the hands of the musicians that reside in the foreground. Markiewicz's work is primarily photographic. She was born in Munich in 1961 to parents born in Poland, and was raised on a diet of universalism and nationalism more than "Jewishness" because of the scarcity of any Jewish community life in Germany in the 1960s and 1970s. She has said of her work that it "is an exploration of an aftermath, of a past which has become a present, of the absence or a traceable reality which has become the presence of memory. I am not concerned with the Holocaust directly, the event, its causes, reasons or details. I am concerned with the ripples, the ramifications, the consequences and our perceptions of it—our place 'in it'" (cited in Feinstein 204). In a mixed-media installation called "Keeper of Accounts" (1989), this presence of the past is visible in a series of photographic images, including that of a moving tram, of an urban railway station, of industrial chimneys, and of an electric locomotive. These are not images from the machinery of transportation of Jews from the past, but images of urban public transportation in the present. For Markiewicz, however, it is impossible for her—and, through her work she insists, for viewers—to understand these images except through the lens of the past, and so when she says on a videotape accompanying the installation that she "avoid[s] public transport in case something goes wrong," that "something" takes on a sinister note. It is sinister in the sense that she feels herself marked as a Jew, regardless of how others see her, due to her received experience. As viewers enter a 1990 installation called "I Don't Celebrate Christmas," they confront their image in a mirror on which the word "Jew" is projected, as if to confront them with an image of how Markiewicz herself sees both her own image and the image of her circumstances, constantly deformed by what has been lost and the reality that has taken its place.

Wendy Kupperman's photographic images function similarly. Born in New York to Holocaust survivors, she received a doctorate in American Studies at Yale, focusing on Holocaust literature. She said during a lecture at the University of Wisconsin at River Falls (23 February 1994) that, growing up, she "thought all adults had numbers and letters tattooed on their forearms" and that they "spoke in hushed foreign tones of terrible losses, of ghettoes and roundups, of hunger and ashes and limestone." During a visit to Poland in 1988, she visited Majdanek, Auschwitz, and the Pawiak Prison in Warsaw, and took a number of photographs that she collected into a group entitled "The Far Country." As if to mirror her childhood understanding of the events spoken of in hushed tones by her parents, the images from "The Far Country" are self-consciously silent about the horror of the experiences whose traces are visible on the Polish landscape. Instead, the images in the photos could have come from anywhere. They depict railroad tracks, chains on a locked gate, the decrepitude of a ruined building interior. The images aren't marked by their connection to a time and place but by their composition in black and white. They are beautiful photos of the ruins of industry, except that when the viewer sees the captions, she realizes that the industry was the efficient machinery of destruction during the war. The Holocaust is not present in the images except as a kind of invisible conceptual pattern in the minds of the artist and of viewers. It's a pattern activated by seeing even the most beautifully constructed images of everyday objects that have become corrupted by the connection to the Holocaust: train tracks (with the transports), locked gates (with the concentration camp), building interior (with the bureaucracy of death).

Deborah Teicholz, for a series of photos entitled "Prayer by the Wall," visited not the sites of the destruction but Israel, the site of redemption in the Jewish historical imagination. An American of Hungarian descent, her identity has been strongly influenced by her father's experience (as an aide to Raoul Wallenberg; her mother is a Holocaust survivor) and her brother's work (as the author of a book about the trial of the suspected camp guard, Jan Demjanjuk, nicknamed "Ivan the Terrible"). She herself, however, makes clear that she was never "there," though by there it's not clear whether she means the location of the destruction or the experience of it. Most of the images in "Prayer by the Wall" include at least some evocation of the western wall of the Temple Mount compound in Jerusalem. The wall is held to be the only remaining structure from the Second Temple, which was destroyed in the first century and replaced, beginning in the seventh and eighth centuries, with Islamic buildings. The site of the western wall (sometimes called the wailing wall) has been a memorial location for Jews: it is where they mourn the loss of the temple and pray for its (and their) redemption. The irony of the images in Teicholz's series is its connection to the Shoah. Two of its principal sections include a triptych whose outer images are railway tracks and whose central one is the furrows of a plowed field. Another triptych depicts piles of cut logs. It also includes objects and cattle branded with numbers, Nazi graffiti, images of decrepit and unused synagogues, and barbed wire. Her point seems to be to evoke for the viewer common images—piles of wood, branded cattle—in the present that, like Kupperman's, also resurrect the horrors of the past—piles of corpses at Belsen, the forearms of Auschwitz survivors—without making direct reference to them at all. One writer who has analyzed Teicholz's images notes that they evoke the memory of the destruction but also evoke redemption (Feinstein 215). If this is true, it raises a number of questions as it does for Markiewicz and Kupperman. If the presence of the past is visible in our everyday surroundings, then whatever redemptive capacity these images have seems full of loss. If, in other words, an Israeli or an American second-generation present involves the triumph of the parents' survival and of the talent and life displayed by these artists, it is a present that also involves a hyperconsciousness of loss, and the worry, in the words of Wendy Kupperman, that something could go wrong. What the viewer sees, in the work of these three artists, unlike that of Samuel Bak, is a memory of the past unmoored from history, from the concreteness of the events. Instead, the events exert a pressure on the present, one that seems inescapable to the artists and that seems vestigial, almost ghostly, to the viewer.

Christian Boltanski

Born in 1944 in Paris to a Christian mother and a Jewish father, Christian Boltanski has been called a second-generation artist of the Holocaust. In terms of chronology, he is indeed a member of the second generation. In terms of his focus, however, it isn't clear that he has in mind to understand the Holocaust, or even its effects. Instead he confronts viewers with the highly problematic state in which the Holocaust has left art. His work is much more highly self-conscious than it is conscious of history. Its focus is aesthetics rather than history, or, to put this another way, Boltanski is more interested in the problem of art than in the problem of history, and with it the problem of the "authentic" self of the artist. In his case, he's a Jew born in France just before the end of the war, but he's not considered a Jew in the eyes of the rabbinical authority in Israel (which sees the question of "who is a Jew" answered from the perspective of the mother's religion, not the father's). The question he's asking is how to create art that isn't his to create. How does an artist, whose identity is open to question, supposed to create an authentic work when he himself doesn't feel authentic?

As Nancy Marmer wrote in *Art in America,* Boltanski has "frequently relied on the photograph's deceptive capacity to function as an 'authentic' trace, a convincing souvenir, or personal experience. In the 'Lessons of Darkness,' he explores the photo's ability to also function as a trace of large historical events, and as a trope for tragedy" (180). He seems, in the uses of portraits and found photos in his exhibits, to reclaim individuals from the faceless anonymity of the disaster, whether it is the Holocaust or some other tragedy. But Boltanski, in using images and portraits interchangeably, is also working *against* the restorative power of naming, as if to suggest that there is no such thing as the authentic photograph, one that we could be sure depicts *this* particular person at *this* particular time, inviolable, sacred, and an equal to the person who is depicted in memory.

Boltanski's "Lessons of Darkness" contains four works completed and shown individually in the middle and late 1980s: "Monuments," "Altar to Lycee Chases," "Altar," and "The Festival of Purim." All four works include found photographic portraits, which he has reshot, sometimes sharply and sometimes with so much blur that it's impossible to see just who is the focus of the photograph. Each of the photos is mounted so that it appears in a series with the others in clusters of tens or hundreds. Most of the photographs are taken from collections: individual and group shots from yearbooks, grammar school portraits, and other institutional collections. Boltanski randomizes the faces, so that the viewer oscillates between seeing them as a mass, and focusing on one or two individual images. In "Archives," first displayed in Kassel in what was then West Germany, Boltanski displayed nearly four hundred black and white photos under glass with black borders. They are portraits, and the dress of those depicted seems to place them at some point in the 1930s or 1940s. Among the otherwise anonymous images—there is no text telling us who is in these photos or when they were originally taken—there is a photo of a man holding up a puppy for a boy on a street corner. It's not easy to see the Star of David worn by the boy, but once the viewer does, she now has her bearings: central Europe during the Third Reich, and this child is a Jewish child slated for destruction. But by placing the image randomly among the anonymity, the question is this: does Boltanski intend for the viewer to recalibrate her experience by contextualizing everything according to this one small image, which could easily have been missed? Or does this image among so many others, which have no reference to the Holocaust at all, mean to decontextualize the single photo, leaving her wondering whether there's anything "special" or significant about this photo in relation to the others? Just what is it that the viewer sees among all these faces?

In "Altar to Lycee Chases," the images are not anonymous. They are taken from the portrait of the class of 1931 from a Jewish high school in Vienna from which the work gets its title. As in "Archives," Boltanski reshoots each of the children's faces, and mounts them on permanent supports, affixing a small desk lamp above each one, so that the faces are not so much illuminated as flood-lit. It makes the images appear spectral, and the viewer gets the uncanny sense—if she moves up close to each—that the individuals in the photos (blurred and badly composed) are being interrogated. Hanging down from each of the lamps are their electrical cords, which—as one moves from the upper images to the lower ones—form a mass of tangled wiring, partially obscuring the faces of the children on the lower rows. In "The Festival of Purim," based on photos of a Purim party in 1939 in a Jewish school in Paris, the viewer gets the same effect, with the lamps burning too brightly on the images of the children. In some cases a set of cinderblocks is installed directly below the mounted photos, as if forming an altar or the detritus of a building.

Just what does Boltanski wish to evoke in these photos? They might as well depict random children from random schools from no particular year in the 1930s or 1940s. Who, he seems to ask, remembers these children? And it's altogether possible that, in an exhibit in France, and in spite of the blurred images, one of the children, grown much older now, might recognize his own image, or that of a friend. In fact, the incessant lighting in the installation might well be asking a question of those depicted, as much as those seeing the depictions: Who are you? Why do you matter? There's no way to identify these individuals except through a kind of sympathetic identification, in which the individual in the photo is unidentifiable except to the extent that the viewer puts herself in the individual's place and extends herself to the self depicted in the photo. These individuals aren't victims, or at the very least, they aren't depicted as victims. The photographs don't function as evidence. To the contrary, Boltanski seems to refuse this sort of victimology, opting instead to put serious pressure on the question of the identity of the victim, the problem of the identity of the artist, the responsibility of those who see the past in the present when in fact there may be nothing of the past to see there.

"Mirroring Evil"

The ethics of Holocaust art is put in question in the exhibit entitled "Mirroring Evil," a collection of pieces shown in the Jewish Museum in New York from 17 March to 30 June 2002. As many critics said at the time, the individual pieces themselves may not have been examples of great art. The fact that the show was put on by the Jewish Museum in New York, and that the collection of pieces was undeniably at the verge of bad taste, or kitsch, or propriety, was what made the show notable. It pushed the boundaries of what an appropriate representation of the Holocaust might be, and of the moral responsibility of the artist, as far as they could go. Add to this the fact that most of the works take the perspective of the perpetrators, and that in most cases the work seemed to revel in the position of the killers and to celebrate them as subjects; and that when suffering was depicted, it was depicted playfully. These facts led James Young to ask a series of questions, questions that should be asked and answered here:

> To what extent . . . are we allowed to consider the potential erotic component in the relationship between Nazi murderers and Jewish victims? What does it mean to "play" Nazis by building your own model concentration camp out of LEGOs? Is this different from "playing" Nazis in the movies? Were Nazis beautiful? And if not, then to what aesthetic and commercial ends have they been depicted over the years in the movie-star images of Dirk Bogarde, Clint Eastwood, Frank Sinatra, Max von Sydow, and Ralph Fiennes? What does it mean for Calvin Klein to sell contemporary perfumes and colognes in the . . . images of the Aryan ideal? And, if this is possible, is it also possible to imagine oneself as an artist drinking a Diet Coke amid emaciated survivors at Buchenwald? Just what are the limits of taste and irony here? And what should they be? Must a depraved crime always lead to such depraved artistic responses? Can such art mirror evil and remain free of evil's stench? Or must the banality of evil, once depicted, lead to the banalization of such images and become a banal art? ("Looking into the Mirrors of Evil" xvi)

Some of the work in the "Mirroring Evil" exhibit tries to juxtapose images we've come to associate with the Holocaust and with its evil, with images we associate only or primarily with traditional art. Christine Borland's sculptured busts of Josef Mengele, for example, seem completely ordinary—half a dozen likenesses, sculpted from clay in the best realist tradition, of a very handsome man—until you realize *whose* likeness you're looking at, and until you read the text accompanying the sculptures. It tells you that many of those who underwent bizarre and tortuous procedures by Mengele were captivated by his beauty, and that some of the medical experiments performed by Mengele at Auschwitz involved the decapitation of his victims. Rudolf Herz's "Zugzwang" involves a checkerboard pattern of alternating images of Adolf Hitler and Marcel Duchamp. The photograph of Hitler was taken by Heinrich Hoffman in 1932, and the photograph of Duchamp was taken by the same photographer twenty years earlier. Again, this is an unremarkable work, until one understands that Hoffman was part of the Third Reich's propaganda machine, and that his photographs of Hitler and other personages in the National Socialist movement served to glamorize the surface of what was an otherwise murderous regime. Duchamp and Hitler are also at entirely opposite ends of the spectrum of, among other things, artistic talent, public demeanor, and fame. Herz seems also to be playing with images: how does the alternation of these two faces, repeated infinitely across what is essentially wallpaper, produce in the viewer an effect that seems to lessen the impact of either of the two images seen individually?

But the questions that began the chapter come into sharpest relief when look-ing at works like Piotr Uklanski's "The Nazis," or Elke Krystufek's "Economical Love" series, where heroic images of Nazis alternate with grotesque female nudes; or in Zbigniew Libera's "Lego Concentration Camp" or in Tom Sachs's wry "Gift-gas Giftset" and "Prada Deathcamp." Uklanski's installation, originally shown in the London Photographer's Gallery, is a series of images from popular films (in-cluding *A Bridge Too Far, Schindler's List, The Eagle has Landed,* and *The Longest Day,* among many others). They're head-and-shoulders shots, some from film stills, and some from theater posters, of actors who have played Nazi officers. They include Robert Duvall, Ralph Fiennes, Yul Brenner, Max von Sydow, and Christopher Plummer. In their high collars, Iron Crosses, and in nearly every case handsome demeanors, these images—like those in the Herz "wallpaper" in-stallation—repeat themselves in an infinite series. Unlike Herz's, which seem to diminish the effect of individual images by placing them into an endless sequence, these images seem instead to gain a kind of power. It's as if the raw maleness, the beauty of masculinity, accumulates a kind of cultural capital. This accumulation isn't unlike the accumulation of Nazis that Hollywood seems to have engaged in since the war. Uklanski seems to confront viewers with their own, and their cul-ture's, apparent obsession with the image of the Nazi. There are, of course, many reasons for this fascination; but it's possible that getting at these reasons is less im-portant for Uklanski than simply focusing attention—relentlessly—upon the ob-session itself. He makes viewers (who, in some cases, playfully tried to name as many of the actors and the movies as they can as they view the series, according to the organizers of the London exhibit) see themselves seeing.

Krystufek's images of Nazis are also taken from film, but hers are paired with other, quite different images. In each of her collages, Nazi officers' images from film stills are paired with at least one other image, that of a nude woman with a camera. The women's images are stylized to various degrees: in the collage subti-tled "Pussy Control," the three Nazi images at the bottom of the page are dwarfed by a large image of a nude woman squatting, with a small camera held to her face. Unlike the Nazis, the woman's image is painted in oils; across her abdomen, between her breasts and pubic hair, is what appears to be a cutout from a maga-zine, printed words on a white background that read "You can't shock us, Damien. That's because you haven't based an entire exhibit on pictures of Nazis." (The words come from a review of another Krystufek show: Damien is to Damien Hirst, a British artist whose work is, in fact, intended to shock.) The woman's image—largely anonymous because of the camera over her face—is painted so that dribbles of paint seem to pour down her body. Two other collages, subtitled "Hitler Hairdo" and "Abstract Expressionism," function in much the same way: Nazi images are paired with female nudes—sometimes painted in outlines, some-times painted in great detail—with cameras and with legs akimbo. In each, text is either painted into the frame, or appears in the frame as printed cutout, text that often undercuts the images' effect, and that at times supports its title or its theme with a kind of brutal irony that is as hard to take as the images themselves.

Part of Krystufek's aim, like Uklanski's, is to bombard the viewer with image after image of the Nazi as if to question his obsession. The difference is that for Krystufek, that insistence is paired with an equal insistence that there is a kind of male erotic fantasy that accompanies the fantasy of the Nazi. In her collages it is women who fantasize, and fetishize, the unquestionably male-identified German officer. But the viewer is also forced to confront an equally fetishized female image, photographed or painted so boldly—some viewers might say grotesquely—that you wonder which should be the object of erotic attraction, the Nazi or the woman making the Nazi image. This isn't Holocaust art so much as it is art that puts elements of the Holocaust to serious question. Remembering that it was the SS who made women strip naked to make their way through selections, that it was women who were the object of the male gaze (not only for prurient purposes, but also for murderous ones), you can imagine a simultaneous pairing of attraction/revulsion in seeing these images. The revulsion comes from the pairing of nude, abject women with images of scowling, handsome Nazis. The attraction comes from the images of women, as if staring from pornographic Web pages. One wonders whether they're photographing the Nazis, or whether they're photographing you as you look at them. Is the evil that Krystufek mirrors the Holocaust, or what we've done with it?

Zbigniew Libera's "Lego Concentration Camp" and Tom Sachs's "Prada Deathcamp" are not so obvious as the photos of Nazis and nudes, but in some ways it's their insidiousness that makes them more problematic. Sachs has created a model of the camp at Auschwitz in cardboard, wire, and adhesive glue. On a "board" the shape of a thick cruciform, the geography of the Auschwitz II camp is replicated to look like a dark version of a Monopoly game. The "pieces" normally reserved for green houses and red hotels are shaped in the form of guard towers, inmate barracks, crematoria, and the infamous entrance through which the trains would pass, all in "deathcamp black." The outside of the "board" is ringed with double rows of miniature barbed wire fence. At the board's center is the logo of the famous Prada house of design (underneath which, in case we were interested in such fidelity, is the house's location, "Milano"); on each of the camp's buildings is a small, but clearly marked Prada logo. If you look carefully enough, you'll also see a tiny train, a locomotive and five boxcars, waiting on the ramp to be unloaded. The only thing missing, it seems, is the Jews.

Libera has also taken an ordinary Lego set, and created scenes from Auschwitz from them: a crematorium and a barracks from Auchwitz II, part of the compound from the original Auschwitz I camp, and special little individual tableaux, including a tiny, black-clad, and helmeted Nazi officer clubbing a white (and skeletonized) camp inmate, a doctor (perhaps meant to be Mengele himself) operating on another camp inmate on a tiny slab, three camp inmates behind tiny electrified barbed wire fences, and another black-clad Nazi officer standing before a stack of presumably dead inmates. Each tableau and each built environment has been placed on a Lego foundation, photographed, and mounted on Lego boxes, and affixed with the "Lego System" trademarks so that they would find themselves at home in any Toys 'R' Us at any mall in the country.

These two exhibits seem to raise the stakes on the idea of "playing Nazi" and "representing the Holocaust." Sachs and Libera are literally inviting viewers to imagine "playing *with*" the Holocaust. In each case, the actuality of the events of the Shoah have, apparently, become so much a part of the everyday—and part of everyday commerce—that the actuality can easily be transformed into objects, and those objects may be manipulated to serve whatever contemporary purposes its consumers wish. Not only can the Holocaust, because it's now part and parcel of our everyday language, be made into an object, the object itself can be manipulated, played with, and recreated so that its outcome might, perhaps, be different. As children play with Legos, visitors can see Libera play with the Holocaust, imagining it as somehow less horrifying, contextualized differently, and easily put away, back into its box, once we're done with it. One way to think about both "Prada Deathcamp" and "Lego Concentration Camp" is that they are meant to "recreate" the Holocaust in vastly different circumstances. They allow us to turn Adorno's dictum, calling poetry after Auschwitz an abomination, on its head: the Holocaust is for recreation, for providing pleasure, now that it no longer troubles us and that the imperative to historical specificity and authenticity no longer holds (the survivors and witnesses so close to disappearing). Sachs and Libera, like all of those whose pieces appeared in the Mirroring Evil exhibit, seem to push Adorno's prohibition to its most logical extreme: here is what happens when the Holocaust is seen as the object of art, as distinct from an object of knowledge.

MUSEUMS

How do museums construct memory? How do they construct individual museum visitors, situating them inside narrative or a community that either naturalizes that "residency" or defamiliarizes it? In the case of Yad Vashem in Jerusalem, the construction of the museum coincided with the foundation of the state of Israel. In 1953, the Knesset passed a special law founding the memorial complex that would commemorate the victims of the Holocaust. The memorial's name comes from a passage in Isaiah: "I will give in my house and within my walls a place and a name (*Yad Vashem*) (LVI: 5). Over the years Yad Vashem has grown to fulfill not only its charge to join place with name, to serve as a memorial to the six million and their families and communities, but also to gather materials to document the Holocaust and to educate Israelis and non-Israelis, Jews and non-Jews.

And these tasks are central to the state itself, a conclusion drawn by James Young in his survey of Holocaust memorials. Young concludes "that as the state grows, so too will its memorial undergirding" (*The Texture of Memory* 250), marking the political nature of the memorials at Yad Vashem, which, as the state evolves, need to grow in number. To this end, Yad Vashem includes a museum that situates the memorials within a historical context, showing the rise of anti-Semitism in Europe, tracing Nazi acts of genocide to the eventual migration of Jews to Israel at the end of the war. Yad Vashem places the visitor inside a narrative of history that marks the very beginning of Israel: it is the first stop on any state visit by foreign dignitaries and is a mandatory part of the training for the Israel security defense force. Over the past fifty years, Yad Vashem's construction has followed the plan of both memorial and museum. Situated on one side of Mount Hertzl, the home of Israel's national cemetery, Yad Vashem is both cemetery and museum, placing each name within a founding national narrative, offering a place where those without physical remains might reside. But although most of the grounds are dedicated to memorial sites, including the Hall of Remembrance, the Valley of the Communities, the Avenue of the Righteous Among the Nations—the most visited site within the complex is the Historical Museum. It is what supplies context to the act of remembrance at Yad Vashem.

The Historical Museum traces the trajectory of the Holocaust, from anti-Semitism, the pogroms, and the extermination camps, to the resistance fighters and liberation, and it concludes with immigration and the rise of the state. Before even entering the full exhibit, the museum presents a more detailed overview of what the specific documentation that follows means in the context of its historical narrative. The historical function of the Museum is clearest just before the section describing liberation from the camps. Before turning a corner around which we encounter the famous picture that includes Elie Wiesel lying in a bunk at Buchenwald, the museum narrates the political problems for Jews immigrating to Palestine during the war. Before we see the liberation, we are confronted with pictures of the Palestinian Mufti stating support for Hitler's Final Solution. Next to this come images of British forces detaining Jewish immigrants in Cyprus. Situated between the resistance fighters and the liberation of the camps, Yad Vashem points toward the trauma of the event through the politics of the founding of Israel, a founding that, as we know, is still very much in negotiation. But the narrative of the museum places the state as the solution to the unrecoverable victims. The state replaces the loss of such remains with its founding narrative.

When leaving the Museum, having passed through the images of liberation and immigration and culminating in a memorial to the numbers of dead from each nation, we confront a warning: "Forgetfulness leads to exile, while remembrance is the secret of redemption." If we define redemption in terms of an act of remembrance, Yad Vashem offers a way into memory in order for redemption to be realized or fulfilled, in order that individual traumas may be gathered up and imbedded into history. And in this context, remembering the correct history—all of its details and motivations—becomes the only way to avoid exile. But the other side of remembrance is forgetfulness, a position that predicates exile itself, making it a place whose ends are more difficult to trace than that of remembrance. For Yad Vashem, the choice of forgetfulness is predicated on choosing *not* to remember—which is a particular act of remembrance itself: denial. By seeing remembrance as oppositional to forgetfulness, the Historical Museum at Yad Vashem offers a universal history of the event that can then stabilize a whole host of other identifications.

Unlike the Historical Museum, the memorials throughout Yad Vashem resist narration. The most visited memorial at Yad Vashem is the Children's Memorial. On a hill above the Historical Museum, we enter the memorial from the summit moving down into a corridor that turns from being open to the sun into a dark enclosed structure, the movement out of sunlight being accompanied by quiet music. The first images in the structure are the faces of children, illuminated faces whose eyes meet ours as we leave the brightness for the dark. The rest of the memorial is quite simple: we turn a corner into an even darker chamber where candlelights are reflected infinitely in glass around us. A voice reading the names of children murdered during the Holocaust echoes through the chamber.

Unlike the museum, the Children's Memorial makes no attempt at constructing a history of children's lives or experiences. It offers no real connection to current politics nor to issues of Jewish immigration to Israel. We don't know any actions of these named children; we aren't given any history or narrative. The memorial refuses to remember these children's stories: to do so would reinvoke the horrors that they suffered. In this instance, the memorial functions neither as a political nor historical act; the Children's Memorial simply gives place to names, names to place. The reading of the names of children in a darkened room with candlelights reflecting infinitely opens up the possibility that that name—that child—could be forgotten, especially considering that the name itself only lasts in the air until the next name is read. The power of the memorial is one that brings us to the brink of forgetfulness, the forgetfulness that is an effect of memory, not something that memory can itself replace.

At Yad Vashem, "the Holocaust" resides in the Historical Museum; its rhetoric places the viewer in the position of having to give up her name in order to identify with Israel's history instead of any particular victim. The Children's Memorial shows that there is no "Holocaust" as such. The faces of Jewish children function to invoke all children even as what they signify—the lives of those envisioned—cannot be known or remembered.

In the United States 1979, a document entitled "Summary of Views Received to Date, Museums and Monuments" was prepared to help guide what was then called the United States Holocaust Memorial Council in how to construct what would eventually become the United States Holocaust Memorial Museum. The memo falls into four parts, reflecting the tensions in the council's understanding of their charge at that early stage: "Living Memorial," "Monument," "Museum," and "Physical Memorial." The memo makes quite explicit the idea that "the Holocaust Memorial should consist of a living memorial *and* a memorial monument," and that it should include, ideally, three parts, "a monument, a museum, and an education center."

One of the reasons the years between 1979 and 1984 were so troubled and the work of the Commission was so painstakingly slow, as Edward Linenthal notes, is that its members were unable to reach a consensus as to just what defined the Holocaust, whose history should be included, how to address the various political and national constituencies (Armenians, the Roma, homosexual and mentally ill victims of the Nazis, to mention a few) that were involved in the history of those years. The museum, which had by 1981 been authorized by Congress, was to be dedicated to "the preservation of Holocaust history, commemoration of the victims, and education regarding the facts and implications of this awesome event." But while the building would house both its memorial and its didactic or historical spaces, "the memorial space is of highest priority as a conceptual challenge. It will serve not only as the symbol of the entire complex, but also as the conceptual link between the memorial museum and the other sacred American monuments located nearby" (2). So while the creation of a collective memory of the events of the Shoah was central, the invocation of memory—the commemoration of victims—and the space devoted to it was crucial.

In May 1984, the question of memory was raised during meetings of the development committee. Two issues were raised: the first was how to connect, in the permanent exhibit and in the space of the museum, the events of the Holocaust to the visitor's contemporary moment, his present; the second was how to allow the visitor to find his point of connection not to the collective experience of "Jews" or "those who were liquidated" but to individual persons. The museum's Director of Museum Development described the Hall of Witness as a place to invoke in visitors "a particular sadness." To do this, she argued for close-up photographs of individuals. She wanted to elicit the viewer to witness, at second hand, a single victim and remember that death as a way of connecting the witness's present with the past. But the designer hired to draw conceptual plans for the museum, makes clear the problem with such an approach:

> I'm afraid that the visitor will look at these photographs and immediately seek to remove them from their own time and space. 'Oh . . . something that happened long ago in a far-off place . . . something that could not happen here.' [. . . U]nless the visitor can relate a message to his own or her own time and space, the story will never penetrate or provoke. (2–3)

The particular "memory" invoked by the photo in the witness will be so strong as to refuse integration into the historical narrative that leads from the Shoah to the present. Rather than give the viewer room to recover from what she has seen so she can move on to other exhibit areas of the museum, he would rather not "give the visitor an opportunity to make a transition upon leaving the area on the camps. I don't want to give the visitor an easy out like that. At the point which the visitor will exit the section on the camps he will be at his most vulnerable. [. . .] If the message you want to convey is sharper than quiet solemnity, then you need to deliver it immediately" (6–7). The danger of letting the visitor off the hook here is that she will isolate what she sees in what amounts to a prison-house of memory, and the effect of what she has witnessed will remain unconnected to her present. The witness's retrospective opinions are impossible to eliminate unless you allow the testimonies and authentic, primary materials speak for themselves. The problem is that there's no guarantee that the secondhand witness will hear what they have to say, since that witness, too, will retrospectively provide a historical context for what they may have to say.

Though the concept proposal for the museum presented in April 1987 was eventually rejected by the development committee, it retained the idea that the museum's aim should be to help "prevent this unspeakable event from becoming, over time, simply one more of the many bloody chapters in the history of the world," and in so doing "help assure that [the Holocaust] remains unique." One part of the plan that was adopted was that the museum would "tell the story twice." The idea was to provide visitors, on the fourth floor of the museum— where the permanent exhibit begins—a capsule history of the Holocaust, which would be told through the use of films and dioramas. On the third and second floors of the museum, which would proceed chronologically from the years beore the rise of National Socialism in Germany through the Final Solution and its aftermath, displays of artifacts and photographs along with explanatory text would provide the visitor with more detail. "The prime motive for this approach of telling the story twice is, of course, to direct attention on the Holocaust at the start." The committee wanted to be sure that there is no doubt left in the visitor's mind that the Holocaust was a unique occurrence, with its own history, and what matters most is that each comes away with a firm sense of that history. What the visitors make of that history is left to them after they leave.

The museum's official story outline, adopted in 1988, has been followed quite closely in the current museum's layout. By this time, its mission is now described not in terms of memory but in terms of description: the permanent exhibit "must describe what the Holocaust was, interpret how it happened, and help to instill in visitors the determination to resist any such tragic horror in the future. In short, *the exhibition must inform the visitor's moral imagination*" (3, original emphasis). In describing the museum's "conceptual" nature, Jesjahu Weinberg—who became the museum's director in 1989—wrote of the building and the development of its exhibits that "the purpose of the Museum is to educate." It intends to do so

> through the dissemination of historical knoweldge on the Holocaust. By the meaningful arrangement of artifacts, photographs, audiovisual displays, and interactive information retrieval facilities, it intends to tell the story of the Holocaust, trying not only to relate to the public the events of this terrible chapter in the history of mankind, but also to expose the moral implications of the story. Thus, the exhibition designers' main task is to design ways of communicating information, to convey messages through the use of two- and three-dimensional visual means. ("The USHMM—A Conceptual Museum" 1, Weinberg 1997-014)

In one committee member's estimation—and in the design the director followed—the historical consciousness of the museum goer can (and in fact should) be manipulated so that the narrative of the Holocaust determines the individual memories the witness recalls. The moral imagination inculcated by the museum's narrative is unmistakably bound by that narrative and by the cultural memory invoked, a distinctly American one. (One of the changes that is most pronounced in the story outline adopted in 1988 is the addition of "American elements into each major area of the Core Exhibition in order to bring the Holocaust story home to American audiences.") The museum's artifacts and photos bring the viewer's attention to individual faces and moments in horror of the events, but the traumatic imagination (not to mention the moral one) is linked to the sweep of the events as a whole. Though certainly less teleological than Yad Vashem in Jerusalem, the U.S. museum has also found a way to guide its visitors, if only in principle if not in practice, to an imagination of the present that is intimately tied to the Holocaust and the destruction of those years. Certainly it is an American museum, located as it is near the national mall in the District of Columbia. But more than that, it is one that has as its aim the creation of a cultural memory and that attempts to leave little room, in spite of its name, for the discontinuity and interruption of the radically particular and fleeting individual memory.

Unless the museum's exhibits somehow make clear the connection between other world events and the Holocaust, the associative memory of individual museum visitors would establish a link between historical events—Bosnia and the Holocaust; evidence of the T-4 campaign in Germany with abortion and the Human Genome Project in the United States—that may appear tenuous but is "authentic" insofar as it is perfectly consistent with the workings of memory. Because the event of the Holocaust was so important for American and other visitors to understand, and the lessons it seemed to imply were so integral to the modern world, it was best to forge just such a cultural memory by establishing the historical narrative of the Holocaust as clearly as they could. The lessons to be learned, and the questions to be asked, could be left to individual museum goers once they left the museum's permanent exhibit. But in spite of the narrative established by the permanent exhibit of the USHMM, "events of the world" like Bosnia, like the attacks of September 11th or the wars in

Iraq and Israel, and like the innumerable events museum visitors carry with them into James Freed's building, intrude upon history, and upon historical memory, and create for the indivual memory images beyond even the witness's reckoning.

Discussion Questions, Part IV

1. Does the fact that some survivors write about what happened to them as fiction make their accounts inauthentic? (Does the fact that Etty Hillesum uses "poetic" language mean that her accounts of life in Westerbork are inauthentic?)

2. If reality isn't a matter of the eyewitness, how might poetry—the most nonmimetic of written genres—get at the "reality" of the Holocaust better than historical accounts?

3. Is Elie Wiesel right to say that Holocaust fiction is a contradiction in terms?

4. Assume for the moment that Berel Lang is right and that it's unethical to represent the Holocaust in anything other than either purely historical, transparent terms or in what he calls the "intransitive" language of fiction. What works of fiction, or poetry, or art, are unethical on his terms?

5. It's been argued that photography is a nearly transparent medium—what's reproduced in the image is what the photographer saw through the lens. If so, wouldn't photographs of the Holocaust (its beginnings, the destruction, its aftermath) be the most unaesthetic of representations? Why or why not?

6. Should atrocity photos be considered art? Why or why not?

7. Which would be the most *ethical* means of producing a representation of the Holocaust: through film or through drama? The most *accurate* means?

8. It's been said that museums create a memorial space through which to experience the effects of the Holocaust. Is the same true for film or drama? Is the same true for visual art?

9. Cynthia Ozick has said that Holocaust artists get themselves into trouble only when they confuse "the rights of history" with "the rights of fiction." What does she mean by this? Find instances of art that seems to confuse the rights of fiction (or art) with the rights of history.

10. If it's true that there are some things or events that simply should not be directly represented—certain aspects of the Holocaust, for example—are there other things or events that should be subject to a prohibition against representation? (Does the work in the "Mirroring Evil" show obey the ban on graven images? Do the paintings of Samuel Bak?)

V | TEACHING

CHAPTER 12

Conclusion: Some Thoughts about Teaching after Auschwitz

This chapter begins with a simple question: what do teachers and students hope to accomplish when speaking, teaching, and writing about the Shoah? In the years since 1945 we've heard a lot of answers: so that we never forget; so that something like the Holocaust can never happen again; so we remember those who perished; so that we can heal or redeem the damage done to the world through anti-Semitism or racial hatred or any number of other causes of genocide. These answers, and others like them, focus our attention on the events of the Holocaust and the ethical consequences of it. And they're compelling and useful answers. But they point to potentially impossible goals. First, we've seen in the chapters that precede this one that knowledge and learning often get in the way of and substitute for the event. By allowing us to believe that the event can be retrieved or adequately represented, the imperative to "remember" sometimes allows us to ignore a problematic fact: what we remember may not be closely related to the event at all, and the event may not be ours to remember. Second, the objects through which we do have access to the event—testimony, documentary evidence, museums and memorials, poetry and fiction—often resist our desire to have them "reflect" what happened. So regardless of what we think we know about the event—any event—the event itself will always be larger and more unmanageable than what could be contained by history, other academic disciplines, or mimetic art. Put simply, conventional accounts of learning may fail, particularly when it comes to the Holocaust.

The fifty-year-old response to the question why we learn about the Shoah is "to remember," to memorialize the dead so that what they suffered will never happen again. We see this imperative enacted concretely at Yad Vashem in Israel. The historical museum contextualizes the Holocaust in terms of a redemption through community, in this case the formation of the Israeli state. Throughout the museum we move through a narrative history of the Holocaust that both rests in and points toward the state itself. Yad Vashem presents redemption as the building of a community, and effectively ties the idea of learning to, if not that particular community, then to community in general. Learning, in other words, seems to be about the forging of a consensus. The example of Yad Vashem points to a problem: everything you learn must either be subsumed to the context in which you learn it—the Holocaust is a horrible step on the way toward Israel—or it falls outside that context and requires another, sometimes competing one. Aspects of the event that are difficult to account for are seen as anomalies. More problematically, the reader's or observer's experience is inevitably tied to the experiences of those whose lives are depicted in a museum, or testimony, or other representation. There's redemption in learning, in the sense that "the dead live through us," but we only learn by connecting what we don't know to what we do. That becomes like this; the Holocaust becomes like _____, and you fill in the blank.

But what about those things we see—aspects of the event that are horrifying or arresting in some other way—that seem to reside outside the pale of what we understand, or that's wholly outside our experience? What about aspects of the Holocaust that seem to resist consensus? Going back to the paradigm of "never forget," what happens when we're confronted with something that is totally alien to us and our memory, that we can't properly "learn" or remember at all? It'd suggest that there is something inherent in events—and perhaps particularly those events of, or related to, the Holocaust—that resist our knowing about them.

Of course, we have clear documentary evidence available that lets us know the operations of the mobile killing squads that followed behind the invasion of the Russian and Polish pale, for instance. There's enough testimonial evidence to let us know something about the experiences of individuals involved in the killing (both survivors and collaborators). But the evidence is not enough to provide us with knowledge of the events. When we teach and when we learn, we engage in a process that names things, events, and objects that we have never seen before. It involves discovering new words, regardless of whether we think of learning as transmission or as creation of knowledge.

A teacher or student may arrive at an understanding of an event, but something is usually missing. Seeing the event isn't the same thing as understanding the event.

Squaring the one with the other—what you saw and what you understand *about* what you saw—often forces aspects of the event out of the equation. In the case of the Holocaust, what often drops out is the horror, or the "why." It is to this problem that some historical and other academic accountings of the Holocaust fall prey. In many of them, the trauma of the event is covered over by an accumulation of detail—facts, figures, footnotes. Other representations of the Holocaust avoid this accretion of detail. Their aim isn't to forge a consensus, or understanding, but to force readers to see things that can't be integrated into any consensus. These works defy academic discourse, the discourse of teaching and learning. These other representations of the Holocaust don't try to construct academic knowledge. Instead, they pose serious questions about what it means to boil the Holocaust down to known quantities. Forging knowledge of the event through consensus—academic or otherwise—won't necessarily recover the lives of the six million or allow us to understand the fact of their murder so that nothing like it ever occurs again. The implications of learning as naming are severe for those of us who were not there on the spot and who have no point of experience to ground that which we learn.

TEACHING AND ETHICS

Sometimes the intensity of the subject matter of the Holocaust interferes with the methods of history, or even of straightforward narrative. One solution, some teachers have argued, is simply to use multiple forms of media and texts—testimonies, histories, film and photography, poetry and drama, fiction and nonfiction prose, art. While none is adequate in and of itself, the effect of them all, in all their overlapping and competing genres, will present an undeniable mass of evidence. But as much as teachers take their jobs to be to recognize the difficulty inherent in creating knowledge, particularly of a limit event like the Holocaust, that job is sometimes met with incredulity, frustration, and a kind of traumatic response. One way to respond, in the face of the complexity of the issues at hand, to what Blanchot calls the "utter burn of history" is to turn your back on it: "Gets on your nerves, seeing that every day" (*Shoah* 93). One way to think of the logic of denial, political and racial agendas notwithstanding, is that it's founded on the premise that something so horrible and counterrational simply cannot be contained by means of the conceptual or logical categories we construct for everyday occurrences. On this logic, the events of the Shoah must conform to some logic that we have overlooked. Maybe the Nazis were responding to the threat of Jewish Bolshevism. Maybe Jews were not systematically killed but died of the starvation that comes in wartime.

One of the problems of devoting a great deal of time studying the Holocaust is that it "gets on your nerves." Once you begin to realize the horror of the events and the difficulty involved in making sense of it, sometimes there's an impulse to tamp it down, to manage it, or to turn away from it. Every time I've taught a course on the Holocaust, at least one or two students become incredibly frustrated with its twists and convolutions of logic and good sense. In one instance, a student simply turned his back on the whole thing. It happened in a course on the Holocaust I co-taught in 1996, one that was focused specifically on the problems of writing the event. The question our class was trying to answer was this: how does an event marked by its apparent counterrationality become written in a logical language? Maybe more fundamentally, the question was: what happens when you or I or historians and novelists commit the Holocaust to writing? The course began with clear documentary evidence that laid out the chronology of the events, and moved on to testimonial accounts of the Holocaust, accounts that gave an impression of the individuals involved in the killing (both survivors and collaborators). What we all began to realize was that that evidence or even explanations *were* not enough to provide a comprehensive knowledge of the events and the experiences of the events comprising the Holocaust.

So we examined the degree to which any attempt to make sense of the event would be *disrupted* by what might be called the event's trace. We read, in the first third of the course, a number of memoirs written by survivors, and sections from several historical accounts—by Hilberg, Dawidowicz, Gilbert, Browning—of the events remembered. Assignments were designed to examine not simply how writing "conveyed" knowledge but how writing may have both created knowledge and stood in its way. As in the case of the Wilkomirski memoir, I encouraged students to investigate the relation between the traumatic or sublime event and the (sometimes precocious) testimony that give historians and laypeople access to it. By the tenth week of a sixteen-week semester, many students were extremely frustrated. Coming into the class, many of them had assumed that we would find a way to name the events of the Holocaust, to pin the Holocaust down so that it could be more or less known. But by putting pressure on the language with which the events of the Shoah were described, we were also putting pressure on the easy relation of language and event, and of experience and knowledge. Far from being able to understand the Holocaust, many students found that as they tried to write what they had learned, they were confounded by that aspect of the Shoah—its irrationality, the vertigo of its unreason—that prevents its being written, named, or known easily, if at all.

It was in the face of this frustration that one student proposed, over an electronic class listserv, a paper that attempted to prove that the Holocaust had not occurred. My knee-jerk response, made on the same listserv, was to tell him that I wanted him to write on something else, in part because of the problems inherent in disproving a negative, and in part because of the disruption such a topic (and the attendant discussion) would cause in the class. The proposal, and the discussions that took place on the listserv, uncovered a curious and troubling ethical dimension of teaching and learning when it comes to the Holocaust. It focused attention on how finding a name for an event—or even finding a way to avoid naming it—works against the effect the event has on individuals. It made everyone in the class understand something about what happens when the effects of an event become so palpable that they force a person to turn away from what he sees, and to turn instead to the much more comfortable realm of "academics," or "argument," or logic.

Many students argued that by writing the argument the student would learn the futility of it (namely, the futility of trying to prove that the Holocaust didn't happen) and, in turn, learn more fully about the event's occurrence. But by offering to write a paper that disproved the Holocaust, it's possible that this student was trying to avoid the very messy and uncomfortable encounter with representation itself. In arguing that the Holocaust did not occur, or that it was exaggerated, the student could build a competing, and negative, narrative of the Holocaust—a narrative of denial—that, like all narratives, runs the risk of keeping trauma and horror at bay. This kind of learning comes at the expense of learning's (ethical) effect. It's an effect that has little to do with logic, but has everything to do with the extralogical, irrational, traumatic underside of events like the Shoah. His proposal might well have prevented him from coming up with a new name for what troubled him so much about the Shoah.

Representations of the Shoah, insofar as they challenge traditional notions of ethics, do so by challenging the rational system of choices moving us—as a "we" or a community—toward the good. It was, after all, otherwise sane and rational people like us who took part in, and stood by during, the slaughter of six million others. And people took part in it because enough of them agreed by consensus that National Socialism and its attendant policies was a good thing. What we see in films like *Shoah* and *Schindler's List,* in both the USHMM and Yad Vashem, in texts like Yehuda Bauer's and Aharon Appelfeld's, is picture after picture of the failure of an ethics based on a consensually agreed-upon "good." But what we also have in those texts is the establishment of an ethics of representation in which the failure of "the good" forces readers, writers, and people of good conscience to find some other way to confront what they've seen or read. While the representation of the Holocaust points to the problems inherent in the logic of rationality, it also forces us to find some other way to come to terms with the horror and illogic of the Holocaust. Logic and morality may fail, but that failure acts as a challenge. And I think it is important for students to deal honestly with that challenge.

Teaching (after) Auschwitz

What are some of the implications of what I've just said about teaching? One has to do with claims that texts like Binjamin Wilkomirski's *Fragments* is tantamount to Holocaust denial, and another has to do with contemporary claims about the relation of writing to reality. What if, as some claim, Wilkomirski's "memories," and the trauma that he so clearly seems to have experienced, are not patently false? Does the ambivalent relation of testimony to knowledge and learning allow for such a reading of the Wilkomirski memoir? It is, in fact, entirely consistent with the idea that the nature of events rendered in discourse can only be established individually. It is impossible to understand whether or not "the Holocaust" occurred in all of its horrible detail on such a paradigm. Any rendering of the event—either through eyewitness testimony, with the broad brushes of history, or through panoramic films like *Schindler's List* or *Shoah*—risks giving us the mistaken impression that what we hear or see in the testimony is what the eyewitness herself saw, or that the individual narrative can substitute for the larger historical narrative. As I've said, this was the point made over and over again during the debates that followed the release of *Schindler's List* in 1994. Reviewers worried that the American viewing public would equate the movie with the event, and conclude that in the end the Holocaust wasn't all that terrible. What was remarkable about nearly every discussion that took place after the film's premiere is that every participant in the debate "saw" something quite different in the film. This is partly due to the nature of taste, but it is also partly due to the nature of the pedagogical enterprise.

For the last forty years—or, if you go back to Aristotle, for the last two thousand—we have simply taken for granted the idea that no argument, no matter how strong and no matter the integrity of the speaker, will settle a matter once and for all. Arguments produce tentative truths that can be later tested for consistency. In this view of knowledge there are few guarantees that what you learn in one "conversation" or testimony will be learned the same way in another. In this view, the successful teacher is the one who can convince his students not that what he says is true, but that what he says, while not necessarily true, has effects that are ultimately related to what actually happened. And this effect is a radically individual one, an effect that is different from person to person, from listener to listener, from student to student. To return to the Wilkomirski narrative, critics are right to say that if we can undermine the authority of the writer of a Holocaust testimony, and say with certainty that he was never there and that he did not see what he claims to have seen, we have eliminated one piece of evidence that we can use to argue that the atrocities of the Shoah occurred. Such testimonies—in the form of eyewitness accounts, documentary evidence, trial transcripts, and diaries—taken together form the tapestry of suffering that we have inherited as the narrative of the Holocaust.

But testimonies establish the credibility of the speaker, and indicate an event as it occurs prior to her ability to speak it, not because they accord with the facts of history (facts that are accessible only through narrative). They do so because they *disrupt* the narrative of history and force the reader, or the interviewer, to see something horrible, perhaps a trace of the traumatic event itself. In the case of the Wilkomirski memoir, we may well be able to undermine the authority of the speaker if we take him to be trying to establish a narrative of the circumstances of the Holocaust that will settle the matter once and for all. And the reverse is also true: his lack of credibility seems to throw open to question the veracity of testimonies of other survivors. But this is not to say that it lessens the traumatic effect of the testimony, or the testimony's ability to indicate something about the nature of the disaster, though that disaster may not be the historical events we call the Shoah.

The pedagogical implications of this are complicated. Holocaust studies has paid a good deal of attention in the last several years to how to teach the Holocaust in high school and university classes, and how representations of the Holocaust can be seen as points of departure for discussions of diversity, or race hatred, or the role of resistance, or any number of other controversial topics. The assumption we generally make in courses like these is that their goal should be the production of knowledge of the events of the Shoah and that, whenever possible, to connect that knowledge with other knowledges—of the dynamics of poverty, or of racism, or of other disasters or genocides. But while there is clear documentary evidence available to substantiate the occurrence of events like the gassings at Chelmno, and though there is enough testimonial evidence to suggest to us the experiences of individuals involved in the killing (both survivors and collaborators), that evidence cannot bring knowledge into accord with the events themselves. I've seen this in writing classes associated with the Holocaust: faced with the enormity of the events as described in halting, incomplete, and yet horrifying testimonies and documents, some students sometimes have had a very difficult time evaluating that writing, let alone trying to find language with which to write themselves. How can you possibly assess the authority of the sources you read, and the character of the witnesses who have written them, when you are shattered by their effect?

The effect of a discourse, of a testimony, cannot function as evidence of the authority or veracity of the witness, if by that we mean "getting it right." But if we take seriously the idea that learning occurs when a witness indicates the way an event exceeds her ability to write or name it, then maybe Holocaust studies courses should not try so hard to produce knowledge—either through analysis of documents, testimonies, and literature, or through the production of essays linking anti-Semitism to contemporary racism. Maybe they should try harder to help students understand the elusiveness of the traumatic experience, and that writing seems to show the event's effects even when it fails to pin the event down as something we can, once and for all, know.

TEACHING AND WRITING AUSCHWITZ AFTER 9/11

It's not true (or only true) that the Holocaust is unwritable or unteachable, some-thing that has become a trope in recent discussions of the events culminating the Final Solution. It's also not true (or only true) that writing or teaching the Holo-caust requires that we engage primarily in ethical debates about the Holocaust's connection with other catastrophes, including the middle passage, ethnic cleans-ing, or 9/11 (though this claim isn't inconsistent with the argument I'll make). To write the Holocaust, to present it in a language that makes relatively clear its ethical and its (perhaps) traumatic effects, we need to make use of genres and modes of writing that are the *farthest* from what might ordinarily be called "au-thentic" narratives. Only those other ways of writing will provide our generation with what might be called a sense of the "real" of the Holocaust. It is just this no-tion that I think is the best defense against a skepticism or relativism whose log-ical culmination is a denial or radical revision of the events of the Shoah.

Let's go back to Lyotard's book *The Differend*. In it Lyotard is asking something like the question we ought to be posing to one another about writing and the Holocaust. He's not asking "Is it possible to write the Holocaust so that it is un-derstood?" He's asking "How is it possible to write the Holocaust so that our un-derstanding of it doesn't lull us into complacency or a more subtle form of denial?" Early on in that book, Lyotard makes a provocative statement: "reality is not a mat-ter of the absolute eyewitness, but a matter of the future" (53). In the context of Auschwitz, this is a distinction between the object of perception and the object of history. When "the Holocaust" is taken as an object of history, we can say that it occurred, and that it occurred in certain ways, because a "relatively stable com-plex of nominatives" or names for it have been developed and widely accepted. As an object of perception—as something that can be pointed to, and that can be established in time and space—it may be put under a great deal of pressure. Those who can say "I was there" have become smaller and smaller in number, and even the testimony of those who were there is subject to error, forgetfulness, and what Berel Lang has called "aestheticization." For "Auschwitz" as an utterance to be real, the writer has to find ways to describe it, to attach other names to it, that—in Lyotard's words—"don't falsify the accepted definition." But just what would the accepted definition of Auschwitz look like?

Many students know full well what it looks like. We've seen *Schindler's List;* we've read *The Diary of a Young Girl* or maybe, before bar or bat mitzvahs, *The Devil's Arithmetic*. Writing the Holocaust is not a conundrum for us because there's a pretty strong paradigm inside of which the event is clearly understand-able. The "fairly stable complex of nominatives" is stable enough for teachers to superimpose upon it another such complex—one that refers to anti-Semitism, or racism, or ethnic cleansing—and the substitution of the Holocaust for Bosnia, or

Crown Heights, or east Jerusalem becomes relatively easy. The eyewitness testimony from Warsaw looks very much like the eyewitness testimony from Ground Zero. It doesn't falsify the accepted definition of either the originary term (Holocaust) or its alternative (the terrorist assault on innocent victims).

But what puts a stick in the metaphorical spokes here is Lyotard's *differend:* an "unstable state of and instant of language wherein something which must be able to be put into phrases cannot yet be" (13). And Auschwitz, which seems to be a clear case of an object of history that has become a stable discursive field over the last fifty years, turns out to be an even clearer case of a *differend.* While "Auschwitz" names an object of history that is more or less stable, its object of perception is far less stable. Eyewitness accounts of the events of the Holocaust—rather than the behemoth of the Holocaust itself—are heterogenous. They differ from one another; they make references to places, to events, to experiences so radically diverse as to be almost completely irreconcilable with the strong narratives we've come to read as "The Holocaust." The diverse names for these aspects of the event, aspects we learn through these testimonies, make consensus impossible. No absolute eyewitness could make all of these aspects of the event concrete, or writable, under a single name. Because the eyewitness is no longer the arbiter of that reality, there must be some other criterion by which the writing (or naming) of Auschwitz can be accomplished.

Moreover, the typical measures with which we would take account of the events don't work anymore. First there is the problem of evidence, which in the closing year of the war the Germans made a methodical attempt to destroy, from burning the records kept at the camps to exhuming and burning the bodies that had been buried in mass graves. The problem of evidence is compounded by the diversity and the confusion of those documents that are left, which makes tracing the policy of the Final Solution—at least in terms of culpability—frustrating. But there is also the so-called problem of enormity: the event was so geographically and politically diverse, and so horrifying to those who could provide even corroborated accounts of the events from country to country, policy to policy, camp to camp, that it almost requires that we invent new historical and ethical categories for it. By what criterion does one measure the catastrophe if it destroys even the instruments we use to measure it?

I taught a course in the fall of 2001 that was meant to work toward some other (as yet undefined) criterion. That course, like the one I taught in 1996, was divided roughly into thirds, and in each section of the course we tested the criteria that have traditionally been used to measure, and to write about, events of history. The first criterion could be called a historical one. If the job of the historian is to gather evidence of events, examine the patterns that run through them, and to construct a reasonable and consistent narrative of events that accounts for most, if not all, of the occurrences indexed by that evidence, then historical writing is meant to provide a broadly accessible and accurate account of what happened for those who weren't there. During the first five weeks of the course, we looked at competing historical accounts of events from the Holocaust, including sections from Christopher Browning's *Ordinary Men* and the entirety of Jan Tomasz Gross's *Neighbors.* We also read and debated Hayden White's now-famous essay about historical emplotment, specifically where he addresses Andreas Hilgruber's book *Two Kinds of Ruin,* where he sets side by side the tragedy of the Shoah and the tragedy of the Wehrmach's destruction in the east by the Soviet army. By what measure, I asked, are historical narratives of the Shoah considered "accurate," or "authentic," or "effective"? We debated how the diversity of evidence could be placed into what Lyotard calls a "stable complex of nominatives" that may be understood and agreed upon by all parties in a debate. The second section of the course was designed to get us even "closer" to the events by examining eyewitness testimonies, diaries, letters, and memoirs written by those who were there on the spot. If historical narratives attempt to wrangle with the heterogenous detritus of history, then on a memorial or testimonial criterion, that detritus—in the form of firsthand accounts—forms history's core. We read Etty Hillesum's diary and letters, we read Abraham Lewin's diary of the Warsaw ghetto, we read Primo Levi's and Paul Steinberg's very different accounts of a year in Auschwitz. In doing so, again we argued and wrote about the testimonial criterion. How can we meaure the eyewitness's account of the events in which he was occupied against other, similar events? How do we account for the inevitable memorial lapses that seeps into those accounts—and the effects of a "traumatic forgetfulness"—in building a "stable complex of nominatives" from them?

In the fall of 2001, we were haunted by the destruction of the World Trade Center in New York and of a section of the Pentagon in Washington. The fact of this more recent catastrophe drove home the weaknesses of both the historical and the testimonial criteria by which we measure history. In the case of 9/11, while we didn't confront the event directly in the class that Tuesday, the images we all saw (I and many of my students spent most of the day on the phone or in front of the TV) seemed indelible. Here was history, playing itself out in front of our eyes. And yet within hours of the catastrophe, we also heard conflicting reports of culpability and of the network of events playing themselves out around the world. Without knowing we'd do so, to illustrate the problems of "parallelism" in historical narratives using Hilgruber's book as its prime example, my students and I took up the parallel versions of the 9/11 attacks that became common within a few days: while it was true that the deaths of thousands of innocent Americans was a tragedy, there was a parallel tragedy in the deaths of thousands of Palestinians and other Arabs in the middle east at the hands of anti-Islamic western (and especially American) interests. Here were accounts of the event that, by many of my students' lights, were simply contradicted by the facts, by what they saw. Yet by many if not most historical criteria, those accounts were perfectly plausible. Students' writing about this problem was heated but always precisely on point: reality here seemed to have nothing to do with the "absolute eyewitness." Here they were, eyewitnesses of a sort to the events of 9/11 and their accounts of what happened were drowned by the "object of history." If this was true with 9/11, was it not also true of the Holocaust?

There was another specter that haunted the class, though I think in reality it only haunted me: that 1996 course in which one of the students proposed the paper arguing that the Holocaust didn't occur. That course's trajectory was more or less the same as this one's: we worked through the question of the criteria by which the Shoah could be written, and the failure of the historical and testimonial criteria had so frustrated students that a few of them wondered whether we weren't creeping into a radical relativism, in which any narrative accounting of events was as good as any other. Students reported, at the conclusion of the course, that while they appreciated the pressure put on historical and testimonial categories of writing, they wanted more discussion of what could be called an "ethical" criterion. After 9/11, and especially after the discussion of Hilgruber and historical parallelism—in which the World Trade Center became the historical equivalent of American and Israeli violence against Arab Muslims—we seemed to skate dangerously close to that same relativism.

What would an ethical criterion look like, and how would it work against the impulse toward relativism and denial that plagued the earlier course? In fact, Lyotard provides an answer in *The Differend*. Reality isn't a matter of the absolute eyewitness but of the future; and to cast history forward, into the future, "the historian must break with the monopoly over history granted to the cognitive regimen of phrases, and he or she must venture forth by lending his or her ear to what is not presentable under the rules of knowledge" (57). What happened matters less than what the narrative of history allows others to see, what effect testimony or narrative has upon the listener. Ideally this effect allows the reader to get a sense of what happened, but not understand it as if it were represented as an image or as something clearly or completely knowable. The effect seems to emerge from the reading or from the reader's "seeing," in which what happened emerges in the present as something altogether new and unprecedented as knowledge. In Lyotard's words, "The scholar can claim to know nothing about [what happened], but the common person has a complex feeling, the one aroused by the negative presentation of the indeterminate" (56).

Auschwitz is the sign of the limit of what can be understood in traditional scholarly categories. The witness, as much as the historian or the sociologist, is charged with "breaking the monopoly over history granted to the cognitive regimen of phrases"—the narrative of history that is well worn, well understood, and that because of this regularity runs the risk of letting us think we can "know what it was like." She must lend an ear "to what is not presentable under the rules of knowledge" (57), things that seem utterly impossible. It requires, to put it another way, a writing in which the impossible can impress itself upon the narrative of history, and works against it. It may require a language other than that of history or memory.

Just what this sort of writing looks like is hard to say. There are a number of possibilities, however, which we explored in the last third of our course: Hayden White has proposed a "middle voice," an intransitive writing that collapses the distance between agent and patient, object and subject, in which the fact of writing in the present is inextricable from the representation of events from the past. Dominick La Capra and, in another context, Geoffrey Hartman have made a case for a mode of writing that records or represents not only the traumatic effect as it registers upon the witness but also the related effect the representation—the testimony—has upon the writer. Aharon Appelfeld, like other writers who were there on the spot, has claimed that the event has had such an effect upon them that they are unable or unwilling to represent it directly, opting instead for representing "before, or after, but not during," and leaving the absent event to register in its effects. What each of these approaches has in common with the others is an inescapable ethical criterion, one suggested by Lyotard. Any writing should make visible not just the object of history but also the object of perception, regardless of their incompatibility. It's precisely this incompatibility—this impasse—that registers as an effect upon the secondhand witness.

It is this sort of writing—whatever it is—that works against the monopoly of the cognitive regimen of phrases. It is this regimen that lulls us into believing that the narrative of the Holocaust is so well-wrought as to admit other possibilities. "A historical discourse is a web of explanations that may give way to an 'other explanation,' if the latter is deemed to account for diversity in a more satisfactory manner" (Vidal-Naquet 97). The problem is that the deniers' and the relativists' accounts seem—on their face at least—to provide a rational sense of the diversity, the heterogeneity, of the evidence from the Holocaust. (What, after all, could be more counterrational than the dehumanization and destruction of six million people?) It is appeals to "free speech" and to "dispassionate inquiry," perverse though this may sound, through which deniers and relativists—even those like my student from 1996—claim to put forward other possibilities. What I've tried to suggest is that writing ought to resist the historical or "authentic" impulse, and should instead function on an ethical criterion. Writing that casts history into the future by lending an ear to what is not presentable under the rules of knowledge may provide us a way out from under the monopoly of academic discourse, and forces us to confront the ways in which we are always and inevitably implicated in events right here, right now.

Discussion Questions, Part V

1. What does studying the Holocaust teach you?

2. What is the relation between learning and remembering? Between "rational" knowledge and "affective" knowledge?

3. What is the relation between learning (about) the Holocaust and denying the Holocaust?

4. How do the academic disciplines, which provide different ways of knowing, help us understand the Holocaust? Do these divisions of knowledge hinder our understanding of the Holocaust in any way?

Bibliography

The following list includes works cited in this book as well as books, essays, and other material that may be helpful for those who want to do further research on the topic of the Holocaust. Like the book, the list isn't exhaustive; it's meant instead to give readers a sense of what material is available in Holocaust studies. The categories generally follow the outline of the book's chapters.

THE HOLOCAUST AND HOLOCAUST STUDIES (CHAPTERS 1–3)

General History

Aly, Götz. "The Planning Intelligentsia and the 'Final Solution.'" *Confronting the Nazi Past: New Debates on Modern German History,* ed. Michael Burleigh. London: Collins and Brown, 1996. 140–53.

Arendt, Hannah. *Eichmann in Jerusalem: A Report on the Banality of Evil.* New York: Viking/Penguin, 1963.

Bartov, Omer. *Eastern Front, 1941–45: German Troops and the Barbarisation of Warfare.* Oxford: St. Antony's/Macmillan, 1985.

———. *Hitler's Army: Soldiers, Nazis, and War in the Third Reich.* New York: Oxford U P, 1991.

Bauer, Yehuda. *Rethinking the Holocaust.* New Haven, CT: Yale U P, 2001.

———. *A History of the Holocaust.* New York: Watts, 1982.

_____. "The Place of the Holocaust in Contemporary History." *Studies in Contemporary Judaism,* Ed. Jonathan Frankel vol. 1. Bloomington: Indiana U P, 1984.

Baumann, Zygmunt. *Modernity and the Holocaust.* Cambridge: Polity Press, 1989.

Berenbaum, Michael, and John K. Roth. *Holocaust: Religious and Philosophical Implications.* New York: Paragon, 1987.

Botwinick, Rita. *History of the Holocaust: From Ideology to Annihilation.* Upper Saddle River, NJ: Prentice Hall, 2001.

Bracher, Karl-Dietrich. *The German Dictatorship: The Origins, Structure, and Effects of National Socialism.* New York: Praeger, 1970.

Bracher, Karl-Dietrich, Wolfgang Sauer, and Gerhard Schulz. *Die Nationalsozialistiche Machtergriefung: Studien zur Erichtung des Totalitären Herrschaftssystems in Deutschland, 1933–34.* Cologne: Wesdeutscher Verlag, 1962.

Breitman, Richard. *Official Secrets.* New York: Hill and Wang, 1998.

Broszat, Martin. *The Hitler State: The Foundation and Development of the Internal Structure of the Third Reich.* London: Longman, 1981.

_____. *Der Nationalsozialismus: Weltanschauung, Programm, und Wirklichkeit.* Stuttgart: n.p., 1960.

Browning, Christopher. *Ordinary Men: Reserve Police Battalion 101 and the Final Solution in Poland.* New York: HarperCollins, 1992.

_____. *The Origins of the Final Solution.* Lincoln/Jerusalem: U Nebraska P/Yad Vashem, 2004.

_____. *Nazi Policy, Jewish Workers, German Killers.* Cambridge: Cambridge U P, 2000.

Dallin, Alexander. *German Rule in Russia 1941–45: A Study of Occupation Policies.* New York: St. Martin's Press, 1957.

Dawidowicz, Lucy. *The War Against the Jews, 1933–45.* New York: Holt, Rinehart, Winston, 1975.

Dwork, Deborah, and Robert Jan Van Pelt. *Holocaust: A History.* New York: Norton, 2002.

Elkana, Yehuda. "The Need to Forget." *Haaretz* (2 March 1988): 4.

Engel, David. *The Holocaust: A History of the Third Reich and the Jews.* New York: Longman, 2000.

Feingold, Henry L. *Bearing Witness: How America and its Jews Responded to the Holocaust.* Syracuse, NY: Syracuse U P, 1995.

Friedlander, Henry. *The Origins of the Nazi Genocide.* Chapel Hill: U of North Carolina P, 1995.

_____. "Step by Step: The Expansion of Murder 1939–1941." *German Studies Review* 17.3 (October 1994): 495–507.

Friedlander, Saul. "Introduction." *Probing the Limits of Representation: Nazism and the "Final Solution"* Ed. Saul Friedlander. Cambridge, MA: Harvard U P, 1992. 1–21.

_____. *Nazi Germany and the Jews.* New York: HarperCollins, 1997.

Gilbert, Martin. *Holocaust: A History of the Jews in Europe During the Second World War.* New York: Henry Holt, 1987.

_____. *Never Again: A History of the Holocaust.* New York: Universe, 2000.

Hilberg, Raul. *The Destruction of the European Jews.* Chicago: Quadrangle, 1961.

_____. "The Ghetto as a Form of Government: An Analysis of Isaiah Trunk's Judenrat." *The Holocaust as Historical Experience,* eds. Yehuda Bauer and Nathan Rotenstreich. New York: Holmes and Meier, 1981. 155–71.

Hoffman, Eva. *Shtetl: The Life and Death of a Small Town and the World of Polish Jews.* Boston: Houghton Mifflin, 1997.

Huttenbach, H. "From the Editor: Towards a conceptual definition of genocide." *Journal of Genocide Research* 4 (2002): 167–175.

Jäckel, Eberhard. *Hitler in History.* Hanover, NH: University Press of New England, 1984.

Levi, Primo. *Survival in Auschwitz.* New York: Vintage, 1996.

_____. *The Drowned and the Saved.* New York: Vintage/Random House, 1987.

Lewin, Abraham. *A Cup of Tears: A Diary of the Warsaw Ghetto.* Ed. Antony Polonsky. Trans. Christopher Hutton. Oxford: Basil Blackwell, 1988.

Marrus, Michael. *The Holocaust in History.* New York: Meridian/Penguin, 1987.

Müller, Filip. *Auschwitz Inferno.* London: Routledge and Kegan Paul, 1979.

Rozett, Robert, and Shmuel Spector. *The Encyclopedia of the Holocaust.* New York: Facts on File, 2000.

Scheffler, Wolfgang. *Judenverfolgung im Dritten Reich.* Frankfurt: Büchergilde Gutenberg, 1960.

Tory, Avraham. *Surviving the Holocuast: The Kovno Ghetto Diary.* Ed. Martin Gilbert, trans. Jerzy Michalowicz. Cambridge, MA: Harvard U P, 1990.

Yahil, Leni. *The Holocaust: The Fate of European Jewry, 1932–1945.* Oxford: Oxford U P, 1990.

Gender, Culture, and Other Groups

Brenner, Rachel Feldhay. *Writing as Resistance: Four Women Confronting the Holocaust— Edith Stein, Simone Weil, Anne Frank, Etty Hillesum.* University Park: Pennsylvania State U P, 1997.

Burleigh, Michael. *Ethics and Extermination: Reflections on Nazi Genocide.* Cambridge: Cambridge U P, 1997.

Dadrian, Kevork N. "The Documentation of the World War I Armenian Massacres in the Proceedings of the Turkish Military Tribunal." *International Journal of Middle East Studies* 23 (1991). 549–576.

Grau, Günther. "Final Solution of the Homosexual Question?" *The Holocaust and History.* Eds. Michael Berenbaum and Abraham J. Peck. Bloomington: Indiana U P, 1998.

Lautmann, Rüdiger. "The Pink Triangle." *The Holocaust and History,* eds. Michael Berenbaum and Abraham J. Peck. Bloomington: Indiana U P, 1998.

Milton, Sybil. "Gypsies and the Holocaust." *History Teacher* 24.4 (1991): 375–86.

_____. "Nazi Politics Toward Roma and Sinti." *Journal of the Gypsy Lore Society* 2.1 (1992): 1–18.

Ofer, Dalia, and Leonore Weitzman, eds. *Women in the Holocaust.* New Haven, CT: Yale U P, 1998.

Proctor, Robert. *Racial Hygiene: Medicine Under the Nazis.* Cambridge, MA: Harvard U P, 1988.

Zimmerman, Michael. *Rassenutopie und Genozid* (Racial Utopia and Genocide). Hamburg: Christians, 1996.

Anti-Semitism

Chamberlain, Houston. *Foundations of the Nineteenth Century.* New York: Fertig, 1968.

Golsan, Richard. *Memory, the Holocaust, and French Justice: The Bousquet and Touvier Affairs.* Hanover, NH: University Press of New England, 1996.

Hellig, Jocelyn. *The Holocaust and Antisemitism: A Short History.* Oxford: Oneworld, 2003.

Lindemann, Albert S. *The Jew Accused: Three Anti-Semitic Affairs (Dreyfus, Beilis, Frank) 1894–1915.* Cambridge: Cambridge U P, 1991.

_____. *Anti-semitism Before the Holocaust.* New York: Longman, 2000.

Massing, Paul W. *Rehearsal for Destruction: A Study of Political Anti-Semitism in Imperial Germany.* New York: Harper and Row, 1949.

Stern, Kenneth S. *Holocaust Denial.* New York: American Jewish Committee, 1993.

Wistrich, Robert S. *Antisemitism: The Longest Hatred.* New York: Schocken, 1991.

Evolution of Holocaust Studies and New Scholarship

Agamben, Giorgio. *Remnants of Auschwitz: The Witness and the Archive.* Trans. David Heller-Roazen. New York: Zone Books, 1999.

Arendt, Hannah. *The Origins of Totalitarianism.* New York: Harcourt Brace, 1951.

Bartov, Omer, ed. *The Holocaust: Origins, Implementation, Aftermath.* New York: Routledge, 2000.

Bartov, Omer. *Germany's War and the Holocaust: Disputed Histories.* Ithaca, NY: Cornell U P, 2003.

Bauer, Yehuda. *Jews For Sale? Nazi-Jewish Negotiations 1933–45.* New Haven: Yale U P, 1994.

———. *Out of the Ashes.* New York: Pergamon, 1989.

Bernard-Donals, Michael and Richard Glejzer, eds. *Witnessing the Disaster: Essays on the Holocaust and Representation.* Madison: U of Wisconsin P, 2003.

Browning, Christopher. *Collected Memories: Holocaust History and Postwar Testimony.* Madison: U of Wisconsin P, 2003.

Cole, Tim. *Selling the Holocaust: From Auschwitz to Schindler's List, How History is Bought, Packaged, and Sold.* New York: Routledge, 1999.

Fackenheim, Emil. "The 614th Commandment." In "Jewish Values in the Post-Holocaust Future: A Symposium." *Judaism* 16 (Summer 1967).

———. *God's Presence in History.* New York: Harper and Row, 1970.

———. *The Jewish Return into History.* New York: Schocken, 1978.

———. *To Mend the World: Foundations of Future Jewish Thought.* Bloomington: Indiana U P, 1994.

Finkelstein, Norman. *The Holocaust Industry: Reflections on the Exploitation of Jewish Suffering.* London: Verso, 2000.

Frankl, Victor. *Man's Search for Meaning: An Introduction to Logotherapy.* New York: Simon and Schuster, 1962.

Gellately, Robert, and Ben Kierman, eds. *The Specter of Genocide: Mass Murder in Historical Perspective.* Cambridge: Cambridge U P, 2003.

Goldhagen, Daniel Jonah. *Hitler's Willing Executioners: Ordinary Germans and the Holocaust.* New York: Knopf, 1996.

Gutman, Israel. *Holocaust and Resistance.* Jerusalem: Yad Vashem, 1970.

Habermas, Jürgen. "A Kind of Settlement of Damages: The Apologetic Tendencies in German History Writing." *Forever in the Shadow of Hitler? The Dispute about the Germans' Understanding of History.* Eds. and trans. James Knowlton and Truett Cates. Atlantic Highlands, NJ: Humanities Press, 1993. 34–44.

Hilgruber, Andreas. *Zweirlei Untergang* (Two Kinds of Ruin). Cologne: Siedler Verlag, 1986.

Hoffman, Eva. *After Such Knowledge: Memory, History, and the Legacy of the Holocaust.* New York: Public Affairs, 2004.

Jorgensen, N. H. "The Definition of Genocide: Joining the Dots in the Light of Recent Practice." *International Criminal Law Review* 1 (2001): 285–313.

Katz, Steven. *The Holocaust and Comparative History.* New York: Leo Baeck Institute, 1993.

Kenan, Orna. *Between Memory and History: The Evolution of Israeli Historiography of the Holocaust.* New York: Peter Lang, 2003.

La Capra, Dominick. "Approaching Limit Events: Siting Agamben." *Witnessing the Disaster: Essays on the Holocaust and Representation.* Eds. Michael Bernard-Donals and Richard Glejzer. Madison: U of Wisconsin P, 2003.

Lang, Berel. *The Future of the Holocaust: Between History and Memory.* Ithaca, NY: Cornell U P, 1999.

Linenthal, Edward. *Preserving Memory: The Struggle to Create the United States Holocaust Memorial Museum.* New York: Penguin, 1994.

Maier, Charles. *The Unmasterable Past: History, the Holocaust, and German National Identity.* Cambridge, MA: Harvard U P, 1988.

Mieder, Wolfgang, and David Scrase. *Reflections on the Holocaust: Festschrift for Raul Hilberg on His Seventy-Fifth Birthday.* Burlington: Center for Holocaust Studies at the University of Vermont, 2001.

Milgram, Stanley. *Obedience to Authority: An Experimental View.* New York: Harper and Row, 1974.

Miller, Judith. *One by One by One: Facing the Holocaust.* New York: Simon and Schuster, 1990.

Mommsen, Hans. "Die Realisierung des Utopischen: die 'Endlosung der Judengfrage' im 'Dritten Reich.'" (The Realization of Utopia: The 'Final Solution of the Jewish Question' in the 'Third Reich') *Geschichte und Gesellschaft* 9.3 (1983): 381–420.

Nolte, Ernst. "Der Vergangenheit, Die Nicht Vergehen Will" (The Past that Will Not Pass). *Frankfurter Allegmaine Zeitung* (6 June 1986): 16.

Novick, Peter. *The Holocaust in American Life.* Boston: Houghton Mifflin, 1999.

Ofer, Dalia. "Israel." *The World Reacts to the Holocaust.* Eds. David Wyman and Charles Rosensveig. Baltimore: Johns Hopkins U P, 1996. 836–923.

O'Neill, Robert J. *The German Army and the Nazi Party 1933–39.* New York: J. H. Heineman, 1966.

Powers, Samantha. *'A Problem from Hell': America in the Age Of Genocide.* Perennial/HarperCollins, 2002.

Rousso, Henry. *The Vichy Syndrome: History and Memory in France Since 1944.* Cambridge, MA: Harvard U P, 1991.

Segev, Tom. *The Seventh Million.* New York: Hill and Wang, 1993.

Solkoff, Norman. *Beginnings, Mass Murder, and the Aftermath of The Holocaust: Where History and Psychology Intersect.* Lanham, MD: University Press of America, 2001.

Todorov, Tzvetan. *Facing the Extreme: Moral Life in the Concentration Camps.* Trans. Arthur Denner and Abigail Pollak. New York: Henry Holt, 1996.

Religion, the Holocaust, and the Churches

Bartov, Omer, and Phyllis Mack, eds. *In God's Name: Genocide and Religion in the Twentieth Century.* New York: Berghahn, 2001.

Friedlander, Henry. *Pius XII and the Third Reich.* New York: Knopf, 1966.

Kirschner, Robert, ed. and trans. *Rabbinic Responsa of the Holocaust Era.* New York: Schocken, 1985.

Lewy, Gunter. *The Catholic Church and Nazi Germany.* New York: McGraw-Hill, 1964.

Littell, Franklin. *The Crucifixion of the Jews.* New York: Harper and Row, 1975.

———, ed. *The German Church Struggle and the Holocaust.* Lewiston, NY: Mellen U P, 1990.

Steigman-Gall, Richard. *The Holy Reich: Nazi Conceptions of Christianity, 1919–1945.* Cambridge: Cambridge U P, 2003.

THEORIES OF HISTORY (CHAPTERS 4 AND 5)

Arendt, Hannah. *Eichmann in Jerusalem: A Report on the Banality of Evil.* New York: Viking/Penguin, 1963.

Bennington, Geoff, Derek Attridge, and Robert Young, eds. *Post-Structuralism and the Question of History.* Cambridge: Cambridge U P, 1987.

Blanchot, Maurice. *The Writing of the Disaster.* Trans. Ann Smock. Lincoln: U of Nebraska P, 1995.

Friedlander, Saul, ed. *Probing the Limits of Representation: Nazism and the "Final Solution."* Cambridge, MA: Harvard U P, 1992.

———. "The 'Final Solution': On the Unease in Historical Interpretation." *Lessons and Legacies: The Meaning of the Holocaust in a Changing World.* Ed. Peter Hayes. Evanston, IL: Northwestern U P, 1991. 19–31.

Funkenstein, Amos. *Perceptions of Jewish History.* Berkeley: U of California P, 1993.

Ginzburg, Carlo. "Just One Witness." *Probing the Limits of Representation: Nazism and the "Final Solution."* Ed. Saul Friedlander. Cambridge, MA: Harvard U P, 1992. 82–96.

Hilberg, Raul. *The Destruction of the European Jews.* Chicago: Quadrangle, 1961.

Hilgruber, Andreas. *Zweirlei Untergang* (Two Kinds of Ruin). Cologne: Siedler Verlag, 1986.

Kracauer, Siegfried. *History: Last Things Before the Last.* New York: Oxford U P, 1969.

Lang, Berel. *Act and Idea in the Nazi Genocide.* Chicago: U of Chicago P, 1990.

Levi, Primo. *The Drowned and the Saved.* Trans. Raymond Rosenthal. New York: Vintage, 1989.

Levinas, Emmanuel. *Otherwise than Being.* Trans. Alphonso Lingis. Pittsburgh, PA: Duquesne U P, 1997.

Lyotard, Jean-Francois. *The Differend: Phrases in Dispute.* Trans. Georges Van Den Abbeele. Minneapolis: U of Minnesota P, 1988.

Mink, Louis O. *Historical Understanding.* Ithaca, NY: Cornell U P, 1987.

Vidal-Naquet, Pierre. *The Jews: History, Memory, and the Present.* Trans. and Ed. Davind Ames Curtis. New York: Columbia U P, 1996.

———. *Assassins of Memory: Essays on the Denial of the Holocaust.* Trans. Jeffrey Mehlman. New York: Columbia U P, 1992.

White, Hayden. "Historical Emplotment and the Problem of Truth." *Probing the Limits of Representation: Nazism and the "Final Solution."* Ed. Saul Friedlander. Cambridge, MA: Harvard U P, 1992. 37–53.

———. *The Content of the Form: Narrative Discourse and Historical Representation.* Baltimore: Johns Hopkins U P, 1987.

———. *Metahistory: The Historical Imagination in Nineteenth Century Europe.* Baltimore: Johns Hopkins U P, 1978.

Swiss Gold

Authers, John, and Richard Wolffe. *The Victims' Fortune.* New York: HarperCollins, 2002.

Levin, Itamar. *The Last Deposit: Swiss Banks and Holocaust Victims' Accounts.* Trans. Natasha Dornberg. Westport, CT: Praeger, 1999.

Ziegler, Jean. *The Swiss, the Gold, and the Dead.* New York: Harcourt, Brace, 1997.

Zweig, Ronald. *German Reparations and the Jewish World.* London: Frank Cass, 1987.

The Holocaust on Trial

Coles, Timothy. *Selling the Holocaust.* New York: Routledge, 2000.

Evans, Richard J. *Lying about Hitler: History, Holocaust, and the David Irving Trial.* New York: Basic Books, 2001.

Finkelstein, Norman G. *The Holocaust Industry: Reflections on the Exploitation of Jewish Suffering.* New York: Verso, 2001.

Fish, Stanley. "Holocaust Denial and Academic Freedom." *Valparaiso Law Review* 35.3 (Summer 2001): 499–524.

Guttenplan, D.D. *The Holocaust on Trial.* New York: Norton, 2001.

Lipstadt, Deborah. *Denying the Holocaust: The Growing Assault on Truth and Memory.* London: Penguin 1993.

Paulsson, Steve. Listserv post 17 July 2002, H-Holocaust.

Schermer, Michael, and Alex Grobman. *Denying History: Who Says the Holocaust Never Happened and Why do They Say It?* Berkeley: U of California P, 2000.

Jedwabne

Gross, Jan T. *Neighbors: The Destruction of the Jewish Community in Jedwabne, Poland.* Princeton, NJ: Princeton U P, 2001.

Gutman, Israel. "Introduction." *Thou Shalt Not Kill: Poles on Jedwabne.* Special issue of *Wiez.* <http://free.ngo.pl/wiez/jedwabne/main.html>

IPN (Polish Institute on National Memory) Report on Jedwabne (English translation). <http://www.ipn.gov.pl/index_eng.html>

Michnik, Adam, and Leon Wieseltier. "An Exchange." *The New Republic,* 4 June 2001: 22.

Polonsky, Antony, and Joanna Michlic. *The Neighbors Respond: The Controversy over the Jedwabne Massacre in Poland.* Princeton, NJ: Princeton U P, 2004.

Strzembosz, Tomasz. "Covered-Up Collaboration." *Thou Shalt Not Kill.* Special issue of *Wiez.* <http://free.ngo.pl/wiez/jedwabne/main.html>

MEMORY, WITNESS, AND TESTIMONY (CHAPTERS 6–8)

Theories of Memory

Bernstein, Susan. "Promiscuous Reading: The Problem of Identification and Anne Frank's Diary." *Witnessing the Disaster: Essays on the Holocaust and Representation.* Eds. Michael Bernard-Donals and Richard Glejzer. Madison: U of Wisconsin P, 2003.

Blanchot, Maurice. *The Writing of the Disaster.* Trans. Ann Smock. Lincoln: U of Nebraska Press, 1995.

Blom, Philip. "In a Country . . ." *The Independent* (London). 30 September 1998. Features 1 +.

Brenner, Rachel. "Writing Herself Against History: Anne Frank's Self-Portrait as a Young Artist." *Modern Judaism* 16 (1996): 1–23.

Caruth, Cathy. "Unclaimed Experience: Trauma and the Possibility of History." *Yale French Studies* 79 (1991): 182–91.

Clendinnen, Inga. *Reading the Holocaust.* Cambridge: Cambridge U P, 1998.

de Certeau, Michel. *The Practice of Everyday Life.* Trans. Steven Rendell. Berkeley: U of California P, 1984.

Felman, Shoshana. "Education in Crisis; or, the Vicissitudes of Teaching." *Trauma.* Ed. Cathy Caruth. Baltimore: Johns Hopkins U P, 1995. 13–60.

Fine, Ellen. "Transmission of Memory: The Post-Holocaust Generation in the Diaspora." *Breaking Crystal.* Ed. Efraim Sicher. Urbana: U of Illinois P, 1998. 201–51.

Friedlander, Saul. *Memory, History, and the Extermination of the Jews of Europe.* Bloomington: Indiana U P, 1993.

Friedlander, Saul, ed. *Probing the Limits of Representation: Nazism and the "Final Solution."* Cambridge, MA: Harvard U P, 1992.

Funkenstein, Amos. "History, Counterhistory, and Memory." *Probing the Limits of Representation.* Ed. Saul Friedlander. Cambridge, MA: Harvard U P, 1994. 31–49.

———. *Perspectives on Jewish History.* Berkeley: U of California P, 1993.

Gruneberg, Michael, and Peter Morris, eds. *Aspects of Memory: Vol. I, The Practical Aspects.* London and New York: Routledge, 1992.

Hatley, James. *Suffering Witness: The Quandary of Responsibility after the Irreparable.* Albany: State U of New York P, 2000.

Hirsch, Marianne. "Surviving Images: Holocaust Photographs and the Work of Postmemory." *Visual Culture and the Holocaust.* Ed. Barbie Zelizer. New Brunswick, NJ: Rutgers U P, 2001. 214–46.

Kant, Immanuel. *Critique of Judgment.* Trans. Werner Pluhar. Indianapolis, IN: Hackett, 1987.

Krell, David. *Of Memory, Reminiscing, and Writing: On the Verge.* Bloomington: Indiana U P, 1990.

La Capra, Dominick. *Representing the Holocaust: History, Theory, Trauma.* Ithaca, NY: Cornell U P, 1994.

———. *History and Memory after Auschwitz.* Ithaca, NY: Cornell U P, 1998.

Lang, Berel, ed. *Writing and the Holocaust.* New York: Holmes and Meier, 1988.

Langer, Lawrence. *Holocaust Testimonies: The Ruins of Memory.* New Haven, CT: Yale U P, 1991.

Levin, Meyer. "The Child Behind the Secret Door." *New York Times Book Review* (15 June 1952): 1, 22.

Lyotard, Jean Francois. *The Differend: Phrases in Dispute.* Trans. Georges Van Den Abbeele, Minneapolis: U of Minnesota P, 1988.

Mink, Louis. *Historical Understanding*. Ithaca, NY: Cornell U P, 1987.

Ozick, "The Rights of History and the Rights of Imagination." *Commentary* 107.3 (1999): 24–7.

Radstone, Susannah, ed. *Memory and Methodology*. Oxford: Berg, 2000.

Roskies, David. *Against the Apocalypse: Responses to Catastrophe in Modern Jewish Culture*. Cambridge, MA: Harvard U P, 1984.

Sicher, Efraim, ed. *Breaking Crystal: Writing and Memory After Auschwitz*. Urbana: U of Illinois P, 1998.

Steiner, George. *The Language of Silence*. New York: Athanaeum, 1982.

Vice, Sue. *Holocaust Fiction*. New York: Routledge, 2000.

Wyschogrod, Edith. *An Ethics of Remembering: History, Heterology, and the Nameless Others*. Chicago: U of Chicago P, 1998.

Yerushalmi, Josef. *Zakhor: Jewish History and Jewish Memory*. Seattle: U of Washington P, 1984.

Testimonies and Diaries

Epstein, Helen. *Children of the Holocaust: Conversations with Sons and Daughters of Survivors*. New York: Penguin, 1979.

———. *Where She Came From: A Daughter's Search for her Mother's History*. New York: Plume/Penguin, 1997.

Fetterman, Leo. *Shoah: Journey from the Ashes*. With Paul M. Howey. Omaha, NE: Six Points Press, 1999.

Fortunoff Video Archive of Survivors of the Holocaust, Yale University. (Individual tapes are referred to by number, as in FVA T-101, for "Fortunoff Video Archive Tape 101.")

Frank, Anne. *The Diary of a Young Girl*. New York: Doubleday, 1952.

Friedlander, Saul. *When Memory Comes*. New York: Noonday/Farrar, Straus & Giroux, 1979.

Gay, Peter. *My German Question: Growing Up in Nazi Berlin*. New Haven: Yale U P, 1998.

Gourevitch, Philip. "The Memory Thief." *The New Yorker* (14 June 1999): 48–68.

Guide to Yale University Library Holocaust Video Testimonies. Vol. I. New York: Fortunoff Video Archive for Holocaust Testimonies/Garland Publishing, 1990.

Hillesum, Etty. *An Interrupted Life: The Diaries of Etty Hillesum 1941–1943*. Intro. Jan G. Gaarlandt. Trans. Arno Pomerans. New York: Pantheon, 1981/1983.

———. *Letters from Westerbork*. Intro. Jan G. Gaarlandt. Trans. Arno Pomerans. New York: Pantheon, 1982/1986.

Klemperer, Victor. *I Will Bear Witness 1942–1945: A Diary of the Nazi Years*. New York: Random House, 1999.

Langer, Lawrence. *Holocaust Testimonies*. New Haven, CT: Yale U P, 1998.

Lanzmann, Claude, dir. *Shoah*. New Yorker Films, 1985.

———. *Shoah: An Oral History of the Holocaust.* New York: Pantheon, 1985.

Lappin, Elena. "The Man with Two Heads." *Granta* 66 (Summer 1999): 7–65.

Levi, Primo. *Survival in Auschwitz.* New York: Vintage, 1996.

Mueller, Filip. *Auschwitz Inferno.* London: Routledge Kegan Paul, 1979.

———. *Eyewitness Auschwitz: Three Years in the Gas Chambers.* Trans. Susanne Flatauer. New York: Stein and Day, 1979.

Ozick, Cynthia. "Rosa." *The Shawl.* New York: Knopf, 1985.

Peskin, Harvey. "Holocaust Denial: A Sequel." *The Nation* 14.269 (19 April 1999): 34.

Spiegelman, Art. *Maus, volume I: My Father Bleeds History.* New York: Pantheon, 1985.

———. *Maus, volume II: And Here My Troubles Began.* New York: Pantheon, 1987.

Vrba, Rudolf, and Alan Bestic. *I Cannot Forgive.* London: Sidgwick & Jackson, 1963.

Wiesel, Elie. *Night.* Trans. Stella Rodway. New York: Avon, 1960.

———. "Everybody's Victim" (review of *The Painted Bird*). *New York Times Book Review* (31 October 1965): 5–6.

Wilkomirski, Benjamin. *Fragments: Memories of a Wartime Childhood.* Trans. Carol Brown Janeway. New York: Schocken 1996.

POETRY AND NARRATIVE (CHAPTER 9)

Amery, Jean. *At the Mind's Limits.* Trans. Sidney and Stella Rosenfeld. Bloomington: Indiana U P, 1980.

Amichai, Yehuda. *The World is a Room and Other Stories.* Philadelphia: Jewish Publication Society of America, 1984.

———. *Not of This Time, Not of This Place.* Trans. Shlomo Katz. New York: Harper and Row, 1968.

Appelfeld, Aharon. *Badenheim 1939.* Trans. Daliya Bilu. Boston: David Godine, 1980.

———. *To the Land of the Cattails.* Trans. Jeffrey Green. New York: Widenfeld and Nicholson, 1986.

Bellow, Saul. *Humboldt's Gift.* New York: Avon, 1973.

Borowski, Tadeusz. *This Way for the Gas, Ladies and Gentlemen.* Trans. Barbara Vedder. New York: Penguin, 1967/1976.

Brown, Jean, Elaine Stevens, and Janet Rubin. *Images from the Holocaust: A Literature Anthology.* Lincolnwood, IL: NTC, 1997.

Celan, Paul. *Poems of Paul Celan.* Trans. Michael Hamburger. New York: Persea, 1988.

Delbo, Charlotte. *Auschwitz and After.* Trans. Rosette Lamont. New Haven, CT: Yale U P, 1995.

Eliach, Yaffa. *Hasidic Tales of the Holocaust.* New York: Oxford U P, 1982.

Englander, Nathan. *For the Relief of Unbearable Urges.* New York: Vintage, 2000.

Foer, Jonathan Safran. *Everything Is Illuminated.* New York: Houghton Mifflin, 2002.

Gershon, Karen. *We Came as Children: A Collective Autobiography.* New York: Harcourt, Brace and World, 1966.

Glatstein, Jacob. *Selected Poems of Yankev Glatshteyn.* Trans. Richard J. Fein. Philadelphia: Jewish Publication Society Of America, 1987.

Goldstein, Rebecca. *Mazel.* Madison: U of Wisconsin P, 2002.

Grossman, David. *See Under: Love.* Trans. Betsy Rosenberg. New York: Farrar, Straus & Giroux, 1989.

Hareven, Shulamith. "Twilight." *Modern Hebrew Literature* 6.3-4 (Winter 1981).

Langer, Lawrence. *Art from the Ashes: A Holocaust Anthology.* Oxford: Oxford UP, 1994.

Levi, Primo. *The Drowned and the Saved.* New York: Vintage/Random House, 1987.

Michaels, Anne. *Fugitive Pieces.* Toronto: McClelland and Stewart, 1996.

Newman, Leslea. "A Letter to Harvey Milk." *A Letter to Harvey Milk: Short Stories.* Ithaca, NY: Firebrand Books, 1988.

Nomberg-Przytyk, Sara. *Auschwitz: True Tales from a Grotesque Land,* eds. Eli Pfefferkorn and David H. Hirsch, trans. Roslyn Hirsch. Chapel Hill: U of North Carolina P, 1985.

Ozick, Cynthia. "Metaphor and Memory." *Metaphor and Memory.* New York: Knopf, 1989. 176–205.

———. *The Shawl.* New York: Knopf, 1989.

Pagis, Dan. *Points of Departure.* Trans. Stephen Mitchell. Philadelphia: Jewish Publication Society of America, 1981.

Raphael, Lev. *Dancing on Tisha B'Av.* New York: St. Martin's, 1999.

Sachs, Nelly. *O the Chimneys.* Trans. Ruth Mead, Matthew Mead, and Michael Hamburger. New York: Farrar, Straus & Giroux, 1967.

Schlink, Bernhard. *The Reader.* Trans. Carol Brown Janeway. New York: Vintage, 1995.

Schneider, Peter. *Vati.* New York: St. Martin's, 1993.

Skibell, Joseph. *A Blessing on the Moon.* Chapel Hill, NC: Algonquin, 1997.

Stollman, Aryeh Lev. *The Far Euphrates.* New York: Riverhead Books, 1997.

Criticism

Bellamy, Elizabeth Jane. "*Humboldt's Gift* and Jewish American Self-Fashioning 'After Auschwitz'." *Witnessing the Disaster: Essays on Representation and the Holocaust.* Eds. Michael Bernard-Donals and Richard Glejzer. Madison: U of Wisconsin P, 2003. 162–82.

Bernard-Donals, Michael, and Richard Glejzer. *Between Witness and Testimony: The Holocaust and the Limits of Representation.* Albany: State U of New York P, 2001.

Bernstein, Michael Andre. *Foregone Conclusions: Against Apocalyptic History.* Berkeley: U of California P, 1994.

Cantor, Jay. "Death and the Image." *Tri/Quarterly* 79 (Fall 1990): 173–95.

Hansen, Miriam Bratu. "*Schindler's List* is not *Shoah:* The Second Commandment, Popular Modernism, and Public Memory." *Critical Inquiry* 22 (Winter 1996): 292–312.

Koch, Gertrud. "The Aesthetic Transformation of the Image of The Unimaginable: Notes on Claude Lanzmann's *Shoah*." *October* 48 (Spring 1989): 15–24.

———. "Mimesis and *Bilderverbot*." *Screen* 34 (Autumn 1993): 211–22.

Lang, Berel. *Act and Idea in the Nazi Genocide*. Chicago: U of Chicago P, 1990.

Langer, Lawrence. *The Holocaust and the Literary Imagination*. New Haven, CT: Yale U P, 1975.

Mintz, Alan. *Hurban: Responses to Catastrophe in Hebrew Literature*. New York: Columbia U P, 1984.

Ozick, Cynthia. "Towards a New Yiddish." *Art and Ardor*. New York: Knopf, 1983. 151–77.

Ramras-Rauch, Gila, and Joseph Michman-Melkman, eds. *Facing the Holocaust: Selected Israeli Fiction*. Philadelphia: Jewish Publication Society, 1985.

Rosen, Alan. "'The Language of Dollars: Multilingualism and the Claims of English in *Hasidic Tales of the Holocaust*." *Witnessing the Disaster: Essays on Representation and the Holocaust*. Eds. Michael Bernard-Donals and Richard Glejzer. Madison: U of Wisconsin P, 2003. 46–74.

Schraepen, Edmond. *Saul Bellow and His Work*. Brussels: Free U of Brussels P, 1978.

Vice, Sue. *Holocaust Fiction*. New York: Routledge, 2000.

Wirth, Andrej. "A Discovery of Tragedy (The Incomplete Account Of Tadeusz Borowski)." *The Polish Review* 12.3 (Summer 1967): 43–51.

Young, James E. *Writing and Rewriting the Holocaust: Narrative and the Consequences of Interpretation*. Bloomington: Indiana U P, 1988.

Drama, Film, Art and Architecture (Chapters 10–11)

Bak, Samuel. *In the Presence of Figures: Recent Paintings*. Display at the Pucker Gallery, Boston, 17 November–30 November 1998.

———. *Landscapes of Jewish Experience I: Paintings by Samuel Bak*. Display at the Pucker Gallery, Boston, 16 October–15 November 1993.

———. *Landscapes of Jewish Experience II: Paintings by Samuel Bak*. Display at the Pucker Gallery, Boston, 12 October–12 November 1996.

Benigni, Roberto, dir. *Life is Beautiful*. Universal Studios, 1998.

Cayrol, Jean. *Night and Fog*. Transcript in Film: Book 2, Films of Peace and War. Ed. Robert Hughes. New York: Grove P, 1962. 234–55.

Delbo, Charlotte. Who Will Carry the Word? *The Theatre of the Holocaust*. Vol. 1. Ed. Robert Skloot. Madison: U of Wisconsin P, 1982. 267–325.

Hampton, Christopher. *George Steiner's The Portage to San Cristobal of A.H.* London: Faber and Faber, 1983.

Hochhuth, Rolf. *The Deputy*. Trans. Richard and Clara Winston. New York: Grove, 1964.

Honnef, Klaus, and Ursula Brenmeyer, eds. *Ende und Anfang: Photographen in Deutsch-land um 1945.* Berlin: Deutsches Historiches Museum, 1995.

Keller, Ulrich. *The Warsaw Ghetto in Photographs.* New York: Dover Publications, 1984.

Klarsfeld, Serge. *French Children of the Holocaust: A Memorial.* New York: New York U P, 1996.

Kleeblatt, Norman. *Mirroring Evil: Nazi Imagery, Recent Art.* New York: The Jewish Museum, Jewish Theological Seminary and Rutgers U P, 2001.

Liss, Andrea. *Trespassing Through Shadows: Memory, Photography, and the Holocaust.* Minneapolis: U of Minnesota P, 1998.

Loshitsky, Yosefa, ed. *Spielberg's Holocaust: Critical Perspectives on Schindler's List.* Bloomington: Indiana U P, 1997.

Milton, Sybil and Roland Klemig, eds. *Archives of the Holocaust. Bildarchiv Preussischer Kulturbesitz, Berlin* (Part I, 1933–39; Part II, 1939–45). New York and London: Garland, 1990.

Resnais, Alain, dir. *Night and Fog.* Images, 1955.

Schumacher, Claude, ed. *Staging the Holocaust: The Shoah in Drama and Performance.* Cambridge: Cambridge U P, 1998.

Sicher, Efraim, ed. *Breaking Crystal: Writing and Memory after Auschwitz.* Urbana: U of Illinois P, 1998.

Skloot, Robert. *The Theatre of the Holocaust.* Vol. 1. Madison: U of Wisconsin P, 1983.

———. *The Theatre of the Holocaust.* Vol. 2. Madison: U of Wisconsin P, 1999.

Spielberg, Steven, dir. *Schindler's List.* Universal Studios, 1993.

Sylvanus, Erwin. *Dr. Korczak and the Children.* Trans. George E. Wellwarth. *Postwar German Theatre.* Ed. Michael Benedikt and George E. Wellwarth. New York: Dutton, 1968.

Tabori, George. *The Cannibals. Theatre of the Holocaust.* Vol. 1. Ed. Robert Skloot. Madison: U of Wisconsin P, 1983. 197–265.

Vishniac, Roman. *A Vanished World.* New York: Farrar, Straus and Giroux, 1983.

———. *Children of a Vanished World.* Berkeley: U of California P, 1999.

———. *Polish Jews: A Pictorial Record.* New York: Schocken, 1947.

Weiss, Peter. *The Investigation.* Trans. Jon Swan and Ulu Grosbard. New York: Atheneum, 1966.

———. "Notes on the Contemporary Theatre." *Essays on German Theatre.* Ed. Margaret Herzfeld-Sander. New York: Continuum, 1985.

Criticism

Cantor, Jay. "Death and the Image." *Tri/Quarterly* 79 (Fall 1990). 173–95.

Feinstein, Steven C. "Artistic Responses of the Second Generation." *Breaking Crystal: Writing and Memory After Auschwitz.,* Ed. Efraim Sicher. Urbana: U of Illinois P, 1998. 201–51.

Hartman, Geoffrey. "Tele-Suffering and Testimony in the Dot Com Era." *Visual Culture and the Holocaust.* Ed. Barbie Zelizer. New Brunswick, NJ: Rutgers U P, 2001. 111–126.

————. "The Cinema Animal: On Spielberg's *Schindler's List.*" *Salmagundi* 106–107 (Spring–Summer 1995). 127–45.

Hoberman, J. "Myth, Movie, and Memory." *Village Voice.* 29 March 1994: 24–31.

Insdorf, Annette. *Indelible Shadows: Film and the Holocaust.* Cambridge: Cambridge U P, 1983.

Loshitsky, Yosefa, ed. *Spielberg's Holocaust: Critical Perspectives on Schindler's List.* Bloomington: Indiana U P, 1997.

Marmer, Nancy. "Boltanski: The Uses of Contradiction." *Art in America* 77.10 (October 1989): 168–84.

Ozick, Cynthia. "Who Owns Anne Frank?" *The New Yorker* (6 October 1997): 76–87.

Patraka, Vivian. *Spectacular Suffering: Theatre, Fascism, and the Holocaust.* Bloomington: Indiana U P, 1999.

Pollock, Griselda. "After the Reapers: Gleaning the Past." *Halala—Autis work.* Bracha Lichtenberg Ettinger. Aix en Provence: Arfiac, 1995. 129–64.

Scarry, Elaine. *The Body in Pain: The Making and Unmaking of the World.* Oxford: Oxford U P, 1985.

Skloot, Robert. *The Darkness We Carry: Drama of the Holocaust.* Madison: U of Wisconsin P, 1988.

Sontag, Susan. "Eye of the Storm." *New York Review of Books* (January 21, 1980).

Young, James. *Writing and Rewriting the Holocaust.* Bloomington: Indiana U P, 1988.

————. *The Texture of Memory.* New Haven, CT: Yale U P, 1994.

————. *At Memory's Edge: Afterimages of the Holocaust in Contemporary Art and Architecture.* New Haven, CT: Yale U P, 1999.

————. "Looking into the Mirrors of Evil." Norman Kleeblatt, *Mirroring Evil: Nazi Imagery, Recent Art.* New York: The Jewish Museum, Jewish Theological Seminary and Rutgers U P, 2001.

Zelizer, Barbie. *Remembering to Forget: Holocaust Memory through the Camera's Eye.* Chicago: U of Chicago P, 1998.

————, ed. *Visual Culture and the Holocaust.* New Brunswick, NJ: Rutgers U P, 2001.

EDUCATION AND ETHICS (CHAPTER 12)

Bernard-Donals, Michael. "Beyond the Question of Authenticity." *PMLA* 116.5 (October 2001): 1302–15.

————. "The Consequences of Holocaust Denial." *Postmodern Sophistry: Stanley Fish and the Critical Enterprise.* Eds. Gary Olson and Lynn Worsham. Albany: State U of New York P, 2003. 243–62.

Flaim, Richard F., and Edwin Reynolds. *The Holocaust and Genocide: A Search for Conscience: A Curriculum Guide.* New York: Anti-defamation League of B'nai B'rith, 1983.

Haynes, Stephen R. *Holocaust Education and the Church-Related College: Restoring Ruptured Traditions.* Westport, CT: Greenwood Press, 1997.

The Journal of Holocaust Education. London: Frank Cass, 1995–.

Kanter, Leona. *Forgetting to Remember: Presenting the Holocaust in American College Social Science and History.* Washington, DC: U.S. Dept. of Education, Office of Educational Research and Improvement, Educational Resources Information Center, 1998.

Lang, Berel. *Act and Idea in the Nazi Genocide.* Chicago: U of Chicago P, 1994.

Lyotard, Jean-Francois. *The Differend: Phrases in Dispute.* Trans. Georges Van Den Abbeele. Minneapolis: U Minnesota P, 1988.

Millen, Rochelle L., et al., eds. *New Perspectives on the Holocaust: A Guide for Teachers and Scholars.* New York: New York U P, 1996.

Roskies, Diane K. *Teaching the Holocaust to Children : A Review and Bibliography.* New York: Ktav, 1975.

Short, Geoffrey. *The Holocaust in the School Curriculum: A European Perspective.* Strasbourg: Council of Europe, 1998.

Totten, Samuel. *Holocaust Education: Issues and Approaches.* Boston: Allyn and Bacon, 2002.

Vidal-Naquet, Pierre. *Assassins of Memory.* New York: Columbia U P, 1992.

United States Holocaust Memorial Museum. *Teaching about the Holocaust: A Resource Book for Educators.* Washington, DC, U.S. Holocaust Memorial Museum, 2001.

Index

Adenauer, Konrad, 10, 23
Adorno, Theodor, 77, 139, 140, 181, 190, 254
Agamben, Giorgio, 47, 68
"Alchemical" (Celan), 208–209
Alexander II, Tsar, 8
Aly, Goetz, 51
American Jewish Committee, 105
American Joint Distribution Committee, 105
Amery, Jean, 64, 194
Amichai, Yehuda
  "Times My Father Died, The," 201–202
Amsterdam, 214
anti-Semitism, 48–51
  and Bolshevism, 56
  in DP camps, 18
  Dreyfus affair, 49
  etymology of, 48
  in Europe, 8, 36, 48–49, 50, 65, 106, 112, 193, 255
  in film, 230, 231
  in France, 8, 27, 36, 37, 60, 82, 88
  in Germany, 3, 6, 9, 12, 48, 62, 67, 161–162, 164
  and history, 7, 48–51, 55, 116
  and Holocaust denial, 94, 118

as ideology, 8, 47, 158, 159
  and Institute for Historical Review, 115
  and Israel, 38
  in literature, 200, 202, 205, 219
  and National Socialism, 50, 59, 67–68
  in Poland, 97, 98, 99, 102, 171
  racial, 8, 49, 50, 211, 263, 270
  in U.S., 28, 36, 112
Applefeld, Aharon, 189, 192–193, 201, 210, 267, 274
  Badenheim 1939, 199–200
  To the Land of the Cattails, 200
Arab, 24, 34, 272, 273
Arendt, Hannah, 29, 33
  banality of evil, 30
  portrayal of Eichmann, 75–77
Aristotle, 268
Armenians, 240, 257; *See also* genocide
Asia, 4
Auschwitz (death camp)
  in art, 251, 253
  French deportations to, 27, 232
  in film, 228
  inhumanity of, 31, 154
  liberation of, 17
  in literature, 191, 194, 195, 196, 197, 218
  photography, 232, 236, 247

Auschwitz (death camp) (*cont.*)
   physical location, 14, 16, 64, 66, 108, 109,
      115, 160, 163, 218, 272,
   in the present, 69, 209, 240
   survivors, 189, 193, 248
   as symbol of the Holocaust, 31, 67, 82–84,
      85, 140, 181, 254, 270–271
   and testimony, 88, 133, 147–148, 151,
      152, 154–157, 180
Auschwitz and After (Delbo), 197–198
Auschwitz: True Tales from a Grotesque Land
      (Nomberg-Przytyk), 196–197
Australia, 12, 66
Austria, 6, 9, 10, 11
authenticity
   and art, 249, 260
   criteria for, 175, 198, 213
   and history, 178–179
   registers of, 171
Authers, John, 111
Autiswork (Ettinger), 242

Babi Yar, 13
Baddeley, Alan, 183
Badenheim 1939 (Appelfeld), 199–200
Bak, Samuel, 241, 242–246, 248, 260
Balfour Declaration, 24
Barbie, Klaus, 36, 60, 82
Barthes, Roland, 80
Bartov, Omer, 51, 63
Bauer, Yehuda, 23, 28, 43, 46, 50, 58, 61, 68,
      117, 267
Bauman, Zygmunt, 50
Beilis, Mendel, 8
Belarus, 4, 6
Belgium, 12, 233, 234
Bellow, Saul, 204–205
   Humboldt's Gift, 205
Belzec (death camp), 14
Ben Gurion, David, 29
Benigni, Roberto
   Life is Beautiful, 229–231
Berenbaum, Michael, 36, 45
Berg, Judith, 118
Bergen-Belsen (concentration camp), 64, 138,
      233, 248
Berlin, 29, 108, 160, 161, 177, 218
   West, 234

Bernstein, Elitsur, 180
Bernstein, Michael André, 200, 202
Bernstein, Susan, 146
Bettelheim, Bruno, 32, 135
Bialystok ghetto, 196
bilderverbot, 189, 192, 197, 198, 199, 206, 213
Birkenau (concentration camp), 154, 195
Blanchot, Maurice, 82, 84–87, 93, 136, 185,
      265
Blom, Philip, 184
bolshevism, 9, 50, 102, 265
Boltanski, Christian, 248–250
Bomba, Abraham, 176–177
Borland, Christine, 251
Bormann, Martin, 21
Borowski, Tadeusz, 64, 197
   This Way for the Gas, Ladies & Gentlemen,
      194–196
Bosnia, 36, 259, 270
Bousquet, René, 60
Bracher, Karl Dietrich, 55, 67
Brack, Viktor, 54
Brazil, 218
Brenner, Rachel, 58
Brenner, Yul, 252
Britain
   British Museum, 231
   and colonization, 25
   emigration policy, 28, 66, 255
   and Final Solution, 16, 21
   Holocaust memoirs, 143, 152, 199
   Holocaust photographs, 232
   and Palestine, 24, 60, 192
   and Suez Canal, 34
   and World War I, 9
Bronfman, Edgar, 106
Broszat, Martin, 56, 59, 67, 115
Browning, Christopher, 44, 48, 56, 63, 266,
      272
Buchenwald (concentration camp), 32, 255
Buna (work camp), 151, 156
Bund, 8, 14, 33, 58, 98
Burleigh, Michael, 52, 53, 54, 57

Cambodia, 36, 45
camps
   concentration, 13, 15 map, 17, 27, 43, 58,
      59, 104, 156, 205, 210, 220

concentration and death, 138, 151, 179, 183, 193, 194, 206, 226
death, 14–15, 15 map, 31, 104, 112, 144, 167, 172, 222, 224, 236, 255
detention, 236
displaced persons (DP), 18, 25, 105, 108, 110, 160, 164, 199
extermination. *See* camp, death
slave labor, 113
Canada, 165, 193
Cannibals, The (Tabori), 220–221
Cantor, Jay, 195, 223
Caruth, Cathy, 135–137, 143, 181, 182
Catherine the Great, 7
Catholicism, 32, 53–54, 101, 163, 208
Carter, Jimmy, 35
Cayrol, Jean, 224
Celan, Paul, 210, 213
  "Alchemical," 208–209
  "Death Fugue," 207–208
Chamberlain, Houston, 8, 49
cheder, 98
Chelmno (city), 158
Chelmno (death camp), 13, 14, 89, 159, 172, 173, 174, 177, 179, 269
Christianity, 53, 218, 227, 244, 248
  anti-Semitism in, 48
  and Judaism, 4, 7
Churchill, Winston, 21
Claims conference, 105–106, 108, 113
Clendinnen, Inga, 153, 154
"Cloud-Jew" (Glatstein), 213
Cold War, 23, 26
Cole, David, 118
Coles, Tim, 103
Communism, 37, 98
Crown Heights, 271
Cuba, 160, 162
Czechoslovakia, 9–11, 163, 228
Czernowitz (ghetto), 207

Dachau (concentration camp), 32, 118, 236
Dadrian, Kevork, 46
Dali, Salvador, 243, 244
Dallin, Alexander, 63
D'Amato, Alfonse, 104, 106
Dawidowicz, Lucy, 35, 55, 56, 266
"Death Fugue" (Celan), 207–208

deCerteau, Michel, 179
deGaulle, Charles, 26, 27
Delbo, Charlotte, 220
  Auschwitz and After, 197–198
  Who Will Carry the Word, 221–222
Demjanjuk, Jan, 247
denazification program, 23–24, 59
Deputy, The (Hochhuth), 217–218
DesPres, Terrence, 79
Destruction of European Jews, The (Hilberg), 28–29
Devil's Arithmetic, The, 270
diaries, 64, 124, 136, 142, 143–151, 185, 272
Diary of a Young Girl (Frank), 64, 124, 142, 144–146, 148, 149, 214–216, 270
Differend, The (Lyotard), 82–84
Dinnerstein, Leonard, 108
Doesseker, Bruno, 180, 181–183; *See also* Wilkomirski, Binjamin
Doesseker, Kurt, 180
Doesseker, Martha, 180
drama, 216–222
Dreyfus, Alfred, 8, 60
Drohobycz (ghetto), 206
Duchamp, Marcel, 251
Duvall, Robert, 252

Egypt, 34, 128, 192
Eichmann, Adolf, 21, 53, 77, 123,
  trial, 27, 28, 29–30, 59, 61, 76–77
Einsatzgruppen, 13, 18, 63, 200, 242, 264
Einsatzkommando, 100, 101
Eisenhower, Dwight, 34, 139
Eizenstadt, Stuart, 110
Eliach, Yaffa, 232
  Hasidic Tales from the Holocaust, 198–199
Elkana, Yehuda, 61
emancipation, 6
endlosung. See Final Solution
England. *See* Britain
Epstein, Helen, 124, 165–167
Ettinger, Bracha, 241–242
  Autiswork, 242
eugenics, 8
Europe
  Central, 4, 6, 193, 207, 249
  destruction of, 128, 201

Europe (*cont.*)
  Eastern, 6, 46, 200
  effects of Holocaust on, 193
  and Holocaust art, 243
  and Holocaust history 3–4, 5 map, 17, 23,
    160, 209, 234
  in Holocaust literature, 204
  Holocaust remembrance, 35, 240
  Jews, 13, 33, 206, 212
  and Jewish culture, 18
  and Jewish emigration, 28, 147
  languages of, 142–143
  map, 17
  Western, 6, 193
euthanasia, 51–54
  gas chambers, 35, 36, 62, 66, 94, 115, 151,
    152, 158, 172, 176, 221, 225
Evian conference, 11, 24, 66
evidence, 250, 271, 274
  documentary, 263, 264, 266, 271
  kinds of, 73, 110, 272
  physical, 71, 100, 116, 117, 123
Exodus (ship), 25
eyewitness, 39, 94, 100, 102, 158, 175, 177,
    189, 190, 271; *See also* testimony, eye-
    witness
Eyewitness Auschwitz (Mueller), 152–153

Fackenheim, Emil, 32, 45, 164
fascism, 37, 77, 193, 217, 230
Faurisson, Robert, 36–37, 80, 82
Felman, Shoshana, 135, 136, 143, 155,
    158
Fetterman, Leo, 160
Fiennes, Ralph, 252
film, 172, 215, 223–231
  documentary, 231
  documentary vs. imaginative, 223–224
  language of, 223–224
Final Solution
  accounts of, 35, 160, 172, 177, 180, 255,
    258
  and anti-Semitism, 30, 54, 173
  denial of, 36
  design of, 28, 51, 65
  documentation of, 21, 71, 224, 234
  effects of, 30, 43, 238
  evidence, 117, 225, 236

  historical accounts of, 56, 73, 97, 114, 115,
    116
  functionaries, 24, 29
  ideology of, 14, 16, 44, 78
  implementation, 14, 32, 35, 48, 51, 110,
    190, 196, 245
  in literature, 208
  logic of, 94, 123, 240
  and personal gain, 105
  questions about, 3
  representation of, 76, 81, 217
  and Soviet gulags, 65
  uniqueness of, 17
  and World War II, 51
  See also Hitler, Adolf; Holocaust
Fine, Ellen, 165
Finkelstein, Norman, 38, 100, 101, 105,
    109–114
Finkielkraut, Alain, 60
Fortunoff Video Archive, 130, 135, 137, 157,
    158, 173
France, 4, 7, 9, 34, 37, 163, 218, 232, 236,
    250
  and concentration camps, 13, 14
  effects of Holocaust in, 26–27
  German occupation of, 12, 26
  and Holocaust studies, 36–37
  reaction to Holocaust, 27, 60, 197
  See also anti-Semitism
Franco, Francisco, 10
Franco-Prussian War, 8, 10
Frank, Anne, 18, 136, 147
  Diary of a Young Girl, 64, 124, 142,
    144–146, 148, 149, 214–216, 270
Frank, Hans, 21, 22, 70, 80, 86
Frank, Otto, 145, 214
Frankl, Viktor, 31
Freed, James, 260
Freud, Sigmund, 161, 182
Friedlander, Henry, 46, 51–52, 54, 108
Friedlander, Saul, 3, 32, 48, 65, 90, 160
  When Memory Comes, 162–164
Funkenstein, Amos, 90–94, 119, 129,

Ganzfried, Daniel, 180
Gay, Peter, 160, 163, 164
  My German Question, 160–162
General Union of Jewish Workers. *See* Bund

genocide
  Armenian, 22, 46–47, 55
  in Bosnia, 36
  in Cambodia, 36, 45
  complicity in, 68
  effects of, 263
  and Holocaust, 43, 46, 75, 190, 270
  and Jedwabne, 171
  meaning of, 22, 44, 47, 217
  representation of, 222
  in Rwanda, 36, 45
  in Yugoslavia, 45
Gerhard, Zeta, 50
German Historical Museum, 233
Germany
  anti-Semitism in, 29
  authors, 201–202, 209
  and camps, 138
  culpability, 24, 59
  culture, 3
  division of, 193
  East, 59
  effects of Holocaust in, 23–24, 259
  emigration of Jews from, 11
  and Holocaust education, 23
  Jews in, 4, 6, 9, 246
  literature, 161–162, 179
  Nazism, 258
  non-aggression pact, 12, 98
  "ordinary" Germans, 62, 68
  politics, 8–10, 43, 51, 55
  Reich, Third, 28, 57, 74, 104, 142, 249,
    251
  Reich, Thousand Year, 193
  Reichsbahn, 14
  Reichsbank, 109
  theater, 217
  West, 23, 59, 249
Gershon, Karen, 209
Gerstein, Kurt, 218
Gestapo, 4, 5 map, 11, 12, 36, 101, 112, 131,
ghetto
  accounts of life in, 81, 126–127, 131
  concentration of Jews, 7, 18
  images of, 236, 247
  living conditions, 14
  organization of, 13–14, 64
  origins of, 28, 51

  as place, 179, 183
  See also Judenrate
Gies, Miep, 145, 214, 215
Gilbert, Martin, 266
Ginzburg, Carlo, 79
Glatstein, Jacob, 210
  "Cloud-Jew," 213
  "Good Night World," 212
  "Smoke," 212–213
Goering, Hermann, 21, 109
Goldhagen, Daniel Jonah, 44, 48, 62, 67–68,
    100
Golsan, Richard, 60
"Good Night World" (Glatstein), 212
Gourevitch, Philip, 183
Grau, Günter, 58
Greece, 4, 14
Gribetz Plan, 107–108, 111
Grosjean, Yvonne, 180
Gross, Jan, 109, 171
  Neighbors, 97–104
Grossman, David
  See Under: Love, 206
Gruenwald, Malkiel, 61
Gutenplan, D.D., 117
Gutman, Israel, 61, 102, 180

Habermas, Jürgen, 67
Hampton, Christopher, 217
  Portage to San Cristóbal of A.H., The,
    218–220
Hansen, Miriam, 189, 190, 223, 224
Hareven, Shulamit, 193, 201
Hartman, Geoffrey, 193, 223, 274
Hasidic Tales from the Holocaust (Eliach),
    198–199
Hasidism, 6, 196
Hebrew, 26, 198, 207, 210, 228, 237
Heer, Hannes, 63
Herz, Rudolf, 251
Herzl, Mount, 26
Heydrich, Paul, 55, 56
Hilberg, Raul, 3, 11, 16, 22, 28, 33, 35,
    51,62, 64, 107, 110, 118, 266
  Destruction of European Jews, The, 28–29
Hilgruber, Andreas, 67, 80, 114, 272,
    273
  Two Kinds of Ruin, 78–79

Hillesum, Etty, 64, 124, 260, 272,
  Interrupted Life, An, 147–149
Himmler, Heinrich, 10, 16, 46, 54–56, 63,
  116, 123
Hindenberg, Chancellor, 10
Hirs, Alfred, 109
Hirsch, Marianne, 165, 193, 231, 241, 242
Hirst, Damien, 252
historical parallelism, 264, 273
History
  and aesthetics, 76, 88, 129, 191
  and authenticity, 99, 116, 182, 183
  collective vs. individual, 88, 138, 238
  consciousness, 73, 91, 129, 221
  description, 71, 73–74, 83, 86–87, 117
  and drama, 219
  effects of, 73, 82, 85, 95, 178
  and ethics, 43, 72, 75, 77
  as event, 77, 125, 181, 225, 263–264
  event vs. telling, 71–72, 75, 89, 95, 105,
    119
  evidence, 73, 97
  and fiction, 197
  functionalism, 56–57
  genres of, 75
  Historikerstreit, 59, 67
  of Holocaust, 3–4, 33, 39, 220, 257
  intentionalism, 55–56
  intentionalism vs. functionalism, 54–57
  as interpretation, 43, 46, 55, 71, 73, 77,
    91, 104, 107, 109, 110, 116
  and language, 74, 77, 78, 84–85, 198, 222
  and memory, 92, 120, 128, 165, 180, 181,
    226
  vs. memory, 124–125
  as narrative, 55, 75, 78–81, 84, 103, 113,
    272–273
  vs. narrative, 72–78
  object of, 270, 273, 274
  past and present, 224, 241, 248
  and reality, 56, 84
  as representation, 73, 75, 81
  and silence, 86
  task of, 46
  and testimony, 83, 88, 92, 128, 137, 182,
    272–273
  and trauma, 181, 205
  and writing, 75–76, 86, 90, 93, 97, 149

Hitler, Adolf, 218
  anti-Semitism, 11, 12, 51, 59
  in art and literature, 204, 218, 251
  and Final Solution, 3, 14, 22, 59, 116, 120,
    173, 255
  as historical figure, 124, 131, 133
  and historiography, 115, 118
  ideological beliefs, 11, 55, 62
  leadership, 9–10, 50, 56, 66, 162
  "posthumous victory," 45, 164
  suicide of, 21
  and Swiss reparations litigation, 108
Hochhuth, Rolf
  Deputy, The, 217–218
Hoess, Rudolf, 21, 109
Hoffman, Eva, 7, 65
Hoffman, Heinrich, 251
Holland, 6, 12, 13, 14, 142, 144, 147
Hollywood, 252
Holocaust
  absence, 140, 201–202, 204
  accounts of, 29, 124, 157, 181, 183, 273
  aesthetics, 81, 192, 248, 270
  art and ethics, 191, 219–220, 243, 250,
    253
  "consciousness," 37
  culpability for, 59–60
  defining, 36, 257
  denial, 36–38, 88, 94, 97, 103, 112, 143,
    170–171, 222, 256, 265, 266–267, 270,
    274, 275
  denial and memory, 118–119
  and disabled persons, 52, 54
  drama, 216–222
  education, 26, 36, 48, 269
  effect vs. event, 203, 220
  effects of, 18, 23–29, 33 143, 154, 166,
    168, 169, 179, 185, 199, 201, 204, 207,
    239, 241, 246, 263, 267, 270
  and ethics, 140, 190, 197, 240, 267, 270
  as event, 43, 103, 157, 198, 201, 232, 248,
    257, 265, 269, 270, 271
  event and narrative, 102, 130, 226
  event vs. image, 191
  evidence for, 39, 184, 268
  fiction, 189, 191, 194, 196, 200, 201, 202,
    205, 260
  and history, 35, 43, 36, 78, 82, 123, 240

and homosexuals, 12, 44, 57, 257
horror of, 47, 183, 190, 200, 205,
    224–225, 265
iconography, 39, 112, 245
imagery, 208, 209–210, 213, 236, 243
"industry," 105, 113, 114
and Israel, 26, 38, 193
knowledge of, 36–37, 167, 184, 264–265,
    269, 275
and language, 39, 48, 69, 74, 82, 84, 89,
    158, 198, 199, 200, 202, 204, 206, 209,
    254, 266
literature, 142, 144, 192, 199,
logic of, 32, 123, 139, 266, 267
memorials, 240, 255, 264
memory, 94, 125, 130, 180, 226, 234
mimesis, 190, 217, 224
motivations for, 45, 47, 50
museums, 240
naming, 27, 38, 213, 249, 264, 266, 267,
    270, 272
narratives of, 169, 185, 193, 193, 199,
    226, 227, 229, 231, 259, 264, 268, 271,
    274
national identity, 59–62, 103
past and present, 177, 221, 225, 246–248,
    257–258
photography, 215
poetry, 206–207, 213
public reception of, 183
resistance, 27, 35, 58
revision, 88
second- and third-generation, 67, 164–169,
    220, 234, 239–241, 242, 248
and silence, 28, 139, 164, 194, 203, 242
stages of, 11, 70
studies, emergence of, 33
studies, backlash, 36–38
survivors, 28, 37, 106, 108, 110, 165, 168,
    198, 204, 206, 210, 222, 239, 242, 247,
    267
and teaching, 263, 265–267, 269
trace of, 266
and trauma, 124, 135, 139, 265, 266
and truth, 184
and uniqueness, 43, 44–48, 73, 75, 77, 83,
    258, 271
and women, 58–59

and writing, 81–87, 160, 266, 270, 273, 274
visual media, 214, 216, 241–253
Holocaust (TV miniseries), 36
Holocaust studies, 20–43, 59–62, 64–66
    intentionalism vs functionalism, 54
Horowitz, Sara, 226
Howe, Irving, 139
Human Genome Project, 259
Humboldt's Gift (Bellow), 205
Hungary, 9, 12, 14, 16, 229

idolatry, 191–192, 198, 213
"If I Only Knew" (Sachs), 209–210
Insdorf, Annette, 223
Institute for Historical Review, 94
Interrupted Life, An (Hillesum), 147–149
Iraq, 34, 260
Irving, David, 97, 115–118
Islam, 4, 24
Israel, 260, 264
    and art, 243, 246
    Eichmann trial, 29, 76–77
    emigration to, 196, 199, 243
    fiction of, 201–213
    founding and independence of, 25, 26, 33,
        59, 254
    Golan Heights, 34
    and Holocaust, 24–26, 60–61, 178–179,
        192, 219
    and Jewish culture, 33, 201, 247
    Lohamei Herut Israel, 24
    Masada, 26, 61
    and memory, 61, 87, 254
    second- and third-generation in, 242, 248
    Six Day War, 33, 34, 35, 36
    survivors in, 28, 199, 228, 240
    Swiss reparations litigation, 105
    Tel Aviv, 89, 176
    and testimony, 163, 165
    and U.S., 34, 38
    War for Independence, 192
    Yad Vashem. *See* Yad Vashem
    Yom Kippur War, 33, 34, 35, 36
    See also Palestine
Italy, 4, 6, 10, 14, 16 42 156, 199, 218,

Jabotinsky, Ze'ev, 24
Jäckel, Eberhard, 55, 67

Jedwabne, Poland, 171
    genocide in, 97–104
    and Germans, 100, 101
Jerusalem, 4, 19, 34, 26, 198, 201, 227, 247,
    254, 259, 271
Jews
    American, 204
    and art, 190, 240
    and camps, 158, 174–175, 176, 177, 196,
        236
    communities, 5 map, 25, 34, 246
    culture, 7, 19, 65, 79, 87, 163, 191, 243
    culture, destruction of, 20, 213
    culture, in Europe, 20, 183, 228
    economic status of, 49, 104
    essentializing of, 59, 74, 76
    in Europe, 6, 49, 61, 143, 159, 198, 218,
        232
    and Germany, 9, 50
    and history, 247
    and Holocaust, 35, 80, 141, 219
    identity, 35, 146, 161, 193, 201, 202, 205,
        218, 231, 246–247
    immigration, 59, 66, 255
    in literature, 154, 205, 211, 212, 218
    Jewish Councils. See Judenrate
    and memory, 244
    Moroccan, 126
    museums, 250, 254,
    organizations, 15, 105
    as people, 108, 200, 208, 248, 249
    Question, Jewish, 3, 7–10, 25, 62
    in Rome, 218
    in Russia, 232
    treatment of, 202, 209, 217, 218, 234
Jordan, 35
Judaism, 45, 49, 130, 145, 149, 200, 212,
    245, 250
Judenrate, 13–14, 25, 28, 64, 70, 127, 144,
    234–235, 235 caption

Kaddish, 125, 153
Kant, Immanuel, 138, 140, 224
kapos, 156
Karski, Jean, 64
Kastner, Rudolf, 61
Kaye, Ephraim, 64
Klarsfeld, Serge, 27, 36, 232, 234, 241, 242

Kleinmann, Alain, 242
Klemperer, Victor, 144
Knesset, 254
Koch, Gertrud, 189–190, 223, 224
Kolbe, Father Maximilian, 218
Kovno (ghetto), 65, 108, 142
Kracauer, Siegfried, 71
Kracow (city), 198
Kracow (ghetto), 227
Krell, David, 128
Kristallnacht, 12, 59
Krystufek, Elke, 252–253
Kupperman, Wendy, 246, 247–248

LaCapra, Dominick, 68, 135, 139–140, 274
Land of the Cattails, The, (Appelfeld), 200
Lang, Berel, 72–78, 84, 185, 190, 191, 199,
    200, 260
Langer, Lawrence, 130–134, 142, 146, 185,
    199
Lanzmann, Claude
    Shoah, 36, 89, 152, 157–159, 171–172,
        172–179, 190, 224, 267, 268
Lappin, Elena, 180, 183, 184
Laub, Dori, 135
Lautmann, Rüdiger, 58
Le Pen, Jean-Marie, 37
League of Nations, 10
lebensraum, 12
Lemkin, Rafael, 22, 44–45, 74
Lenin, Vladimir, 98, 101
Levi, Primo
    and authenticity, 184
    gray zone, 44, 68, 77
    "Letters from Germans," 67
    memory and witnessing, 133–134, 135
    Survival in Auschwitz, 155–157, 194, 197
    and writing of Holocaust, 64, 120, 124,
        142, 151, 207, 272
Levin, Itamar, 106, 111
Levin, Meyer, 144
Lewin, Abraham
    diary of, 65, 71, 80–81, 85, 86, 124, 136,
        142, 149–151, 197, 272
Lewy, Gunter, 32
Liberia, Zbigniew, 252, 253
Life is Beautiful (Benigni), 229–231
Lindemann, Albert, 49–50

Linenthal, Edward, 36, 66, 240, 257
Lipstadt, Deborah, 97, 115–118
Liss, Andrea, 240
Lithuania, 9, 232
Littell, Franklin, 32
Lodz, 7, 177
Lodz (ghetto), 136, 150, 232
London, 231
    Photographer's Gallery, 252
Loshitsky, Yosefa, 223
Luxembourg, 12
Lyotard, Jean-François, 119, 217, 274
    Differend, The, 82–84, 139, 181, 270, 271, 273

Madagascar, 12
Majdanek (death camp), 14, 113, 180, 247
Mandaag, Sieg, 233–234
Markiewicz, Lily, 246–247, 248
Marmer, Nancy, 249
Marr, Wilhelm, 48–49
Maus (Spiegelman), 167–169
May Laws, 8
Megged, Aharon, 87
Meltzer, Ewald, 52–53
memoir, 126, 160–164, 182, 266
memorials, 256, 257, 263
memoribuchen, 99
memory
    absent, 91, 169, 240
    art and, 214, 246
    and authenticity, 193, 224, 268
    collective, 36, 67, 90, 102, 103–104, 126, 234, 236, 238, 257
    collective and individual, 94, 98
    collective, Jewish, 125, 127, 243
    cultural, 259
    denial of, 118, 119
    direct, 36, 236, 239, 240, 241
    envy, 224
    failure of, 97–98, 134, 145, 259
    false, 180
    and history, 73, 87, 123, 136, 142, 162, 260, 274
    individual, 93, 94, 113, 117, 126, 168, 259, 260,
    instruments of, 158–159, 171, 172, 231, 234
    kinds of, 90, 92, 130, 183

vs. knowledge, 126
and language, 91, 128, 129, 134
loss of, 128, 130, 165–166, 167, 185, 234, 242, 245, 256
and narrative, 129, 193
object of, 242
post-memory, 193, 241–242, 253
problem of, 124–130, 225
and remembering, 87, 91, 134, 255, 257
and time, 122–123, 141, 151, 165, 173, 177
and tradition, 126, 128
and writing, 93, 127, 128, 130, 163, 181, 185
Mengele, Joseph, 197, 251, 253
metaphor, 191–192, 194, 197
"Metaphor and Memory" (Ozick), 191–192
Michman-Melkman, Joseph, 201
Michnik, Adam, 102
middle ages, 4, 13, 51, 90, 92, 127, 173
Middle East, 33, 272
middle passage, 270
Milgram, Stanley, 30–31, 33
Miller, Judith, 35
Milosevic, Slobodan, 45
Milton, Sybil, 46
Mink, Louis, 72, 90
Mintz, Alan, 200
"Mirroring Evil," 250–254, 260
Mizocz, 242
Mommsen, Hans, 56, 67
Monowitz (work camp), 151
Morris, Benny, 26
Mueller, Filip, 64, 151, 154
    Eyewitness Auschwitz, 152–153
Müller, Klaus-Jürgen, 63
Munch, Edvard, 206
Munich, 9, 243, 246
Muselmann, 68–69
museums, 254–260, 263
My German Question (Gay), 160–162

narrative
    and ethics, 259
    evaluation of, 79
    and events, 81, 182
    historical, 77, 194
    individual vs. historical, 268
    kinds of, 79, 87

narrative (*cont.*)
  and language, 81, 155, 196
  and memory, 153, 167
  telling, 229–230
  See also, History, and narrative; Holocaust,
    narratives of
Nasser, Gamel Abdel, 34
National Alliance, 116
National Socialism. *See* Nazi
Naumann, Klaus, 63
Nazi
  and camps, 172, 173
  crimes, 16, 82, 94, 106–107, 113, 153,
    190, 200, 206, 257
  culpability, 59, 175–176, 212
  ideology of, 29, 37, 50, 51, 59, 78, 88
  ideology, racial, 46, 52, 54, 57, 65, 177,
    211, 263, 270
  images of, 230, 248, 252, 253, 254
  and Jews, 30, 61
  in literature, 205, 211
  neo-, 118
  perpetrators, 17–18, 24, 70, 175–176, 218,
    227, 251
  policy, 7, 29, 46, 51, 127, 267
  policy, Final Solution, 13, 15, 62, 81, 110,
    123, 156, 217
  political movement, 9–10, 251, 258
  politics, 9, 25, 26, 265
  propaganda ministry, 52, 232
  resistance to, 194
  rise of, 10–11
  state, 3, 9–10, 63–64, 65, 74, 107, 117,
    218
  war efforts, 18, 27, 62, 98, 109, 145, 147,
    171, 209, 232, 243
  See also SA; SS
Neighbors (Gross), 97–104
New York, 203, 247
New Yorker, 29, 183, 214
Niebrzydowski, Antoni, 103
Niemoller, Pastor, 16
Night and Fog (code name), 13
Night and Fog (Resnais), 27, 224–226
9/11/2001, 259, 270, 271, 272, 273
Nolte, Ernst, 67
Nomberg-Przytyk, Sara
  *Auschwitz: True Tales from a Grotesque
    Land,* 196–197

Novick, Peter, 29, 37, 38, 112, 144
  "olympics of suffering," 105
Nuremburg Laws, 11, 28, 51, 123
Nuremburg trials, 23, 21–22, 29, 44, 109

O'Neill, Robert, 63
Ofer, Dalia, 58, 61
Omar, Caliph, 51
Oneg Shabbas, 71, 126, 144, 149
Ophuls, Marcel
  Sorrow and the Pity, The, 27
Order Police, 117
Ozick, Cynthia, 124, 191, 193, 195, 197,
    214–215, 260
  "Metaphor and Memory," 191–192
  "Rosa," 203–204
  "Shawl, The" 203

Pagis, Dan, 213
  "Testimony," 211–212
  "Written in Pencil in a Sealed Railway
    Car," 210
pale of settlement, 5 map, 7, 8, 98, 234, 234,
    264
Palestine
  Arab identity, 33
  deportation of Jews to, 12
  effects of Holocaust on, 24–26, 219
  Irgun, 16, 24
  and Israel, 35, 272
  Jewish Agency for, 24, 25
  Jewish emigration to, 12, 28, 60, 199, 210
  and Jewish redemption, 128, 201
  Mandatory, 9, 192
  mufti, 255
  sabras, 25, 61
  See also Israel
Papon, Maurice, 60
Paris, 207, 248, 250
  Peace Conference. *See* Versailles Treaty
partition, 59
Patraka, Vivian, 217, 222
Paulsson, Steve, 101
Pétain, Henri Phillipe, 26, 27
photography, 231–238, 241–253, 260
Piekarz, Jakov, 102
Pillier, Verena, 180
Pius XII, Pope, 53, 218
Plaszow (concentration camp), 228

Plummer, Christopher, 252
Podchlebnik, Mordechai (Michael), 173, 179
pogroms, 7, 12, 18, 36, 48, 56, 127, 255
Poland
    artists and authors from, 196, 212, 246
    camps, 13, 138, 236
    effect of Holocaust in, 193, 198
    German invasion of, 11–12, 24, 46, 98
    ghettoes in, 22
    Institute of National Memory (IPN), 99–100, 171
    Jews in, 6, 9, 13, 18, 218, 228
    in literature, 167, 203
    in photographs, 242, 247
    pogroms, 18
    politics in, 8
    See also Auschwitz; Warsaw
Pollock, Griselda, 241
Pol Pot, 45
Portage to San Cristóbal of A.H., The (Hampton), 218–220
Prague, 162
Princeton University, 205
Proctor, Robert, 51
Prodchlebnik, Simon, 89
Protestantism, 32, 53
Prussia, 6, 7
    Prussian Archives, 242, 234, 243, 241

Raczymow, Henri, 165
Ramras-Rauch, Gilda, 201
Representation
    aesthetic, 126, 192, 215, 217, 220, 254
    direct, 200, 206
    effect vs. image of, 210
    and ethics, 39, 250, 260, 263, 267
    and history, 45, 191, 226, 229, 258
    kinds of, 239–240
    limits of, 217, 189–190, 223
    mass media, 37–38
    and naming, 87, 265
    past and present, 168, 250, 274
    See also, bilderverbot; idolatry
Resnais, Alain
    Night and Fog, 27, 224–226
responsa, 64
Ringelblum, Emmanuel, 64, 124, 149
Roehm, Ernst, 57

Roma, 12, 46, 54, 240, 257; See also Sinti
Romania, 9, 10, 12, 14, 199, 207, 210
Rome, 218, 127
Rommel, Irwin, 16
Roosevelt, Eleanor, 145
Roosevelt, Franklin, 21
"Rosa" (Ozick), 203–204
Rosen, Alan, 198
Rosey, Paul, 109
Roskies, David, 125–127, 153
Rothschild, Lionel de, 6
Rousso, Henry, 60
Rudashevski, Yitskhok, 127
Rumkowski, Chaim, 64
Russia. See Soviet Union
Rwanda, 36, 45

SA, 57
Sachenhausen (concentration camp), 45
Sachs, Nelly, 213
    "If I Only Knew," 209–210
Sachs, Tom, 252, 253
Sadowski, Roman, 101
Scarry, Elaine, 217
Scheffler, Wolfgang, 59
Schindlerjuden, 226–228
Schindler's List (Spielberg), 140, 157, 226–229, 267, 268, 270
Schlink, Bernhard, 190
Schulmann, Jacob, 177–178
Schultz, Bruno, 206
Schutzstaffeln. See SS
See Under: Love (Grossman), 206
Segal, Lore, 193
Segev, Tom, 26, 61
Shandler, Jeffrey, 223
"Shawl, The" (Ozick), 203
Shermer, Michael, 118
Shoah (Lanzmann), 36, 89, 152, 157–159, 171–172, 172–179, 190, 224, 267, 268
shtetl, 6, 18, 65
Sicher, Efraim, 240
Simon, Irene, 237
Six Day War. See Israel, Six Day War
614th Commandment, 32
Skloot, Robert, 216, 218
Smith, Bradley, 118, 119
"Smoke" (Glatstein), 212–213
Sobibor (death camp), 14

Social Darwinism, 8, 12
Sonderkommand, 64, 151, 152–153, 155
Sontag, Susan, 216
Sophie's Choice (Styron), 37
Sorrow and the Pity, The (Ophuls), 27
Soviet Union
    and Final Solution, 21, 46
    German invasion of, 12–13, 98, 199, 232
    and Hitler's corpse, 218
    in Holocaust literature, 196, 197
    Jews in, 4, 6, 9, 13
    occupation of Eastern Europe, 23
    pogroms, 8
    political alliances, 34
    Red Army, 16, 272
    Revolution of 1917, 9, 50
Spanish Civil War, 10
Spiegelman, Art, 79, 124
    Maus, 167–169
Spielberg, Steven, 36, 157
    Schindler's List, 36, 140, 157, 190,
        226–229, 267, 268, 270
Srebnik, Simon, 89, 172–173, 179
SS
    in camps, 65, 156, 253
    and euthanasia, 13, 53
    expansion of, 10
    and Final Solution, 12, 56, 62, 64, 112
    in literature, 133, 206, 218, 221
    records of, 43, 55, 117
    testimony of, 175–176
Stalin, Josef, 23, 218–219, 240
Star of David, 5 map, 28, 218, 234, 236, 237,
    245, 249
Steinberg, Paul, 272
Stern, Itzhak, 226
Stocker, Adolf, 8
Strzembosz, Tomasz, 100, 101–102
sturmabteilung. *See* SA
Styron, William
    Sophie's Choice, 37
sublime, 138–140
Suchomel, Franz, 175–176
Survival in Auschwitz (Levi), 155–157
survivors, 43, 151, 193, 227
Survivors of the Shoah Foundation, 157, 158
Sweden, 209
Switzerland, 6, 104–114, 163, 172, 180

Sylvanus, Erwin, 220
Szlezinski, Bronislaw, 97, 100
Szold, Henrietta, 58

T-4 campaign, 13, 44, 52, 53, 259
Tabori, George, 222
    Cannibals, The, 220–221
Talmud, 205, 212
testimony
    and aesthetics, 156, 211
    and authenticity, 131, 141, 171–173, 181,
        185
    coherence of, 132, 174
    and denial, 222
    effect of, 136, 183–184, 274
    as evidence, 184, 185, 263, 264, 266,
    eyewitness, 72, 137, 143, 175, 181, 202,
        260, 268, 271, 272
    and interpretation of, 99, 184
    and language, 132, 138, 155, 178, 181
    and memory, 137, 155, 159, 182
    and narrative, 71, 137, 229
    nature of, 138, 156
    oral, 157–159
    oral vs. written, 133, 134, 185
    problems of, 170
    second generation, 167
    and theater, 217
    and time, 173, 177
    and trauma, 97, 134–138, 269
    and witnessing, 130, 140, 178
    written, 151–157, 181
"Testimony" (Pagis), 211–212
This Way for the Gas, Ladies & Gentlemen
    (Borowski), 194–196
Thucydides, 88
Tiecholz, Deborah, 246, 247–248
"Times My Father Died, The" (Amichai),
    201–202
Todorov, Tzvetan, 32, 65
Tomasz, Jan, 272
Torah, 45, 150
Tory, Avraham, 65, 142
Touvier, Paul, 60
Treblinka (death camp), 14, 65, 70, 86, 158,
    159, 175–176
Turkey, 4
Two Kinds of Ruin (Hilgruber), 78–79

Uklanski, Piotr, 252, 253
Ukraine, 46
Umschlagplatz, 70, 86
United Arab Republic, 34
United Nations, 25, 34
United States
  anti-Semitism in, 66
  effects of Holocaust in, 27–29
  English language, 143
  Fortunoff Video Archive. *See* Fortunoff
    Video Archive
  and Holocaust art, 243
  Holocaust denial, 37
  Holocaust literature, 144, 152, 160, 162,
    165, 199, 219
  Holocaust Memorial Museum and Coun-
    cil, 35–36, 66, 126, 157, 198, 231, 232,
    240, 242, 256, 257, 267
  Holocaust remembrance, 35, 36
  Holocaust response, 16, 24, 28, 66, 114
  Holocaust studies, 193
  and Israel, 34, 38
  nationalism, 59
  President's Commission to the Holocaust, 35
  racism in, 116
  and World War I, 9
univers concentrationnaire, 156, 194, 196, 200
Unterscharführer, 175–176

Van Pelt, Robert Jan, 115
Versailles Treaty, 9, 10, 21
Vice, Sue, 153, 198
Vichy, 26, 37, 60
  Vichy France, 26, 27
Vidal-Naquet, Pierre, 60, 78, 93, 129
  intransigence of history, 87–90
Vienna, 200, 249
Vietnam War, 221
Vilna, 7, 8, 242
Vilna (ghetto), 243
Vishniack Roman, 232
Volcker, Paul, 107, 111
von Galen, Clemens August Graf, 53
von Sydow, Max, 252

Wallenburg, Raoul, 247
War for Independence, Israel, 192
Warsaw, 7, 194, 203, 204, 234, 236, 247, 271

Warsaw (ghetto), 113, 124, 142, 144, 149, 158,
    180, 232, 234, 243, 244 caption, 272
  accounts of, 80
  liquidation of, 70, 85
  Pawiak Prison, 247
  uprising, 14, 35, 163
Wasersztajn, Szmul, 102
Weber, Ernst, 109
Wehrmacht, 43, 62–63, 67, 79, 117, 272
Weinberg, Jesjahu, 258
Weitzman, Leonore, 58
Westerbork (work camp), 64, 147, 148, 260
Wetzel, Erhard, 46
When Memory Comes Back (Friedlander),
    162–164
White, Hayden, 78–81, 184, 272, 274
Who Will Carry the Word (Delbo), 221–222
Wiesel, Elie, 35, 37, 64, 142, 240, 255,
    260
  Night, 151, 153–155, 194, 197
Wieseltier, Leon, 102
Wilhelm, Hans-Heinrich, 62
Wilkomirski, Binjamin, 179, 181, 184, 266,
    269
  Fragments, 172, 179–185, 268
Wirth, Andrej, 195
Wise, Stephen, 66
Wistrich, Robert, 48
witness
  acts of, 136, 146, 231
  and aesthetics, 148, 198
  complicity of, 176, 217
  and ethics, 134, 273
  event and telling, 175
  and history, 148, 183
  and Holocaust denial, 118
  language of, 142, 150, 155, 156, 157, 173,
    169, 198, 222, 227
  and memory, 118–119, 157, 185
  and narrative, 132, 227, 233
  reaction of, 161, 219
  refusals to, 233
  secondhand, 146, 147, 170, 215, 216, 220,
    222, 225, 229
  and silence, 136
  and testimony, 103, 130–134, 151, 182,
    226, 229
  and time, 168

witness (*cont.*)
  and visual media, 214
  and writing, 182
Wolffe, Richard, 111
World Jewish Congress (WJC), 66, 104, 105,
    106, 114
World Jewish Restoration Organization
    (WJRO), 106, 110, 112, 113
World War I, 9, 21, 26, 27, 46, 50, 55, 127,
    202
World War II 26, 51, 73, 89, 104, 120, 213,
    231
writing, intransitive, 80–81
"Written in Pencil in a Sealed Railway Car"
    (Pagis), 210
Wyschogrod, Edith, 138

yad vashem, 87, 89
Yad Vashem, 28, 61, 102, 157, 196, 231, 254,
    255–256, 259, 264, 267

Yahil, Leni, 61–62
yellow star. *See* Star of David
Yerushalmi, Josef, 7, 87, 90, 125, 126, 127,
    128, 129
Yiddish, 18, 194, 204, 207, 212, 213
yizkor books, 99, 125, 126
Yom Ha Shoah, 126
Yom Kippur War, 33, 34, 35, 36
Young, James, 189, 198, 240, 251,
    255
Yugoslavia, 45

Zegal, Jehoszua, 81
Zelizer, Barbie, 231, 233, 234
Ziegler, Jean, 105, 108, 111
Zimbardo, Philip, 31
Zimmerman, Michael, 46
Zionism, 8, 9, 14, 24, 25, 33, 49, 58,
    144
Zweig, Ronald, 105